C000108707

The
Threshold
Perspective

Michael I Finesilver

© **Pathway Initiatives Ltd** England (2018)
ISBN 978-1-900034-14-2
www.pathwayinitiatives.co.uk

All rights reserved.
Parts of this publication may be reproduced in various forms
after obtaining the written permission of the publisher.

CONTENTS

2

CHARTS & DIAGRAMS

Fakery Unlimited: a clear sign...
Not a new phenomenon,
but in the spotlight like never before.

Fake news - propaganda regarding events on the mass media
world stage concerning

Fake politics - with puppet figurehead leaders
of nation states waging

Fake wars - to justify the legalised protection rackets
of State ruling elites in

Fake nations - of mixed ethnic groups and religions,
many adopting

Fake identities - in order to seek better life opportunities
through obtaining

Fake passports - into a wider world that's now deeply addicted to

Fake money - issued as debt by a global financial syndicate,
promoting

Fake economics - in a fraudulent, rigged global system
of **fake financing**, while

Fake spirituality - offered by some religious organisations
encourages

Fake worshipping - as a trade-off for those seeking

Fake forgiveness - for their bad deeds and thoughts,
and **fake healing** as they chase

Fake honour - in prizes, privileges, **fake status** and
fake qualifications in a world of

Fake emotions - with **fake sincerity** and **fake images**
on display, indicating

Fake values - producing the widening rich/poor divide.
... and then there are all the **fake *Facebook* 'friends'** etc etc...

Fakery on this scale is an indicator, a symptom of humanity having lost its way and its natural sense of identity, reality and authenticity, leaving the disempowered, vulnerable majority open to exploitation by a selfish minority.

So, now's the time to abandon all that fakery and start to rediscover what this life on Earth is actually all about, ie to find real, lasting fulfilment through living and sharing in more balanced and just ways... instead of struggling on through complicated tangles of conflicting cultures, misdirected aspirations and man-made toxic environments.

Meanwhile, fake, powerless governments, funded by fraudulent financiers, continue to **BLUFF** and hype up public anxiety, pointing loaded guns at their enemies' heads, such that just one shot could trigger an irreversible chain reaction of mass killing and deadly nuclear radiation.

So, the **dilemma** for humanity is how to resolve a seemingly irresolvable **deadlock** between opposed forces that has left it stranded, stuck between the proverbial rock and a hard place. Learning how to evolve **beyond fakery and bluffing** is an integral theme of this book.

INTRODUCTION

This book is intended to make certain empowering knowledge as widely available as possible. That knowledge is essentially an all-inclusive and penetrating worldview that reveals a coherent pattern of forces at work behind every worldly situation. It's a perspective from which many of the distortions and inconsistencies in human thinking and behaviour can be understood as the result of imbalances... as is explained further on.

The special kind of non-religious, intuitive understanding involved is sometimes called *gnosis* (see Glossary, page 413). The outcome is a potentially life-changing and world-changing perspective that combines:
(a) an all-inclusive **overview** which sets any particular situation in its greater context, and
(b) psychological **insight** that can penetrate to the motivating heart of any situation.

But because it's a big and powerful, yet essentially simple vision, it needs time to be pondered upon and considered with care. It's not an idea to be hastily consumed before its significance has been realised. So anyone in a hurry to devour this and move swiftly on had better perhaps abandon the idea now.

In the current deeply troubled phase of human evolution, this book offers an unusual *diagnosis* and *prognosis* plus a few proposals regarding the much needed rebalancing and healing of humankind. It involves seeking out, identifying and addressing the deeper factors behind the many superficial symptoms, and is concerned with understanding and healing – not with blaming or condemning.

The approach is neither *pro-* nor *anti-* any particular belief systems, organisations or people. It's offered as plain speaking, **need-to-know** information about a wide range of topics, and includes some unfamiliar insights concerning politics, money, sex, religion,

8

psychology, health, science, history, the occult and more. A **Brief Summary** is included on page 382.

The book is divided into three main parts plus, at the end, some extra information referred to in the main text and some notes about the author.

Part One: the Knowledge

The unique worldview referred to above is called the **Threshold perspective**. And the essential knowledge it reveals is that three simple universal principles govern how the whole cosmos, including humankind, originated and how it all continues to function.

Awareness of those three principles has resulted in several significant revelations. These include an enhanced awareness of individual and cosmic human *identity*, ie who and what humans are... beyond these physical bodies, names, titles and other labels. That's because the universal principles at work are not yet widely recognised or taught as part of normal education, and are certainly not part of mainstream media output.

Familiarity with this fundamental knowledge does not diminish one's appreciation of the beauty, subtlety, scale and power of the cosmos. Another benefit is an understanding of *cosmic time* as a spiral of alternating eras of *contraction/descent* and *expansion/ascent*.

Throughout this work, all issues are addressed from the *Threshold* perspective. Which means it's free from the prejudices and partisan biases of any particular cultures or belief systems. It's concerned with how to gain a deeper understanding of this world, and with the practical necessities for enabling all humankind to live in more fulfilling ways than at present.

Part Two: the World

This section briefly reviews how it is that despite the many ongoing advances in digital and other technologies, several basic *psychological* problems of humankind remain unresolved, due to ignorance of the universal basics. As a consequence, humanity's troubled condition of inner turmoil continues to find expression in various outer symptoms.

Yet amidst all this, the beginnings of a potentially more balanced, sane and just world can also be detected. For example, some creative, out-of-the-box thinking is already being directed towards addressing major problems such as illness, pollution, war and weaponry, money, poverty, migration, food production, safe and clean energy provision etc.

Part Three: Applying the knowledge

To optimise satisfaction and fulfilment in this life requires an ongoing quest to maintain some *balance* in all areas of life, including cancelling out extreme *deficiency* and *excess*. And it is possible to attune one's consciousness to the coherent rhythms of the primal, pulsating, natural forces, and to harness their power for the benefit of all humankind.

That's because being in *resonance*, ie in harmony and rhythm, with those cosmic forces enables *healing* to occur and a basic *happiness* or joy in life to be experienced. But when there's *dissonance*, ie discordant clashing, there's usually trouble. So, most pathological situations can potentially be rebalanced and healed to some extent when approached from the *Threshold* perspective.

The *Threshold*

The *Threshold* referred to in this work is not a physical border or a boundary in space. It's a level of being that's experienced at the interface, the border zone between (a) the gross *physical-material* realm of space and time and (b) the subtle *pre-physical* realm of thinking and consciousness. It's the realm of potential, not yet materialised phenomena and *life*, ie *vitality*... which is essentially the difference between yourself and a corpse.

The *Threshold* perspective, therefore, offers a worldview that extends beyond the limited *out-look* of a unit of consciousness *looking out* through the eyes of a physical body, which gives only a ground level, mainly *horizontal* perspective. Mentally ascending and descending to and from the *Threshold* also provides a *vertical* range of awareness levels.

The section, *Guns and Money in the USA*, shows how viewing a problem from different levels gives different perspectives which enable a situation to be read in a variety of ways. Each of them highlights a different aspect of the situation as apparently the most significant. So, to think coherently, there has to be some awareness of the different perspectives involved.

There's nothing complicated, abstract or obscure about the *Threshold* perspective and the understanding it brings. To benefit from it simply requires being open to a radically different way of thinking about this world and finding fulfilment in being your own unique self. Trying to force-fit it into a rigidly established mindset will bring little or no benefit. So, the challenge for anyone first encountering it is: *'Are you willing to look at this world from a perspective more inclusive than your own familiar, comfort zone viewpoint?'* And that's because...

**"No problem can be solved
from the same level of consciousness
that created it"**
Albert Einstein
(NB The author does not endorse some of Einstein's ideas regarding physics.)

So, how do you get to this *Threshold*? For ultimately you can't fool yourself with fakery. So, it first requires being honest with yourself and with the world in general, living a life that's broadly in resonance with the rhythms of nature and the cosmos... more of which later.

Once a start is made, an all-inclusive 'bigger picture' *context* becomes accessible, which highlights numerous previously unseen connections. And so, a coherent pattern emerges from what would otherwise be an incoherent mixture of scenarios and events.

But, alarm bells...

An urgent and overriding need has meanwhile become increasingly apparent. It's the need to address the troubled and fast deteriorating condition of humankind as a whole, and the resulting damage being inflicted on this planet. From acknowledging that need,
s then arise, such as: *How best to apply the Threshold perspective to investigating the main factors behind this situation?* and *What would be the most effective ways to begin healing it?*

There is thus a main, primary theme in this work, but it can't be separated from a secondary theme, which is driven by a simple, widely known but also widely ignored fact:

**There are billions of human beings on this planet
unnecessarily suffering
in dire *deficiency* of the basics for a simple, balanced,
fulfilling life...
while others are living self-indulgently and wastefully
in varying degrees of *excess,*
the overall result being continuing conflict and damage
that harms all humanity.**

Yet that gross imbalance, with all the troubles it brings, is not inevitable. There exist more than enough available natural resources to meet the natural needs of all people on Earth. And humanity now has the technical know-how and the capability to resolve this tragic situation, which is a major factor, for example, in the current *mass migration* crisis (page 274). So, while most people are being kept preoccupied with other matters, their fate is being decided by certain others who have no concern for the general wellbeing of humankind.

How is it, then, that humankind is being frightened and distracted from taking the necessary steps to create a more balanced, just and healthy world?

The more deeply that problem is investigated, the darker the story becomes. Yet the *Threshold* perspective also reveals how all such problems can be resolved, once certain vital knowledge is more widely shared and appreciated. For it then becomes clear how all earthly phenomena, including all human activities, fit into a pattern – once thinking extends beyond the cultural *mind-boxes* (page 20) within which most are trapped without even realising it.

It has already been mentioned that a radically different way of thinking is required. But achieving that liberation involves daring to venture into unfamiliar areas. The claims made for the mode of thinking described in this work may seem extravagant. The test is to try its potential out for a while. Or it can, of course, be ignored or rejected. Either way, no one, having once encountered it, can then claim to be unaware of it. So, where is all this leading?

It's about preparing for the incoming era

How is Threshold thinking different from other ways of addressing challenging situations?
Threshold awareness involves understanding how each earthly life is an integral part of this one living, evolving system, ie the cosmos. And given that a major cosmic *transition* is under way, the emphasis in this work is on clearing the path and preparing for the next phase in that process.

Viewing the world from the *Threshold*, which gives an all-encompassing **overview**, makes it possible to zoom in and focus on any particular situation, penetrating to the psychological heart of it, while in the process developing new skills of observation and judgement.

Insight is thus gained into how the primal forces involved might be affecting human motivation in particular situations. *Weather forecasting* involves something similar, on a more mundane level, in working out how local weather patterns will be affected by the interaction of major atmospheric forces. And looking out beyond this planet, it can also be sensed how the cosmos is alive and conscious, although perhaps not in ways that would normally be recognised by humans incarnated in dense, earthly, physical bodies.

True power and *false* power
True power comes through being in resonance and rhythm with the pulsating of the cosmos – optimally attuned and in balance, 'in the zone', centred in the calm at the eye of the storm.
This brings a 'vertical', elevating sense of balance, poise and ease... and optimum health. Any system is able to achieve maximum power and efficiency and express its full potential when it functions as a harmonious unity. Otherwise there's conflict and breakdown.
Likewise, minds need to be free and not boxed into compartments of prejudiced thinking, whether political, economic, religious, ethnic, scientific, artistic or whatever.

False power is a superficial, shallow, 'horizontal' substitute for true power, since no amount of dominating or controlling other peoples' lives or using artificial means is in itself ultimately fulfilling. Neither is blaming, taking revenge nor assuming an attitude of inherent superiority – these being essentially relics of our individual and collective childhood, ie signs of immaturity. *False power* creates imbalance, insecurity, fear and stress, and is ultimately self-defeating. To be at the *Threshold* is to transcend all such limitation, to move beyond childish competitive rivalry, jealousy, envy and infantile selfish greed... and to begin to know *true power*.

But simultaneously...
The other major aspect of this work is concerned with why humankind collectively now finds itself off balance, out of tune and out of step with the rhythms of the natural world and the pulsating

cosmos. The problem is primarily the result of the difficulties presented by the era of *'descent into matter'* (page 45).

This era has involved humankind in a long process of conflict and learning by experience. Like waves on a great ocean, certain groups of humans rise to prominence and for a while affect many other lives, only to sink back and remerge with the ocean.

A significant part of the process has been, and still is, the long running three-way conflict still being fought out between three major religious groups: Jews, Christians and Muslims (page 128). Together, they form a three-way system of conflicting *undercurrents* that have caused disruptions in all aspects of world affairs. The *Threshold* perspective reveals a clear pattern behind this complex and troubled situation.

The *superiority* delusion and the money spell

Many groups of people throughout human history have had a sense that they were there to perform a special role in the world or in the 'greater plan'. And in certain ways this may have contained an element of truth. But in some cases that sensing has been misinterpreted and corrupted into a primitive, immature attitude of *superiority* and contempt for others.

So, when a small minority of the human species still indoctrinates its young with that warped idea, and is driven to behave in manipulative financial ways that result in worldwide conflict, poverty, disease and the trashing of this planet – and is being allowed to continue doing so – some deeper understanding and preventive action is urgently required.

Yet presently, hardly anyone dares to speak plainly about these matters in public. Why? Because having an endless supply of money enables the financial elite to pay for a nonstop stream of clever PR media trickery to mask what's going on. So, how does that work?

Briefly, the existing widespread *fear* – primarily resulting from *ignorance* of how the cosmos functions at its more subtle levels – continues to be exploited through a huge *bluff*. That is, a grand, global deception, a *confidence trick*, based on that minority retaining control of the world's supply of the addictive, imaginary stuff called *money*.

For just as empire building has usually involved violent wars and land grabbing, other kinds of empires can be gained by more subtle, covert means, such as the manipulation of *money*.

Most of humankind has thus been unwittingly set up, through clever exploitation of the mass media and education systems, to be the *losers* in an elaborately rigged, lifelong game of financial '*Let's pretend*'. And the ultimate *winners* are always the central bank money-mongers, just like casino operators who always end up fleecing the ever hopeful gamblers.

Most money today is *fiat money*, which means it has no intrinsic value and is not backed up with gold or silver, but is made legal tender only by order of the State authorities. This huge bluff dates back to the historical fraudulent trickery of the goldsmiths, explained on page 176 and in other sources, online and in print. The *nation state* racket is described on page 197.

So, who is responsible for all this trickery that's been allowed to continue for so long?

Humanity's unspoken problem: Zionists rule from behind the scenes

The diverse and widely scattered class of people calling themselves Jews today are overwhelmingly dominated by the descendants of an earlier mass conversion to Judaism. Now known as Ashkenazi Jews, they have been extremely influential in the world. And as is explained later, their special role in human history becomes clear when viewed from the *Threshold* perspective.

The Ashkenazi elite are the main force behind *Zionism*, a political/
religious belief system addressed later in this work. These days it's
widely recognised, but not in public, that a small group of *financial*
Zionists has in effect gained monopoly control of the world's money
supply. Which has enabled them, along with the more *politically*
motivated Zionists, to control, from behind the scenes, the Federal
administration of the USA and most other national governments, as
well as media corporations and other key industries.

But such a major imbalance has inevitably had a deeply damaging
effect on all life on Earth... although this will, naturally and in due
course, be adjusted. In the meantime, it's a hugely significant factor
in world affairs, affecting all human lives one way or another. Yet in
the mainstream news media this highly influential strand of the
human species is never directly referred to, and so is 'invisible', ie
not in most people's day to day awareness. The reasons for this are
made clear further on in this work.

Another dimension

It is possible, however, to see this situation in a different way. That's
because now is a time of major cosmic *transition*, which presents an
opportunity for Jews to move on from claiming to be God's *chosen*
people – ie superior and deserving favoured treatment – to choosing
a more balanced and responsible role for the next, very different
phase of human evolving.

For the incoming era is characterised by certain qualities that are
quite distinct from those of the departing one. And the resulting
changes are bringing to an end what has long been a crucial
evolutionary role in the world for the Jews, a role not previously
recognised, it seems.

This crucial subject will therefore be addressed directly, since it deals
with **certain key factors of which many Jews and non-Jews are not
yet aware,** but which affect all humanity. Also offered is some insight

17

into how things could work out for that ancient culture. All of which has huge implications for the rest of humanity.

Breaking the spell

So, like a children's storybook *spell* that's waiting to be broken, this situation awaits some honest, open exposure – for the good of <u>all</u> humanity, including Jews. And there <u>is</u> a way out: a practical and potentially inspiring path of *redemption* is described later. However, that doesn't guarantee it will be an easy path, just as the simplicity of the three universal *Threshold* principles doesn't mean that they'll be easy to apply in all situations.

So closely interwoven are the two themes of this work that they are, in effect, inseparable, although for the sake of clarity it would be preferable to address them separately. Therefore, they have to be addressed together: applying the power of the *Threshold* perspective to overcome what's preventing the problem from being more widely appreciated.

Another challenging factor in the current situation is that the big universal principles involved are so broad and inclusive that they can seem remote and not connected to people's everyday lives. Making those necessary connections is one of the main aims of this work.

What to do?

To get to grips with these matters, you don't have to be an expert of some kind – just as you don't have to be a psychiatrist to instinctively sense when someone is lying or deceiving, or be a trained medic to recognise that someone is seriously ill. So, how best to make a start? First, refer back to the three basic *Threshold* principles (page 30), and then dispel a few major delusions that are still being widely promoted. These include:

Four great bluffs

Here are four great *bluffs*, four delusional, corrupted claims that have evolved into major **scams**, still being perpetrated on humanity by certain minorities.

1. *Territorial land-grab claims* to exclusive, hereditary, so-called 'ownership' of areas of the Earth's surface by states and others.
2. *Supremacy religions*, organisations of self-selecting *divinity agents*, claiming to represent the will of a divine being.
3. *The 'debt money' trick*, a deceitful conjuring illusion that entices and entraps much of humankind in debt.
4. *Materialistic 'boysworld' science* (page 337), which lost its way attempting to counter the superstition and bigotry inherent in certain religious institutions.

Then, having gained some awareness of what's going on, what are the options here and now?

Three basic options

1. **Actively support the status quo** by participating in the ongoing charade, while powerless politicians act out the pretence of governing, in a crass double act with the mainstream media, blessed by religious authorities, and all within a corrupt, rigged, greed-driven system, cleverly controlled by a global financial syndicate (page 201).

Obvious examples would be pursuing a career serving the State or in a commercial corporation, since the primary function of these institutions is to maintain the current status quo of power, authority, wealth and privilege. Which therefore implicates all mainstream news media professionals as accomplices in a major ongoing cover-up operation... OR

2. **Passively and unquestioningly comply** with the existing status quo, allowing the insanity and injustices to continue and worsen, unchallenged by any moral, ethical or radical alternative thinking and action... OR

3. **Work practically and systematically towards creating a more sane and balanced world** – by helping to develop local and global networks of cooperative relationships, individual and collective, with a common, inspiring, long term aim of de-centralised self-governance, as proposed in the **One Humanity** project (page 304). The challenge here is to enhance the empowering sense of *unity*-in-a-greater-purpose over the disempowering effect of *division* and fragmentation, which 'divide and rule' elites will always try to exploit.

The spell is now broken

So, from here on, **the whole subject is out in the open**, exposed for honest, thorough investigation, discussion and resolving at all levels, and without childish recrimination and retaliation for disagreeing... responses which only confuse and prolong the process. That's because **the spell is now broken and the conspiracy of silence is ended**.

Which will encourage people to speak out openly without fear, regardless of their different perspectives... although plenty of resistance to this unstoppable process is still to be expected. So... *Can the Threshold perspective enable us to understand better the main factors behind the present dysfunctional state of humankind, and so bring some much needed healing?*

The simple answer is, 'Most certainly, yes'. The *Threshold perspective*, described a few pages further on, reveals that **there is coherence, ie a consistent pattern, throughout this apparently chaotic and random cosmos**. And that empowering realisation brings new meaning to the term *human nature*, as well as to what *normal* could mean in the future.

What practical difference can the *Threshold* perspective make?

For some, accessing and appreciating its subtle power amounts to 'raising your game', ie an instant 'upgrade' in understanding and sensitivity, and an overall enabling effect. For others, it brings a more gradual realisation of their increasing ability to discern what's superficial from what's more profound and could bring deeper fulfilment in this life.

Mind-boxes, repetition and fixed ideas

In the name of *education* and *upbringing*, most people as infants are, figuratively speaking, fitted with pre-programmed, imagination-limiting *mind-boxes*. Thereafter, the cultural indoctrination they receive through them is continuously reinforced by the mass media.

The result is that they've become so used to hearing and repeating certain fixed ideas and attitudes, they tend to consider them 'normal' and don't bother to question them or the assumptions behind them. Today electronic screens of all kinds are being used to severely limit people's vision and imagination, not least through **information overload**. And yet... many people have a sense that **something vital is lacking** in their lives and worldview.

Ruling, financial and other elites maintain their privileged positions and lifestyles by exploiting, dominating and feeding off divided and discontented populations. They maintain this state of affairs by continuously setting people against one another in hyped up fear, anxiety and enmity in an ethos of competitive, rivalry-driven jealousy etc.

For example, there's the familiar, media-hyped, competitiveness and rivalry that's promoted in many sports, and in trivial, childish, 'fun' quizzes, cooking, dancing and other activities... which all subtly feed into that divided-and-ruled mentality.

Also, many people are finding that despite all the smart technology they now have, and on which they are becoming increasingly dependent to the point of addiction, just living from day to day is becoming increasingly complicated, confusing and stressful.

Change is inevitable, but...

There <u>are</u> better options for humanity as a whole, once the awakening reaches a critical level of awareness. However, like a big ship turning around, it will take time and perseverance for humankind collectively to change direction. But as part of the natural cosmic tendency towards a state of **equilibrium**, inevitably, it will happen.

The *Threshold* perspective reveals how and why there will be resistance and negative reaction to change, and how the challenges it presents can be overcome. For if humanity **needs** to know something, although at first it may not **want** to hear about it, making that information accessible becomes a matter of responsibility for those who already have it.

So, this work is offered here and now for anyone who's prepared to think 'out of the box', ie beyond the limitations that ruling elites try to impose in order to prevent people radically questioning the status quo and discovering their potential for a more fulfilling life.

In this venture, a major challenge is learning how to connect the big ideas and principles with the worldly details of everyday life on Earth. The views of experts who only deal with the nuts and bolts and mechanisms of the current dysfunctional status quo are thus of limited value. An all-inclusive *bigger picture* perspective is required.

For example, take the question, *'What is this earthly life really all about?'*. The bigger picture answer is, *'It's about each individual's part in the **redemption** of all physical matter and energy back into universal consciousness, from which it originally emerged'*... and how this plays out in the everyday details of each person's life and humanity's collective evolving.

Also, what may appear obvious to some may not be appreciated by others who have been taught to accept without question only what they've been told by by those they've been persuaded to regard as *the authorities*. So they tend to respond to unorthodox thinking in a negative way.

With that in mind, some of the information presented in this book cannot, due to its non-physical nature, be backed up with hard physical evidence, such as times, places, names and numbers. It's general soundness and accuracy, however, can be verified by 'reading' any situation with the benefit of the enhanced **Threshold** *overview* and *insight*, as explained later. Certain subtle esoteric connections between the cosmic and earthly realms are not included.

Most of the worldly examples included are observations of humankind in the westernised world, especially in the UK and USA, since these cultures are the most familiar to the author.

If the tone of this work seems somewhat impersonal or detached, that's because the thinking comes from a level of consciousness beyond normal worldly interaction, and is therefore free from the limitations of physicality, emotions and fixed ideas concerning this or that. However, there is a section near the end entitled *'The Author as Beginner'* which gives some personal insight into where, figuratively speaking, the author of this book is coming from.

The generous use of italics and bold characters in the text is to highlight certain words, phrases and ideas expressing the unfamiliar *Threshold* perspective.

Fakery: a later chapter focuses on the year 2016, when *fake news* became *the news*. The obvious conclusion to be drawn from that development is a realisation of the need to think BEYOND the present, familiar status quo and the typical boxed-in mindset it produces. For ultimately, you can't fool yourself by faking your way through this life. So, to progress beyond today's futile fakery towards a more balanced, sane life and world, read on.

PART ONE

THE KNOWLEDGE

Three simple, universal principles account for the formation and functioning of this living, evolving cosmos and all that it comprises.

Can it really be that simple that just three universal principles account for a recognisable, coherent pattern throughout the whole cosmos and in all situations within it? If so, it follows that any problem – however complicated, obscure, slippery or deadlocked – can be resolved by applying the three essential principles... but without them, a fully coherent understanding cannot be reached.

The three principles, **consciousness**, **polarity** and **resonance**, are outlined a few pages further on. But in advance of that, a question arises.

*Isn't simplifying everything down to a few basic principles a typically **masculine** way of thinking – unlike the **feminine** way of appreciating the complexity inherent in any situation?*

This question concerns what the **polarity** of *masculine* and *feminine* means, a question dealt with more fully on page 34. It involves recognising first that the *masculine* and the *feminine* are a complementary pair of **universals**, ie two recognisable, complementary, polar opposite sets of qualities **both of which are present in every living creature**. They are <u>not</u>, therefore, the same thing as the specific *gender* of each individual, whether male, female or any other denomination, since each individual is a unique combination of *masculine* and *feminine* qualities.

Appreciating this basic distinction is crucial for applying *Threshold* thinking. So, how would a *feminine* version of the opening proposition work out? It would amount to proceeding in the opposite direction from the *masculine,* top-down approach.

It would involve starting from a given situation in all its complexity, and from there trying to find a way back to a previous set of circumstances in order to find out what happened in between. For the earlier situation would also have been a combination of the basics, ie *consciousness, polarity* and *resonance,* but in a different configuration.

Problem-solvers such as detectives, agony aunts, psychotherapists and counsellors deal with challenging, complex situations in which there is usually some kind of imbalance and unresolved conflict. So, they try to identify the main factors that have created the disharmony, and then seek practical ways to rebalance things as best they can in the circumstances... rather than start out by simply trying to apply a few general principles to the situation. A combination of both approaches is thus the optimum method of investigating.

Another linked question: *Does the stark **simplicity** of the three principles make this whole approach not credible to those who think only in terms of today's highly **complicated** world?*

And a cautionary thought: The *Threshold* perspective is <u>not</u> some kind of ultimate, complete, final answer to every problem. It offers ways to resolve many of humanity's current troubles. And as part of the ongoing evolving of human consciousness, it opens up a range of potential questions which have yet to be articulated.

All these themes will be addressed by working through a variety of situations and topics. So, down to basics, and first, how it all began, followed by the three universal *Threshold* principles.

How did the cosmos begin?

Big bang, black holes, dark matter and *dark energy,* presented as serious scientific terms, are a just few examples of the pre-adolescent *'boysworld science'* mentality still prevailing in the early 21st century. They illustrate the boyish fascination with dramatic explosions and dark, unsolved mysteries. For those wry humorous names involving *darkness* and *blackness* clearly indicate a lack of understanding of the phenomena under consideration.

By contrast, here's a very different perspective on the formation of the cosmos. Obviously, there can be no hard, definitive, physical 'proof' or 'disproof' of this account. But careful, open-minded observation does enable certain universal principles, outlined in the next chapter, to be inferred and tested.

The Becoming
of Cosmos out of Chaos

Universal consciousness, formless and beyond the scope of limited, earthbound minds, focused on a point within itself... for reasons beyond present human understanding. This **focal point** then instantly became the originating centre of a **pre-physical** *spherical* wave, in the way that a **physical** pebble hitting calm water creates an initial *circular* radiating wave.

The spherical wave extended outwards, creating a sphere of a magnitude proportionate to the power of the initiating impulse in the given medium. At maximum expansion, there began a contracting inwards, and the resulting sphere became a potential **cosmos** (in Greek, kosmos means 'order') within that pre-physical medium of **chaos** (khaos means 'formless void, space or matrix').

So between the periphery and centre of this primal sphere, a vital **dynamic** was set up, a rhythmical pulsating of inward and outward waves, creating spherical standing waves, generated by the universal tendency towards **equilibrium** and eventual cosmic **redemption**.

That primal two-way dynamic is pure, raw, pre-physical, potential **ENERGY**, which is constantly **mutable**, ie changeable, according to the prevailing balance of forces affecting any situation.

And it's this primal dynamic that powers the universal rhythmical **pulsation**, the **CONTRACTION** and **EXPANSION**, driven by the two primal cosmic forces: inward, contracting **GRAVITY** and outward, expanding **LEVITY**.

Then from that primary **polarity** arise secondary polarities, such as **density** and **rarity**, gravity-dominated **magnetism** and levity-dominated **electricity,** and the universal **masculine** and **feminine**.

From there, a cooling, slowing, solidifying and fragmenting process produces all the temporarily separated phenomena that constitute this physical world. An earthly version of this would be a flow of hot, liquid, volcanic lava cooling and solidifying into rocks.

In the process of universal consciousness becoming dense physical matter, an intermediate ***pre-physical*** level of existence comes into being, functioning as an enabling ***medium***. It arises from the rhythmical pulsating interaction between the expanding force of *levity* and the contracting force of *gravity*. The result is a dynamic, spherical 'field' of ***potential energy***, which is convertible into physical energy (called *kinetic* energy in physics).

This medium has long been called the ***aether*** or ***quintessence***. It's what the ***quantum vacuum*** of contemporary physics essentially is. A physical hint of the fluid nature of the *aether* is the *aurora borealis*, ie mobile electric plasma manifesting as visible light at the border zone between the *pre-physical* realm and the *physical-material* world.

The interface zone where the polar opposite cosmic forces of *gravity* and *levity* meet and interact is the ***Threshold***, a key concept of this work. It's where there's a continuous interchange between:

(a) the expansive, unlimited, *pre-physical*, timeless realm of *levity* and increasing *rarity*, and
(b) the contracting *gravity-bound* world of *dense physical* matter in 3D 'box' space.

A dynamic 2-dimensional reality behind the 3D world

Contracting, expanding, contracting, expanding... everything, everywhere is *pulsating*: inward towards the centre, outward towards the periphery, in multiple coordinated rhythms. Everything is thus vibrating, but in another dimension, a different kind of space from the familiar physical 3D *box space* with its height, width and depth, corners, angles and edges.

That primeval medium is **D2D** (**dynamic 2-dimensional space**), the **pre-physical** space of primal *expansion/contraction*. It's a spheroidal world of continuous pulsation between the centre and periphery of each sub-spheroid, all within the original, all-encompassing, pulsating spheroidal cosmos. (A *spheroid* here means something approximately spherical)

These pre-physical spheroids function as *resonant cavities* – producing the legendary *music of the spheres* – like tuned, earthly musical instruments or other vessels, as Pythagoras demonstrated some two and a half thousand years ago.

So, *pre-physical* space, as a manifestation of universal consciousness, can be inferred as being conscious and responsive in ways beyond the current comprehension of earthbound humans... who can, however, read and measure certain physical signs and gain a limited understanding of it.

That kind of awareness implies the existence of a range of levels of consciousness in the cosmos and, therefore, the possible presence of non-physical, conscious beings. These could be accessible to certain incarnate humans whose minds are not locked into a limiting, materialistic mindset, and could be benevolent, neutral or malevolent.

At the limits of human comprehension, where the terms **infinity** (space) and **eternity** (time) serve as signposts to an unknown **beyond**, further questions arise which cannot as yet be answered in worldly terms. For example:
'**What prompts universal consciousness to *focus* in on itself and create *focal points?*'**, ie centres of *gravity/contraction* which in response *expand* with the polar opposite force of *levity*, according to the universal tendency towards *equilibrium* between the two forces.

The archetypal **torus** form (page 341) offers a clue as to how energy is shaped by the dynamics of the two universal forces into temporarily distinct forms, which may then materialise or not.

The Identity Continuum (page 427) hints at how an individual, a single *unit* of consciousness, can become aware of being part of the limitless, all-inclusive *universal consciousness*. Then further information about the Threshold and how we experience it follows. But first, a few basics, necessary for appreciating this unfamiliar worldview.

The
Three
Universal
Principles

1. Consciousness

Universal consciousness, briefly summarised, is the most fundamental, primordial state of being conceivable by incarnate human beings. Indefinable, unlimited in its potential and not quantifiable, it focuses within itself, creating *focal points* which temporarily exist as distinct units of *individual consciousness*, ie potential beings of many kinds, including humans

The cosmos is a primal manifestation of such an impulse, although what may have preceded it presently seems beyond human comprehension. The creator gods of religious systems worldwide seem broadly to allude to universal consciousness.

So, each living creature is, in essence, one unit of consciousness, an individual centre of gravity, clothed in physical matter and generating its own unique *sphere of influence*. Consciousness, therefore, is <u>not</u> the product of electrical and chemical processes in a physical brain. For in the longer cosmic story the brain is a much later development, while human evolution is fundamentally the the evolving of human consciousness.

There also exists a spectrum of levels of consciousness: from deep sleep, through normal waking, to 'higher' states which may be experienced when in a *transcendent* mode of being.

A very basic transcendent experience would be to mentally rise above your present earthly situation and look down on it in a detached way, seeing yourself down there within it. The overview enables you to see how the various elements in the situation relate to each other.

In everyday language, the terms to 'be conscious' or 'lose consciousness' are mostly used only with reference to the normal waking state of physical, here and now self-awareness. But then people also speak of *sub-conscious, superconscious* and *unconscious* mental processes.

Meditation, in its many forms, is about accessing the more subtle levels of consciousness and experiencing a state of inner balance.

Meanwhile, the '*all is energy*' idea of materialistic scientists amounts to an acknowledgement that there's more to this world than just physical matter. The problem there is that it hasn't yet been widely realised that energy is a manifestation of universal consciousness, (as is explained in <u>*Threshold Science*</u>).

And it's the <u>*pre-physical*</u> level of being, at which ideas and thinking occur, that accounts for the ease with which some people can influence other people's consciousness, individually and collectively. This is demonstrated by, for example, hypnotists, conjurers, performing artists and charismatic speakers, and in the power of advertising and propaganda.

Individually, the consciousness of each incarnate human being, while embodied in physical matter, tends to be limited to a unique *out-look* from that singular *view-point*. By contrast, when discarnate or having an out-of-body experience, the resulting 'surround' vision would enable one to survey a situation from all around it at once, as well as look outward into cosmic space. Then, when one's attention is drawn to a particular location, that spot can be focused on from an appropriate view-point at the periphery.

A <u>physical</u> parallel of that sense of surrounding an inner space could be a person's awareness of his or her own heart, pulsating at the functional centre of the body. Or, in a more artificial way, there's the experience of medical scanning equipment enabling one to monitor the ongoing action inside one's own body.

This more evolved way of comprehending the world is essentially the *Threshold* perspective.

The 'brainism' fallacy

Meanwhile, Western materialistic scientists are still vainly trying to reduce consciousness and psychology – given that *psyche* means the non-physical *soul* – down to a kind of *'brainism'*, ie the misconception that electrical and chemical processes in the brain are the original cause of all our conscious experiencing.

'How does the brain give rise to consciousness?' is the so-called 'hard problem' that contemporary scientists investigating consciousness are still asking. Such is their continuing hope of finding a way to explain a non-physical reality in physical-material terms. Which is why their models and theories simply can't handle the range, complexity, fluidity and spontaneity of the human psyche, and so inevitably prove inadequate.

Measurable physical processes may well be detected occurring simultaneously with reported conscious experiences, but they are not in any way identical with it. They are the outer, gross manifestations of more subtle inner processes – just as:
- the tail doesn't wag the dog into a state of excitement,
- a high body temperature is not the cause but a symptom of a fevered condition, and
- a fluttering flag isn't causing the wind to blow.

Also, stimulating inner experiences artificially by applying an electric current to the brain only works if the capacity for those experiences already exists.

From a practical engineering perspective, the brain is bodily matter accumulated in the skull and utilised as an instrument for registering, ordering and processing information. It doesn't itself *think* – just as some component part of a car cannot decide it's time to go for a drive – although robotic models can be pre-programmed to appear self-motivating.

Relatively recent medical-scientific discoveries concerning the *'heart brain'* or *cardiac plexus* add a further dimension to the subject. It's a plexus of nerves which has been found to respond to events and stimuli prior to the brain in the skull (page 399).

So, since consciousness defies any precise definition of what it <u>is</u>, we build up an impression of it by approaching it from various angles. For while all the matter constituting our physical bodies is continuously disintegrating and being replaced, our individual sense of identity, our *consciousness*, persists.

2. *Polarity*

Polarity, the second universal *Threshold* principle, is essentially a simple idea. It says that in any situation there are always two fundamental, opposite and complementary forces at work, and therefore two perspectives involved. The primal polarity is the dynamic rhythmical **contracting** and **expanding** of the living, pulsating cosmos (see diagram, page 343). *Multi-polar* situations are lower order subsidiaries of that fundamental phenomenon.

These polar opposite movements are expressions of the universal complementary cosmic forces, *gravity* and *levity*... although levity has long been a jettisoned word in materialistic science. Examples of levity in action are the ascending of heat, as in a flame, a helium-filled balloon and the 'upward' growth of plants, all drawn away from Earth's centre of *gravity*.

Polarity thus refers to the kind of *duality* ('two-ness') that comprises <u>a pair of complementary opposites within a greater *unity*</u> or wholeness, such as the *north* and *south* poles of planet Earth. And each always includes an element of the other, its polar opposite. The following chart serves as a *'polarity lens'* for appreciating the opposed complementary qualities of any situation in the everyday world.

The universal principle of
POLARITY

Contraction	*Expansion*
Gravity	*Levity*
Yang	*Yin*
Masculine	*Feminine*
Focusing	*Radiating*
Probing	*Yielding*
Penetrating	*Accommodating*
Centralising	*Decentralising*
Uniformity	*Diversity*
Density	*Rarity*
Magnetism	*Electricity*
Containing	*Releasing*
Inhibiting	*Expressing*
Descent	*Ascent*
Systole	*Diastole*
Alkali	*Acid*

(Universal *masculine/feminine* polarity is not the same as individual *male/female* gender)

Binary duality, by contrast, involves two opposites being treated as **mutually exclusive** by ignoring what's common to both, **as if** nothing unites them. It's the *either/or* logic of *yes/no, on/off, zero/one, black/white, us/them* etc. And it's the basis of all **digital** technology, which essentially comprises systems of lifeless, sterile, sandcastle-

34

like information, inherently unstable, however fine the granular 'building block' *bits* of which they're composed.

The universal principle of **polarity** applies at all scales, from the microcosmic to the macrocosmic, as well as to the experiencing of *pleasure* and *anxiety* (see the chart, page 36), which has many health and balance implications regarding *wellness* and *illness*. Other examples can be found throughout this book.

Regarding **time**, the cosmos is currently in a **transition** phase between the departing era of **descent into matter** (*contraction/ gravity*) and its polar opposite, the incoming era of **ascent out of matter** (*expansion/levity*) (page 46).

Contracting *gravity* and expanding *levity* find expression in the living world as the **masculine** and **feminine** universals. So, every individual creature, of whatever *gender* category in the spectrum from **male**-ness to **female**-ness, is **a unique combination of both** of the universal, polar opposite qualities, *masculinity* and *femininity*.

Thus domineering, forceful, typically *masculine* tendencies, and manipulative, controlling *feminine* tendencies occur in all gender types. But an inability or unwillingness to distinguish biological *gender* types from universal *masculine* and *feminine* qualities leaves one unable to appreciate fully the *Threshold* principle of *polarity*.

Certain strands of humankind also express a recognisably predominant *masculine* or *feminine* quality. For example, broadly, **Hindu/Indian** and **Hebrew/Jewish** cultures have a predominantly **feminine** character, while **Arab** and **Chinese** cultures display a predominantly **masculine** character.

Polarity also incorporates the quality of **three-ness**, as follows:
- the **no-thing-ness/all-ness** of **universal consciousness**, symbolised as **zero**, includes...
- the **one-ness** of the **cosmos** which itself pulsates with

P O L A R I T Y
of
Pleasure/Anxiety
via the autonomic (involuntary) nervous system

Expansion	*Tendency*	Contraction
Opening up, outreaching	*Attitude*	Closing down, withdrawing
Retarded	*Heart action*	Accelerated
Decreased	*Blood pressure*	Increased
Dilated	*Peripheral vessels*	Constricted
Constricted	*Pupils*	Dilated
Increased	*Saliva secretion*	Decreased
Relaxed, toned	*Muscles*	Paralysed
Bright	*Eyes*	Dry
Dry, smooth	*Skin*	Cold sweat, goose bumps
Slow	*Pulse*	Fast
Inhibited secretion	*Adrenalin*	Stimulated secretion
Increased	*Sexual sensation*	Decreased
Pleasure	*Experience*	*Anxiety*

- the **two-ness** of contracting **gravity** and expanding **levity**,
- with **three-ness** manifesting as the two polar opposite forces continuously interacting within the original unity, inherently tending towards an *equilibrium* state.

3. Resonance

Many kinds of *resonance*, physical and psychological, occur or are used in a variety of different ways, natural and man-made. In humans, resonance is experienced when there's *sympathy* or *empathy* between hearts and minds, and in the *aesthetic* vibratory effects of music, the other arts and design.

Chladni patterns (see YouTube) demonstrate visibly how musical tones can cause randomly scattered iron filings to form corresponding patterns when the surface on which the iron filings rest vibrates in *resonance* with the musical tones. The resulting rhythmical waves of energy passing across it organise the particles into a particular pattern.

Healing can be understood as a *reconfiguration* in tune with the harmonics of the cosmos. Thus an important area of enquiry regarding **resonance** is the subject of **wellness** and **illness**, and whether or not people, individually and collectively, are living in harmonious **resonance** with the rhythms of nature and the cosmos, as well as with other creatures. That is to say, do their ways of living create a more harmonious world or are they *dissonant* and clashing, causing discord, division, conflict, damage and pain?

Resonance is implied when, for example:
- Mentally, people are said to be '*on the same wavelength*'.
- Politically, people are '*singing from the same song sheet*'.

So, **CONSCIOUSNESS, POLARITY and RESONANCE, as a dynamic triad, are the three fundamental working principles of the cosmos.** Everything and anything, however complex or subtle, can be traced back and ultimately understood in terms of this combination.

RESONANCE

The Polarity of Resonance

	Consonance	Dissonance
Physical:	Attraction /	Repulsion
Emotional:	Harmony /	Conflict
Mental:	Agreement /	Disagreement
Spiritual:	Unity /	Division

Psychological Resonance

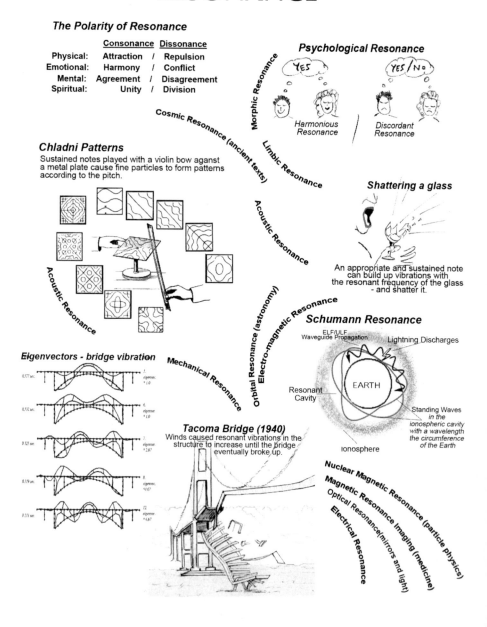

Harmonious Resonance / Discordant Resonance

Morphic Resonance

Cosmic Resonance (ancient texts)

Limbic Resonance

Acoustic Resonance

Chladni Patterns

Sustained notes played with a violin bow aganst a metal plate cause fine particles to form patterns according to the pitch.

Acoustic Resonance

Shattering a glass

An appropriate and sustained note can build up vibrations with the resonant frequency of the glass - and shatter it.

Orbital Resonance (astronomy)

Electro-magnetic Resonance

Schumann Resonance

ELF/ULF Waveguide Propagation

Lightning Discharges

Resonant Cavity

EARTH

Standing Waves in the ionospheric cavity with a wavelength the circumference of the Earth

Ionosphere

Eigenvectors - bridge vibration

Mechanical Resonance

Tacoma Bridge (1940)

Winds caused resonant vibrations in the structure to increase until the bridge eventually broke up.

Nuclear Magnetic Resonance (particle physics)

Magnetic Resonance Imaging (medicine)

Optical Resonance(mirrors and light)

Electrical Resonance

Together they demonstrate that there is **coherence** behind the apparently incoherent disorder and randomness in this troubled world. Therefore, humans can choose whether or not to create more coherent *resonance* in their own lives and in the world they inhabit.

It's all about *balance* and *equilibrium*

The three principles are thus all about the cosmos working towards a harmonious balance between the primal forces of *contraction and expansion*, ie towards an **equilibrium** state, and ultimately the **redemption** of all matter and energy back into universal consciousness.

Viewed in their greater context, the three universal *Threshold* principles are therefore the bare essentials for understanding how the whole cosmos, in all its complexity, works. Together they account for the richness and diversity of all the cultures, myths, legends, stories, dramas and characters, beings of all kinds, languages, symbols, poems, songs and theories that have emerged in the evolving of human consciousness on Earth.

Two of the most influential predictive books of the 20th century, *Brave New World* by Aldous Huxley and *1984* by George Orwell, represent a pair of *polar opposite* pessimistic visions. Huxley portrayed the softer, pathologically distorted, *descent era feminine* qualities to be expected, while Orwell set out the pathologically distorted, harsh, *descent era masculine* qualities already on display then in the Soviet Union. *1984* could be read as predicting the current **temporary** *masculine* push-back against the **long term** trend of the *transition* process towards increasing *feminine* influence (page 197). Thus the early 21st century regression into nationalism and the rise of so-called *anti-globalism*.

Next, a look at the nature of the *Threshold*, the key to a whole new way of thinking and understanding how the world works.

What is this *Threshold*?

The *Threshold* referred to in this work is not to be found at a particular location or altitude in physical space. As already mentioned, it's the level of awareness experienced at the border zone between the pre-physical realm and the world of physical matter - more like the temperature thresholds at which *liquid* water is transformed into *solid* ice or *gaseous* steam.

The *Threshold* Initiation

Accessing the *Threshold* perspective for the first time is a kind of *initiation* into functioning at a 'higher' level of consciousness than the familiar everyday range. For you can't raise your game while mentally and emotionally weighed down by *descent era* ways and thinking.

It involves adopting, at least temporarily, the *three universal principles* outlined earlier. All major spiritual disciplines *resonate* with these principles, even though they may not expressly acknowledge them. So, for a start, an open mind, a desire to be in harmonious resonance with the cosmos, a strong will and some perseverance are all that is needed.

The power of this knowledge enables life choices to be made from options that previously may not have seemed available. However, becoming familiar with this new power can at first feel challenging because, in the process, your sense of *individual* identity is significantly expanded, yet without you losing your distinctive individual qualities.

Until it's directly experienced, the power and value of the *Threshold* perspective obviously cannot be judged other than indirectly - such as through the reported experiences of other people. A parallel but lesser experience might be one's first glimpse through a telescope or microscope, falling in love for the first time or making a major artistic or scientific breakthrough – all life-changing, mind-expanding, worldview-enhancing experiences.

What benefits can this *Threshold perspective* bring?

The **Threshold** *perspective* gives an all-round, all-inclusive view of the world, combining a comprehensive **overview** with some penetrating psychological **insight**. And that brings an enhanced ability to look both inwards into earthly life and outwards into the wider cosmos.

An *overview* is essentially a *masculine, gravity*-dominated, vertical perspective, looking inwards from the periphery towards the centre. *Insight* is more *feminine*, empathy-influenced, sensing of *resonances*, whether harmonious or discordant.

The *Threshold* perspective cannot thus be part of any exclusive, partisan or divisive belief system, whether religious, scientific, political or commercial. It's *transcendent*. Which is to say, it's a view from beyond the limited scope of your personal **mind-box**, ie the set of constraints upon thinking that was installed through mass education and the mass media when you were too young to realise it was happening.

As a transcendent perspective, it enables you to view things from beyond the prejudices of dogmatic conventional thinking, and to realise that all human beings are interconnected and related as sub-centres of the *one cosmos*... itself formed within the great '*no-thing-ness*' that is *universal consciousness*.

A practical example of a transcendent understanding is seeing the *water cycle* as one whole continuous, cyclical process. It involves witnessing the rising of water vapour from the Earth's surface in warm temperatures, and its subsequent falling as rain, hail or snow when cooled in the atmosphere, forming rivers which in turn wet the Earth's surface. That is, instead of simply thinking at different times, '*Now the weather's warm and the ground is dry, now it's cold and the ground is wet.*'

41

So, with the help of the three simple guiding principles outlined earlier, it is possible to navigate a way through the current turmoil, and begin to formulate radical new solutions to what otherwise seem to be unresolvable problems that affect all aspects of our lives. These range from earthly practical matters to abstract mathematical and philosophical problems.

Zoom out/zoom in

Zooming out, ie mentally moving away from a centre of attention, provides a range of *overview* perspectives on humankind as a whole. So, from way beyond any horizontal, ground level view, the human species can be observed, for example:

- As if it were an extended family, sharing common ancestors. So, all alliances, factions and feuds among different groups can be observed from above as patterns of interaction.

- As if it were an 'ant colony',ie a vibrant mass of indistinguishable individuals. Thus large scale patterns and complex rhythms, not apparent from closer in, can be detected.

- As if it were a single organism of many interacting, interdependent 'cells' and structures, enabling their coordinated functioning to be appreciated.

Zooming in enables one to focus on any point within the whole cosmos and attune to the core motives, attitudes, feelings, hidden assumptions and other psychological factors at work.

The *horizontal* and the *vertical* dimensions

Given that understanding, the current rivalry, hostile competing, fighting and blaming among different strands of humankind look like symptoms of a collective *psychological* disorder which urgently requires some deep self-healing. And that requires addressing the problem in two distinct dimensions.

First, there's the ground level, earthbound, *horizontal* dimension which includes all personal and group interaction, harmonious and dissonant. Then there's the *vertical* dimension in which various levels of psychological development and evolving can be recognised.

One other major challenge is that the inherent **simplicity** of the three basic *Threshold* principles may at first seem not at all credible to some people. These would be people who have grown up and been educated in *descent era* cultures long blighted by **inertia.** For that results in rigid traditions and institutions that create a false impression of static permanence in this ever-evolving cosmos. And that mismatch results in **complicated,** confused thinking.

Accessing the *Threshold*

You don't need any special abilities to appreciate the power of the *Threshold* perspective. You don't have to be especially clever. And it doesn't involve anything mystical or religious. It's not something you can just buy or master on a weekend course, and there's no neat trick or technique you can learn to perform in order to get there more quickly.

Also, it won't happen if it's approached in a detached, intellectual or cynical way. In order to engage in this mode of thinking, what's required is **a genuinely open and wholehearted attitude**. Why? Because it necessarily involves your **intuition**, which functions at a 'higher', more inspired and inclusive level than your analysing *intellect*... which serves your intuition.

So, if you're willing and ready to venture into a greater dimension of your own being, it can be life-changing. But this is no ordinary knowledge, and does involve thinking in an unfamiliar way. Which may sound challenging... but, like any new activity, once you've tried it out for a while, you could start to appreciate the difference for yourself.

One essential part of the process is abandoning old and now redundant habits and attitudes. So, when challenging situations arise, you see them in their broader context, and they no longer instantly cause paralysing fear, inhibiting anxiety, hostility, anger or weakness. You may also experience a new sense of direction, purpose and meaning in your life. And be prepared for some unexpected subtle changes in yourself, as your mind opens up to new ideas, and certain old habits simply fall away. It then becomes possible to see through all kinds of distorted thinking and to examine the assumptions behind them, ie notions that have long been unquestioningly accepted as just 'the way it is', and so haven't yet been considered worth seriously investigating or abandoning.

'Aha, now I see it!' – the *stereograph* experience

The *stereograph* experience offers a simplified hint of how it feels to first encounter the *Threshold* perspective. A stereograph is a flat two dimensional image of what at first appears to be a patternless spread of dots, blobs and/or other shapes, familiar and unfamiliar.

However, when you gaze at this in a relaxed, non-focused, non-analytical way for a while, you may suddenly behold there a striking three dimensional image which wasn't apparent before, even though the physical 2D picture hasn't changed at all.

This *'Aha, now I see it!'* experience indicates a shift in perception, ie in *consciousness*, as the mind merges various visual clues and gains a whole new, coherent, 'in-depth' perspective on whatever the 'hidden' picture portrays.

Next, a brief look at a way of understanding *sequence* and *time* on the cosmic scale - necessary for recognising the pattern behind the unfolding sagas of world affairs and individual lives.

Cosmic time

and the turbulent *transition*

from **descent** to **ascent**...

Time has several meanings. It can refer to a particular **moment** or *date*, the **duration** or *period* between occasions, or endless **eternity**. Then there's the difference between the *objective, quantified* time of date, hours, minutes etc and the *subjective, qualitative* experiencing of time passing, including *imagined* time, *past, present* and *future*.

All these distinct notions of time can also be considered aspects of one all-inclusive, continuous process. For the general idea of time relates back to humans sensing the rhythmic pulsating of nature in various repetitive, cyclical patterns, such as the rhythms of their own bodies and lifespans, day and night, the sequence of seasons, the movements of the sun and moon and the changing configurations of stars in the night sky.

Another aspect is the apparent 'speeding up' in the passing of time that many people are currently experiencing, which is an effect of the ongoing **transition** between cosmic eras. And the sensing of this *transition*, as an ongoing, here-and-now moment or event, is what many contemporary artists, scientists and creatives of all kinds are trying to express in their work.

The *descent into matter* era

A key notion in *Threshold* thinking is that pre-physical **cosmic time** – so far as limited human minds can presently grasp ideas on this scale – consists of an alternating, cyclical sequence of eras, each broadly dominated by either *contraction* or *expansion*. And that's in contrast to the linear, physical-material 'arrow of time' idea.

The present departing era is one of **contraction**, which is being superseded by an incoming era of **expansion**. The current phase marks the **transition** between the two.

The *contracting* era is characterised by a cosmic process of **descent into** matter. That is, the 'descending' of consciousness and energy from conditions of *rarity* into increasing *density*, and thus from a faster to a slower rate of pulsation, as described on page 45. Energy is thus drawn 'downwards' by **gravity**, ie inwards towards the centre, resulting in contraction, cooling and condensation into the physical-material realm of matter.

The *descent into matter* has thus been an unbalanced era in which the universal *masculine* has been dominant, affecting all gender denominations. Consequently, humankind has been living in what has predominantly been a *'man's world'*, in which the emphasis has been on focusing, probing, penetrating, centralising, uniformity, mechanical and abstract thinking, quantifying and enforcing... ie the products of *contraction* and *gravity*. And that has resulted in a general lack of empathy with the counterbalancing range of *feminine* human qualities.

The emergence of the biblical figure *Abraham*, which means 'exalted father of a multitude', can be understood as symbolising the rise to dominance of the universal *masculine*, as the *descent into matter* proceeded. This would have been recorded by male scribes, presenting it as the forming of a new nation with a historic mission.

Origins of dis-ease
The context was thus a shifting from a fluid, free-flowing, aethereal, predominantly *feminine* world to an increasingly physical-material, static, *masculine* world of fragmentation and separateness. The easy flow of energy became increasingly obstructed and blocked, and a previous blissful state of oneness with the cosmos became reduced to experiencing limited 'doses' of pleasure only within particular sets of circumstances.

In this deprived condition of imbalance, *dissonance* and unease, various pathological patterns developed and evolved – as humankind's earliest primal *diseases*, including cancer (pages 45, 110).

The *ascent out of matter*

The *descent into matter* era, as already indicated, is now being superseded by a phase of *transition* into its polar opposite, an era of **ascent out of matter**. This will be increasingly characterised by the ways of the universal f*eminine*: radiating, expanding, diversifying, accommodating, fluid, subtle, intuitive, manipulative, enticing and influencing. The changes are bringing about a profound rebalancing throughout the whole gender spectrum.

As a consequence, in conflict situations, instead of gross physical force automatically being used, there has been an increasing emphasis on *soft power* and subtly winning over 'hearts and minds'. And with nuclear war not a viable option – given the *MAD* (**m***utually* **a***ssured* **d***estruction*) factor – messy, expensive, physical warfare is increasingly being replaced by digital *information wars*, fought in cyberspace, involving propaganda, disinformation and currency wars in the financial arena... along with remote-controlled, weaponised drones.

Worldwide there is now an unmistakeable pattern of previously stable *descent era* institutions disintegrating, along with ever increasing numbers of women now taking on roles previously occupied only by men. And that has exposed a pattern of gender inequality regarding pay for work done, highlighting the depth of a long established and hidden imbalance.

Thus more and more women are no longer willing to be treated as inferior human beings at the mercy of men, or as the property of men... although such assumptions still persist in various old, redundant traditions, customs and laws from the *descent* era.

Another sign of rebalancing and shifting priorities in the current transitional phase is a growing appreciation of the significance of the many forms of *mental* illness – long treated as less important than physical illness – and how this affects all aspects of people's lives, including the realisation that it's a major factor behind many physical and social ills.

The *Threshold* view reveals that the *ascent out of matter* is an evolutionary process through which the physical cosmos and all that it comprises is becoming less dense as its rate of pulsation and vibration accelerates. This is part of a yet greater process of **redemption** back into universal consciousness.

It's the polar opposite of the *pre-physical* realm *contracting* and **manifesting** in physical form, and will involve everything reverting first to a more fluid, pre-physical, *aethereal* state, and eventually back into universal consciousness.
This is the cosmic context, the greater pattern behind what has been labelled **global warming**, a process experienced on Earth as **climate change** and **extreme weather**. For expansion normally results in the release of heat. And humankind, swept along as part of the speeding-up process, is a contributing factor... ie consuming more and exacerbating the changes while still unable or unwilling collectively to acknowledge this and act responsibly.

Cosmologists have observed physical signs of an increase in expansive *levity* (so-called *dark energy*) relative to contracting *gravity*, and have interpreted this as evidence that the universe is expanding (or *'inflating'*) at an increasing rate. Meanwhile, one sign of humankind responding to this development is a tendency to behave in more frantic, hurried ways and speak faster. However, more words per minute do not necessarily deliver clearer information, and can more easily result in misunderstandings.

Meanwhile, in this troubled *transition* phase
The cosmos has an inherent natural tendency towards a state of **equilibrium** between the forces of *contraction* and *expansion*. And

so, the *descent* era dominance of humanity's *masculine* aspect over its *feminine* aspect has produced many distortions of life on Earth.

Consequently, in response, there have been many ways in which that imbalance has been countered. For example, in living systems, in response to inhibited, static, unwholesome conditions due to inertia, resulting from chronic *contraction,* an extreme kind of *expansion* is the tendency to multiply and spread. Such is the essential nature of *cancerous* growths and *infestations* of vermin (page 110).

The reaction to extreme *expansion* is normally a tendency towards extreme *contraction*. For example, in economics, the standard response to a period of *expansive,* 'cheap' money, over-indulgent borrowing and spending, and the resulting *inflation* is the imposition of a policy of so-called *austerity,* in which the supply of money, and therefore economic activity, *contract.*

The ideal in most situations is thus an appropriate, dynamic state of *equilibrium* between *impetus* and *inertia,* since some inertia is necessary to provide stability and structure.

So, two cautionary thoughts. First, an excessive predominance of the universal *feminine* over the *masculine* would bring many problems of a polar opposite kind to those experienced throughout the *masculine*-dominated *descent* era. Second, when **expansion** proceeds too fast or too far for some people, it provokes a backlash, a push back in the opposite direction, ie a temporary **contraction**, as part of the universal tendency towards *equilibrium.*

This is what's happening on Earth in the early 21st century, as the predominantly *feminine ascent* era begins to take effect, prompting a *masculine* and therefore predominantly *male* reactionary backlash. And that explains the temporary resurgence of regressive, authoritarian, centralising, so-called **populist** political movements, which broadly represent a step backwards in the direction of dictatorships and **fascism**.

This reaction is mostly against what in the westernised world are called *liberal* values. These represent a compromising but basically conservative attitude. They are also promoted by the greed-driven and predominantly *feminine* (not *female*) global central banking syndicate which controls the world's money supply, and thus most national governments (page 201).

Greed can be understood as a symptom of certain psychological and social factors (page 86).

The mass media follow the money trail
Presently the immature attitude of selfish, fear-driven *greed* is being continuously promoted through the mass media as admirably 'smart'. Why? Because it's an important part of the long term strategy of those who have monopoly control of the world's money supply, money they issue as interest-bearing **debt**... enabling them to exert mass mind control through the media they fund and therefore control.

The purpose of the strategy is to keep humankind disempowered and addictively dependent on this *debt money*, which, when you think it through, doesn't actually exist. Conjured up out of nothing, it's imaginary, an illusion, just a shared idea which has for centuries been cleverly and fraudulently exploited by a small minority in order to (a) pursue a secretive long term *supremacy* agenda, and (b) in the process, make themselves and their accomplices rich.

Yet presently, the pathological mindset of all those who choose to live way in excess of their real, natural needs while fully aware that other humans are struggling to survive in a state of dire deficiency, is still being glorified as successful, admirable and something to be emulated. This is similar to the systematic indoctrination of young children by impressing them with superficial appearances of success, glory or pleasure which they then try to emulate.

'Follow the money' is a well known line of enquiry in investigative work of all kinds. It's also a useful guide in seeking out the source of

50

humanity's worldwide money-related troubles. For it soon becomes clear to an open-minded observer that those who exclusively control the world's money supply intend that humankind should remain dependent on and therefore preoccupied with this *debt money*... rather than with investigating the huge fraud that it is.

So, humankind's collective debt is ultimately owed to the few who continue to delude themselves that they are the smartest people on Earth and therefore inherently *superior* to all other human beings. But that delusional fantasy is approaching a dramatic end, with the outcome still in the balance. Meanwhile, they carry on relentlessly pushing and scheming to eliminate all possible rivals by whatever means they can, while keeping everyone else distracted, fighting amongst themselves and therefore disempowered.

The *redemption* path

It has been mentioned that the *ascent out of matter* is part of a cosmic evolutionary process of *redemption* back into universal consciousness.

Regarding this *redemption* process, a long journey of return through many generations, the first major 'milestone' could be the proposed implementation of something like the project labelled **One Humanity** (page 304). It refers to a future phase in which, as a priority, all real human needs are being met so that nobody has to live in deficiency and, simultaneously, no one lives way in excess of their natural human needs.

For by then a more sane and balanced value system will have evolved, under which all surviving humans will be able to live and thrive together on Earth... because it will have become clear that no other way is viable in the longer run.

Identity: This I Am

What defines my essential identity - if not this body, a name and a few other labels? Here's a view from the *Threshold* perspective.

Individual I

*...am one focal point of **universal consciousness**, one single unit of self-conscious life, and am therefore connected to every other individual being through our shared greater unity.*
('In-dividual' means 'not divisible'.)
*So each individual being is one unique yet integral part of the one **universal I**.*

Universal I

*...is a name which **individual I** use to identify with the all-inclusive **universal consciousness**. At the universal level of existence, there are no separate, isolated beings, in the way that there appear to be on the physical level.*

***Universal I** incorporate the many individual lives embodied in physical matter on Earth. These are shaped by the flow of primal energy resulting from the continuous interaction of **levity** and **gravity**, just as mountains and riverbeds are sculpted by wind and water.*

*The **focal point** of each individual being is within the heart, the centre where the upper and lower circuits of energy and blood-flow cross over. For through generations, body-forms adapt to changing cosmic and earthly conditions.*

***Individual I** am thus much more than a complex lump of physical matter, made of cosmic stardust which, according to modern Western science, is somehow supposed to generate the mysterious something known as **consciousness**.*

*I **am** consciousness which, at its lower levels of vibration, manifests as physical matter. Realising this bi-**polarity** of human identity clarifies the notion of 'mixed motives' in the dynamic between **individual** and **universal** will or **selfish** and **altruistic** behaviour.*

Individual I and humankind

Individual I can think of myself physically as one cell among trillions of other such cells, growing increasingly aware of the diseased condition of our common host organism. How best to serve the self-healing of this complex being, humankind, starts with gaining some understanding of its nature, it's origins and the troubles afflicting it.

Spirit, soul and ego

Spirit is the essential 'fire' of universal consciousness, the vital 'spark' in each individual.

Soul refers to an individual unit of consciousness carrying its own archive of experiences on its own 'homeward' journey towards eventual redemption into universal consciousness.

Ego is the Latin word for 'I', for referring to one's own individual identity. However, since Sigmund Freud used the term in the early 20th century, the 'ego' has become an unflattering term, implying immature, personal self-centredness.

No going back

Once it's realised that each **individual** human being has a **universal** dimension, there's no going back to separated, fragmented ways of thinking about identity, for **individual I** am also one integral part of **Universal I**.

Realising this 'two in oneness' regarding oneself could potentially cause a schizoid split, but that's prevented by knowing that **polarity always exists within a greater unity**.

The Identity Continuum (page 427) is an attempt to summarise the 'two in oneness' of universal I and individual I. For with that awareness, a correspondence can be appreciated between:

(A) *individual development* from infancy, through childhood, adolescence and adulthood to, perhaps, mature, wise seniority... and
(B) *human evolution* from early, primitive, animal-like ways to psychologically, socially and
    ecologically well balanced societies.

This pattern of correspondence, called *recapitulation*, is summarised on page 81. And out of an all-inclusive awareness of one's dual *identity*, a more inclusive sense of morality and ethics can emerge, ie a natural, intuitive feeling for what are called *good* and *evil*.

Good is *balance*, *Evil* is *imbalance*
Good is essentially a state of **equilibrium** or **equipoise**, ie the maintaining of a dynamic balance between the polar opposite forces, *contraction* and *expansion*, in any situation, however complex or simple.

Evil, in any particular situation, can be understood as essentially a state of **imbalance** between the two polar opposites. Too much of one and too little of the other, either way, produces the distortions and stresses which result in *evil* in one form or another. So, there are basically two kinds of evil:
(a) **Excessive contraction**/*gravity*/*masculine qualities*/*yang*/*descent*... resulting in dark, dense, restricting, threatening, materialistic, centralising, *satanic* tendencies.
(b) **Excessive expansion**/*levity*/*feminine qualities*/*yin*/*ascent*... resulting in dazzling, over-ambitious, extravagant, high-flying, enticing, diffusing, *luciferic* tendencies.
All situations labelled *evil* can be seen as the result of such imbalances.

Thus the optimum way to overcome evil is to **rebalance** the whole situation – not condemn, blame or impose 'solutions' in a partisan way.

Simply punishing 'evil-doers', however instantly gratifying that may be, tends to create and feed spirals of vengeance, defiance and resentment, thereby prolonging the trouble. History recounts many examples of evil regimes being overthrown, only for the conduct of their successors, the vengeful victors, to be even more extreme and evil... having become a distorted mirror image of their defeated enemy.

The origins of *good* and *evil* are symbolised in the biblical *Garden of Eden* story. Viewed from the *Threshold*, the cosmic **descent into matter**, humanised in Christian doctrine as the **fall of man**, brought to an end a state of fluid, aethereal, pre-physical, pre-gender existence for evolving humanity. The division into polar opposite living forms (page 61), broadly symbolised by Adam and Eve, signified the beginning of the inertia-bound, fragmented and conflicted, physical-material mentality that still inhibits most human activity.

The more advanced are responsible for the less advanced

Each human being is identifiable as a unique *individual* unit, one *focal point* of universal consciousness, clothed in physical matter, on a long journey of *redemption* through many lifetimes... on the way to redemption back into *universal* consciousness.

So, from the perspective of humanity's collective destiny, those who have travelled further along this route have a clear responsibility to help those following behind, still passing through an earlier stage of the journey. Why? Because neglecting the needs of the less evolved – either deliberately or out of naive unawareness – ultimately harms all humankind... even though how that works out may not be obvious from a ground level viewpoint.

Descent era religions and spirituality

The 'descent' of individual units of universal consciousness into the world of dense physical matter, ie incarnation, has resulted in many temporarily experiencing a sense of disconnection, detachment and separation from their source... like particles of spray temporarily separated from the ocean.

One consequence is a deep longing, at different levels of awareness, to reconnect with the source in order to rediscover the lost sense of completeness and fulfilment. Partially isolated in this way, some humans developed the habit/tradition of naming and worshipping that 'higher' dimension of themselves AS IF it were a separate entity, a supreme being, requiring intermediaries, such as priests, rabbis or imams, to act as go-betweens or agents.

Once people become aware of their disconnection and realise that they can re-connect, the need for such go-betweens and other compensatory substitutes diminishes significantly.

The broad insights of this section also shed light on why so many people are confused about and obsessively fascinated with **sex** and **gender**, the next topic.

Sex and Gender: a fuller understanding

"What sex is, why it evolved and how it works are the biggest unsolved problems in biology." Steve Jones, eminent UK biologist, in The Language of Genes (1993).

But first...

The *polarity* of the complementary cosmic forces, contracting *gravity* and expanding *levity,* is a fundamental working principle of the cosmos. In the living world this polarity manifests as the complementary relationship between the universal *masculine* and *feminine*. So, each creature, of whatever gender – *male, female* or *other* – is a unique combination of <u>both</u>.

How did biological *male/female* gender originate?

Physical life forms first manifest at the <u>pre</u>-*physical* level of existence - that is, the dynamic intermediate level between pure consciousness and the physical-material world. It's the timeless dimension that has been known for centuries as the *aether*, or more recently in physics as the *quantum vacuum* or *quintessence*. It's the realm of <u>potential</u> energy.

A *pre-physical* living form is thus a kind of 'blueprint' design of what may later become a physical creature. And the biological emergence of *male, female* and less clearly defined forms has naturally evolved from the primary *polarity* of centripetal, penetrating *masculine gravity* and centrifugal, accommodating *feminine levity*.

In the accompanying diagram:
(a) The archetypal spherical <u>torus</u> form unites *inner* and *outer* surfaces, symbolising a continuously circulating *inward/outward* flow of energy, expressing the most basic motion of pulsating living forms, *contraction/expansion*.
(b) the point within the spherical *torus* where the two vortices connect represents one particular *focal point* of universal consciousness.

The two vortices on the axis of the torus are being pulled in opposite directions:
(a) **Inward** - drawn towards the centre of the cosmos by the force of *gravity*, and
(b) **Outward** - drawn towards the periphery of the cosmos, by the force of *levity*.

At a crucial stage in the *descent into matter* process, the two vortices are pulled apart by the opposed forces of *levity* and *gravity*. And so, two separate, polar opposite entities are formed, the one drawn towards the cosmic *centre*, the other towards the cosmic *periphery*.

These two *pre-physical* forms are manifestations of the complementary polar opposites:
(a) the outer, *gravity*-powered, inward-probing and penetrating, universal **masculine** and
(b) the inner, *levity*-powered, outward-opening and accommodating, universal **feminine**...
both of which subsequently become physicalised into a range of physical gender forms.

This *polarity* in separate physical bodies is demonstrated, for example, in:
- the *outer* genital organs of males and the *inner* genital organs of females, and
- the dynamics of **expansion** in the erectile penis, clitoris and nipples when *charged up* with energy and fluids, and **contraction** in the polar opposite *discharging* mode.

Diagram warning: The accompanying static, flat 2D diagram is not a pictorial representation of any particular physical forms or living processes. It's intended to portray symbolically the *dynamic* interplay between contracting *gravity* and expanding *levity* in the formative process. The **polarity** of these two universal principles applies at all scales, from macro to micro.

Earthly sex has a cosmic dimension

One universal factor is the constant tendency of the cosmos towards establishing a state of balance or **equilibrium** between the two complementary polar opposite forces: focusing, penetrating *gravity* and radiating, accommodating *levity* – just as organisms tend to maintain an ideal body temperature while adapting to inner and outer changes.

In the 'Origins of Gender' diagram on page 61, the inward-spiralling, *gravity*-dominated, pre-physical vortex form represents '*masculine*' energy being drawn towards the centre of the cosmos. Its most direct and attractive route is through the *levity*-dominated '*feminine*' vortex form, which opens up as it reaches out away from its own and the cosmic centre, drawn towards reunion with the wider cosmos. In performing this function, it draws into itself the inward-spiralling *masculine* vortex form. The outcome is potentially a state of *equilibrium* between *gravity* and *levity*.

When these *pre-physical* energy forms manifest as living, physical-material creatures, the cosmic significance of the *male* and *female* roles in sexual union, ie copulation, is obvious. Then, if the energy flow between the two organisms is not obstructed by muscular tension, emotional inhibition or other factors, the two pulsating cosmic forces mutually combine in an act rhythmical union. And the climax, as they temporarily fuse into one natural energy circuit, is what's known as **orgasm**.

To understand the magic, vital ingredient, ie the true reality and power of sex and sexuality, is to realise how the universal polar opposite forces of the cosmos rhythmically interact in a natural energy discharge and flow between two aroused and willing individuals, ie in full, uninhibited, unfaked orgasm.

Orgasm has nothing to do with outer, physical appearances and dramatised performances, and it's not about shape, size, cosmetics, gymnastics, marathons or vocalising. Nor is it about wealth or social status, since it's not something that can be bought or stolen. And it's not about personal power politics... or shallow, instant gratification, like junk food.

Orgasm is a peak experience of **resonance** with the rhythmic pulsating of the cosmos. It's when the universal, complementary cosmic forces of gravity and levity, as the universal *masculine* and *feminine,* temporarily fuse into one complete circuit of free-flowing bio-energy.

So, this shared moment of supreme, pulsating climax is no trivial, insignificant event, despite all the embarrassment and jokes, due to the associated inhibition and frustration. It's when the power of the inner fire is physically expressed and fully experienced... or not. For that experience can be drastically limited by the inhibiting and de-sensitising effects of emotional wounding and *muscular armouring* (see page 108).

These are significant factors in understanding why and how certain emotionally repressed people can only experience sexual pleasure after their reaching out has had to break through the barrier that is their own armouring, and in the process has become callous anger or violent rage. Simply condemning or punishing this affliction only perpetuates the problem, which may be reproduced through generations and be accepted, unquestioned, as 'normal'.

A similar pattern seems to apply to the sexual abuse of children. However, disgust and anger on the part of parents – naturally fearful for their children's safety, but lacking a deeper understanding of this disturbing symptom – only tend to perpetuate the problem. For it's likely to make potential abusers more devious, as they seek compensatory substitutes for the pleasure of touch/sharing/love etc that was absent or forbidden in their early years.

The human dimension
So, sexual activity always has consequences, short term and long term, for the lives of the participants. The consequences may be beneficial or damaging for either or both, and the need for

Gender: the Evolving of Male and Female Forms
from pre-physical energy-flow patterns

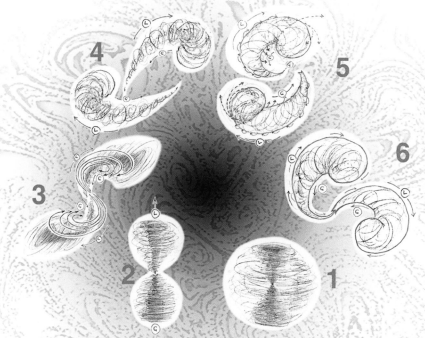

This static 2D diagram comprises a sequence of dynamic pre-physical energy-flow patterns, showing the evolving of archetypal male and female forms within the living, pulsating cosmos.

Gravity, the universal contracting, inward force becomes the universal *masculine* principle.
Levity, the universal expanding, outward force becomes the universal *feminine* principle.
Pre-physical: the intermediate dimension between consciousness and matter.
Torus: an archetypal, dynamic energy form with a single surface that unites *'inner'* and *'outer'*.
Vortex (vortices): a spiralling form contracting into and expanding from a point.
NB The universal *masculine* and *feminine* principles are uniquely combined in each individual of whatever gender.

1   A primal, pre-physical, spherical **torus**, formed by the polar opposite cosmic forces of **gravity** and **levity**, creates along its axis two pre-physical vortices, joined at its centre point.(The basics are explained in *Notes from the Threshold/The Becoming*)

2   The two vortices are being pulled apart, one drawn towards the centre of Earth by *gravity*, the other towards the periphery of the cosmos by *levity*.

3/4 As the 2 vortices begin to condense, separate and evolve into distinct forms, in the one closer to Earth the predominant 'inward' force of *gravity* opens up an aperture/orifice at the point of separation. Correspondingly, this inward pull results in a protruding extension of the other evolving form as it is pulled away. The functional difference between them marks the origin of the 2 complementary forms of genitalia and the 2 archetypal biological genders, **female** and **male.**

5   Energy patterns of a potential male and female, with their potential for growth and forward movement.

6   The reunion and fusion of penetrating *masculine-gravity* and accommodating *feminine-levity* forces into one temporarily complete circuit of living, pulsating energy flow.

awareness of possible outcomes involves responsibilities for both.

Human sexual activity can therefore be understood broadly on **two levels**. On the *biological* level, there's the basic instinctive animal urge to discharge a build-up of natural bio-energy through copulation with an available and compatible partner.

On the 'higher' level of self-aware human beings, much depends on the attitude and feelings of each towards the other life involved in this intimately shared experience, and whether either or both are willing, pro-active participants or not. This is where issues of satisfaction, frustration or displeasure arise.

It's an evolving process

In the early stages of the *descent into matter* – after the separation into physical male and female forms – humankind would have still retained some characteristics and a collective memory of its earlier pre-solid matter state, ie when it was less dense and more fluid. That softer, more *feminine*, flowing quality in early humankind suggests the likelihood of a tendency towards over-indulgence in sexual gratification... which would have had its consequences, including sexually transmitted diseases.

An evolutionary adaptive response to that would have been a phase of sexual restraint, probably instigated by humankind's wiser spiritual guides. But as the increasingly *masculine*-dominated *descent into matter* era proceeded, bringing with it a tendency towards increasing density and inertia, that attitude of restraint, promoted by certain religious leaders, would have become increasingly dominant, restrictive and rigid.

Eventually an ethos of condemnation, punishment and self-denial regarding 'sins of the flesh' would have arisen, creating a situation in which the suppression of natural physical pleasure in the body became an ideal... with the kind of long term results already mentioned.

Viewed from the *Threshold*, liberating changes in attitude and increased diversity are signs of humankind, while currently still in its **collective adolescence**, rejecting the old status quo. Which means experimenting, in a typically individualistic but natural adolescent way, with a fascinating spectrum of possible gender identities and roles... yet still within the confused, ambivalent setting indicated at the beginning of this chapter. Which suggests a growing realisation that personal identity is more than just a physical matter.

Addiction to sex

This deep and complex subject can only briefly be considered here. Addiction to sex involves a state of consciousness in which consideration for a sexual partner as a human being tends to be overridden by an insatiable, lustful desire for the pleasurable sensations of sex. But given that full, natural *orgasm* is one of the most intensely pleasurable physical-emotional experiences possible this addiction mostly seems to involve a craving for compromised, lesser substitutes for the full experience.

The *Threshold* perspective brings an understanding of the powerful cosmic forces driving all sexual urges. So, given some awareness of the possible consequences of following those urges – ie personal, social and biological consequences – humans now have an enhanced **power of choice** regarding sexual activity. However, having that power also inevitably involves personal responsibility.

Meanwhile, many contemporary societies, especially Christian ones, remain deeply confused and troubled about how to accept in an affirmative way this vital, primal element of human nature – and so treat sexual activity that's practiced not solely for procreation as 'sinful'. Which tends to add to both the guilt-ridden **inhibition** and the worldwide rebellious **defiance** about sex. The result is an adolescent-like **ambivalence** of opposed extremes.

An addiction to sex seems to occur especially in the context of unfulfilled lives that lack wholehearted deep love or a profound sense of oneness with the cosmos and nature. So, for example:

- There's the widespread **suppression** of sexuality in many societies that results in an obsessive **fascination** with all things sexual.
- There's the **denial** and **secrecy** that results in its polar opposite, ie **explicit** and exaggerated expressions and displays of sexuality.
- There's the cold, clinical, **biological** 'sex education' which teaches about **procreation** and sexually transmitted **diseases**.
- And, by contrast, there's the range of **idealised, cosmeticised** images of people indulging in a carefree, **irresponsible** sex life.
- Then there's the disempowering **frustration** resulting from a lack of natural, fulfilling sexual involvement... which, combined with a desperate urge to exercise some **power** over weaker and more vulnerable individuals, can result in **sexual abuse** of various kinds.

...And all this along with the 'forbidden fruit' of **pornography**, in its many forms, now produced on a massive scale and available globally through the internet, to feed the voracious, insatiable appetite of sexually unsatisfied lives all over the world.

'Sex' and 'porn' are said to be the most common words typed into internet search engines, and a global online 'cyber-sex' industry provides unlimited substitute stimulation for voyeurs. All of which says plenty about the power of this natural drive, the widespread lack of sexual fulfilment and the lack of any deeper understanding of sex and sexuality.

This is why there are so many glamorised 'body image' and 'sexual performance' products being promoted and sold... and particularly targeted at those most vulnerable and exploitable. The word 'sexy' is widely used to denote anything with an appealing, fascinating quality. And the 'can't get enough' attitude in adverts is where addiction, obsession and selfish greed merge.

Callous exploitation of the vulnerable has been one of the tragic social consequences of the worldwide addiction to sex. For example, children are exploited and abused by adults, the poor by the wealthy, and, overwhelmingly, females by males, such that human trafficking has become a major worldwide industry.

Historically, the repressed **sexual frustration** of young males has long been exploited by **military** and **religious orders** for their own purposes.

Paedophilia, which literally means 'a fondness for children', has become a corrupted term as a result of the widespread confusion and anxiety about sex. When sexuality has been suppressed in childhood, accompanied by embarrassment and inhibition, and further poisoned with guilt, the problems this creates may continue into physical adulthood, for example as an **obsessive, insatiable curiosity and fascination** with bodies and their sexual organs... whether of children or adults.

So, in this much confused world the widespread addictive craving for sexual stimulation is understandable. Distorted sexual desires and the many corresponding subcultures that have arisen worldwide are largely the result of emotional damage due to ignorance of the deeper meaning of sex.

Yet when all this is viewed from the *Threshold* perspective, a coherent pattern emerges. For sex is a comm-union, a unifying coming together. The more committed and fuller the shared experience, the more powerful the energy flow. This means that in well balanced lives there's less need for compensatory substitutes and less chance of an addiction to sex.

How did something as natural as sex become such a loaded subject?

In the *Breast Cancer* section of _Threshold Wellness/Illness,_ a scenario is presented which links prehistoric times and troubles with the range of clues to be found in the various forms of *cancer* prevalent today. **Inhibition**, in a variety of forms attributable to different causes, stands out as a common **emotional** factor behind the various **physical** manifestations of the disease.

This understanding is affirmed by realising that the breasts are outer expressions or extensions of the **heart**. For situated at the centre of the chest - where love, sadness and longing are experienced and nurturing impulses are generated - is the *pre-physical* heart, which functions at a more subtle level than the physical heart, situated towards the left side. (The connection between the two is another subject ripe for some investigative research.)

And that provides a vital clue regarding the incidence of breast cancer in sexually confused, inhibited, breast-obsessed societies, ie those in which female breasts and nipples have acquired an iconic *sexual* status. It also connects with how female breasts, in a male-dominated world, have come to be treated like ornaments for attracting **orally** unsatisfied males in *peep show* enticement games of *hide and seek*.

And then there are the many variations on this *oral* theme, all to do with people stuffing things in their mouth for emotional comfort and compensatory pleasure. All of which suggests a deep psychological problem of **guilt within humankind regarding sex and experiencing pleasure**. This appears to be connected historically to the influence of certain religious institutions as they became inertia-bound, although there can be no final proof or disproof in these matters.

One symptom is the still widespread intolerant, disapproving attitude of *denial*, *withholding* and *inhibition*, ie **contraction**. This results in the suppression of natural physical pleasure in the body... which includes the whole broad area of sexuality. Consequently, *descent era* ignorance and the *masculine* tendency towards *contraction*, emotional inhibition and dogmatism have created a long history of confusion, guilt and sexual frustration, accompanied by much condemnation and punishment for so-called 'sins of the flesh'.

The result has thus been much suffering due to many related symptoms, physical and psychological, individual and social. The 2018 emergence of the '***incel***' (*involuntarily celibate*) phenomenon via the internet was one more sign of old, deep, dark problems now surfacing in this the case anger of sexual frustration.

Today, within the still male-dominated Christian Church - as well as in other religious and secular institutions, including the military - there remain many signs of this troubling problem. As a consequence, there's turbulence and confusion worldwide concerning sexuality and gender, reflected in a continuing flow of revelations of perverse sexual gratification and exploitation, ie **abuse**, previously kept hidden by 'the authorities'.

Through centuries the overall situation became increasingly confused by taboos on the whole subject. Consequently, a deep misunderstanding about the problem has become normalised into a widespread false assumption that *'This is simply how it is'*. And that accounts for such notions as 'forbidden fruit', 'dirty' jokes, 'naughty but nice' etc, which demonstrate the confusing ambivalence created by all the fraught, hostile intolerance, based on ignorance, prejudice, guilt, shame and fear.

Sexual confusion and frustration tend to leave people discontented and psychologically weakened. They are then exploitable, politically, commercially and psycho-spiritually. And that dissatisfaction accounts for the myriad distortions of natural sexuality normally labelled as *perverse* or *obscene*, some of which are also decreed illegal, punishable offences.

When such unbalanced ways have become so familiar and embedded in a culture that they are statistically 'normal', they tend not to be recognised as symptoms of a deep sickness in that society, or as a sign of the troubled state of humanity. Further evidence of this is the vast quantity of so-called *pornographic* material being produced and consumed worldwide.

So, given the amount of sexual material of all kinds readily accessible online, from now on it will no longer be acceptable for certain fundamental questions to be ignored, glossed over or rejected because of the unease or embarrassment of some parents, teachers and others... who are themselves mentally trapped in belief systems not fit to handle today's challenges. Thus the need for some enlightened improvements in what presently passes for so-called **sex education** in most countries.

Then in 2017, an age-old unresolved conundrum suddenly became a hot media topic, especially in the UK and USA...

What is acceptable or '*inappropriate*' sexual conduct?

For any complex problem to be adequately resolved, it has to be considered in its *context*. And the relevant context here is the current phase of cosmic *transition*, described earlier, and a general lack of awareness of the cosmic evolutionary origins of sex and gender.

On Earth the *transition* is working through in an uneasy rebalancing of the dynamic between the two polar opposite principles, the universal *masculine* and *feminine*. That is to say, it's being acted out in the endless variety of personal relationships among the many human gender categories.

And that lack of awareness is resulting in unbalanced, inconsistent thinking and behaviour: sometimes driven by fear, inhibition, guilt or coyness (*contraction*), sometimes by irresponsible, reckless bravado (*expansion*), and mostly by combinations of these polar opposite tendencies.

Another factor in today's upfront, multicultural, online world, is the widespread confusion and conflict resulting from different traditions, each with its own system of beliefs, values and procedures, colliding and interacting. Added to that is the endless diversity of personalities, character, experience and understanding... along with the increasing unwillingness of women to be treated as inferior, sexually exploitable human beings.

All of which, taken together, have made the business of developing mature personal relationships, especially regarding sex, a minefield of potential misunderstandings and offence. Thus the wide range of views on what is acceptable or inappropriate behaviour.

If the *Threshold* understanding of sex and gender were common knowledge, and **self-defence** – psychological and physical – were part of a normal education, then relationships could develop in more mutually self-confident and creative ways... less fraught with fear, guilt or anxiety about inadequacy, succeeding or failing, winning or losing etc. There would also be less faking and trivialising in order to conceal people's ignorance and unease.

The gender spectrum

Within the natural evolutionary process, numerous adaptive mutations continuously emerge, resulting in a **spectrum** ranging between extreme *maleness* and extreme *femaleness*.

From the late 20th century, the shift from an era of *descent into matter* towards one of *ascent out of matter* has been marked by a relaxing of attitudes towards *gender*. That is to say, the previous **binary**, **'either/or'** idea that *'Men are men, women are women, and any blurring of that distinction is a problem'* is gradually being replaced by a recognition that there exist naturally a broad spectrum both of gender and sexuality.

In the past, the simplistic binary distinction of *male* or *female* was made more flexible in such expressions as 'his *feminine* side' or 'her *masculine* side' – which did not imply that such a man was womanly or such a woman was manly. So, in general, how harmonious or otherwise any personal relationship turns out to be may depend on how the *masculine* and *feminine* qualities in each partner mutually balance out.

And recently, significant technological advances in surgery and hormonal treatments have greatly enhanced the range of gender options and transitions possible. The vocabulary is therefore also evolving rapidly. So for now, here are just two basic terms:

Transgender: an umbrella term for all gender identities that are not simply '*male* or *female*'.

Non-binary: an umbrella term for those who refuse to identify themselves as either male or female. Numerous other terms are also now in use for defining specific gender identities.

Becoming over-concerned with superficial individual differences is a typical *adolescent* trait, part of establishing one's own distinctive ***identity***. Along with gender, the endless sub-categories of styles, fashions and preferences in clothes, cosmetics, music, vocabulary etc are evidence of this. Similarly, humankind's *collective adolescence* is revealed in the numerous denominations within various religions.

Such over-focussing on worldly details can be a weakness that distracts people's attention away from a more profound and empowering awareness of their own deeper/higher sense of *identity*. That is, as one *individual* unit of consciousness, a unique *focal point* of the all-inclusive *universal* consciousness. It can also leave those individuals who feel out of place in their own bodies and/or in their societies vulnerable... and vulnerable people are exploitable.

One outcome has been that as humankind passes through its current phase of immature greed-driven commercialisation and monetisation, the marketing of 'gender options' has become a highly profitable business, such has been the upsurge in demand.

Another dimension of this complex subject is the question of ***reincarnation***, ie what qualities, experiences and unresolved issues may have been carried over into this lifetime from previous lifetimes. On a larger scale, the evolutionary shift from an era of *masculine*-dominated *descent* to a more *feminine*-influenced one of *ascent* brings major **psychological** challenges for everyone, regardless of gender. And that includes the potential for greater fulfilment or greater loss and suffering, as individuals and cultures either successfully adapt or fail to adapt... part of the business of the next chapter.

Threshold Psychology
The science of consciousness

This subject is at the heart of all *Threshold* knowledge and thinking. It's therefore an integral part of every topic addressed in this book, including identity, wellness and illness, sex and gender, politics, finance, economics, evolution, artificial intelligence, spirituality and more.

That's because from the *Threshold* perspective, the first universal principle of the cosmos is the *primacy of consciousness*. Which means that for incarnate humans, *universal consciousness* – by whatever name it is known, spiritual or scientific – is the ultimate reality, and everything in the cosmos is therefore a manifestation of it.

Psyche is an ancient Greek word for the *soul*, the *pre-physical* dimension of every human being, each of whom can be understood as one *focal point* of universal consciousness. So, *Threshold psychology* is the primary discipline, the main stem from which all others branch out. It serves as the hub, the unifying, linking element that connects all other disciplines.

As a subject on its own, it could fill several volumes, but for present purposes, just a few brief glimpses into a few key areas will have to suffice. Without this essential, fundamental knowledge, other disciplines remain incomplete and unbalanced, and therefore tend to suffer from anomalies, paradoxes, conundrums and enigmas.

Being all-inclusive, *Threshold* psychology is concerned with both:
(a) big, open-ended questions, such as '*What is my true identity, beyond this body, my name and my genealogy?*','*How do I fit into the bigger cosmic picture?*' and '*What are we all doing here on Earth?*', and

(b) specific, personal questions, such as 'Why do some individuals take an instant dislike to certain people while others do the opposite, and some do neither?'

Along with **consciousness**, the other two universal *Threshold* principles, **polarity** and **resonance**, are also essential elements of *Threshold Psychology*.

Polarity and *resonance* in psychology

These are the two main factors that account for how compatible or incompatible, friendly or hostile, and trusting or mistrusting people are. Which in turn affect how in tune with the rhythms of nature and the cosmos their lives are, and so, how well or unwell they are.

Polarity here is about how the interaction between the two primal forces, *expansion* and *contraction*, works out in each individual, each group and each relationship. And that includes the dynamic between people's *masculine/yang* and *feminine/yin* aspects, regardless of their individual gender.
It illustrates the dynamics of people's *motivation*, ie between selfishness and altruism, their varying *emotional* states, their desires, passions, hopes, ambitions, regrets, fears, and anxieties. It's also a way of gauging people's honesty or deceitfulness, and how tense or relaxed, how vain or modest, how courageous or risk-averse they are and so on.

Resonance and its polar opposite, *dissonance* (page 37), describe how certain tonal and rhythmical qualities affect lives and relationships positively or negatively, and so tend either to connect and unite or separate and divide people.

Overview and *insight*

So, in order to investigate any human situation, what's needed first is a combination of:
(a) an all-inclusive **overview** of the whole situation within its broader context, and

(b)   some penetrating *insight* into the motivation at the heart of it. Then the details, connections and mechanisms in between can be filled in as appropriate.

The ultimate *Threshold* **overview** is described in **The Becoming of Cosmos out of Chaos** (page 26) and is later developed in the section on **Natural Involution/Evolution** (page 354), all derived from the three fundamental *Threshold* principles. The story throughout the *masculine* and *gravity*-dominated *descent* era has been one of humanity focussing and gaining increasing knowledge of the gross, dense, physical-material world... but, in the process, losing other, more subtle and complex faculties, such as the navigational abilities of migrating birds.

Insight from the *Threshold* reveals how each *focal point* of universal consciousness at the heart of each individual creature, is continuously seeking to experience, however misguidedly, some 'feelgood' *resonance* with the cosmos – ie is trying to 'make the most' of this lifetime with whatever 'assets', physical and non-physical, can be worked with in the present circumstances.

The Integrity Ladder diagram (next page) shows how people's everyday, ground-level choices are linked to their higher, guiding principles, whether or not they're aware of the continuity connecting the 'vertical' range of levels of their consciousness. Also, each level gives a different perspective on the world, highlighting different factors and features, as the most prominent and therefore the most important.

Which is why there is often a lack of meaningful communication in dialogues between people viewing a situation from different levels, resulting in them seeing it in a different context, each according to their own assumptions and priorities.

Context is crucial - since nothing happens out of nothing
An essential element of all *Threshold* investigating is the **context** of the situation under consideration. And the ultimate context here is

The Integrity Ladder

The Ladder connects our everyday choices and decisions
with our highest guiding principles, and vice versa,
enabling consistency and integrity.

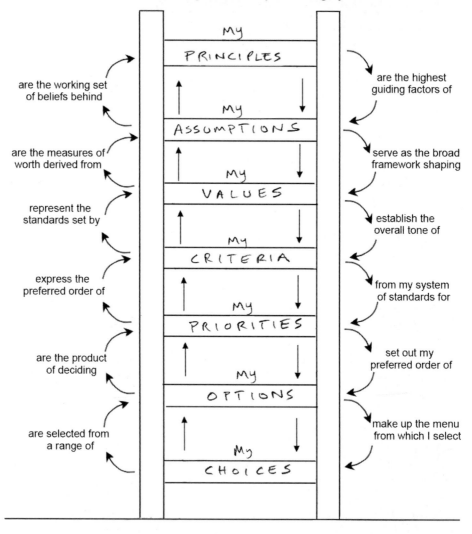

the constantly changing panorama of cosmic and human evolution, described earlier, which affects both the subtle and the more obvious dynamics of all earthly human activity.

Nothing simply happens out of nothing, since all phenomena, physical and non-physical, occur within particular sets of circumstances, ie their *context*. Each person, as one unique unit of human consciousness embodied in physical matter, is therefore the product of a complex combination of factors. And these factors are constantly changing.

Briefly revising a few basics, the predominant characteristic of the currently departing cosmic era of *descent into matter* is **contraction**. That means contracting *gravity* dominating its polar opposite force, expanding *levity*, which naturally displays a constant tendency to restore a state of **equilibrium** between them. The main contrasting qualities of the two polar opposite forces are displayed on page 34.

When thinking is restricted within a boxed in, limited context, the result is usually an inadequate, unappealing range of options. Thinking *out-of-the-box,* ie **beyond** the present context and its related assumptions, then becomes a more appealing proposition and perhaps the only game-changing way ahead, despite being more challenging and risky.

There is a natural evolutionary human urge to excel in whatever ways one can. But that's hindered by the density, inertia and fragmentation resulting from the *descent into matter*. These impulses are thus obstructed, causing some people to feel frustrated and believe that they're in competition with rivals on a similar quest. Which creates an atmosphere of hostility and conflict, rather than harmonious cooperation.

One victim of the *descent era*

Think of a typically *expansive*, confident, outgoing, assertive, expressive and successful individual. Then, by contrast, think of a child whose natural urge to express and excel was suppressed, inhibited and had to be contained because of the restrictions imposed – an example of withdrawal inward, ie *contraction*. The outcome could well be a person with low self-esteem, ie a self-image of an insignificant, powerless person, unworthy of respect.

But held captive within that inhibited, constrained person lurks an awesome *anger monster* – the product of years of suppression and containment – which could suddenly break out and use its destructive power to cause general disruption and wreck relationships.

The result of this continuous inner conflict between *expansion* and *contraction* is a life of anxious, emotional hyper-sensitivity, in which vital energy is depleted by the constant need for *vigilance* and by the muscular *tension* required in order to mask and contain that danger.

The inevitable outcome is chronic fatigue, irritability and other symptoms, which in turn feed back into the already troubled body-mind and perpetuate a general pattern of under-performance. Any creative, expressive or spontaneous behaviour tends to be limited to certain familiar, emotionally safe, comfort zone activities in which to excel.

Also, the fear of failure and dreading the loss of one's basic human dignity can result in a defensive, *self-protective* attitude towards the world in general, and a rejecting of any expectations of successful achievements. Such personalities tend to be exploitable by those skilled at manipulating, for their own advantage, other people's submissive powerlessness and pre-programming regarding who is *superior* and who is *inferior* in their society.

And that leads on to questions about **hierarchies** and the complex subject of **mind control**, which is a major topic on its own, involving such questions as which kinds of people are more susceptible to *hypnosis, programming, bullying, suggestion* etc, and how these various techniques actually work.

Hierarchies in a multi-level world

Just about everyone is familiar with *hierarchies* of one kind or another, ie systems of ranking in order of status, power, authority, wealth, privileges, giftedness etc. It might be a social class or a caste system, an order of seniority within an organisation, or a league table based on results achieved. And at the top level of a hierarchy is its **elite** group.

The *Threshold* perspective reveals a clear distinction between two kinds of *hierarchy*, and therefore two kinds of *elite*. And that suggests a choice as to what kind of hierarchy and world different people would prefer... and be prepared to work towards. One points towards a sane and more balanced future, the other is a reflection of the familiar present and deeply flawed world.

- **Natural hierarchies** of inherent abilities, attributes, talents, qualities and characteristics – develop through accumulated experience and learning. They affirm that everyone has something to offer the world from their own perspective. Such hierarchies tend to have **wise elites**, comprising proven, competent, impartial, altruistic individuals who do not seek material rewards. Their fulfilment comes through the honour and respect they get for taking on and fulfilling such responsibilities. (See *OH*, page 304) OR...

- **Man-made hierarchies**, arising out of *descent era* ignorance of the basic *Threshold* principles, tend to be based on fear, insecurity and anxiety. So, they involve power-lust, competitive rivalry, hostility, domination, manipulation, vanity and greed. They tend to be headed by **elites**, driven by primitive self-interest and partisanship, who crave worldly power, material rewards and wealth beyond their natural human needs.

Elites can thus be wise or unwise, humble or arrogant, altruistic or selfish. Also, the term *elitism* does not imply that all hierarchies and elites are unjust and unnatural. Each human being's unique history, has resulted in that person reaching a certain level on the evolutionary scale of maturity, learning, balance and wisdom. Symbolically, this can be pictured as a staircase with steps representing degrees, up to the highest levels reachable.

Those who reach the higher levels will have experienced all the levels below on the way up. So, they will have had the chance to gain a more inclusive worldview... enabling **but not guaranteeing greater understanding and wisdom** than is possible from the lower levels.

However, this does <u>not</u> imply that people at higher levels of development are inherently *superior* human beings who therefore deserve privileges, authority and material wealth in excess of their natural needs, while others are left to suffer in deficiency... despite the still common tendency to accept such unjust situations as natural and inevitable.

That tendency is the result of mass indoctrination throughout the *descent* era by ruling elites (who are not necessarily the most evolved humans) attempting to justify their privileged lifestyles and status as protectors and leaders. And so, certain dynasties have remained committed to preserving their exclusive, hereditary *bloodlines* – as part of their tribal/medieval, tradition-bound mentality of '**superior us** over **inferior them**', ie being '*winners*'.

The *Threshold* perspective brings the realisation that reaching a higher level naturally incurs an obligation to assume a certain degree of personal responsibility for the wellbeing of those at lower levels. So, any selfish exploiting of one's worldly advantages, in order to gain material wealth, status, power, authority, control or privileges, while neglecting the needs of the less evolved, amounts to failing both oneself and all humankind.

How does that moral obligation fit into the bigger picture? The evolutionary function of the cosmic tendency towards **equilibrium** – in this case, the balancing out of **deficiency** and **excess** – is to reduce the stress and suffering due to imbalance, and so enable humanity to proceed more efficiently towards its eventual **redemption**, as summarised earlier.

Addiction to winning

In English there exists a range of words concerning *winning* – which suggests how important the idea has been throughout the *descent* era. They include *success, victory, triumph, defeat, conquer, vanquish, overcome, beat* etc.

The *addiction* can be traced back to the natural childhood and primitive striving to establish one's individual identity and place in various social pecking orders. In contemporary adult society it can be seen, for example, in career rivalry, arguing, debating, bargaining, negotiating, competitive sports and gambling. Players and spectators alike can become obsessed with and addicted to the thrill of winning which generates a false sense of power and pride, however hollow and misguided, in not being a 'loser'.

But **what's natural in childhood can become dangerous and toxic in adulthood** – as *ASS* (page 89). The striving of children to be the best in a particular activity is natural and mostly beneficial – that is, while they're children, testing their development against others. In adult life, however, if the desire to win remains an unsatisfied craving, including the desire to defeat rivals or enemies, it can create serious problems for the whole society. That's why when competitive games and sports serve as substitute combat activities, these ritualised contests and battles can become highly charged emotionally for all involved.

As a classic divide-and-rule trick, the role of 'winner' has long been greatly glamorised and hyped up in the mass media, while the shadow side of this is a callous disregard for the 'losers', ie most of

79

humanity. Thus the cheating and fraud, often very creative, in all areas of life, and the use of performance enhancing drugs etc in many competitive activities.

The adrenaline-endorphin rush of excitement from being totally in the moment, and gaining some immediate acclaim, reward or relief for overcoming a particular challenge, can be such a powerful experience that a craving to repeat it develops into a habit. The addiction will then take the form of that particular activity. It's also closely related to *ASS, Addictive Superiority Syndrome* (page 89).

Risk takers of all sorts are familiar with the process. Comedians, for example, speak of an addiction to winning laughs from their audiences – at the risk of 'dying', ie failing, while performing.

So, when a significant number of people share an addictive affinity for a particular competitive pursuit, it may become an accepted tradition, institutionalised within that society's culture. **The amount of such rivalry in a society indicates how immature it still is**, and how its rulers are exploiting that weakness by promoting competition in all areas of life, as a *divide-and-rule* technique. It's especially obvious in politics, commerce, sport, education and even in the arts. And it's no accident – it's a basic *ASS* technique of mass mind control.

Recapitulation (page 81) in this case, is a kind of repeating of a process from humankind's earlier evolutionary history that's re-run in each individual's infancy and childhood years. The amount of competitive rivalry in a society indicates how immature it still is, and how its rulers are exploiting that weakness by promoting competition in all areas of life, as a *divide-and-rule* technique. It's especially obvious in politics, commerce, sport, education and even in the arts, and is no accident – it's a basic *ASS* technique of mass mind control.

Addiction to gambling
This is closely related to the addiction to *winning* and risk-taking, and involves a fascination with successfully predicting the outcome

of particular situations. The form it takes depends upon the motives of the gambler, which could be selfish or altruistic.

The financial circumstances of the gambler are also significant. For the poor, it may represent a chance, however remote, of some relief or escape from poverty, while for the rich and poor it may simply be the passing thrill of winning a trivial game of chance.

On a global scale, *descent era* ruling elites gamble continuously in order to maintain the status quo, under which they consider themselves to be 'winning'. This they do by keeping the odds well stacked against a more balanced, just and healthy world. But once the old *debt money* system disintegrates and is abandoned, resulting in the decline and fall of *SCAB*, so the old territorial state ruling elites' grip over increasingly discontented and aware populations will also weaken, increasing the odds against their survival.

Recapitulation (Re-living earlier developmental stages)

In this context, the word refers to:
(a) how individuals re-enact phases from earlier periods of their current life cycle, and
(b) how these re-enactments represent earlier phases in the evolving of humanity as a whole.

Some adults, in their behaviour, clearly display the attitudes and ways of the *infant*, the *child* and the *adolescent* they once were, while these displays also correspond to earlier, more primitive stages in the evolving of humankind. For example, and much simplified:

- The **baby**, totally dependent for its survival, represents primitive, vulnerable humankind.

- The self-centred, dependent **infant**, beginning to evolve a sense of individual identity,
 ie of 'self and other', represents early settlement-based, tribal humankind.

- The **child**, establishing his/her status in various *pecking order* hierarchies, represents humankind in its *'us v. them'* phase of tribal competitive rivalry. This is when humans learn the trick of lying and deceiving others in various ways, and first experience the passing thrill of false power it can bring. For example, *'I'm the king of the castle, you're the dirty rascal...'* is a traditional children's triumphant chant about *sovereignty* claims

- The **pre-adolescent**, fascinated with status, secrecy, cliques, symbols, codes and numbers, loosely represents *medieval* humankind, living in organised towns and city states with formal, hierarchical structures of governance, religion, trading, moneylending and arts.

- The **adolescent**, a mixture of infantile, childish and adult qualities, typically displays volatile emotions and extreme attitudes while seeking *independence* – yet without fully appreciating the benefits of *inter*dependence. This phase corresponds with the emergence of industrialised nation states, central banks, corporations, organised religions, and political *'separatist'* movements, pushing to assert their own unique identity. In the early 21st century, most of humankind, with exceptions, is still at this challenging stage.

- The **young adult** shows *empathy* in an increasingly mature ability and willingness to 'walk in someone else's shoes', ie to identify with other people's feelings and perspectives.
  An example would be if 'innocent' citizens in a particular country could see themselves
  through the eyes of a person they've labelled as a 'terrorist', realising that the 'terrorist'
  sees them as biased, hypocritical accomplices, responsible for electing leaders who act in
  hostile ways toward the so-called terrorist's people.

- The **mature adult**, with qualities of balanced, responsible, <u>non-partisan</u> leadership, parenting, mentoring, counselling etc, represents a stage that most of humankind hasn't yet reached. An important lesson learned by this stage is not to be manipulated or 'bullied' psychologically by less developed humans who threaten trouble if their self-centred wishes are not granted. Here humankind still has much to learn.

- The **wise elder** represents wisdom, mature compassion, inspiration, guidance etc – again, qualities that most of humankind hasn't yet manifested.

Stuck at a lower level: ie an earlier stage of development

Given that understanding, it's evident that many physically mature human beings who continue to think and behave in immature ways have become stuck at a certain earlier stage in their own personal development, a stage that also corresponds to an earlier one in humanity's collective evolving. Old biblical images of a mature God, or one of his earthly agents, as the *shepherd* with humankind as his *flock of sheep*, confirm this understanding.

There are some who consider themselves 'anti-competition', perhaps after witnessing the ugliness or experiencing the unpleasantness of some forms of *descent era* competition. But that does not take into account the fact that *competition* comes in various forms which can include 'opponents' agreeing to strive against one another, enabling them both to excel through testing their own and each other's limits. Such competing is therefore ultimately a *cooperative* endeavour (see page 291, regarding *sport*). Also, people can compete in endeavours that benefit their whole society, so that everyone 'wins' one way or another.

Class and caste systems – of *winners* and *losers*

Hierarchy problems arise when knowledge of the basic *Threshold* principles has been lost, a consequence of the *inertia* that's an unavoidable result of the *descent into matter*. The resulting distortion in thinking has then encouraged some people to falsely imagine that they are inherently *superior* human beings who somehow have an automatic right to special privileges, wealth, status, authority, power and so on.

Referring back to **recapitulation**, this tendency is a sign of a basic immaturity which has become tradition-bound and institutionalised, such that it's widely regarded as a kind of inevitable, unquestionable, unchangeable, natural reality... simply 'the way things are'.

Obvious examples would be the rigid *class* and *caste* systems in which elite groups try to evade the responsibilities that come with reaching higher levels of evolvement. This is, in effect, *negligence*. The rigidity and callousness is the result of *descent era* **inertia** hardening people's mental processes. And when such patterns are allowed to evolve, toxic cultures of *superiority* and *inferiority* arise, prompting further troubles – a theme developed later.

In these cases, it's usually the 'winners' – ie those with the wealth, the weaponry and the know-how regarding *mind control* and *governance* – who write a society's laws and its history in ways that favour themselves. And according to their own agendas, they decide what's to be included in and excluded from the education of their young, as well as what subjects are taboo for the mass communicators.

For *descent era* ruling elites, if unchecked, tend to steer a course towards some kind of neo-feudal/fascist set-up, drastically reducing the 'upwardly aspiring' middle classes. The resulting mass underclass of disempowered, deprived, distracted and discontented citizens can then be divided, controlled and ruled through force and clever use of the mass media.

Such is the intent behind the **democracy delusion** (page 225) that's still being promoted in the westernised world. There the so-called '*will of the people*' is manipulated through the mass media in

84

numbers game elections, subtly corrupted by clever PR mind-control tricks.

The basic method is to deprive the mass majority of an education that empowers them to examine and question the status quo in a systematic and radical way. And so they remain unable to recognise how they are being tricked and exploited. Deeper questions thus arise about the responsibilities of being one of the more evolved human beings:

- *Should humans who are more evolved be allowed legally to exploit for their own worldly advantage those they know are currently less evolved... or is there an overriding, natural, universal, human obligation to support and help educate the less advantaged?*

- *In any disputed situation, are the lives of the more advanced humans being guided by compassion and wisdom, or by arrogance and selfishness, like discontented older children bullying and tricking younger children... because they still can without being punished?*

- *Are **lying** and **cheating**, techniques first discovered in **infancy** to be effective in achieving short term goals, socially acceptable behaviour, eg when justified as not actually illegal?*

- *Is a young, less evolved life worth less than that of an older, more evolved one?*

Or, in more direct and personal terms:

- *Are you willing to continue being indoctrinated and misguided into behaving like an insecure, fear-driven, selfish child, trained to be deferential and submissive towards authority figures and wealthy individuals, however unbalanced and misguided they may be, OR...*

- *Do you yearn for a more meaningful and fulfilling life, not constrained, corrupted or harmed by the toxic effects of the currently unbalanced, distorted world order on Earth?*

(If you do, you could try working steadily through this potentially empowering book.)

These questions lead on to a crucial question that many people would prefer to ignore.

How have *so many people* come to feel *disempowered* and *ignorant*?

Referring back to *One victim of the descent era* (page 75), most people feel they have little influence, individually and collectively, on world events, whether it's a question of 'Who's in charge?', 'Who gets what?', 'Who to believe?' etc... or in trying to cope with the ever deteriorating state of our earthly environment.

Keeping humanity preoccupied with these concerns and in endless rivalry and competition has so far been an effective diversionary tactic, a distraction, used by certain minorities.

They are the current ruling elites worldwide, who have thus been able to maintain their privileged positions, however bad things may be for the majority they rule over.

These few always appear to have smarter ways of operating than the rest. They know how to keep 'winning' and stay on top, despite all kinds of setbacks. And so they've kept the deprived, divided and disempowered 'many' in ignorance and fear, disheartened, deeply discontented, insecure, and greedily craving over-indulgence by way of compensation. As a result, all on Earth continue to suffer, in varying degrees, the consequences of this unbalanced situation.

Greed

Greed itself arises as **a symptom of a deep *fear* of deprivation, poverty and failure**. Which together create an ***anxious*** feeling of *insecurity*, itself due to a sense of **vulnerability** that results from **ignorance** of how the whole cosmos works. The resulting lack of fulfilment generates a discontented feeling of **emptiness** in this life, and a craving to acquire and consume **compensatory comforts** of one kind or another to remedy that uneasy feeling.

Infantile, greed-driven behaviour by adults usually results in bad outcomes one way or another, whether in one's personal life, career or the wider society. That's because it distorts the natural balancing tendency towards an *equilibrium* state between any extremes of deficiency and excess in each life.

Lack of *trust* undermines all relationships
The psychology of personal relationships is too complex a subject for this book, but a couple of key points stand out. Through the experience gained in developing close personal relationships, an individual can progress from the mentality of *infantile* and *child*-like **dependency**, through an *adolescent*-like quest for **independence** and **autonomy**, to mature, *adult* **inter-dependence**.

An essential ingredient for progressing through this process is an appreciation of the value of TRUST, ie the special quality in relationships that can create a lasting mutual bond of *confidence* (page 170).

So, in the light of the three basic *Threshold* principles, and with an awareness of the current shift from an era of *descent* into one of *ascent*... what is going on?

There's a major *addiction* problem
Briefly, an *addiction* is a longing for relief or for some kind of satisfaction, a longing which has degenerated into a repetitive craving for some substitute for that satisfaction. It amounts to being enslaved to a desire – which means being psychologically trapped in a distorted state of consciousness, with a habitual craving to indulge in some kind of self-gratification.

Addiction to sex has already been addressed (page 63). Other addictive patterns are addressed elsewhere in this work, including *addiction to winning, food, drugs, money, gambling, violence* and *weaponry, territory* and *property*, and *artificial/digital/virtual worlds.*

Most modern societies seem to treat the more familiar addictions as a certain kind of enemy which has to be attacked and defeated, whether it's a substance or an activity. The crucial questions <u>not</u> normally asked concern what's lacking in people's lives such that they feel deeply unfulfilled and in need of some extra 'magic' to enliven their existence... or at least relieve their misery. Here the *Threshold* perspective can bring insight and healing.

Whose problem is it?

From the *Threshold* perspective, it becomes clear that humanity is presently being subtly controlled, exploited and dominated by a small group of addicts whose pathological condition means they cannot avoid making life worse for everyone else. That is, so long as they're allowed to continue indulging their habit.

What is that habit? It's their addictive attachment to acting out **a delusion that they are inherently superior to the rest of humankind**, and therefore have a God-given right to excessive wealth, unjustifiable privileges and unmerited authority to rule over all nations.

As with most addictions, their **symptoms** can be understood as **substitutes** which compensate
for a **lack** of something more profound, ie a lack of *resonance* with the cosmos and therefore a lack of any deep sense of **fulfilment** in their lives. Also, their elite culture, with its high expectations of success and supremacy, does not gladly tolerate failure by its members to live up to its ambitious standards.

And since substitutes cannot satisfactorily fill that psychological gap, that emptiness, the result is **a constant craving for more control** over life on Earth – at whatever cost to the rest of the world, friend or foe.

So it all comes down to doing whatever it takes to feed the addictive habit, to stay ahead of the game and at least maintain the status quo of *superiority/inferiority*. And if that involves damaging other people's lives and the natural environment, so be it. It has to be done. *'This is our destiny'* – or at least, so it seems to the addicts.

This psycho-pathological condition is at the root of many familiar problems in human relationships, whether interpersonal or collective, ie concerning family, tribal, religious, ethnic or national identities. And that in turn affects people's sense of harmony, allegiance, loyalty and duty, or discord, difference, rivalry and enmity.

What to call this condition?

A *syndrome* is a group of symptoms that characterise a specific disorder. Syndrome names are used as concise descriptions of various behaviour patterns. Their use became common in late 20th century US psychiatry, when targeting specific symptom patterns with profitable pharmaceutical 'fixes' became the fashionable approach - instead of treating the whole person in the context of his or her whole life so far.

By contrast, the *Threshold* perspective, with its *overview* and *insight*, always includes the broader context of any specific symptoms observed, because there's always both an *individual* and a *universal* dimension. And since the condition in question here is an extremely addictive one with its own clear pathological symptom pattern, ie an attitude of **superiority**, an appropriate contemporary name for it is...

Addictive Superiority Syndrome (ASS)

However, to name a pattern of symptoms in this way is not to condemn or imply any blame. It's simply an attempt to describe it as something clearly recognisable. Other well known examples of syndromes are AIDS and SARS.

How does addiction happen?

The *descent into matter* has left humanity fragmented into isolated units of consciousness, a collection of individuals whose awareness has become disconnected from the oneness of the cosmos and thus from their ultimate identity, *universal consciousness*, ie their *universal I*. And that lack creates a feeling of insecurity, along with a desire to rediscover the power and reassuring pleasure of the lost sense of unity.

As a consequence, many people feel unfulfilled, dulled, inhibited and frustrated, and are seeking some form of compensation for what seems to be missing in their lives. Making do with substitutes or medical relief can then seem to be the best compromise. The outcome then tends to be a balancing act between opposed emotional states, treated with what are essentially either 'uppers' or 'downers' of one sort or another.

How do attitudes of *superiority* start?

Being born into a culture which promotes the notion of **us** being inherently better than **them** encourages a general attitude of *superiority*. But how is that attitude actually formed?

The *descent into matter* has produced a world of density and inertia, a world in which physical action and outcomes tend to lag behind thoughts and intentions. The resulting delay can cause frustration and a feeling of being constantly thwarted or failing.

Sometimes people catch unwelcome *reflections* of their own failings through glimpsing these in other people, while not consciously realising that this is happening. And one way of dealing with such discomforting experiences is <u>not</u> to acknowledge the reflecting, but instead to **project the *feelings* of discontent and failure back on to** the 'reflector', thereby gaining a false kind of comfort from imagining oneself to be *superior* to that person.

For some, this attitude has become a habit, a way of life, which has evolved into various *ASS* cultures of falsely assumed *superiority* over others. In extreme cases, this mentality can manifest in violent attacks on the vulnerable or elderly by individuals who are deeply disturbed by reflections of their own unacknowledged sense of vulnerability, and feel impelled to attack or eliminate the immediate cause of that uncomfortable feeling.

Typical ASS symptoms

- **Arrogance:** the unmerited, unearned, *'I deserve this'* attitude of privileged superiority, expecting and demanding subservience, deference and obedience from all 'inferiors'.
- **Ruthlessness:** a callous disregard for justice and the needs, sensitivities and wellbeing of others – all in the pursuit of maintaining *superiority*.
- **Excessive greed:** claiming exclusive rights over land, resources, property and money...
as substitutes, compensating for an inner/spiritual emptiness.
- **An obsessive fixation** on all indicators of status and prestige etc in relation to those seen as rivals.
- **Corrupt patronage:** distributing privileges to buy assistance in maintaining the status quo.
- **Protection racketeering:** eg nation states providing non-refusable *protection*: military, social, financial... (page 195)
in return for taxes, service, loyalty and obedience to the ruling elite (the State, gangsters...).
- **False mythologies,** fed into the culture to maintain loyal support for the status quo.
- **Dominance** and **control**, through the old *IFDR* method of *'Ignorance, Fear, Divide & Rule'*:
  Ignorance of empowering knowledge weakens already deprived and oppressed peoples.
  Fear is generated through the threat of violence, deprivation, prison and various enemies.

Divide and rule works by setting all individuals and groups in mutual competitive rivalry, and by exploiting the '*stick and carrot*', ie punishments and prizes, trouble and treats..

In this way the potential political power of the 'many', the 99.9%, can be cancelled out.
(By contrast, in **cooperatives** collective power amounts to more than the sum of the parts.)

Addiction to violence and weaponry

A sign of addiction to violence is when it's perceived as the only practical way to resolve conflicts – whether between individuals or groups. **Releasing bound up emotional and physical tensions** in a violent way seems to bring at least some temporary relief. And the powerful feelings may either be directed at others, or be self-inflicted in cases of self-harm and suicide.

Violence can become an integral part of a culture when it has long been treated as acceptable – as in some domestic violence – and reinforced in traditional ritualised ceremonies, or where fear-driven weapon carrying becomes institutionalised as normal. It may be directed in a military way at 'enemies', external or internal, or be channelled into relatively safe and culturally acceptable activities like certain physical sports.

In general, **weapons provide an addictive form of *artificial empowerment*,** a substitute to compensate for feelings of weakness and vulnerability in pathologically unbalanced societies. However, the use of weapons by disempowered people tends to bring all kinds of unintended consequences and trouble, such as disproportionately violent responses to emotional upsets and discontent, as in the numerous mass shootings across the USA (page 283).

Individually, there's the fear and anger of some young people who carry weapons as they seek to establish their own sense of security, identity and status in the world. But this addiction, sometimes due to immaturity and ignorance, is also hyped up and exploited by the hugely profitable arms industry, at both international and local levels.

Then there is the unprovoked violence perpetrated against weaker, more vulnerable people. Individuals who find it too disturbing to see, in others, reflections of their own weaknesses, may violently project the resulting anger in themselves back on to their innocent victims.

Lording it - hard head and thick skin required

ASS regimes - whether political, military, religious, scientific, medical or commercial - all have certain *descent era* characteristics in common. Consequently, they cannot offer any deep or lasting fulfilment to those whose lives they govern and control. Hostility, rivalry, cheating, treachery and revenge are thus normal features of *ASS* societies. And that prompts crucial questions about whose lives are currently being blighted by whom and how.

ASS ruling elites have a tendency to establish exclusive bloodline dynasties, dedicated to **maintaining their dominant status... ie their** *superiority*. **This position requires them to be psychologically de-sensitised, ie emotionally hardened and callous, not showing any signs of weakness, such as genuine feelings of compassion or sympathy.**

Over centuries such regimes have kept their subjects ignorant, fearful, divided and ruled, conditioning mass populations into deference and loyalty, in awe of the 'authorities'. Recently, in wealthier, more informed societies, the style of control has become more subtle, more persuasive, in a *feminine* way, through clever use of psychology and the mass media.

In this way, the privileged *ASS* lifestyle has continued to be presented as a sign of success, with humankind remaining divided and exploited by self-appointing elites and dictators lording it over their submissive inferiors, their subjects.

Caste and class systems are frozen ASS hierarchies

Out of the insecure, anxious *ASS* mentality of the *descent* era, many sub-cultures have arisen, each with its own distinct ethos of distorted aspirations and ambitions regarding *status*. And many people, in aspiring to appear 'better' or *superior* in various ways, like children, compare themselves with others whom they think of as rivals or competitors.

This is natural in childhood, in the animal kingdom and in primitive societies where competing to establish one's place in this or that pecking order is how status is worked out. But when such an attitude persists into human adulthood and becomes normalised, such societies solidify into rigid hierarchies of **superiority**, known as **caste** and **class** systems.

Politically, *ASS* progresses broadly in the direction of so-called **populism** and nationalism, sometimes labelled the '**far right**'. This tendency is reflected in the distorted ambitions of certain minorities to rule over a **neo-feudal fascist** world.

What is *fascism*? In essence, it's deep discontent on a mass scale that's being exploited and manipulated by a ruthless, opportunistic leadership, which directs people's anger, resentment frustration and longings against targeted 'enemies', internal and external. Those feelings tend to result from a long term sense of powerlessness at having been continuously conned and let down, as they naively see it, by politicians. So, what's the trick? How is it actually done?

The **fascist democracy trick** (*populist politics*, page 227) is to use the mind-manipulating power of the mass media to stir up and exploit a combination of gut level anger and fantasy longings in the most educationally deprived voters in the population, ie the **numerical majority of the electorate**. Legitimised by that mathematical measure of support, however unwise, the State, financial and corporate sectors can then merge into the typical tyrannical fascist set-up.

To prevent this kind of exploitation of weaknesses in the constitutional status quo, and to halt the ongoing decline into fascism, difficult, searching questions have to be asked. For a start:
- *How to enable the deprived mass majorities worldwide to realise how they are being callously manipulated and exploited?*
- *How to highlight the silent approval of those who for now feel they are benefitting from the status quo?*

Obviously, any such questions will be unwelcome to many. But without such radical changes in humanity's collective mindset, the present situation can only deteriorate. And once again, the 'smart, educated and politically aware' classes will be deluded and fooled because they can't think beyond their fear of losing their current worldly advantages. Variations on this theme are developed in the section of this book that focuses on politics and economics.

ASS: a symptom of the *descent into matter*
The tone of contemporary politics, finance and and economics worldwide is thus still characterised 'at the top' by a mixture of corrupt power-lusting, greed and fear, resulting in bullying, deceiving, cheating, posturing, sabotaging, blackmailing etc. This is the the complicated *ASS* 'game' that most people have grown up in and call the 'real world'... because it has become so familiar that they're now conditioned and, in a way, addicted to it. For it's still basically about the childhood desire to 'win' and be a 'winner', not a 'loser'.

Yet such is the poisonous power of **fear** – of losing, falling, failing, being shamed or blamed etc – that despite all the harmful effects of this way of life, many would rather stick with the status quo than risk losing what they feel are their present advantages. So they hang on to their various 'winnings', however these were acquired, since in *ASS* societies these are the measures of worldly success and superiority. This is *descent era* **inertia** inhibiting lives.

ASS: an <u>emotional</u> dis-ease

Emotional intelligence has become a common term, indicating a growing appreciation of the *emotional* origins of many physical and social ills. The 'down side' of that awakening has been it's callous exploitation for commercial gain.

Huge profits are being made by pharmaceutical corporations and other drug dealers **monetising**, ie selling various instant *emotional fixes* for **artificially medicalised** states of mind. An obvious example is the mass marketing of Ritalin and other similar drugs for the symptoms now labelled as *ADHD* (Attention Deficit Hyperactivity Disorder). Which is a reminder that the deep discontent these callous exploiters are attempting, in their superficial and short term way, **to fix but not heal** is essentially a troubled state of **consciousness**.

So, from the *Threshold* perspective, Western psychiatric medicine still seems doggedly incompetent in its attempts to address *emotional* conditions, which are, essentially, unbalanced, unstable, *expanding/contracting* states of consciousness. Focusing on the outer *physical* and the *intellectual* (*cognitive*) symptoms of *emotional* problems, it has little to offer in the way of resolving the worldwide *ASS* problem. Also, since many authority figures and medical professionals themselves clearly display *ASS* symptoms, any official recognition of it as a significant syndrome is unlikely in the foreseeable future.

Politically, clever ruling elites, in mass manipulating their citizens' emotional ups and downs, always keep a few spots of *optimistic hope* shining... to feed people's yearnings amidst the confusion, struggle and lack of fulfilment in their lives. And that's because certain dark truths about so-called *governments* continue to be concealed.

A common delusion: governments serve 'the people'

Seen from the *Threshold*, one major delusion in humankind's ongoing self-deception is **the fantasy that governments work for the**

good of the people they supposedly represent. For these politicians only gain the chance to act out the vanity-driven pretence of 'governing' once they've committed to serve first the interests of the hidden ruling elite.

Such elites, sometimes known collectively as the ***deep state***, consist of those who command and control the workings of the *state* from behind the scenes. They include mainly the global financial syndicate (page 201), to which almost all nation states are deeply in debt, the land-claiming elites, the military and the major religious authorities.

These privileged individuals, who know how to exploit the vanity of ambitious politicians and the rhythmical moodswings of the public, are also constantly competing among themselves for supremacy in psychological war games of mass mind control, with humankind as their expendable 'assets'.

Through their control of the mass media, elites will thus tolerate so-called 'democratically elected governments', and let them inevitably fail, only to be replaced by another set of compliant puppets.

So, in effect:
> **Elected 'governments' are allowed exist in order to:**
> **(a) sell to the public the agenda of their hidden, ruling elite sponsors, and then**
> **(b) try to implement that agenda as best they can until they eventually fail.**

All the while, public opinion polls and elections serve as *weather vanes* for measuring trends and influencing the public *mood*, so that the elite can stay a step or two ahead and cling on to their privileged positions. That trend includes taking full advantage of the rapid advances happening in digital technology, especially in telecommunications... and in particular, smart mobile phones which have enabled, over just a few decades, a vast, parallel, online, virtual *screenworld* to come into existence and take over people's lives.

Bullying & its victims

Bullying is another aspect of the **ASS** condition. It's a psycho-pathological relic of the dark *descent era,* a primitive, callous practice which tends to damage the lives of its *victims* and their descendants.

It's a way of compensating for a lack of any significant power or authority. By intimidating or exerting force of one kind or another over others who seem vulnerable, a false sense of power and **superiority** over them is created. It's how some insecure individuals project unwelcome reflections of their own vulnerability back on to their victims...with a vengeance.

Victims of bullying may themselves later become bullies, repeating the same pattern –
perhaps in even more extreme or subtle ways – and so perpetuate spirals of trouble and vengeance through generations. Or they may end up as weakened, vulnerable, conflict-avoiding, timid individuals whose passive demeanour tends to invite further victimisation of one sort or another.

Tolerating bullying encourages the perpetrators to make it a potentially *addictive* habit. And emotionally wounded victims may themselves develop a callous indifference to the suffering of others and remain detached, uninvolved onlookers or passers-by when they see others suffering. However, some do overcome the ill effects and try to help heal this sickness known as 'bullying'.

Were *self-defence*, physical and psychological, an essential part of normal education, there would be far fewer opportunities for bullying and victimisation, including the many varieties of sexual harassment and abuse, to occur and flourish.

'Honour' killings, so-called, look like another variation on the same theme. Discontented parents, trapped within a constrictive, authoritarian culture, conspire to prevent their young from enjoying freedom of choice in their relationships. So, in the name of

'tradition', men, acting out a fantasy of **dominance** and false power, and women, exercising a distorted, pathological form of **manipulative control**, collude in inflicting their unhappiness on the next generation.

Vital, practical questions regarding ASS

Are you willing to allow humanity to continue being blighted by the pathological craving of a bunch of superiority addicts to feed their sick ASS habit?

In response to which some might argue:
But all humans suffer in varying degrees from this ASS tendency. So, doesn't that make the whole idea of ASS meaningless?

But that argument can also be taken to affirm the view from the **Threshold** perspective that...
... Since all people experience some superiority feelings, all are potentially ASS addicts. Which is why all people can identify with ASS behaviour and understand it, however offensive it may appear when observed in others. And since the ASS problem can be understood, it can be overcome.

Therefore, if each individual is an essential part of the ASS problem, then potentially each is an essential part of the solution, ie the healing. So, the options are:
Remain part of the problem OR become part of the solution.

Most people have at times felt that they are 'better', in some way, than certain other people. So, most people are able to understand how this feeling of superiority can grow out of control, and into a pathological belief that they therefore deserve all kinds of privileges.

History is full of famous instances of such delusional behaviour. And although reminders of this may not be welcome, what is now known cannot later be un-known... although memories can fade. So, what kind of attitude and thinking could enable a start to be made towards making the much needed changes?

It doesn't have to be like this

The *Threshold* perspective brings the realisation that human beings are capable of thinking and behaving in more balanced and fulfilling ways than they have been while dominated by *descent era* ruling elites. They will be able to experience a more natural, harmonious kind of *power* than the fragile, unsatisfying, *false* sense of power many naively seek as compensation for the lack of fulfilment in their lives within their present cultures.

Healing is much more than symptom-fixing

Merely eliminating the obvious symptoms of any illness is at best only temporary.

For example:

- **Removing or concealing** the outer manifestations of inner, deeper imbalances merely results in other substitute symptoms instead.
- **Cosmeticising**, ie creating a false image of beauty or wellness, is a cover-up, a temporary disguise, and not a cure.

A screen-sized world... of pre-set menus offering unlimited distractions

Increasingly, humankind's worldview is being systematically filtered and reduced down to the scale of images on electronic screens of digital phones, computers and TVs. As a consequence, the lives of billions of people worldwide are increasingly lacking direct, multi-sensory interaction with one another, with the natural world and with the cosmos.

Instead, much of that missed experience and learning is being substituted with 'virtual' simulations. These include the self-indulgent pursuit of **fantasy involvement and interaction** of all kinds, including sex and violence, as well as standard entertainment material. **Addictive dependence** on these is clearly a symptom of a much deeper human problem.

To feed that hunger, an increasing number of profit-driven, easily accessible, online platforms are now being provided for billions of disempowered people to get some kind of instant gratification... as compensation for the emptiness of their lives. And much of this appears to be through self-expression and self-promotion – whether driven by goodwill, ambition, greed, sentimentality, hostility, vengeance or mischief. In the process, people can accumulate numerous 'friends' and instantly let their likes, dislikes and moods be known to the world... as notably demonstrated by USA President Trump.

But as a result, many young people are also tending to become isolated, self-centred and either excessively aggressive or passive... and thus exploitable by clever mind manipulators.
And that will continue as long as they unquestioningly allow themselves to be fed a toxic diet of biased misinformation and disinformation in the form of commercial advertising, partisan propaganda and various other kinds of indoctrination.

With the many rapid advances in digital technology, distinguishing between what is real and true, as opposed to what is fake or make-believe, is becoming increasingly difficult. And that has multiplied the variety of fantasies being acted out online, and in the real world, by all kinds of people presenting themselves in whatever ways they choose.

The confusion resulting from trying to discern what is authentic or illusory, beneficial or harmful, liberating or entrapping suggests that it's not happening entirely by chance. It looks increasingly as though humankind is being subtly misled, disempowered and steered towards accepting a centralised authoritarian world in which a small, privileged elite is aiming, through mass mind control, to rule over a neo-feudal, fascist-style, global empire.

And one part of preparing the ground for that pathological fantasy world is the generous funding and encouraging of young, talented, ambitious creators of **digital fantasy games** and other highly addictive distractions – designed to grab young people's attention so that the hidden, long term agenda can be pursued more easily. This is just one of many methods for shaping minds, manufacturing consent and promoting willing participation in that process.

One simple trick, for example, in influencing a screen-viewer's impression of who or what is most important in any situation is to make that person or object appear larger, brighter or in the foreground of the picture.

Languages reveal hidden assumptions and prejudices

The ways in which people think about and try to understand the world is deeply influenced, ie shaped and coloured, by the *languages* and *vocabularies* they learn to use in the different departments of their lives. That's why languages tend to be manipulated and distorted, for good or otherwise, by people who are acutely aware of the power of words, and are skilled at exploiting that power.

Poetry and other creative writing are obvious examples, as are **propaganda** and **advertising** which can be devious in concealing the purposes and strategies behind their usage. The lack of words concerning certain subjects and the ambiguity of other words also reveal much about a particular culture and its values.

The English language, for example, as a legacy of the *masculine*-dominated *descent* era, suffers from a severe lack of precise, meaningful words for various kinds of adult human **relationships**. Thus the common use and misuse of such inadequate terms as *girlfriend, boyfriend, lover, womaniser, mistress, gay* etc. More mature, *feminine*-influenced, *ascent era* societies will develop richer vocabularies for the subtleties of this complex area of people's lives. Clarifying the *Threshold* perspective has required introducing some new terminology.

The basic function of language in general concerns people seeking some kind of **resonance** between and amongst themselves, and establishing broadly agreed patterns of visual, audio and tactile signals to convey and communicate thoughts and feelings, whether friendly or hostile.

As they evolve, so they develop increasing complexity and subtlety. Then there's the peculiar vocabulary of so-called '***swearing***' – or what the broadcasting media quaintly call 'strong language'. It normally combines references to the sacred, the sexual and bodily eliminatory organs and their functions. These words have come to carry a peculiar power of their own, and are used to add emphasis to whatever is being said, whether expressing anger, surprise, defiance or ridicule.

And that's at least partly because they're loaded with conventional disapproval when used in that way. For they can cause embarrassment and unease to some people who have grown up in cultures that overlay these matters with feelings of disgust, shame and guilt.

Why do psychologists ignore so many crucial issues?

The simple answer is short-sighted self-interest, ie careers, funding, status and reputations. For the issues described above require a kind of thinking and questioning which the hidden sponsors of nation states, media corporations and education systems do <u>not</u> want to encourage. For that could inspire some deep questioning of their role in the present dysfunctional status quo on Earth.

Nudge psychology offers an emotionally safer career path at this time of *transition*. It's all about positive reinforcement through indirect, subtle suggestions and prompts, as ways of influencing the behaviour and decision making of individuals and groups. It's thus a more *feminine* way of persuading than the typically unsubtle *masculine* ways of the *descent* era.

The *Wellness/Illness* Spectrum

What does *wellness* mean... beyond *not* being *ill*?

This chapter is inseparably linked with the contents of the previous one on *Threshold Psychology*, since a person's mental, emotional and physical states are closely interrelated.

And that concurs with ancient traditional healing systems, such as Chinese *acupuncture* and Indian *ayurveda*, which explicitly work on the subtle *pre-physical* as well as the gross *physical-material* level of each individual, as also does the healing system of *homeopathy*.

The intention here is to demonstrate in a 21st century way that there is a basic, coherent pattern to be found behind many of the conditions normally labelled simply as '*illnesses*', and how *wellness* is much more than merely an absence of any obvious symptoms of illness.

Equilibrium: between e*xpansion* and *contraction*

As stated in the previous section on *Threshold Psychology*, nothing happens out of nothing. All symptoms, physical and psychological, occur in a unique context of time and place, arising out of particular sets of circumstances. So, each person, as one unique unit of individual human consciousness, is a complex energy system embodied in physical matter, the product of a combination of continuously changing factors.

Keeping well is thus a lifelong balancing act. It's the ongoing attempt to remain stable and poised while being pulled and pushed on different levels of one's being by the polar opposite forces of *expansion* and *contraction*. However, these forces, acting upon humanity, do naturally tend towards an *equilibrium* state.

Equilibrium, therefore, is the guiding principle. For each individual has some awareness at all times, perhaps unconsciously, of what he or she needs in order to maintain a balance between *contraction* and *expansion*, *yang* and *yin*, *alkali* and *acid* etc. For example, excessive stress, resulting in *contraction*, causes the body to produce extra acid in order to maintain its chemical balance. But excessive acid in the body can have various detrimental effects.

A life of **excessive** consumption keeps people distracted through continuously having to attend to the **consequences** of seeking to consume or possess more than they need for a natural, fulfilling life. **Deficiency**, by contrast, leaves one weakened and vulnerable to illness and exploitation, resulting in a continuous struggle to function in a relatively balanced way.

So, wellness involves balancing various pairs of complementary opposites, such as *expression/inhibition, releasing/containing, relaxing/tensing, flexibility/rigidity, soft/hard, mobile/static* etc... all variations of *expansion/contraction*.

Healing is not symptom-fixing

Merely eliminating the obvious symptoms of any illness is at best only temporary. For example:

- *Removing* **or** *concealing* the outer manifestations of inner, deeper imbalances merely results in other substitute instead.
- *Cosmeticising*, ie creating a false image of beauty or wellness, is a cover-up, a temporary disguise, and not a cure.

Healing is therefore all about restoring to the whole body-mind system a balanced, harmonious *resonance* with the rhythms of nature and the cosmos. This involves **reconfiguring one's life** into the optimum pattern possible in the present circumstances, which does not necessarily mean a *cure,* ie eliminating a particular set of symptoms.

For in the current *transition* phase from an era of *masculine*-dominated *descent* to one of increasingly *feminine*-influenced *ascent,* a corresponding shift in attitudes to illness is now possible. Instead of this or that medical condition being treated as an **enemy** that has to be fought and battled with – for example, in the context of a so-called 'war on cancer' – an illness can be thought of as a true *friend* telling you something you need to know about yourself and your life, even though that message may at first come as unwelcome news. It may, for example, draw attention to some previously unquestioned habits, imbalances, inhibitions or fears.

Also, merely *naming* an observed set of symptoms with an official medical label does not itself constitute a useful *diagnosis*. Nor is it equivalent to understanding:
 - what that condition *means* in terms of a person's whole life so far, or
(b) how the circumstances, physical and psychological, in which the condition arose might be adapted to enable healing.

Wellness, therefore, is the state of being in *harmonious resonance*, physically and psychologically, with the cosmos and the natural world. Such an optimum condition is sometimes described as being 'at one' with the world.

In all living systems, any changes in that balance affect the functioning of the whole system. Which makes keeping *well* a continuous, dynamic *balancing act*. So, *wellness* is all about qualities, relative proportions and adapting.

Illness occurs when a person is out of balance and therefore not in harmonious *resonance* with the cosmos, ie is out of tune and out of step with the rhythms of nature... resulting in various forms of stress, inhibition, damage, suffering and depletion of natural vitality.

Ease/Unease/Disease
Ease is an untroubled state of being in harmonious *resonance* with nature and the cosmos.
Un-ease is the experience of that resonance becoming disturbed, dulled or discordant.
Dis-ease occurs when *dissonance*, the polar opposite of harmonious resonance, results in imbalance and symptoms which cause suffering

and disrupt a life's optimum expression.

All these distinctions indicate how, behind many 'illnesses', ie *physical* symptom patterns, there's a history of **emotional** trouble, ie a disturbance in *consciousness* which has manifested physically. Where in the body these symptoms occur and in what form varies with each individual situation. For every emotional reaction, major or minor, produces a corresponding chemical reaction in the body. And repetition over time produces patterns of effects, ie *symptoms*.

Symptoms, serving as **warning signs**, therefore indicate that presently all is not well in a life – like flashing red warning lights. Inflammation, eruptions and chronic fatigue are obvious examples. So, it's necessary first to acknowledge any symptoms instead of ignoring them. Then they can be read as clues as to what might be wrong and what might be a better way of maintaining physical and psychological *wellness*.

The *Threshold* perspective enables the meaning of symptom patterns to be detected through thinking in terms of how the primal cosmic forces interact at the everyday level of earthly living. Here are a few basic examples of familiar symptoms viewed from that perspective.

- *Arthritic joints*: the result of chronic inhibition and containment, ie unexpressed feelings, causing energy to be obstructed and fluids to crystallise and solidify – with painful effect.
- *Muscular armouring*, as described on page 108, is a clearly recognisable symptom.
- *Shivering/shuddering/shaking* can be understood as the *releasing* of tension and stored up stress energy in *waves* generated by the basic organic *pulsating* of each living creature.
- *Epileptic fits*: the involuntary, out-of-control releasing of pulsating energy, held trapped within an inhibited body until it can no longer be physically contained. The convulsions can be seen as functionally related to the natural rhythms of the orgasm reflex.

Susceptibility and a **predisposition** to certain pathological conditions indicate weaknesses and imbalances in a person's psychological and physical constitution. Some can result in particular vulnerabilities and therefore a tendency to suffer particular forms of illness. Also, mental *inertia* and rigidity, effects of the *descent* era, leave some people unable or unwilling to recognise the *emotional* factors behind their *physical* symptoms.

One sub-system of the pulsating *cosmic* energy system is the rhythmical circulating of blood throughout the body via the beating *heart*. This is a reminder that **the physical heart is not a pump**, despite orthodox medical teaching. It is itself pumped and acts as a servo-mechanism, regulating the blood flow according to the body's fluctuating energy needs, powered by the rhythmical *expanding* and *contracting* of the whole, living cosmos. The non-physical heart, as the centre of one's very being as an individual, is referred to briefly on page 436.

The *armouring –> anger –> anxiety –> depression* loop

This is a familiar, self-perpetuating, psycho-physical spiral of misery which can be very difficult to halt, reverse or prevent, especially for those lacking an understanding of the emotional/physical dynamics involved.

When an emotionally vulnerable person reaches out to connect with the world but gets no response, is rejected or is met with hostility, the ***psychological pain*** experienced causes a reflex **contraction**, ie a withdrawing inward, mentally and physically. With repetition, this becomes outwardly recognisable as ***inhibition***, ie an uneasy, withholding self-restraint.

If this withdrawing tendency becomes a regular, fear-driven reaction, the effect over time is a pattern of chronically tensed, rigid muscles and a lack of natural vitality in certain regions of the body, depending on the unique character of the individual in question. The result is a kind of ***armouring***, physical and psychological – a protective shell that anaesthetises and shields you from emotional pain. However, it also leaves the essential you trapped within an inflexible, 'armoured' physical body, prone to discomfort, pain and restricted functionality.

Psychologically, this protection against further emotional wounding may also result in a callous insensitivity to other people's feelings and produce a tendency towards hollow, insincere, empty words or hypocrisy. Also, as a de-sensitised barrier, it may prevent you from fully experiencing pleasure and from expressing your feelings, which remain trapped and contained within.

Thus it **inhibits** natural curiosity and so makes lives seem dulled, isolated and shut off from the world. Then, when these powerful but contained feelings seek expression, they have to force their way out through the armouring, which turns such impulses into **anger**. And this anger itself may be *inhibited* if displays of anger are considered socially unacceptable.

As a consequence, the undischarged energy of that suppressed 'explosive' anger may remain in the individual as an unsettling condition of free-floating **anxiety** (page 108). **Anxiety** is a psycho-physical sense of unease which undermines self-confidence and mental stability, and results in various physical symptoms. It's a depleting, self-reinforcing condition which leaves people anxious to avoid anxiety-provoking situations.

Should the pattern become established as an ongoing 'way of life' – along with the resulting **depletion** of vitality and energy, a general feeling of **dissatisfaction** and a sense of **pessimism** – it may degenerate into what's called **depression**. And that can then feed back, reinforcing the general attitude of *contraction*, keeping the whole process going in a kind of loop.

A typical example of *armouring* is the **throat** becoming chronically tight in order to prevent uncontrolled outbursts of anger or other emotions. But this inhibits breathing and constricts or dulls the voice. It also results in various other symptoms, including heart problems, blood pressure, a suppressed immune system and all the troubles that can follow from these.

That's just one example of **contraction** and **expansion** being out of balance, and consequently resulting in multiple problems, because the psychological and physical dimensions are inseparable. Also, when one is weakened and frustrated by such imbalances, sometimes there's a tendency to project one's unhappiness, in a hostile way, on to others who are not the cause and perhaps are also not in a position to defend themselves.

Healing muscular armouring involves systematically dissolving the chronic tension and *releasing* the affected parts. That brings a growing sense of all round relief, ease and renewed vitality, as the circulation of energy and fluids recharges the system and helps the whole body/mind to *reconfigure* itself into optimum functioning and form. Which means being able to be soft/flexible/mobile or hard/rigid/stable as appropriate.

Social versions of **armouring** exist in the form of walls and barriers, although a wall built around a city to protect the citizens within from the threat of external enemies may also have a containing, imprisoning effect on those citizens. A 'mental wall', built around the minds of citizens and/or members of a cultural or religious group, also has an insulating effect.

A variation of this condition exists when the shock or pain of a traumatic experience has become physicalised and lodged somewhere in the body, subsequently causing some otherwise unaccountable malfunctioning of one kind or another. Healing this kind of trouble may be possible through regularly repeating some general *releasing* procedures. And in many healing and therapy situations, awareness of the **recapitulation** process can be useful (page 81).

The cancer process
The general *cancer* process, in its many variations, is hinted at on

page 120 with particular regard to the connection between inhibition and *breast cancer*. The subject is also addressed in _Threshold Wellness/Illness_. where the question of how to handle this life crisis is raised.

Crisis psychology and healing

A *crisis* is a crucial, critical turning point, involving both jeopardy and opportunity. From the *Threshold* perspective, crises are necessary stages or initiations in all evolving lives, and are the basis of endless dramas – both in in everyday life and in various art-forms. For example, suddenly and unexpectedly being diagnosed with a potentially terminal medical condition tends to trigger a sense of crisis.

What is then crucial is how the person concerned and those close to her or him respond. An overwhelming fear of death and a strong desire to revert to how things were before the crisis, perhaps by removing or suppressing the symptoms, is likely to result in the disease recurring one way or another, despite any temporary relief.

By contrast, pausing to radically re-evaluate one's most basic attitudes and previously unquestioned assumptions – along with expressing gratitude for whatever has been of real value in this life so far – can create a positive outlook with the potential for healing in one way or another. This generally involves looking forward to the next phase of this lifetime, including preparing for a 'good death' (page 379), whenever that may occur.

Emotional hygiene

One pro-active way of counteracting the tendency towards muscular armouring and various other ills is to practice daily some form of **emotional hygiene**. This involves regularly discharging the day's build-up of contained anger and stress, since **no amount of *physical* cleansing and exercise or *mental* distraction is a substitute for regular *emotional* cleansing**.

It's the regulated releasing, as a daily routine, of inhibited, suppressed, negative feelings contained within the body. Emptying this 'reservoir' effectively prevents such build-ups and their ill-effects, as well as certain kinds of sleeping problems, with all their longer term consequences.

For each day, a person tends to accumulate undischarged mental, emotional and physical energy. And that energy, if contained and suppressed, has ill effects, one way and another, on the whole body/mind system, depending on the current susceptibilities and predispositions of the individual... especially if the pattern becomes chronic, ie long term, and extreme.

Ignoring, denying or 'fixing' symptoms by concealing or physically eliminating them are all ways of failing to address the deeper problems behind their outer manifestations. The result is often the manifesting of even more troubling symptoms... until the real problem is addressed.

Diet and nutrition

Diet is an aspect of human health that is radically changing in the ongoing transition from the **density** and darkness of an era of *descent into matter* to the relative **lightness** of an era of *ascent out of matter*. This unfolding development can be witnessed as humankind gradually abandons the habit of consuming *dense*, heavy food such as animal and dairy products, in favour of vegetables, fruits and more liquid nutrition.

Various researchers have found statistical correspondences between people consuming highly processed food and the incidence of different illnesses, including cancers, diabetes and obesity. But the orthodox medical profession lacks the *insight* and perhaps the will to investigate the deeper reasons for this pattern.

The missing link between the numbers and how they arise can, however, in general be traced back to people feeling unfulfilled and discontented in their lives in different ways. In response, they seek the instant gratification, comfort and convenience that processed foods are cleverly designed to provide – that is, in a shallow, short-term way which leaves an addictive craving for more of the same to fill the 'inner' emptiness.

Addiction to food, in that context, can be seen as a highly significant problem for human health and wellbeing everywhere. And it coincides with how, in the current phase of *transition*, diet has increasingly become a target for profit-driven commercial organisations. The result is many new health problems worldwide, some referred to in the following pages. Next, a few major health issues which are currently receiving much medical, media and therefore government attention.

The *Type 2 Diabetes* epidemic
A symptom of *transition* stress
Type 2 diabetes is a diet-related illness that has become a major world health problem. But when viewed from the *Threshold* perspective, it can be broadly understood and overcome.

The 'bigger picture' context
The cosmos is currently passing through a crucial **transition** phase. This is characterised by the currently departing materialistic era on Earth beginning to be superseded by the early signs of a very different and more subtle incoming era of **expansion** and diversity. The relevant political, economic, financial, religious and scientific issues regarding this are dealt with elsewhere in this work.

Throughout the *descent into matter* era, the differences between the small minorities of humans living in *excess* and the mass majority living in *deficiency* have resulted in bitter resentment and a corrupting, divisive desire on the part of the poor to emulate the excesses of the wealthy. Which leaves the poor vulnerable to divide-and-rule exploitation, and so maintains the unbalanced, unhealthy status quo.

The connection between **poverty** and **illness** therefore represents a major problem. For currently, billions of human beings worldwide are unnecessarily suffering as a result of being deprived of the essentials for a basic balanced, healthy life, while others carry on living in excess of their natural needs. And **that tragic situation is being callously exploited as a commercial opportunity for pharmaceutical corporations and others to make big profits, unhindered by powerless governments**.

The current phase is being increasingly influenced by the universal *feminine*, while still characterised by various distorted ways of the departing *masculine*-dominated *descent* era. For example, there now exists the enticing digital online marketplace where just about anything you might desire can be found – on offer, either to buy or to experience by simply typing a few digits on an electronic keyboard. Or you can walk into physical supermarkets where all kinds of products are enticingly laid out within easy reach.

Also today, plastic money cards allow people to indulge in instant gratification, ie 'have it now, pay later'. Thus there are millions of traders in the world, competing to sell their wares, many prepared to compromise quality, safety, reliability etc, in order to keep their prices 'competitive' so as to make a profit.

In that context, billions of already educationally deprived, unfulfilled and discontented people continue to seek substitutes as compensation for what's lacking in their lives. And in response, 'the market' is offering a vast range of junk foods, drinks and distracting entertainment, much of it designed to be *addictive*, to get people hooked and craving more.

The broader picture shows an increasing proportion of humankind worldwide ending up in an overweight and dysfunctional condition. And these individuals are more likely to lead their children by example, even if unintentionally, into habits which result in yet more obesity and *Type 2 diabetes*.

What does *Type 2 Diabetes* indicate regarding today's world?

Excessive *sweetening* in many junk and comfort foods is a substitute and short term 'fix' for a **lack of love** (sweetness) and for **depleted energy** levels resulting from all kinds of imbalances, physical and emotional.

Excessively *salty* (*yang*) foods may then be desired as a polar opposite reaction, in response to the excess of (*yin*) sweetness, and so may contribute to an unstable, volatile oscillating between the two extremes.

Physically, overconsumption of sweet foods and drinks results in an excess of sugar in the blood such that the pancreas cannot produce enough insulin to maintain a healthy *acid/alkali* balance. The liver can store some of this excess, but once it is overloaded, the result is fatty deposits accumulating in certain parts of the body and an overweight person.

That condition can then itself cause further discomfort, unease and problems which may prompt the seeking of more junk and comfort food as compensation... in a 'downward' spiral that results in *obesity* and the pathological condition known as *Type 2 Diabetes*. The polar opposite ill effects of an excessive intake of salt are also well known.

There may also be other contributing factors, such as various forms of electromagnetic and chemical **pollution** which human senses can't consciously detect, but which affect various subtle human faculties. The lack of scientific research into these areas, and therefore the lack of conclusive evidence, indicates how certain commercial interests are determined to maintain the status quo and consequently their profits.

Meanwhile, orthodox medical practice in the main offers only superficial and physical responses, and little or nothing to address the critical *emotional* and *socio-economic* factors.

The *Dementia/Altzheimer's* Epidemic

In the natural ageing process of gradual biological degeneration, many of the symptoms normally diagnosed as **dementia** are essentially an extreme and simultaneous *polarising* of:

(a) **contraction**/withdrawing/slowing/deadening/hardening/rigidifying etc... and

(b) **expansion**/releasing/loosening/disconnecting/separating/disintegrating etc...

The result is an apparent loss of normal coherence and efficiency in thinking and behaviour patterns, which vary from individual to individual. Yet certain common *cultural* and *environmental* factors can clearly be detected and could be independently researched. For example, there are the many unnatural, invisible pollutants in the air and water, referred to regarding *Type 2 diabetes*, which affect all people's mental and physical faculties.

Then there are the many inconsistencies in the values, rules and conventions within most societies and cultures. These become more of a problem to cope with as ageing restricts some people's mental agility and competence at dealing with new challenges.

A broad view

Dementia is especially prevalent in western Europe, where the idea of a *welfare state* is most
developed, and therefore more people tend to live longer. However, in these societies there are still many suffering from dementia who are poor and in some cases homeless, struggling to survive without the basic help they badly need.

At the same time, there's a financially secure minority of older people whose health and accommodation needs are taken care of, and who now have fewer personal responsibilities. Consequently, some of them may appear to be just living out safe but superficial, directionless lives of leisure, drifting along in a world of undemanding activities and light entertainment, filling in time with distractions and repetitive routines.

In that cushioned condition, if unchallenged mentally or emotionally, there's little or no impetus to seek a deeper understanding of themselves and the world... for example, in preparing for the prospect and experience of their own approaching dying and death.

This indicates how in the western world there are many cultures which are now technologically advanced but psychologically and esoterically retarded. Once again it's a situation the world's dominant *financiers* are manipulatively exploiting for their own advantage through their ultimate control the world's money supply.

And that links to **the lie, much peddled by governments, that there is only a finite amount of money available - eg for much needed public health, medical and social services** - when the potential supply of this imaginary stuff called money is actually limitless, through the centuries old *money trick* (page 185).

Thus all the political talk about *austerity* and countries 'having to live within their means' is a deceitful confidence trick, a pretence the State 'authorities' are obliged to act out. And that results in widespread neglect of the sick and elderly, including *dementia* sufferers.

Bipolar disorder/Manic depression

Obviously related to the universal *polarity* principle, this is a common condition in which a person lacking psychological stability and balance involuntarily alternates between the two polar opposite moods, *expansive* **mania** and *contracting* **depression**. The imbalance that results in these extreme moodswings indicates that humankind collectively is still passing through its volatile *adolescent* phase.

Drugs: personal *polarity* regulators

Drugs are substances which, when ingested or injected, bring about significant physical and psychological change. They can be:
- medical or recreational,
- natural or synthetic,
- *expansive* **stimulants** (*uppers*) or *contractive* **inhibitors** (*downers*) or **stabilisers**,
- bringers of relief from suffering or a means to getting high, ie transcending normal waking   consciousness.

Alcohol is *expansive*: releasing, relaxing, loosening, a solvent, ie *yin* in effect. As such, it can bring some temporary emotional relief to people who tend to feel tense, inhibited, contained or anxious, or are in discomfort or pain of some kind... that is, in a **contracted** state, feeling trapped in the dulling density of a *gravity*-dominated body and world.

It's an example of the universal principle of *polarity* – in the form of a pro-active, temporary adjustment towards an optimum state of *equilibrium*. An *addictive dependency* on *alcohol*, however, brings a hazardous loss of self-control over one's whole life.

The huge global drugs trade includes – as well as alcohol, tobacco and pharmaceuticals – all the non-legalised varieties, natural and synthetic. This is the *supply* part of the trade, where **there's always profitable business to be done... so long as at the *demand* end widespread discontent, unhappiness and illness continue**. Categorising and legalising this or that substance is no substitute for understanding and addressing the psychology of *addiction*.

A *statistical* fabrication: *alcohol* consumption implicated in *breast cancer*

One deeply flawed aspect of contemporary medical thinking is to be found in the misuse of **statistical data**, especially in attempts to connect particular medical conditions with certain lifestyle habits or substances. *Statistics* are always based on the past, and as such are

118

dead information, since numbers and proportions themselves convey no qualities of *will* or *feeling*, whatever the subject matter being measured. Statistics can also be manipulated for particular purposes.

Medical *co-incidences* and *mathematical correlations* can be presented to imply a *causal* connection which may be completely fallacious... but effective in grabbing media headlines and funding. For example, an abstract *mathematical **probability*** of alcohol consumers developing breast cancer has been conjured up. But that approach omits any reference to the deeper, underlying **emotional** factors behind both the compulsion to consume alcohol and the cancerous process itself.

So, to put that omission in its broader context, here's a brief account of how an ongoing cancerous process may be boosted secondarily by excessive consumption of alcohol. (A deeper, more subtle understanding of **cancer**, and **breast cancer** in particular, is available in the online work-in-progress, *Threshold Wellness/Illness*.

Cancer is a process that tends to occur when a **contracting**, **inhibiting** reaction becomes chronic and focused in a particular part of the body – in this case, the breasts. They then become devitalised, allowing unregulated, *expansive* cancerous growth. For the breasts can be understood as outer physical expressions, ie outgrowths or extensions, of the **heart**, which itself has been recognised throughout human history as the inner centre where humans experience feelings of **love** and **nurturing... but also emotional pain and loss**. So when, for emotional self-protection, the sensitivity of the heart is dulled, the breasts are likewise affected and become vulnerable to the cancer process.

Opioid addiction, bringing instant but temporary relief from suffering and unhappiness, is becoming a major global *depopulation* factor (page 214), given the easy availability and cheapness of the required ingredients, and the speed of communications in the 21st century.

PART TWO

THE WORLD

First, what to do about
the huge, invisible
elephant
on the world stage?

Before proceeding any further, it's necessary to acknowledge one major obstacle to any clear understanding of current world affairs. The obstacle in question overshadows and distorts the lives of just about everyone on Earth, but remains unaddressed. However, from the *Threshold* perspective, it's possible to recognise the forces behind this phenomenon, as is explained later in this work.

The obstacle is a **secretive global financial syndicate** which controls the world's supply of *money* through a worldwide web of debt, quietly spun over centuries, now with a branch, ie a ***central bank***, lodged in almost every country on the planet (page 201).

Its web incorporates the three international *arch-banks* – the IMF (International Monetary Fund), the World Bank and BIS (Bank for International Settlements, the central bank of the central banks). These operate at a level above the more familiar commercial banks. With virtually every nation state deeply and inescapably in debt to it, this syndicate is able, from behind the scenes, to control governments and corporations, and so influence and affect the lives of most people on Earth.

As such, it's a major distorting factor which has a toxic effect on all social, political and economic affairs. For this manipulative minority also uses its financial power to prohibit any mention in the mass media - much of which it controls - of its own existence, its motives and how it abuses this privileged position it has achieved.

Gagging always has an unhealthy effect on all concerned, either directly or indirectly. But such is the power that this minority is now able to exert on people in positions of authority worldwide – through' career fear', the threat of 'reputation damage', bribery, blackmail and worse – there's little chance of any significant healing for humanity until the spell is broken. So, the world continues to stagger from crisis to crisis... until enough people realise the futility of all global supremacy agendas when viewed from the *Threshold*.

In various countries this elite is a key part of what has been called the **deep state**. That is the covert alliance of financial, military and industrial interests who, in effect, dictate what the puppet government in each country is required to do and what it's not allowed to do.

So, simply recognising how this huge 'elephant' is affecting all aspects of world affairs has an empowering effect. It may prompt some people into pursuing more balanced and fulfilling ways of living... ways preferable to remaining passively dependent on an arbitrary and corrupt supply of imaginary money tokens, and on powerless puppet governments that are themselves at the mercy of the current global moneylending elite., the world's creditor

For so long as humankind remains spellbound, tricked into a state of addictive dependence on this imaginary *debt money,* it's troubles will persist. On page 178 there's a stark quote from **Lord Stamp**, a former director of the Bank of England, which summarises the basic situation then and now. It ends with *"...if you wish to remain the slaves of bankers and pay the cost of your own slavery, let them continue to create deposits (ie create money as debt)."*

So...

How would it feel
to realise that all through your adult life
you've been tricked and deceived
about money, finance and funding?

Would you wonder whether this deceit,
by institutions and trusted authority figures –
state and commercial, religious and educational –
was deliberate or due to their ignorance?

Would you feel
- angry at the perpetrators of such deceit?
- angry at yourself for having been a victim of the deceit?
- angry at the messengers who deliver unwelcome news?
OR
- would you be willing to let the scam continue
unchallenged,
and yourself become cynical and tempted
to become a career trickster yourself
since it's obviously easy to con lots of people,
once you know how?
OR...
would you like to be wiser and living a more aware
and fulfilling life,
grateful to no longer be addicted to money
or engaging in 'us v. them' politics,
and be free from supremacy-preaching religious propaganda?

How to sort out the *morals* and *ethics* of all this?

To understand how all this fits into the bigger *cosmic* picture requires
the all-encompassing *Threshold* perspective or something
comparable, as will become apparent. For example, a deeper
understanding of *good* and *evil* (page 54) is revealed when they are
viewed as aspects of *balance* and *imbalance* in the greater context of
cosmic evolution.

Also, the knowledge that we are presently living in a time of turbulent **transition** from a cosmic era of '*descent into matter*' – which has resulted in a male-dominated, inertia-bound world – towards a polar opposite one of '*ascent out of matter*' helps explain many otherwise inexplicable phenomena.

From the *Threshold* perspective, it's soon realised that *deception*, *blaming* and *vengeance* are immature and ultimately counter-productive behaviours, the consequences of which can then be addressed in a balanced, constructive, non-partisan way. And that includes identifying and dealing with the perpetrators of unnecessary damage to other people's lives and to their environment.

Similarly comes the realisation that most of humankind is still in its **collective adolescence**, ie in transition from its childhood into adulthood (see *Recapitulation*, page 81). Which explains why so much childish and infantile behaviour by individuals in physically adult bodies is statistically 'normal', and why prominent figures in public and financial affairs often display typically adolescent traits.

Also, recognising this 'inner child' as still present and active in an adult, doesn't have to involve condemning or blaming. It's simply a matter of acknowledging the situation and responding appropriately - for example, by not allowing such people to hold positions of significant power, authority or responsibility.

Territoriality: an old tribal mentality in a global era

In this early 21st century phase of transition out of the cosmic era of *descent into matter*, the primitive mentality of **territoriality** still dominates many cultures. The densifying and *inertia* that are part of the now departing *descent* process have resulted in ignorance, insecurity and fear, which in turn breed hostile defensive aggression and acquisitive greed.

In that context, animal-like territoriality became a political and legal necessity for privileged ruling elites in their roles as *protectors* of the citizens over whom they ruled.

In the earlier stages of the *descent* era, it's widely assumed that humans mostly lived in **nomadic** groups. And from that shifting perspective, attitudes to the land, rivers, seas and the resources they contained would have been functional and communal rather than possessive.

But gradually the *descent* process brought increasingly static ways of living and a sense of stability, resulting in **settled communities**. Then, working on the land would have bred an awareness of the value of particular parts of Earth's surface and coastal waters to a community. In that context, defending those areas from invaders would have become a shared priority, alongside the establishing of new social orders and hierarchies.

Taking the British Isles as an example, next came the phase broadly labelled *medieval*, during which many further developments took place. Existing social hierarchies, traditions and customs became consolidated and enshrined in laws and institutions – established and controlled for their own benefit by those already in positions of power. When William the Conqueror, in the 11th century, claimed the crown and ownership of all the land, his supporters – members of the feudal aristocracy and the Church – were rewarded with their portions.

Next, the **industrial age** formalised and reinforced the notion of property and territorial rights, alongside the formalising of money-mongering through banks, and especially through an emerging all-powerful *central banking syndicate*. This process eventually led to the mass moneylending of the current **post-industrial, electrical/ digital** phase.

Through all these developments, the ruling elite partnership of (a) gross (*masculine*) **territoriality** and (b) subtle (*feminine*) **finance** has kept people politically submissive by applying the age old *IFDR* method of *i*gnorance, *f*ear, *d*ivide and *r*ule. Which in this case has meant keeping whole populations pre-occupied and distracted, competing amongst themselves for deliberately contrived shortages of money and the necessities for life.

And so the two groups, *territorial* and *financial*, out of necessity, have colluded. 'Landowners' have long exploited their stable, tangible, *material* assets – through rent, crops, forestry, mining rights etc – to acquire plenty of the intangible, *non-material*, fluid asset called *money*. Conversely, the money-mongers have used their profits to acquire more *physically permanent* and secure assets in the form of land and property.

In the longer view, today's notion of '***private property***' is a *descent era* idea from humanity's collective early childhood. So, given how all things, material and non-material, eventually revert back into a non-physical state, territoriality is merely a **temporary** phenomenon.

The *descent* era, meanwhile, is beginning to recede noticeably, as the qualities of the incoming *ascent out of matter* era become increasingly significant, and the universal *polarity* principle points to a rebalancing of the cosmic forces of *expansion* and *contraction* and an eventual *equilibrium* state.

However, in the meantime, the notions of *territorial rights* and *property ownership* have become embedded in the minds of disempowered, insecure citizens... providing a seductive illusion of private *home ownership*. So, along with the corrupt and distorted global system of non-existent money and protection racket nation states, *territoriality* and *property ladders* are still very much part of the current confused tangle that defines contemporary life on Earth.

Addiction to territory and property

Privileged elites have for centuries exploited the material benefits and advantages resulting from their ancestors' land-grabs, which were then 'legalised' in property laws, passed in order to protect their gains. And in today's frantic, confused and distracted world, the gross injustices regarding land and property 'ownership' are mostly overlooked without question.

In the UK, for example, 70% of the land is claimed by less than 1% of the population. But such facts remain widely ignored, seemingly because the implications are too challenging to be taken on board by most supposedly rational, logical people... who choose not to question the divine right claimed by monarchs, states and others to 'own' areas of the Earth's surface.

That tends to create an ethos of defensive possessiveness regarding property, characterised by envy, ruthless ambition and a cynical lack of responsibility for the planet. Which together amount to a pathological *addiction* and a major build-up of trouble ahead.

Yet a wholly different sense of responsibility arises when an altruistic impetus to alleviate real human suffering, due to unnecessary deprivation, prompts action. This is **charity**, plain and simple. It's about humanity behaving in an adult, compassionate way by providing some suitable static or mobile accommodation, ie **a dwelling, for everyone according to their real, natural, human needs**.

Technically, it's a do-able task, once it's treated as a priority over other projects which are more about vanity and selfish greed. So, a resolution of this addiction and its ill-effects is simple in principle, although in practice a very challenging prospect. For **the undeniable, simple justice of the idea transcends any petty resentment, envy, jealousy** or other negativity, and can be an empowering force.

Yet before this idea begins to take hold, it will inevitably be dismissed by some as naively idealistic. However, without **an inspiring vision of life beyond the current unwholesome status quo**, most of humankind can easily be kept entrapped and disempowered by those who feel they are doing OK and don't want to risk losing their present 'advantages'.

A balanced and just way to start healing the addiction to territory and property would be to introduce a universal system of **temporary usage, according to real and present need**... bringing to an end all arbitrary and exclusive but unjustifiable territorial claims, whether by addicted dynasties, other privileged groups or individuals.

The *One Humanity* proposal (page 305) provides a practical starting point for progressing beyond this mess. It incorporates a more just, fair and all-inclusive worldwide system of organising who lives where and in what circumstances, **according to real, natural human needs**. For that is now a technologically viable possibility.

These matters are still a major part of the background to the next topic, the forces behind the long-running, three-way conflict in the Middle East, a hugely complicated problem of claims and counter-claims concerning religion, nationality and *territorial* rights.

Three undercurrents
distorting world affairs

From two-ness to three-ness

As has already been described, the primal **polarity** in the cosmos is the opposition of the forces of *contraction* and *expansion* (page 34), which manifest as *gravity* and *levity,* and in the living world as the complementary qualities of the universal *masculine* and universal *feminine*.

Among human societies, the **masculine/feminine** polarity is clearly recognisable in the broad contrast between the more *masculine* **Chinese** Confucian culture and the more *feminine* **Indian** Hindu culture, as is explained next. There's a similar contrast between the ancient and predominantly *masculine* **Arab** cultures and the more *feminine* **Hebrews** whose roots go back to a prehistoric *matrilineal* culture which featured powerful goddesses.

Within that *bi-polarity*, **Christianity** serves as an intermediate third factor, expressing the *masculine* and *feminine* in roughly equal proportions, including many variations. This brought the quality of *three-ness* into the basic two-way polarity, increasing at least the potential for humankind to eventually achieve a state of *equilibrium*.

But before proceeding with that triangular situation, here's a brief look at an ancient *polarity* which is a vital part of the greater context, as viewed from the *Threshold* perspective.

First, China and India: two ancient *polar opposite* cultures

In what follows, some insight into the two ancient, conglomerate cultures, *China* and *India*, is needed. And the insight offered here, from the *Threshold* perspective, unsurprisingly, differs from the views and interpretations of observers within the mainstream media and institutions. For present purposes, it's also much simplified.

As all wise individuals know, there are many paths leading to the proverbial mountain top, where all cultures converge and affirm, each in their own way, certain fundamental principles of human existence. The combination of three universal principles introduced earlier incorporates that basic, non-partisan knowledge.

Two-ness first

The **Chinese** Confucian culture has the predominantly *yang*, **masculine**, centralising quality of the *descent* era, and, in terms of broad social structure, is male-dominated. Being an expression of *gravity*, it focuses inwards from the periphery towards the centre, *contracting*, probing, penetrating and enforcing *uniformity* in order to **dominate,** with grand ideas, plans and a linear sense of order and logic.

Here the State is the dominant force, and dissenters are perceived as a major threat, condemned as **terrorists**, **separatists** or **insurgents** etc. Chinese communities in other lands tend to be exclusive and self-contained.

The Hindu **Indian** tradition has a more **feminine**, yin, expansive, diversifying quality, which has persisted and influenced affairs throughout the *masculine*-dominated *descent* era. The **feminine** – radiant, expansive, opening outwards, and so more vulnerable, with a subtle earthy sensitivity for feelings and details – tends to attract, accommodate, nurture, manipulate, create and elaborate in order to **control**.

So, *diversity*, individual enterprise and creativity are tolerated and encouraged. Also, Hindu Indians in other lands tend to adapt and merge into the local culture.

The *Threshold* perspective affirms how the predominant quality is always partly counterbalanced by its polar opposite. And that's also affirmed in ancient Chinese **Taoist** philosophy, which transcends the bias of the later, *descent era* philosophy of *Confucianism*.

Taoism honours the integrity of the <u>one</u>, timeless, '**indescribable**

way' of infinite variations, while Indian **Hinduism** incorporates a multitude of diverse deities in a complex hierarchy, ultimately united in one supreme, timeless being, Brahma.

But in the incoming, expansive *ascent* era, both of these huge conglomerates face eventual disintegration: China through *implosion* due to factional in-fighting, ie predominantly **contraction**, India through *explosion* due to independence-seeking secessions, ie **expansion**.

Broadly viewed, all human cultures are swept along in the cosmic evolutionary tide, which alternates between polar opposite eras of *descent into matter* and *ascent out of matter*. Phases of this tide 'turning', such as the present time, are periods of extra turbulence, when the significance and destiny of different cultures can change in many ways.

...And then, three-ness

Turning to the Middle East, three distinct 'streams' emerged and evolved into separate, contrasting cultures, yet remained closely intertwined. These were the three related groups now broadly known as **Jews**, **Christians** and **Muslims**.

Common characteristics of all three date back long before recorded human history, and together they've played a significant role in the evolving of human consciousness. But their historic rivalry has also resulted in *ASS* (page 90) claims to **superiority** by each, claims which have been periodically challenged by the competing claims of the others.

During the *descent into matter* era, at their earthly, mass-following level, leaders of all three have indulged in divisive, intolerant, corrupt politics, preaching the *superiority* of their organisation and appealing to people's survival instincts by cultivating fear, rivalry, conflict and fantasies of glory in order to bolster their own status.

In the 21st century, the three have remained powerful *undercurrents* to all world affairs, like three hyper-sensitive, highly reactive creatures, each with its own rival claim: **Jews** as *the chosen*, **Muslims** as *the righteous*, **Christians** as *the saved*. And overlaid on this seething middle layer of intense religious, tribal and ethnic rivalries, is a superficial layer of *territorial nation states*, spread out like a patchwork blanket.

Meanwhile, at the 'higher', intuitive, esoteric level of pure wisdom-seeking, the three cultures converge in affirming, in their own ways, an ultimate, transcendent unity, over-arching, underlying and permeating the whole situation.

Jerusalem

Jerusalem is where the three rival cultures have historically converged, and remains the focal point of their conflicting interests. It's where the *higher-spiritual* and *earthly-territorial* dimensions have yet to be reconciled, as humanity struggles towards eventually transcending its present *adolescent* extremist ways. Consequently, this little place, as a microcosm of *descent* era humanity, is still brewing up a potent mix of Old Testament, New Testament and Quranic passions.

Three cultures in need of some rebalancing

Viewing humankind today as a tormented, suffering being in need of some deep healing, the triad of troubled cultures display three key symptom patterns, simplified here as:
- the *Jewish* pattern: behaviour indicating a delusion of *superiority*, with a craving for global **control**,
- the *Muslim* pattern: behaviour indicating over-zealous, *self-righteous* ambition, seeking total **domination**,
- the *Christian* pattern: behaviour indicating a confused and disempowered state of moral **ambivalence**.

In the fragmentation resulting from the *descent into matter*, they've each sub-divided into numerous factions, creating endless further complications. Meanwhile, the **inertia**, resulting from the *descent*, has hardened attitudes and materialised 'higher' aspirations into rigid, earthly *territorial* claims and ambitions.

The outcome is **a three-way conflict of mutual mistrust and hostility**, a seemingly irresolvable, deadlocked, triangular struggle. As a result, their *ASS* rivalries are the *undercurrents* to many current world problems, despite their attempts to operate behind various flags, proxies, alliances, fronts etc.

My enemy's enemy...

...Having emerged during humankind's troubled *pre-adolescence*, the three-way dynamic still works on the old double-negative maxim from the *descent* era: *'My enemy's enemy is my friend'*.

Consequently, lies, mistrust, jealousy, betrayal and vengeance govern most of the action, and account for much of the obscure, twisted, coded and loaded language used.
And so:
- **Jews** seek global *supremacy* through their monopoly control of the world's money supply.
- **Muslims** explicitly seek to establish a *caliphate*, an all-powerful worldwide Islamic state.
- **Christians** strive to 'save' humankind from 'sin' through a worldwide network of *churches*.

From *Notes from the Threshold* (no longer available)

Why are Jews focused on in this book?

First, these three labels are used here only for convenience as broad terms of reference. Each refers to a broad class of people with a diverse mix of backgrounds, beliefs and traditions. The reason why the problems posed for humanity by Jews are addressed at greater length than those posed by Muslims and Christians is that, at this critical stage of human history, the distorting influence of certain Jews in world affairs has grown out of all proportion.

Especially significant have been the **Ashkenazi Zionist** descendants of the East European/West Asian **Khazars** who converted to Judaism around the 8th century. A predominantly *masculine*, medieval, warrior culture, they have since then taken over and dominated the worldwide Jewish network, becoming highly influential and notorious for their manipulative behind-the-scenes **meddling** in world affairs while **accusing others, especially the Russian state**, of the same. But they are now a fading force, as will be explained.

From the *Threshold* perspective, the *Khazari/Ashkenazi* (*K/A*) conversion to Judaism had a major effect on Hebrew/Jewish culture, creating a uniquely versatile and effective combination of *feminine* and *masculine* qualities... the significance of which will also be explained.

However, linking present day troubles on Earth with events centuries and even millennia ago cannot be an exact science – especially with regard to authentication, given the many records, translations and interpretations now available. So, some simplifying and inferring are inevitable. Nevertheless, by joining up certain well established dots, key patterns can be detected. For, not surprisingly, there's a complex and much disputed back story to contemporary Jewish culture.

The invisible, fragile Jewish empire: now in decline
The increasing proportion of secular, materialistic attitudes in the world has broadly coincided with the increasing global influence of Jews as the world's financiers. And since the 1960s, through a range of financial intermediaries, they have been making *credit*, ie borrowing money at interest, ever more easily and widely available.

As a consequence, billions of people worldwide have been enticed into debt and become addictively dependent on borrowed 'Jewish' *debt money* (page 207). The overall result is today's global, out-of-control, incalculable, unredeemable *debt crisis*. Which could continue until enough people stop believing in this imaginary *money*, and stop buying into the glamorised image of a consumer lifestyle in a monetised world, controlled by a secretive, Jewish moneylending syndicate.

At some point this huge, elaborate scam is doomed to collapse, because it's essentially like a *pyramid selling* or *Ponzi investment* scheme... which always eventually run out of money. And meanwhile, the historic Jewish talent for infiltrating and influencing royalty, State institutions, secret societies and major industries continues to leave a tangled, distorted and messy legacy... for the pioneers of a future, more balanced and sane world to clear up.

Can infinite money power buy '*security*'?

The financial power resulting from its control of the world's money supply has enabled the predominantly *masculine* Khazari/Ashkenazi/Zionist government of Israel to equip itself with the most effective weaponry available... both for defence and in pursuit of its territorial strategy which extends way beyond Palestine. But this has not brought any sense of security, peace or ease to most of the Israeli population. Which is not surprising, since such outcomes have never been a part of the longer term 'Zionist' agenda, despite all the official talk of local political solutions involving one or two states.

So, not for the first time, ordinary Jews have been realising that material wealth which for a while enables them to be the oppressor and persecutor, rather than be the poor, oppressed and persecuted, does <u>not</u> itself bring genuine happiness or deep, lasting fulfilment.

Immature, selfish behaviour is clear evidence that humanity overall has not yet emerged from a combination of its collective infancy, childhood and adolescence... even though a more mature, 'bigger picture' perspective is now available that sets these things in their greater context and brings some revealing insight into their causes. For nothing happens out of nothing.

With the benefit of that perspective, thinking the situation through in an unprejudiced and balanced way reveals why and how those who call themselves Jews have encountered so much hostility through the centuries. And it doesn't involve blaming the Jews or anyone else, as the next chapter explains.

It's no use simply blaming 'the Jews'
for the world's many problems

The broader context

First, a brief reminder of the 'bigger picture' context. The cosmos, including humankind, is passing through a phase of *transition* from an era of *descent into matter* to one of *ascent out of* matter, involving timespans unimaginably long for most earthbound human minds to comprehend.

The two eras represent the *contracting* and *expanding* of the cosmos, expressing the alternating of the complementary cosmic forces, *gravity* and *levity*. In the living world, these two forces can be recognised in the **universal qualities** of *masculine* and *feminine* – not to be confused with the **specific gender** of individuals, each of whom is always a unique combination of the two universals.

The cosmos naturally tends towards a state of *equilibrium* between its polar opposite forces. And during the now departing era of *descent into matter*, gravity and the universal *masculine* qualities have predominated over *levity* and the universal *feminine* qualities. But as the current *transition* phase proceeds towards an era of *ascent*, the reverse tendency will prevail. And that's of special significance to the originally *feminine* Jewish culture.

However, Jews in general seem unaware that their culture is essentially an expression of that universal quality. So, as the victims of much hostility and persecution, they have continued to consistently undermine and sabotage the *masculine* dominance inherent in, for example, the institution known as the *nation state*.

All of which serves as a reminder to any investigator that in order to resolve a major human problem without creating a worse one, you first have to understand the forces at work in some depth, although not necessarily in minute detail. You can then **transcend** all the divisions and trouble, for these always occur within a greater unity.

History: Who writes the back story?

Viewed historically, Jewish culture – tribal, fiercely intense, calculating and exceptionally creative – is traceable back to humanity's collective childhood in an earlier phase of the *descent* era. It's also a primarily *feminine* culture, being *matrilineal* which means that only people with a *Jewish mother* can be accepted as authentic Jews.

Today that tribal quality is still present and active, but covered with a thin veneer of contemporary Western ways and technology. But, unlike Muslims and Christians, Jews rarely air their deeper differences in public. On mother's orders, these are strictly kept 'in the family' – as a survival strategy, through making a display of unity and concealing divisions.

From that mixture has been contrived the **Jewish State of Israel**, ever seeking to grab more territory, regardless of the loss and suffering inflicted on native Palestinians in that process of expansion. And even though worldwide there's now a growing realisation that Zionists are responsible for much unnecessary suffering all over the planet, simply blaming them achieves nothing except reinforce their intention to carry on doing what they do.

That's because their intense indoctrination, typical of more primitive *descent* era cultures, leaves Jews deeply loyal, hyper-sensitive and reactive to anything that could be perceived, rightly or wrongly, as critical, hostile or offensive to them. So, in today's interconnected, over-stressed and highly weaponised world, evolving beyond that emotionally immature *us v. them* mentality is an urgent necessity. Otherwise, oversimplifying can confuse the situation further. For...

There are Jews and there are Jews

Just as there are Catholic, Orthodox, Protestant and other *Christians*, and there are Shia, Sunni and other *Muslims*, there is also a wide variety of distinct groups who call themselves *Jews*. It has recently been conclusively shown that there never has been a single 'Jewish' people, nation or race (see below, page 138). **Benjamin Freedman**, an exleading Zionist, had already explained the origins of the word *Jew* in a famous 1961 speech in New York (See References, page 396).

The word **Jew** is an anglicised version of *Judahite*, a member of the ancient tribe of *Judah*, and *Judean*, someone from *Judea* in Palestine. From these, *Jew* has been adopted as a catch-all, umbrella term, **a label creating a false impression of a single, united people or nation**... whereas Jews have been shown to be, historically, a hybrid collection of diverse peoples who share some common beliefs and practices (see below). Also, *Jew* and *Zionist* have very different meanings, despite the attempts of some to blur that crucial distinction. So, given this exposé of a long-running identity fiction...

What has *'Jewish'* come to mean today?

What *jewishness* has come to mean today incorporates *religious*, *ethnic* and *nationalistic* loyalties – including atheists and secular, Likud-led, Israeli governments – in a complicated and conveniently confusing tangle of permutations. And it's this *feminine* tendency towards fluid *diversity* – unlike typically *masculine* rigid *uniformity* – that enables all kinds of arbitrary and inconsistent attitudes to be rationalised and justified. Thus the familiar tricky, ever-shifting but tenacious Jewish style of arguing and negotiating.

What the added aggressive presence of Khazari Ashkenazis created in Jewish communities around the world was **a uniquely resilient and versatile combination of *feminine* and *masculine* qualities which has so far proved too subtle, confusing, intense and strong-willed for most non-Jews to handle**. It has also enabled the K/A elite to stay a step or two ahead of the rest of inertia-bound, *descent era* humankind. And since Ashkenazis now form the overwhelming majority of 'Jews' in the world, they have taken on a controlling leadership role.

The outstanding achievements of Ashkenazis in certain areas of human activity – ie those requiring particular intellectual skills, self-discipline and creative adaptability – seem to be linked to this unique combination of *masculine* and *feminine* qualities, as is evidenced in the high proportion of Jewish Nobel Prize winners, writers, musicians and artists.

The historic '*Jewish people*' - an elaborate fiction

Recently, it has become increasingly clear that much of **the claimed history of the so-called Jewish people is an elaborate fictional back story**. The whole subject has been thoroughly researched by Professor of History at Tel Aviv University, Shlomo Sand, and laid out in his controversial books **The Invention of the Jewish People** *and* **The Invention of the Land of Israel** (see References).

He describes how over centuries an epic tale has been concocted by scribes at various times and places, in a long running attempt to create a romantic legend of 'the Jews' as one people or nation whose unique culture has survived numerous troubled times through being favoured by God. Sand's account is about a hybrid collection of diverse, intermixed tribes and peoples, misled into believing that a metaphysical, symbolic '*holy land*' could be repackaged and sold as a *territorial* claim to a promised earthly '*homeland*' in Palestine.

Professor Sand's findings counter the Zionists' nationalistic and territorial claims that the 'Jewish people' have a historic, exclusive, God-given right to occupy Palestine as their 'spiritual' homeland... and therefore to terrorise, slaughter and forcibly expel thousands of Palestinians who have been living there for centuries without any need for formal statehood.

He also describes how in the past the supposedly exclusive Jews interbred with other groups, including the medieval Turkic **Khazari** converts... whose **Ashkenazi** descendants now constitute the overwhelming majority of Jews worldwide yet have no **semitic** roots. And that unavoidably links up with searching questions about the artificially manufactured ***anti-semitism*** trick (page 155).

The Myth of the Jewish Race by Dr Raphael Patai, a highly respected anthropologist (see References), was published back in 1975.

Promoting the fictional idea of a distinctive and united but widely scattered 'Jewish' people or nation has long been the strategy of the *K/A* leadership. For that has so far provided them with effective cover within which to pursue their Khazari agenda, while outwardly living as Ashkenazi Jews.

Another dimension has been added to this topic in the growing claims by various people of **African** descent today to be authentic descendants of ancient Hebrews or Israelites from biblical times. They imply an authenticity superior to that of the later Khazari/ Ashkenazi converts, who have thus been labelled **'fake Jews'**.

For historians attempting to disentangle the many complicated strands and trace back tribal and local 'origins', this is inevitably a highly speculative field of research... prompting **differing and disputed interpretations of DNA 'evidence' by opposed factions**. Thus it has begun to look like another branch of *statistics*, a discipline notorious for producing numbers that are manipulable according to the purposes and assumptions of interested parties.

But overall, a whole new perspective has now been introduced into this fluid, open-ended, evolving subject. Also being increasingly highlighted is the *polarity* of the *universal masculine* and *feminine*.

The Hebrew Goddess, for example, is another authoritative book by Dr. Raphael Patai. Here he traces the long saga of Jewish culture back to an ancient *matrilineal* (ie predominantly *feminine*) Hebrew culture involving goddesses, whose influence was eliminated as the predominantly *masculine descent* era proceeded, and males took over various significant roles previously performed by females.

And that *feminine* quality, much distorted as a result of its suppression throughout the *descent* era, can be witnessed in the early 21st century ***smothering* of the Palestinian people**, particularly in Gaza, in a callous, merciless and cruel form of **torture**.

Today, old Jewish prayers worshipping a ***male God*** as an **all-**

powerful *father figure* and ***king*** help preserve a child-like mentality of *dependency*, typical of an earlier, more primitive phase of human evolution. Then there's the biblical figure of Abraham as a revered father figure (page 46). So, there's much untangling still to be done, since...

All is not as it seems - or as is claimed, given that:

- Yes, Jews have been so successful at manipulating money and debt they've gained monopoly control of the world's **money** supply, enabling them to control governments and corporations... thus affecting just about everybody's life in some way.

- Yes, they do consequently control much of the world's **news** and **entertainment** industry, state and commercial, thereby affecting how billions of people think and behave, while also influencing who gets selected for leading roles and key jobs.

- Yes, they do have a long term **agenda**, inspired by propaganda in the Old Testament and other texts, the aim of which is to ruthlessly and mercilessly gain dominant **control** over all humankind.

- Yes, there is **racism** and **apartheid** in Israel/Palestine, mostly inflicted by the majority Ashkenazi Jews on Arabs, Ethiopian Jews and other minorities whom they treat as inferior human beings. Which is, in effect, *ASS* (page 90) in action.

- And yes, Israel does have nuclear weapons, despite neither affirming nor denying this, and does continue to condemn other states, especially Iran, for seeking to be similarly armed.

Also, as a result of the Jewish diaspora, there has evolved, over centuries, a complex global network, known as the *sayanim* (page 167). Its effect is to prevent humankind from resolving certain core problems and from developing more balanced ways of living on Earth. And one useful lesson learned from awareness of this is that trying to unravel that tangled net by tugging at separate strands only complicates the problem, creating further tangles.

So, to deal with the whole situation, it's necessary to view it in its broader context and over a long timescale. So, how to make sense of all this and decide what's best for humanity as a whole – without becoming trapped in prejudiced, biased, partisan ways of thinking about people and the world?

The key to understanding 'the Jewish problem'

The *Threshold* perspective, which is not limited to an earthbound, ground level view, reveals that...

**The cosmic function of the essentially *feminine* Jewish culture
during the now departing era of *descent into matter*
has been to provide a counterbalancing force on Earth
to the natural predominance of the *universal masculine*.
But now, in the ongoing *transition* from that era
towards a polar opposite one of *ascent out of matter*,
the previous subversive, sabotaging role of the Jews
is becoming redundant.**

The cosmic rebalancing process works 'down' from a level way beyond earthly human morality and ethics, and therefore beyond any blaming and counter-blaming. It also naturally involves some alternating, as it gradually progresses towards an **equilibrium** state between *contraction* (as the universal *masculine*) and *expansion* (as the universal *feminine*). Jewish culture, however, has remained locked into what is now a redundant pattern, no longer serving the natural progression of the cosmos towards a state of *equilibrium*.

The influx of the Khazars (see next section) also added an extra dimension to Jewish culture). So, as humanity begins to realise what's been going on, and human consciousness evolves towards an equilibrium state, ie a more equal dynamic balance between its *masculine* and its *feminine* aspects, a decline in the power of Jews to influence world affairs is to be expected.

141

And in response to that cosmic shift, worldwide resistance, especially among *males*, is temporarily intensifying. Thus the wave of old style, 'strong man/dictator' politicians appearing on the world stage, along with the rise of ultra-conservative religious elements.

Yet the age old '*Jewish problem*' still hasn't been fully thought through

Without the benefit of the *Threshold* perspective, most thinking people who call themselves 'Jews' still seem unable to clearly and fully think through their troubled position in the world. And a big part of the problem is that, in the 21st century, they seem to be clinging on to what is essentially a tribal/medieval, 'us versus them' mentality regarding the rest of humankind.

As mentioned earlier, the progression of the *masculine*-dominated *descent into matter* era left the ancient predominantly *feminine* culture that was later labelled *Jewish* struggling to counter that imbalance in whatever ways it could. Males were gradually taking over leading roles in society earlier performed by females, and the *inertia* effect of the *descent into matter* was causing attitudes to harden and rigidify.

All this contributed to the emergence of the psychological condition described in this work as **ASS**, *Addictive Superiority Syndrome*... which appears to be, although not exclusively, a major Jewish problem.

Which is why many 'Jews' have found that an inbred assumption of their **superiority** over non-Jews has not brought ease, joy or a sense of security into their lives. Material and financial wealth, accompanied by an arrogant manner, based on anxiety, self-pity and vengeance is not a formula for healing troubled souls. So, what's at the heart of all this?

Even today, many 'Jews' appear to have been so effectively indoctrinated with a deep, unquestioning sense of tribal **loyalty** that this tends to override personal differences, integrity and honesty.

Consequently, many have learnt how to play the part of the tragic, persecuted victim, while doggedly arguing the case for Israel and disregarding the blatant moral and ethical failings of its various governments regarding the Palestinian people since 1948. All of which together amount to a mentality of **collective denial**.

They also haven't yet realised why the power and influence of their *K/A* Zionist leadership is now in decline, as evidenced by its increasingly desperate and extreme strategies and tactics. The resulting confusion has left many 'Jews' still unaware of how the '*Beyond Zion to Khazaria*' agenda of the fanatical *K/A* ruling elite is being relentlessly pursued... **in the name of all Jews worldwide**.

So, ordinary Jews everywhere are now suffering the increasingly disturbing consequences of their **misplaced, unquestioning loyalty**, which has so far resulted in them passively complying with that longer term, separate *K/A* agenda.

Fooled by a simple *labelling trick*, ie the *K/A* Jewish **identity scam**, what the world's Jews have been left with is a widely mistrusted and disliked Israeli government – headed by a coalition of **secular conservatives, strategically aligned with some extremist *religious* conservatives** – who together stoke up and politically feed off the insecurity, fear and anger of those Israelis still opting for 'protection' by politicians posing as 'Big Daddy' father figures.

However, once you look behind the frontage at what's really going on, you can see **the lost and fearful many** being easily misled through a high-tech but spiritually barren desert by **a few dedicated fanatics**, using a combination of threats and false comforts.

And in that context, the ***anti-semitism* trick** (page 156), along with the legacy of the *Nazi holocaust* story, can be seen serving as **distracting diversions** from the shame and unease of many 'Jews' worldwide about what's being perpetrated in their name.

The *Threshold* perspective, meanwhile, provides a powerful *overview* and penetrating *insight* during this exceptional phase of *transition*. It reveals how, given the basically *feminine*, expansive, diversifying nature of Jewish culture, a major dissipation and diluting is due.

And given how the influx of the Khazaris (see next section) added an extra dimension to Jewish culture, the next key question concerns the emergence of **Zionism** in the 19th century and the **Khazari/Ashkenazi/Zionists**... who assumed leadership of world jewry and for a while have been major players behind the scenes in world affairs. So...

Who are these *Zionists*...
apart from certain Christians who've been persuaded that an <u>earthly</u> *homeland* for the 'Jews' in Palestine is equivalent to the biblical promise of a <u>spiritual</u> *holy land*?

They are primarily *Khazari Ashkenazis*. But can they ever be authentic Jews?
Evidence of the ongoing cosmic shift from an era of *descent into matter* to one of *ascent out of matter* is clear. So, a crucial factor in how this works out will be the state of mind of many uneasy Jewish people around the world, as they awaken to an uncomfortable realisation.

And that realisation will be that much of their unease is the result of the medieval-minded, domineering ambitions of a particularly ruthless element among them, known as the **Ashkenazim**, descendants of a people called the **Khazars**. So, who are or were the Khazars?

Historically, they are understood to have been a powerful warrior people, between the 7th and 10th centuries CE, occupying a country called **Khazaria**, which was approximately where Ukraine now exists. In the 8th century they were allegedly converted to Judaism

144

by their own leadership for strategic political purposes. In the 10th century the Khazars were conquered by what is now Russia, and many moved west into Europe. So, there's a clue as to why control of **Ukraine** continues to be such a bitterly disputed geopolitical issue.

Benjamin Freedman (1890-1984) concisely explained the background to this little mentioned strand of modern history in his 1961 speech (page 396), and again in a 1974 speech to US military personnel. That was before Arthur Koestler's book, *The Thirteenth Tribe*, also addressed the history of the Khazari/Ashkenazis.

So, that strategic conversion still presents a major paradox, given that Jews have generally not been open to converts – although with individual exceptions – since a much earlier, more *feminine*-influenced phase of the *descent* era.

Crucial questions thus remain as to whether these converts and their current leadership could ever be authentic Jews. It's crucial because certain *Khazars* took their predominantly *masculine* culture into Europe, where they became the driving force of what later emerged as the ***Zionist*** movement, a territorial, land-grabbing, *political* faction, founded in the late 19th century. Zionism thus imposed on the *religion* of Judaism a ruthlessly ambitious policy of promoting a Jewish State in Palestine, despite fierce opposition from many Jews.

What started as a kind of *merger* later became a *takeover* or *hijack* by this grafted-on, medieval, *masculine* hard 'shell'. Since when, it has dominated and 'protected' the essentially *feminine* Jewish culture, which itself has long wielded considerable *soft power* through its manipulative skills with *money* and as *confidants* and *advisors* to ruling elites. Both of these roles have a long history of prompting public resentment in their host countries.

Zionists are not universally liked or supported by **non-Zionist Jews**, who nevertheless are normally **trained to remain loyal** to the overall Jewish cause. So, any ***anti-Zionist Jews*** who don't want to be identified with Zionism have to explicitly dissociate themselves from it. Otherwise they remain complicit in allowing the **Khazari Ashkenazis** to use their adopted jewishness as cover, ie as a protective shield for their greater ambitions beyond Palestine.

First stop, Palestine... destination Ukraine/Khazaria 02?

The questions arise: *Are the K/A plotting a takeover of Ukraine – to make it the new Khazaria – after which the 'Holy Land/Homeland' in Palestine can be abandoned, having served its purpose as a stepping stone? Then, who will leave and who'll stay, loyal to whom?*

This sheds light on the current 'American' (ie K/A) foreign policy, which is aimed at disruption in Ukraine... but is proving to be badly misguided, due to ignorance of the greater cosmic forces at work.

What does Zionism look like from the *Threshold*?

Winston Churchill, in 1920, **eloquently described** that apparently paradoxical combination of characteristics in Jewish culture, as he saw it – quoted by Douglas Reed in his book *The Controversy of Zion* (see page 392 of this book). But lacking the *Threshold* perspective, Churchill **couldn't explain** what he'd observed.

That requires observing Zionism <u>not</u> from a ground level, *'us v. them'* perspective, but with the *overview* and *insight* available from the *Threshold*. Open-ended questions then arise, such as:
- *Could all that fervour, determination and creativity of the K/A Zionists be serving <u>all</u> humanity, instead of acting as a partisan, subversive and divisive force?*
- *How can they best be helped to redirect their formidable willpower, energy, and talents away from an unachievable medieval fantasy ambition driven by a hunger for vengeance?*

As stated earlier, to overcome a major problem without creating a worse one, you have to probe and understand it in some depth. So, here's a question for non-Jewish people who have so far not given much thought to Zionism and its implications.

**How do you respond to the idea
that a small *minority* of fanatics
currently *control* much of this world,
because they know they can *exploit your unwillingness*
to *believe* the *extremes* to which they'll go
in pursuing their *supremacist* agenda?**

Zionism: a tribal/medieval mentality in the 21st century

In the longer view of cosmic evolution and shifting land masses on Earth, the relatively recent violent, land-grabbing **occupation** and **ethnic cleansing** by Zionists in Palestine reveal a primitive, animal-like, tribal/medieval mentality... seething away behind the superficially civilised image of a modern, well funded, hi-tech and well armed Jewish State of Israel.

It has also become clear that the price of this worldly 'success' has been much insecurity and a severe lack of happiness and fulfilment among most ordinary Jews – a situation which looks likely to continue until a significant number have the courage to openly question and start the much-needed healing process.

In 1948, **Albert Einstein** and various other leading Jewish thinkers described the ideology behind the newly formed **Jewish State of Israel** as **akin to that of Nazis and Fascists.** https://archive.org/details/AlbertEinsteinLetterToTheNewYorkTimes.December41948. The extremist faction in question was part of a ruthless, violent group known as *Revisionist Zionists*, which in 1973 converted itself into the secular political **Likud Party**.

Zionism's two functions

To summarise, there are two distinct aspects of the passing phenomenon known as Zionism.

1. **Its earthly human form**: *Zionism* is a primitive, nationalistic, political, belief system, promoting the interests of the Jewish State of Israel in Palestine. It's headed by a K/A elite, convinced that they are *superior* to all other human beings. And that's justified by Old

147

Testament propaganda about Israelites being God's 'chosen' people, who therefore assume that they deserve special worldly privileges.

2. **Its cosmic evolutionary function**: With the grafting on of the *masculine* K/A Zionists' *protective shell*, the essentially *feminine* Jewish culture – already serving as a counterbalance to the universal *masculine* principle – became a much more significant force in the world... although Zionism itself has now peaked and is beginning to fade.

Broadly, there are three kinds of Zionists

1. *Political* **Zionists**: medieval-minded, 'us v. them', territorial nationalists, demonstrating an essentially **masculine** quality. Eg the war-mongering USA *neo-conservatives (neo-cons)*.
2. *Financial* **Zionists**: primarily the money-mongering, global financial syndicate, **SCAB**, with its *descent era* **feminine** qualities, supported by *neo-liberals* in the USA.
3. *Religious* **Zionists**: including ultra-conservative orthodox Jews and certain Christians, primarily concerned with the coming to pass of certain biblical 'prophecies' in the Middle East.

The vendetta against Russia

Although Khazaria was conquered and overrun by Russia back in the 10th century, when many Khazars moved west into Europe, one legacy is still a *K/A* hunger for revenge against Russia. And it's that which seems to have prompted certain historical events not normally viewed in this light. They include the 1917 Russian revolution, allegedly funded by European Jewish bankers, and the ongoing anti-Russia campaign of the Zionist-controlled US government. Russians choose to refer only to '*American*' hostility because they are aware that Jews still control the world's, and therefore Russia's money.

Courageous investigators, insiders and observers reveal...

Further insight into humanity's Zionist problem is included on page 389 in a short extract from **Whose Promised Land?** by **Colin Chapman**. Also referred to is the work of two respected and well qualified 20th century writers, **Benjamin H Freedman** and **Douglas Reed**, and a contemporary independent 21st century investigative journalist, **Brandon Martinez**. (page 395).

Benjamin H Freedman (1890-1984) was a Jewish, high level political confidant of US presidents and other leading figures, and an insider at the highest levels of Jewish/Zionist activities in the US. But he withdrew in disgust at the shameful conduct of the Zionists in the 1940s. In a famous speech in 1961, later published in **Facts Are Facts** (page 396), he said, "... *here in the United States, the Zionists and their co-religionists have complete control of our government... ...the Zionists and their co-religionists rule this United States as though they were the absolute monarchs of this country.*"

Douglas Reed was a controversial writer and, in the mid-20th century, a senior foreign correspondent of The Times (London), which was then still a prestigious newspaper prior to being taken over in 1981 by a populist supporter of Zionism. Reed's **The Controversy of Zion** is a detailed and extensively documented history of Zionism, focusing on the *political* aspect of the story.

Through his in-depth investigations, he would, however, have been fully aware of the shadowy, manipulative manoeuvrings concerning finance and debt that were going on behind the superficial, political theatricals. These included the 'granting' of 'independence' by nation state colonial powers to various less developed countries... which then found themselves starting out inescapably in debt to and therefore under the control of *SCAB*. Israel was not part of that pattern.

Professor Shlomo Sand has already been mentioned (page 139).

Professor Joseph P Farrell, in his book *Babylon's Bankers*, explains how the so-called 'economic cycles' of *expansion/boom* and *contraction/bust* have continued to be orchestrated by those he calls Babylon's Bankers, ie the financial Zionist elite, *SCAB*... at the expense of the rest of humankind. For through funding and controlling the world's mass media and education systems, *SCAB* has kept most of humankind ignorant of the relationship between the 'economic cycles' and certain natural rhythms.

Any mention of **Henry Ford**, founder of the Ford Motor Company, regarding the influence of Jews in 20th century North America, is guaranteed to prompt choruses of 'Anti-semitism!'. Yet he did directly experience hostile Jewish financiers trying to take control of his empire. And regardless of the merits or otherwise of his production methods and his extremely conservative political, patriotic and religious outlook, one of his famous quotes is:
"It is perhaps well enough that the people of the nation do not know or understand our banking and monetary system, for if they did I believe there would be a revolution before tomorrow morning."

Kay (Katherine) Griggs, the Christian ex-wife of a violent, alcoholic US Marine colonel – in a long interview, later posted (by others) on YouTube – unsensationally tells of a hidden, toxic corrupt world, seething with sexual perversion, drugs and murderous violence at the higher levels of the US military and government, especially involving Zionists and certain Freemasons.

A 21st century *Exodus*: liberation from the *ASS* mind trap
Although this work may at first appear to some people to be expressing an *anti-Jewish* attitude, what it's offering is the opposite. It's proposing an alternative, positive and creative way forward – that is, instead of passively complying with the misguided, K/A led, Jewish 'mission', which is now dragging this world towards an avoidable catastrophe for all humankind.

But first, the extent and the dark depth of the current problem has to be appreciated in order to get a measure of the challenges involved.
For example, it might at first seem inconceivable to many Jews and non-Jews today to ask the following question:
Could the calculating ruthlessness of the Zionist elite in the 1940s have led them to utilise what has been labelled the 'Nazi holocaust'

as part of a long term plan...?
- *First, to win world sympathy for the Jews, as persecuted victims seeking a 'return' to what they'd been led to believe was their spiritual and physical homeland, and*
- *Second, to prompt the migration of millions of European Jews to Palestine in order to occupy and forcefully take it over – which was the explicit aim of the Zionist movement?*

For in order to overcome the unwillingness of many Jews in Europe and America to leave their settled lives for an uninviting restart in 1940s Palestine, the Zionist leadership had to strongly incentivise them one way or another and appeal to the deeply inbred Jewish sense of *loyalty*. And in making all this do-able, it certainly helped to have an unlimited supply of money available, through having gained monopolistic control of the world's money supply.

Such a perspective serves as a reminder of the natural fact that **no human beings own or have any exclusive rights over any part of this planet**. And that applies to royal and aristocratic dynasties, nation states, plutocracies, religious orders and any other groups, including Zionists, who make such claims. For traditions, customs and documents are, in essence, only 'frozen' ideas and practices, products of the *inertia* of the *descent* era.

It follows, then, that all ruling elites and others claiming divinely ordained *superiority* and special privileges, such as *territorial* rights, are **BLUFFING**. For such assertions ultimately rely on the threat of violent force or financial penalties.

Sufficient land and resources exist on Earth for all humans to live a healthy and fulfilling life. So, it's not necessary today for anyone to suffer in real deficiency while others live in excess of their real natural needs. A practical, visionary way forward towards the necessary rebalancing is proposed later in the **One Humanity** section (page 305). But back with the main theme...

Who's ready to renounce Zionism?

All along, the Zionist leadership - with its domineering, *masculine* attitude, ambition and unrelenting determination - has been exploiting the traditional **loyalty** deeply inbred in Jews around the world. For the predominantly *feminine*, family-based, tribal, Hebrew culture instills in each new generation a reluctance to betray the pivotal Jewish mother at the centre of domestic family life, while the stern father figure God looks down from above.

Since Judaism is a *matrilineal* culture, it presents a challenging prospect for those Jews who long to liberate themselves from this psychological entrapment, but don't want to provoke a strong emotional reaction which could result in them being excommunicated and/or persecuted one way or another.

Consequently, how they respond to this dilemma carries huge potential significance for all humanity, although such individuals may not presently be aware of this. The reason is the extensive worldwide control still currently being subtly and secretly exercised by highly motivated Zionists, and the resulting damage and suffering.

However, as the cosmic *transition* phase proceeds on Earth, the Ashkenazis, whose intelligence and creativity came to excel in the later stages of the *descent* era, are likely to find themselves increasingly out of touch with the times and less influential than they were. That is, unless they radically adapt their ways – which does <u>not</u> mean cosmetically adopting a superficially different style and image while maintaining the same basic attitude.

One example of them losing the plot was the way they miscalculated the outcome of the 2016 US presidential election. Which left them having to improvise ways to try and control the maverick, unpredictable President Trump, who had devised a winning formula for the 'numbers game' *democracy delusion* (page 226), previously able to be 'managed', ie controlled, by just a select few K/A Zionists.

In summary:

If you sense that you are the victim of some clever trickery, you need to understand how the trickery works in order to overcome it. Viewed from the *Threshold*, the *K/A* Zionists' trick has been to combine four key elements into an effective mind-controlling programme.

1. An old, **tribal** era, supremacy **religion** and belief system, dominated by a stern, harsh, father figure God.
2. **Primitive**, animal-like **territoriality**, introducing the idea of a *'promised land'* on Earth.
3. **Medieval**, 'us v. them' **nationalism**, starting with a 'successful' Jewish State of Israel in Palestine
4. **Financial** control and **exploitation** of money wherever possible.

The destination: a form of **globalism** which amounts to a neo-feudal system of world governance. Thus through a combination of manipulation and bullying, the unspoken *Khazaria 02* project continues to be supported by millions of 'Jews' worldwide, unaware of how their goodwill and loyalty is being callously exploited.

A key part of the trick has been to 're-interpret' the ancient biblical ideal of a **symbolic/spiritual** *Holy Land* into a physical **earthly homeland** for the widely scattered Jews... to be acquired through a territorial land grab in Palestine. However, that move can now be seen as part of a longer term K/A strategy to establish a first base, a stepping stone, on the way to reinstalling the medieval state of *Khazaria* in what's approximately Ukraine today.

By the early 20th century, *SCAB*'s control of both the world's money supply and the US Federal Administration enabled the Zionists to manipulate US military power into assisting the British in World War One... in return for a commitment to have Palestine as their *promised land*. Which temporarily reinforced the fantasy idea that God had delivered on his biblical promise... only for the 'milk and honey' later to turn sour and bitter. (See Freedman's revealing 1961 speech, referred to on page 395.) The secretive financial exploitation of the UK state in WW1 is revealed at <u>https:bankunderground.co.uk/</u>

2017/08/08/your-country-needs-funds-the-extraordinary-story-of-britains-early-efforts-to-finance-the-first-world-war/.

The outcome in the early 21st century is a medieval, *masculine, descent era* culture of dominance, ambition and vengeance in the coalition of militant secular politicians and religious extremists ruling over Israel... temporarily reinforcing the inbred, fear-driven loyalty of most Jews... who have so far found themselves powerless to heal this sick situation. One example of this **bullying** tendency can be seen in the policy of the so-called USA government (ie the *K/A neo-con* elite) towards Muslim Iran, which is seen as a threat to the very existence of The Jewish State of Israel.

A short term prognosis: Zionists still rule, but not for much longer

Just as the Jewish/Zionist phenomenon must inevitably change through time, likewise, other religious movements will either adapt and evolve or wither and fade into obscurity.

For as the current *transition* phase progresses, the excessive male violence and ambition that has characterised certain sections of the **Muslim** world will gradually be neutralised, as a result of the increasing influence of Muslim women. Which could lead to a new surge of creative inspiration, echoing the great medieval blossoming of Islamic culture, but this time heralding a more mature balance between the qualities of the *universal masculine* and *universal feminine*.

Also, once the **Christian** Church has grown out of its ambivalent adolescent confusion about sex and gender, and has moved beyond the futile *'creation versus evolution'* dispute, the essential Christian message of love, compassion and inclusion could prevail. But first, some honest confessing and apologising for the dark history of *'Churchianity'* will be necessary, given all the persecution and cruelty that has been perpetrated in the name of Christianity. Which leaves one clever, and so far extremely successful, *Jewish*, mind-manipulating **bluff**..

154

The *Anti-semitism* trick

Anti-semitism is a term that does not make sense, given what it's intended to imply, ie a hatred of Jews. According to Encyclopaedia Britannica, *"Although the term now has wide currency, it is a misnomer* (a wrong or inaccurate name), *since it implies a discrimination against all Semites. Arabs and other peoples are also Semites..."* So, it's a deliberately confusing and misleading term.

Like numerous other nonsensical catchphrases, hooks, labels and brand names, artificially conjured up for propaganda purposes or commercial adverts, *anti-semitism* is an ingeniously contrived term, first used in late 19th century Germany. It primarily serves as a shield, to deflect hostility directed at Jews and Zionists away from them and towards some so-called **semitic** peoples – which literally means certain groups or tribes in the Middle East, **including Arabs and Jews**, who speak or once spoke a local **semitic language**.

Yet paradoxically, **the overwhelming majority of Jews in the world, the *Khazari Ashkenazis* from western Asia/eastern Europe, have *no semitic roots*, ie no direct ancestral linkage with the Middle East.** Which, in effect, exposes the whole *anti-semitism* strategy as a hollow, hyped-up, naming and blaming trick that plays on people's emotions, guilt and lack of factual knowledge.

Thus it has become a kind of **trap** which also, however, entraps Jews in a warped *victim* mentality and uses their fear and sense of loyalty to protect the unspoken long term agenda of the Khazari Ashkenazis.

After many years of persistent repetition by the Zionist-controlled mainstream media, the term has become normalised into everyday language. And as a further subtle twist, the spelling is now being deliberately changed by some writers, omitting the hyphen to make *antisemitism* look like a normal English word, such as antiseptic or antibiotic.

From the *Threshold*, the almost meaningless but emotionally loaded notion of *anti-semitism* can be viewed on several different levels...

that is, beyond the familiar ground-level, blaming and disputing:

1. At the lowest level, in response to any unfavourable comments about Jews or Israel, there are the familiar self-pitying accusations of *victimisation* and racist hatred.

2. That response tends to be backed up with emotional *appeals for sympathy* by referring to the *Nazi holocaust*, even though certain often repeated 'facts' and and figures about it have been seriously disputed as politically motivated exaggerations.

3. From one level up, such accusations and appeals can be seen as *diversionary tactics* to distract attention away from:

    (a) the **guilt and shame of many Jews** regarding the conduct of the Israeli government pre- and post-1948,
    (b) the crucial but avoided question of **why Jews have been persecuted through many centuries**.

4. From a yet higher level, the answer to that question can be seen as a **list** of typical 'Jewish' characteristics * that have long been widely disliked and resented (see below).

5. And that leads on to a further question: *What does that list of typically Jewish ways reveal about **the bigger picture factors** accounting for this particular strand of humankind?*

The main factor, regarding the *universal masculine* and *feminine* and the natural tendency of the cosmos towards an *equilibrium* state, is summarised on page 38.

* In response to the key question, *Why have Jews been persecuted for centuries?* (a subject ripe for some in-depth, unbiased research), here's a brief checklist of certain attitudes, normally suppressed in public. That is, a few common unfavourable perceptions of Jews as people who somehow seem to be smarter and more successful than most, especially regarding the following:

156

1. **Money** and **property**, and therefore the wielding of 'behind the scenes' **influence** at the higher' levels of societies.
2. **Two-faced**, double-dealing, manipulative secrecy and dishonesty:
(a) as persecuted **victims**, seeking sympathy and special treatment, through the *anti-semitism trick* and the efforts of the '*holocaust industry*'** (see Shulamit Aloni, below), while also
(b) as **superior beings**, with an arrogant, exclusive and contemptuous attitude towards non-Jews, as in the explicit malevolence of the 'sacred' *Talmud* teachings (page 401).

The Holocaust Industry: *Reflections on the Exploitation of Jewish Suffering* by Norman G. Finkelstein, an Israeli Jew (2000) ISBN 9781859843239SECA, plus a short video of him at
s://www.youtube.com/watch?v=aun2O2U0uvU

3. **Moneylending for profit:** through Zionist/Jewish control of the world's money supply.
4. **Mass media control**: especially of major news and entertainment corporations.
5. **Anti-Russia propaganda** – because of a centuries-old vengeance grudge (page 148).
6. **Anti-Iran propaganda** – because of regional rivalry for power and control.
7. **Ukraine takeover ambitions:** to re-establish Khazaria (page 147).
8. **Global governance ambitions**: via 'independent' set-ups, such as the Bilderberg Group, WTO, Chatham House (UK), Council on Foreign Relations and Trilateral Commission (USA), plus numerous secret networks and institutions – administrative, commercial and educational.
9. **Preventing any open, 'truth-seeking'**, discussion or questioning about the above subjects.

Shulamit Aloni, an Israeli ex-government minister concisely summarised how *anti-semitism* and the *holocaust* story are two of the favourite propaganda tricks used by Israeli Jews. (See YouTube https://www.youtube.com/watch?v=RFB0pJYO-QA).

And so the cry of *"Anti-semitism!"* has been adopted as the automatic reflex reaction of many Jews and Jewish organisations to any less than favourable references to Jewish people or Israel. It's now regularly exploited like an emotive, unthinking *conditioned reflex*, triggering instant condemnation and guilt, in order to protect Jews and Israel from criticism or penetrating investigation. (See two examples in the *2016* chapter, page 273) By 2016, it was beginning to show some signs of *desperation*.

Psychologically, it's a sign of a self-centred, hyper-sensitive, artificially contrived, **victim mentality**... part of the primitive, 'all or nothing' attitude, **'You're either with us or you're against us!'**. Which is itself an echo of the ancient *tribal* world of humanity's collective childhood, still typical of various Jewish organisations, including the Israeli government.

Thus the implicit claim by Jews that they are an exceptionally deserving special case. Which indicates a deep collective unease and an understandable sense of **identity insecurity** – that is, for a basically *feminine* culture which has long had to survive by whatever means it could through a mostly hostile, *masculine*-dominated era.

So, at ground level there's still a broad swathe of inbred, unquestioning, loyal support for what many naively choose to believe is simply the 'Jewish/Zionist cause'... while not recognising it as the dark, unmentionable, Khazari/Ashkenazi agenda, involving various crimes against humanity, perpetrated in the name of all Jews.

A superficial yet significant indicator of the desire of many Jews to avoid being identified as Jewish is the high proportion of Eastern European Ashkenazi Jews who have changed their names to more typically western or western-sounding names. Hundreds of examples, including many Hollywood celebrities, are listed online.

Various other cultures are similarly still stuck at that emotionally primitive stage of their development... **but they do not have control of the world's money supply.**

Resolving the three-way tussle
The crucial first steps (of a long journey)

As already stated, it's not the purpose of this work to blame or demonise any individuals or groups. Each culture has its own unique qualities, talents and strengths to contribute to human destiny. Also, any long term solutions to the problems of humankind unavoidably require the participation of all those who may currently be seen as troublesome to the rest.

So, how to start the healing process and build up some momentum? This is where it becomes very testing for all concerned. Why? Because some radical re-thinking is required from all involved, given the current worldwide inertia of politically impotent, puppet-like, elected politicians, including presidents and prime ministers... all controlled by unseen puppeteers.

The *Threshold* perspective on the historic three-way tangle reveals how 21st century hi-tech humanity, at this time of *transition*, has lost the fierce, upfront, partisan edge, ie the intensity and ambition of earlier *descent* era cultures. Which is why it's inept at dealing with:
(a) the predominantly *masculine*, medieval and violent fundamentalist **Muslim** mentality,
(b) the predominantly *feminine*, devious, manipulative and fiercely loyal **Jewish** mentality,
(c) the idealistic but *ambivalent*, morally confused and compromised **Christian** mentality.

Each of these *descent era* cultures represents a particular kind of *imbalance*, resulting in a long term, inherent **lack of fulfilment for its people** and therefore **three-way trouble**.

Also revealed are the ways in which westernised societies are being outmanoeuvred, provoked and intimidated, such that they themselves are regressing back into more primitive, tribal/medieval ways. So, how to address this as yet unresolved triangular problem?

- First, recognise and acknowledge that there is a problem that requires urgent attention.

- Second, try to understand the problem from the transcendent *Threshold* perspective through gaining (a) an **overview** of the whole situation within its greater cosmic context, and (b) some penetrating **insight** into the motivating forces at the heart of it.

- Third, take the path towards an optimum state of **equilibrium** between the primal forces,   ie a balance that's fair and beneficial to all humankind and in harmony with nature. Simple in principle, not so simple to put into practice.

One essential part of any resolution has to be an explicit commitment by all who agree to involve themselves in pioneering the necessary changes that they will publicly denounce:
(a) all divisive, partisan, supremacy-seeking claims wherever and whenever they occur, and
(b) all incitement to 'us versus them' exclusion and violence – except in extreme cases of genuine self-defence.

Today, many signs of the disintegration of the old and the emergence of the new can be witnessed. All over the world people are hungry for fresh inspiration, instead of re-runs of old, failed policies. Also, subtle but profound changes in the human psyche can be detected emerging, which imply the coming of a very different kind of world. The empowering *Threshold* perspective can help those seeking to create a more balanced and sane world.

Big changes are due: for better or worse?
Changes could start to happen quickly once the old *SCAB* 'money trick' fails and the present global *debt money* system begins to disintegrate and collapse. For that will leave Israel increasingly **isolated, unfunded and vulnerable**, surrounded by hostile, vengeful neighbours, although in the short term still heavily armed and in possession of nuclear weapons.

When it's realised that that the whole 'Israel in Palestine' project was stage one of a longer term Khazari/Ashkenazi strategy, the current *'We are the deserving, infallible winners'* mentality will start to dissipate, as trust in the K/A leadership wanes.

By early 2018 there were noticeable signs of increasing desperation in the Zionists' bluff as they pursued their faltering agenda. For decades Israel had dominated the Middle East region through the apparent invulnerability of its Air Force. But in 2018 that imbalance was abruptly adjusted when one of its fighter planes was shot down over Syria, presumably with the assistance of Russian weaponry. This marked a significant shift in the regional balance of power and influence.

False flag-type sabotaging operations around the world were not having the intended effect. One example was the Israeli/US accusation of an alleged 'chemical attack' by Syrian State forces, with the support of Russia and Iran, on a medical centre in Syria. This event was later revealed to have been staged, filmed and reported as a propaganda stunt by a fake volunteer organisation known as the *White Helmets*, allegedly funded by wealthy Zionist sympathisers.

Simultaneously, there was an alleged 'chemical nerve agent' attack on two Russians in Salisbury, England... implicitly blamed, without any conclusive evidence, on Russian agents. And in May 2018, the Israeli army's massacre of over fifty Palestinians in response to a protest demonstration was condemned worldwide by governments and the public.

Looking ahead, as the world status quo continues disintegrating, nation states everywhere will be squabbling amongst themselves, stuck in the selfish partisan mindset of the old order, trying to negotiate a new global money system that's acceptable to each. With this in mind, the radical proposals concerning money in the **One Humanity** chapter (page 305) could be useful in planning ahead in order to pre-empt the approaching crisis.

Regarding timescales, all this will take as long as it takes, depending on how quickly or slowly humanity as a whole awakens to its collective potential.

So, looking further ahead...

Politically, the *Threshold* proposals include the careful dismantling of all nation states and replacing them with a decentralised, global, regional and local system of autonomous communities, more suited to a grown-up, hi-tech, ecologically aware humanity in the latter 21st century and beyond.

Financially, SCAB would cease to exist, and instead there would be a radically different kind of transitional, interim *money system*, **not based on debt** and designed to operate until humanity has grown out of its childish dependency on imaginary money tokens. This would replace *fear-and-greed* financial *economics* with a system that prioritises satisfying all real natural need and eliminates living in excess of real natural need... until an ecologically and socially balanced global *equilibrium* has been achieved.

Religious supremacy-seeking will be exposed as a perverse, divisive form of spiritual politics and be abandoned in favour of ways more in harmonious *resonance* with the cosmos and nature. And together, these developments will converge into...

A critical moment of destiny for Zionists everywhere

Given the mass of corroborating evidence now available regarding the destabilising influence of Zionism on world affairs, a critical *tipping point* seems imminent. For it's clear that Ashkenazis in general do have some exceptional abilities and talents which have made them the most 'successful' group of people on Earth, in worldly terms, during the latter stages of the *descent into matter* era... at least according to certain measures of 'success'.

And a key part of that success has been their controlling influence as sponsors and directors of the 24/7 soap that's acted out on the mass media *world stage* by an ever changing cast of actors... while they remain hidden and in control behind the scenery. BUT that era, with its distorted values, is now passing away, ending their assumption of an inherent 'superiority' and the kudos of admiration, respect and wealth associated with it.

So, as humankind awakens and starts to radically rethink the meaning of life on Earth, Zionists and Jews face a crucial choice:
A. Doggedly carry on pursuing a deluded and damaging fantasy agenda of *supremacy* that's doomed eventually to fail disastrously, or instead...

B. Turn their considerable talents, strengths and will power to assisting in the healing of all humankind, helping to redirect world affairs towards a more sane, balanced path.

However, this requires, first, some deep self-healing... to enable the abandoning of old *ASS* habits (page 90) and manipulative, fear-driven, selfish greed. But where to start? Perhaps by recognising the fundamental changes to life on Earth are occurring, as part of the ongoing cosmic *transition* from an era of *descent into matter* to one of *ascent out of matter*.

For, when the present global money system does eventually collapse, in the absence of a fair and transparent replacement, many different schemes will inevitably arise, some driven by pathological ambitions to dominate or control human destiny locally, regionally and globally.
Dealing with such schemes will require competent, well prepared, non-partisan and accountable professionals, explicitly acting on behalf of all humanity (See *OH*, page 304)

Although the inglorious history of ruthless, Zionist, supremacy-seeking will not be forgotten, forgiveness and reconciliation are possible over time... if a new phase of *reparations* were to begin. For an adult kind of ***forgiving-without-forgetting*** is feasible amongst people who've progressed beyond emotionally immature, 'us v.

them' reflex responding. Then automatic vengeance-seeking and the persistent to justifying of misguided prejudices can be left behind.

A new role as healers?

So, here's an opportunity for former Zionists worldwide to seize the initiative – by wisely abandoning their unachievable medieval fantasy of global supremacy and going instead for a greater prize. Instead of rigidly adhering to an ancient, tunnel vision, partisan agenda, they could, in humanity's moment of need, rise to the occasion and use their unique talents to play a new leading role – as prime agents in the healing of all people on Earth.

In the *transition* from a cosmic era of *descent into matter* and *masculine* predominance into one of *ascent out of matter* and the predominating influence of the universal *feminine*, **the uniquely Jewish combination of the universal *feminine* and *masculine* could greatly enrich the collective consciousness of all humankind.** But this would involve the present *masculine* monotheism evolving into a more balanced, diverse understanding of divinity.

By example, it would also demonstrate to other supremacy-seeking groups that their time is up too, that their fantasy ambitions of global domination cannot be fulfilled, and that continuing relentlessly to pursue them can only result in further pain, suffering and damage all round... without achieving their goals.

Understanding the situation in this way brings the realisation that **Jews and Zionists, as well as others with misguided ambitions, presently need some dedicated assistance in adapting to this** *transition* **phase** – rather than being resented, ignored, feared or treated as alien enemies. And that kind of help, a mature form of *tough love*, can only come from people who've already achieved a state of unselfish inner balance and strength.

However...

Should this opportunity be refused or ignored, today's Zionists could face the prospect of being abandoned by many previously loyal Jews around the world, who are now beginning to realise how they and previous generations have been cleverly mind-controlled and manipulated for centuries. Which will herald the rapid demise of the Zionist financial syndicate, *SCAB*, and consequently, the Jewish State of Israel in Palestine which it funds.

In the short term, meanwhile, Zionist attempts to pursue their global supremacy strategy can be expected to continue through the mass media outlets and education systems they control. For *SCAB* still remains the ultimate source of all major funding and sponsorship, despite the well known fact that its 'debt money' is totally imaginary, ie an elaborate *confidence* trick.

Of course, Jews are not the only problem...
Obviously, there are many other troubled and troublesome factions within the dysfunctional human family. For example, in contrast to the uniquely Jewish combination of original Hebrew *feminine* qualities with *masculine* qualities superimposed, there are other major cultures creating problems for humanity – some predominantly *masculine*, some predominantly *feminine*.

But the harmful effects of these others could more easily be handled and neutralised if virtually the whole human species were not now so corrupted by and addictively dependent on *SCAB*'s **debt money**. For, as already explained, this fact is a key part of the massive *confidence trick* being performed by the Khazari/Ashkenazi/Zionists' financial arm, which has managed over time to subtly persuade people everywhere that life on Earth without its *debt money* is unthinkable and that there is no viable alternative... that is, until the emergence of *crypto-currencies* and the alternative idea of the *blockchain* (page 192).

The *sayanim* (the global Jewish support network)
Another significant factor in this ongoing story are the **sayanim**, the alleged global network of loyal individuals and groups, scattered all over the world as a result of the Jewish diaspora. They are committed

to and actively support the Jewish/Israeli cause. Through this unofficial system, a small number of Khazari/Ashkenazi Zionists are able to mind-control millions of people worldwide through influencing their mass media and education systems.

The Talmud: sacred text / toxic reality?
This is the primary written source of instructions for rabbis on 'how to be a good Jew'. However, it does contain some extremely toxic and malevolent sentiments (page 401).

The Jewish State of Israel: just a stepping stone?
Central to all Zionist/Jewish affairs today is the Jewish State of Israel, established in Palestine in 1948. Since when, there has been continuous strife and suffering there as a result of the Zionists' violently enforced occupation and their ***ethnic cleansing* of native Palestinians**. However, behind the labels 'Zionist' and 'Israel' there's an unspoken territorial agenda that's aimed way beyond Palestine, beyond a 'Greater Israel' and beyond the Middle East (page 147).

All of which serves as a reminder that perhaps no location on Earth has experienced more continuous ideological conflict through the centuries than Palestine and Jerusalem. So now, with the benefit of the *Threshold* perspective, a key question can be addressed in a non-partisan, balanced way...

Is there
a *coherent pattern*
behind the tangled politics
of the
M i d d l e
E a s t ?

The *polarity* behind the basic three-way battle for supremacy in the Middle East has already been sketched out. There's the predominantly *masculine* Muslim culture, the predominantly *feminine* Jewish culture, and the ambivalent, confused and compromised Christian culture. Each is currently in a state of flux, as the influence and authority of its *feminine* aspect increases through the ongoing cosmic *transition* phase. Meanwhile, each still retains various distorted characteristics of the departing *masculine*-dominated *descent* era, including various unavoidably distorted *feminine* characteristics.

Appreciating that pattern immediately brings some coherence to viewing the long running, tangled conflict in the Middle East and to its wider implications. And realising that the current turbulent transitional phase is part of a process of deep cleansing and healing brings insight into the current surfacing of various dark, long 'buried', primitive human attributes.

For example, there's the temporary rising to prominence on the mass media *world stage* of certain tribal and medieval cultures, along with various extreme and violent fundamentalist groups in different parts of the world.

They represent the primitive, 'us v. them' mentality of humanity's childhood that's still active within 21st century 'western' societies... which themselves have become 'softer' and less able to deal with this unavoidable clash of cultures. (See *recapitulation*, page 81). Humankind, still in its **collective adolescence**, is thus experiencing much misunderstanding, trouble and confusion.

Adolescent humanity: a phase of turmoil

Typical **adolescent** characteristics, common across many cultures worldwide, include:
- volatile, self-centred, extreme emotions,
- an oscillating between hyper-sensitivity and a callous indifference to the feelings of others,
- an individualistic desire for *independence* from parental authority, while lacking a mature appreciation of natural *inter-dependence*,
- passionate *idealism* alternating with sceptical *indifference*, and
- a heightened awareness regarding sexuality, gender and personal relationships.

A typical adolescent ideological awakening tends to involve:
- First, a natural youthful seeking, based on an emerging sense of *conviction*, perhaps inspired by encountering an unfamiliar worldview.

- Next, welcoming an opportunity to identify with, belong to, feel valued in and formally commit to an organisation with a strong, clear message about good and evil in the world, plus a definite set of rules and an ethos of order and discipline.

- Then, having any unresolved discontent, bottled up anger, frustration and yearnings either released in a healing way, or harnessed and re-directed at targeted enemies.

Political *resonance* - despite superficial differences

Resonance is the third universal *Threshold* principle. It can be witnessed in either:

- the **straightforward, positive** way in which certain ideas seem to inspire and unite some people in support of this or that cause, OR
- the **distorted, double-negative** way in which unlikely allies, such as Wahhabi **Muslims** and Zionist **Jews**, recognise in each other a primitive craving for power, control and supremacy. This explains their current strategic alliance of mutual convenience. It also helps explain why the Zionist-controlled US government favours the ruling elite of Saudi Arabia... beyond oil and weapons trading

How can ordinary people help resolve the problem?

Imagine that while in your local market place you've become aware of a small team of confidence tricksters at work, openly but fraudulently taking money from people who are not aware of how the deception works. Would you choose to let people know what's going on? Or would you look away and let this 'daylight robbery' of unsuspecting victims continue so that they, in their ignorance, become confused, angry and suspicious?

This is the kind of dilemma, but on a much larger scale, that faces those who start to see through the grand scams, ie the fraudulent bluffs being perpetrated behind various political, financial and economic fronts. That is, along with the orthodox religious, scientific and medical authorities which help prop up the current status quo of wealth, authority and privilege. It's a dilemma because choosing to do nothing means assisting the tricksters by allowing them to carry on conning the public.

However, the scams of confidence tricksters are usually fragile balancing acts that can easily be brought down once they're recognised. And that clearly is the case with the present world status quo... once the general **ignorance** of how the cosmos works and the resulting **fear** are overcome.

So, what do the many dissatisfied people worldwide need – especially those who feel they're ready to move on from the present set-up? An inspiring vision of a viable alternative and a sense that it is eventually achievable. That's what's on offer in the **One Humanity (OH)** chapter (page 304).

It offers a path that requires courage, conviction, compassion, perseverance and a willingness to think 'out of the box', ie creatively beyond your normal comfort zone... in order to connect with others who are similarly seeking a more fulfilling life. Thus it involves the emotionally risky business of cultivating deeper, stronger human relationships. Which in turn requires developing your intuitive and instinctive sensing of the honesty and integrity, or otherwise, of people... including yourself.

For example, some self-questioning could start with:
- *Do I want to be part of the much needed, long term healing of humankind OR will I look the other way and remain part of the present inertia-bound sickness?*

- *Am I content to continue being deceived, misled and exploited by certain unknown others?*

- *How can I maintain a positive, creative outlook while being constantly on the alert for such strategies?*

So, yes, there <u>is</u> a way out of the present insanity. But it comes at a price, since nothing of real value in this life is gained without some cost. And the price here is the requirement to start pro-actively cultivating that rare and precious human quality: **TRUST**.

So, is this the deal?
'*The price of overcoming*
the present world insanity
is the cultivation of **TRUST**.'

The answer is, '**Yes, that is the deal**'– ie cultivating mutual *trust*, instead of passively consenting to be divided and ruled. It involves no longer being tricked into competitive rivalry and enmity, which inevitably result in *mistrust* and endless spirals of hostility, deception, betrayal, conflict and vengeance... ie unhappiness.

TRUST is the essential quality in relationships that can create a shared and lasting bond of *confidence* during the current turbulent *transition* from an era of *descent into matter* to one of *ascent out of matter*. It can't be be bought or obtained by force or clever arguments. It has to be earned by consistent mutual confidence-building behaviour... although it can temporarily be gained by deceit... as most voters and consumers well know.

The challenge is essentially about understanding and healing a deeply troubled situation –instead of blaming and condemning others, or assuming that most of the troubles people experience are inevitable or natural. For *trust* and *mistrust* essentially work through *instinct* and *intuition*, both of which operate on levels *beyond* people's normal, rational *intellect*.

How long until there's a noticeable difference?

Question: '*How long might it take for a small but significant minority of humankind to rise above the current worldwide, childish, descent era squabbling and competing?*'.

Answer: It will take as long as it takes. That's because it involves people growing out of their child-like dependence on and unquestioning loyalty to parent-like authority figures – whether tribal, national, religious, commercial etc. For those kinds of leaderships always require enemies and/or rivals, in order to justify their own positions of authority and superiority... and so prolong the dependency culture.

So, here and now, with no short term prospect of a dramatic overall improvement in human behaviour, a clear choice faces each human being: Be a pro-active participant in the long term healing of humankind OR be part of the current collective inertia and sickness.

Pioneering **OH** groups could, in the meantime, demonstrate how it is possible, and would be infinitely more fulfilling, to live on this planet in more balanced and harmonious ways. That means by starting to live according to just a few simple practical principles that unite rather than divide. For the longer the current *descent era* insanity of a divided-and-ruled, debt-ridden, decaying world is allowed to continue, the more difficult and dangerous it will be for future generations to tackle the ever-increasing clean-up and healing work needed.

People will no longer be automatically identified as belonging to and owing loyalty to this or that group of people. For each person is primarily a human being and a citizen of planet Earth. Therefore, anyone could adopt a new global identity as an *Earth Citizen*.

Traditional cultures could still be honoured in a diverse *One Humanity* world – for example, in ceremonial and sporting events – so long as they don't promote, explicitly or implicitly, any exclusive, divisive, doctrines of inherent *superiority* over other humans.

Overall, the evolutionary direction of travel is towards rejecting the fantasy ambitions of those who cannot resist certain immature *false power* urges, such as the craving to be 'in charge', 'top dog' or simply a 'winner' in deluded worldly power games... whether in public or behind the scenes, and whether or not they claim divine authority for their efforts.

Next, a major common factor in all these troubles... MONEY.

Money Trouble

"Money trouble here, money trouble there,
Everywhere trouble in a money bubble world"
(From *There's No Such Thing as Money* by Threshold Pilot)

**In this chapter, simply and without jargon, the *Threshold*
perspective focuses on how the basic 'nuts and bolts' workings of a
money system can be exploited in corrupt ways by people who are
motivated and able to do so. Some understanding of this is
necessary in order to start planning how to carefully dismantle and
replace the present corrupt set-up.**

For a start, a few simple, basic questions:

- *Since money is, in essence, a non-physical human creation,
  arbitrarily conjured up out of nothing, how come there are
  'shortages' of it worldwide, resulting in billions of people suffering
  in deficiency of life's essentials while others live in excess of their
  natural needs?*

- *How come, amidst all the complaining and blaming about
  shortages of funding for this or that, nobody points, **in public**, to
  those who are actively responsible for this preventable, tragic
  situation... which hasn't arisen simply by chance?*

- *How come virtually all nation states are deeply and inextricably in
  debt to SCAB, the world's primary moneylender, ie the global loan
  shark?*

- *So, since there's really no such thing as money, isn't it now just
  part of an elaborate conjuring trick to maintain the status quo of
  wealth, privilege and power in the world?*

Money: an elaborate illusion

From serving as a useful measure of value and a convenient means
of exchange, money has long been hijacked, abused and corrupted

in an elaborate global **confidence trick**. Money is essentially an abstract idea, imaginary, a fantasy based on a shared belief, what some would call a *social construct*. It's an example of a thought-form being collectively treated as though it were physically real.

The pretence works through the use of symbolic *tokens*, each valued as a specific number of identical *units* like points scored in a game. These can be gained or lost, and so increased or decreased in total in the 'money game'. The resulting *score* is the *balance* or total value of monetary wealth held or owed. This also allows money, under the present system, to serve as a store of value (eg as savings).

A money system makes trading convenient by enabling everything to have a monetary *price*. And when a group of people agree to share the pretence that a certain form of money exists, the system of token units used in that system is called its *currency*. So money, as a means of exchange, has no inherent moral value and is ethically neutral.

From utility to exploitation
In the *descent into matter* era, as societies became more complex, so money systems became more complicated and multi-levelled, providing increasing scope for deception, cheating, theft, fraud and so on. Also, money has taken many forms, including stones, lumps of clay, notched sticks and even cigarettes (when scarce and in demand), as well as metal coins and paper, so long as there was *confidence* that they could be exchanged for other desired things.

Credit, as physical evidence of mutual trust regarding the future payment of a debt, has long been another form of money. Money has thus enabled more complex trading to go on than simple exchange *bartering*.

But then money began to be traded as a **unique commodity** itself – which could be lent and borrowed for a price, ie at negotiable rates of *interest*. And as societies became ever more complex trading systems, *moneylending* evolved into the more formal, organised and profitable business of **banking**. Consequently, **debt** became a significant factor in world affairs.

Another key factor is that money doesn't decay, and its units are homogeneous, ie one is worth exactly the same as another. Which encouraged the practice of hoarding and exploiting one's monetary wealth –at least until the late 20th century era of easy credit for the mass of humanity.

Now that almost all money worldwide is issued in the form of interest-bearing loans created and granted by the **central bank** lodged in each country, **it's to the global central banking syndicate that virtually all money is all ultimately owed**. And so the world, in effect, functions on *debt money*, through loans, mortgages, card credit etc.

Only a tiny percentage of the total money supply today is created free from debt, and that's the physical notes and coins still issued, interest-free, directly by nation states, along with some newly emerging and evolving digital currencies, still in their infancy.

Bankrupt world?

Bankrupt means broken and unable to pay outstanding debts. Since 2007, the world's money system has been haunted by talk of financial collapse, bankrupt corporations and bankrupt states, sinking ever deeper into 'sovereign debt'. (See *'When small-time greed brought down the world's banking system...' almost* on page 406).

However, from the *Threshold* it's clear that with a more radical and balanced approach, this whole debt money system could simply be abandoned as unfit for humanity's needs, and be replaced by a very different system, based on very different assumptions and values. That is, when people have finally had enough of all the unnecessary stress and trouble, and realise that a system <u>not</u> rigged in favour of the most selfish and greedy would much better serve humanity as a whole.

A brief overview of the unwholesome world of *banking* is thus due, in order to start planning how to carefully dismantle and replace it. For humanity now needs to better understand and move beyond that miasma of deception and fraud, that 'parallel universe' which the mass media and educators are required to promote.

The less than glorious origins of banking

In Europe through the middle ages, charging interest on loans, ie **usury**, was considered immoral, evil, a sin, and was forbidden by the main religions. The Jews, however, came up with a convenient biblical interpretation which served as a loop-hole, allowing them to practise **usury** – at least on non-Jews.

And it's this historic linking of the Jews with profiteering through money dealing that mainly accounts for the unfavourable reputation they've retained through the centuries. Implicit in this is also a general dislike of certain manipulative ways. The *New Testament* tells of the Jew, Jesus, attacking the Jewish money-changers who were conducting their business within the sacred temple.

The historic *confidence trick* of the goldsmiths

Back when goldsmiths were offering secure storage for the gold of the wealthy, they would issue credit notes for the value of the gold they held and charge a rate of interest per annum on the amount, as a kind of rent, for the service. Soon these notes themselves began to be exchanged and traded in the wider world, as convenient, portable substitutes for the actual gold they represented. As such, they became an early form of paper *money*, while the gold stayed safely stored away. So, inevitably, **confidence** in the goldsmiths and the overall system was essential.

However, the goldsmiths began to realise that they could get away with issuing credit notes well in excess of the value of the gold they actually held, so long as they kept enough for the occasional client wanting to reclaim some gold. It didn't require great mathematical ability to realise that by means of this scam, this **money trick**, they could quickly become very wealthy. They could issue and charge interest on numerous 'money' notes, which **created profits out of nothing**, since their face value was **not backed up by the equivalent in actual gold**.

'Fractional reserve' banking is the current pseudo-technical term for banks holding in reserve gold only worth a *fraction* of the 'money' they're lending out. The word *'credit'* comes from *credo* (Latin for *'I believe'*). So any borrower of money has to believe in the value of what the lender is offering, and the lender has to believe that the loan and the interest due on it will be repaid. In this belief system, they each have to have **confidence** that the other is **credit**-worthy. Today this **confidence trick** is still key to the success of the global *central banking* business.

Then came the money manipulators who knew how to exploit other people's ignorance, beliefs and naivety to their own advantage. That was when **this imaginary money itself began to be traded as a unique commodity** which could be lent and borrowed for a price, ie at negotiable rates of **compound interest**.

This kind of interest, at an agreed percentage, is charged annually on the total amount currently owing, ie including interest previously charged. So, the debt is continuously growing. By contrast, **simple interest** is charged only on the original amount lent.

As societies became ever more complex trading systems, **moneylending** evolved into the more formal, organised and profitable business of **banking.** As a consequence, **debt** became a significant factor in world affairs.

Forged: an *uneasy alliance*
Through time, ruling dynasties became increasingly indebted to their bankers, as they sought to continue financing their wars, rivalries and lavish 'royal' lifestyles. Eventually they found themselves obliged to grant official, legally sanctioned permission for the bank they were dependent on to expand its money-making scam.

Thus arose the uneasy alliance of bloodline dynasties and money-lending bankers, a pragmatic 'loveless marriage of convenience'.

SCAB is born

In 1694 the *Bank of England* was set up as banker to the then Kingdom of England, an event seen by some as the handing over of English sovereignty to a group of financiers. That, in effect, created the kind of monopolistic institution now known as a *central bank*.

Later the already wealthy Rothschild family business moved in to this set-up, thereby becoming an influential part of the English governing elite... all this back when the British Empire was a powerful force in the world.

They then set up other central bank 'branches' across Europe, and in the mid 20th century established three **arch-banks**: the **World Bank**, **IMF** and **BIS**. This financial empire was, in effect, a global **syndicate of central and arch-banks (SCAB)**, which can be symbolically represented as a spider at the centre of a worldwide web of debt and influence that it had long been weaving. (see diagram, page 201)

The Rothschilds: first international bankers

Back in the late 18th century, Mayer Amschel Rothschild, original founder of the *syndicate* of *central and arch-banks*, reportedly said:

> *"Let me issue and control a nation's money, and I care not who writes its laws."*

And in Britain, since then, there has been a continuous line of barons called **Rothschild**.

Which puts in perspective the pretentious posturing of presidents, prime ministers and their so-called governments as *leaders* and *protectors* of 'the people', and as executive decision makers... when, in reality, they're wholly dependent on the central banking syndicate, *SCAB*, for the money they require to carry on the pretence of governing.

Lord Stamp, a former director of the Bank of England, summarised the situation very frankly.

"… The Bankers own the earth. Take it away from them, but leave them the power to create deposits, and with a flick of the pen they will create enough deposits to buy it back again.

*However, take it away from them, and all the great fortunes like mine will disappear. And they ought to disappear, for this would be a happier and better world to live in. But, **if you wish to remain the slaves of bankers and pay the cost of your own slavery, let them continue to create deposits** (ie create money as debt). "*

Speaking at the University of Texas in 1927. Ref: *The Legalized Crime of Banking* (1958) by Silas W. Adams

The takeover of North America

After the decline of the British Empire, when North America was heading to be the next major 'world power', various Jewish financiers moved in and, by exploiting their wealth and banking skills, took control of most of the major US industries. Crucially, those included the entertainment industry, ie movies, theatre, radio and TV, as well as the news gathering, news distribution and news broadcasting business. As a consequence, the mass communications business was largely under their control.

And by cleverly exploiting the immense power of these media, they've been able to mass indoctrinate American and many other minds worldwide into attitudes and beliefs that serve the long term Zionist/Jewish agenda. This has proved so effective that now, when mainstream news media mouths speak of 'American' policy or 'American' interests in the wider world, it usually means Zionist and Israeli interests... cloaked in the American flag.

Back in 1913, a group of European Jewish banking families had deviously contrived to set up a US *central bank*, which they deceptively called the Federal Reserve, despite it being a non-Federal, private business. This was a vital part of enticing Americans into becoming obsessed with and addicted to the money exclusively supplied at interest by this private bank.

Also highly influential was the infamous *Jewish Mafia*, about which plenty of information is available online.

Addiction to money

Humanity's addictive state of dependency on money will persist only as long as enough people continue to believe that money has some kind of objective existence, and continue to fantasise that if they could get enough of it they'd be able to obtain whatever they desire – whether that means possessions, privileges, status or a (false) sense of security.

So, until a sufficient number of people realise how the *money trick* has been working for centuries to make a few people very rich and keep the rest poor and struggling, the delusion will continue. For some, it starts with childhood stories of magically empowering golden coins or eggs which imply that money can solve all our problems and end our worries. That idea is then encouraged to grow into an unquestioning belief and faith in the *'greed creed'* of financial capitalism, ie classical *economics*.

Having been brought up in such a context, many people find it too challenging at first to even consider thinking beyond a mindset within which everything has a monetary value, a price. To them it seems 'unrealistic' to consider the possibility of a **post-money era** that functions according to a very different set of **human** values. Eventually, however the idea of humanity kicking the money habit does begin to make sense, as part of a broader solution... but certainly not as a simple, instant fix.

Banks are insolvent

In general, banks, as moneymongers, run on a continuous inflow and outflow of 'money' – borrowing and lending – while holding minimal *reserves*, ie nowhere near enough to meet any mass withdrawal of funds by depositors. This, as explained earlier, is *fractional reserve* banking, in which only a fraction of the total amount lent is held in reserve as capital.

So they are, in effect, permanently *insolvent*, which creates an ongoing sense of insecurity. Yet within this highly contrived environment of fear and greed, banks make huge profits.
However, the trick can work only as long as there's *confidence* in the *supply* of money. In financial terms, this can last only as long as that supply remains *'liquid'*, ie 'on tap', readily available to borrow.

It's the *central bank* in each country that controls the supply, the *liquidity*, which it can allow to continue flowing or shut off at will. And whether the outcome is an *upturn or downturn* in an economy, the central bank, ie the 'local' branch of *SCAB*, still profits.

'Higher' and 'lower' status banks

1. **SCAB**, through some shrewd and devious manoeuvring over centuries, has established itself in the dominant position worldwide in relation to other banks. However, this fact is largely obscured in order to protect the *SCAB* people and their dependents whose privileged lifestyles depend on the status quo being maintained. That's because should the *victims* of this great money scam, ie the mass of humanity, discover what's been going on, their attitude towards *SCAB* would change dramatically.

2. The **commercial banks**, below *SCAB* in the hierarchy, are essentially money-mongers, along with a range of other financial intermediaries. They borrow money at a lower rate than that at which they lend it. There are basically two kinds of commercial bank, sometimes combined within one.
(a) **Retail banks**, also known as 'safe', 'high street' banks or clearing banks, deal with the general public's normal borrowing, saving, loans, mortgages etc.
(b) **Investment banks**, or *merchant banks*, get involved in more speculative, financial gambling, extreme examples of which contributed to the crisis of 2007/8 (page 406).

After the electronic globalisation of financial markets in the 1980s, the two kinds of banking became intertwined in major financial institutions worldwide. Which meant a loss of separation between sober, 'low risk, low return' *retail* banking and intoxicating 'high risk, high return' *investment* banking, with its *big bonuses* culture based on gambling with ordinary people's savings.

As *SCAB* allowed the 'expansive' era of 'easy money' and credit to continue worldwide,
commercial banks and others grew increasingly greedy, speculative, reckless and fraudulent –
for example, gambling with money taken from clients' accounts without authorisation.
Frantic, competitive, short-term greed overrode sober, long term judgement – until in 2007/8 the financial bubble this created burst.

Then, after the shock, there were some token gestures towards stability and the previous separation of functions. But with other large businesses, such as supermarkets, moving into *financial services*, the meaning of the term 'bank' itself was becoming less clear.

So, who owes what to whom... in a world that currently runs on debt?

The *national debt,* also known as the ***sovereign*** or ***public*** or ***government debt*** is what each **state** owes to the **SCAB central bank** lodged in its territory. And since states need to keep borrowing more in order to pay off just part of the ever-accumulating interest due on this debt, it's an indicator of the power relationship between each *state* and the *syndicate*.

That ever increasing debt due on its borrowing is the unspoken reason why economic *'growth'* is taken to be a normal requirement for a state to maintain its financial status.
And the growing interest on the borrowing is a constant part the **annual *budget deficit*** that governments vainly pledge to reduce,

since the taxes the State is able to collect are not sufficient to meet that obligation.

In the West, this long running two-way conflict of interests has created a deep **fault line**. Essentially, it's humanity's *masculine* aspect set against its *feminine* aspect. This clash of two irreconcilable, and now redundant, value systems has been symbolised as flag v. credit card, patriot v. mercenary, society v. economy, duty v. greed, welfare v. market etc.

The gross *descent era masculine* **politics** of dominance and force has been outmanoeuvred by the more subtle *descent era feminine* **economics** of greed, moneylending and debt. So, powerless governments try to straddle the two incompatibles to create an illusion of authority and unity in their so-called *policies*. Thus the continuous tension between the State's **fiscal** policy, ie its taxing and spending, and the central bank's **monetary** policy, ie setting the rates at which they'll lend money.

Who is 'the *taxpayer'*?
Caught between the two conflicting forces are the 'protected' and exploited citizens who are required pay the state its protection money, normally called *taxes*.Labelled as **the taxpayer'** these citizens are thus forced to contribute to the interest payments due on the *sovereign debt* that the State owes to the *central bank*, the creditor lodged in its territory.

Also, the taxes that citizens pay amount to significantly more than the cost of meeting real needs, since they have to fund the ruling elite's privileged lifestyle of palaces, servants, banquets and travel etc. And just as a government's primary obligation is <u>not</u> to the electorate but to its creditors, so the *State* does <u>not</u> use its tax revenues primarily for the benefit of its citizens. Therefore, the idea of *the taxpayer* 'owning' or even having a stake in this or that 'national' or 'public' asset is a delusion and a pretence.

'*The markets*': gambling arenas in cyberspace

Within this corrupt set-up, the balance of power between the state and the financial elite has long been shifting. Humanity's addiction to money has resulted in a pathologically **monetised** world, ie it operates according to a value system which dictates that everything has a *price* – *ie monetary* value predominates. Which suits those who control the money.

In this belief system – this 'religion' with its blessed, wealthy, deserving *winners* and its cursed, poor, unfortunate *losers* – one recent development has been the worldwide epidemic of financial *gambling addiction*... and especially the proliferation of high-tech, online, short term speculating, pretentiously called *trading*. Excited by greed and fear and the desire to be a winner, professionals and amateurs have been drawn into risk 'games' where fortunes can be won and lost in an instant while sitting in front of a computer screen.

The *cyberspace* casino for this addictive pursuit is where millions of speculators around the world swarm like parasites to play *the markets* (see the diagram, page 202). So, all the while, the addicted gamblers obsessively feed on rumour, gossip, sentiment and leaks, tending to react in a herd-like way to the endless flow of up and down numbers... like insecure, emotionally volatile, fashion-conscious teenagers, desperate to appear 'successful'.

Overshadowing all that is the mysterious, superhuman entity known as *The Market*, revered by economists as though it were a kind of ultimate authority, an oracle or arbiter of all things financial. The *market forces* it generates stimulate selfish greed and fear, an attitude referred to in the mainstream media '*business friendly*'.

Coded language conceals deceit

The alleged *Rothschild* quote on page 217 eloquently illustrates why elected governments are powerless, and always end up failing those who voted for them. It points to how those politicians, supposedly competing to be in charge of the populations they'll serve, are actually competing for roles which require them to sell the *SCAB* agenda to the electorate. That's why this is not discussed in public by political and economics experts, who fear jeopardising their own careers by speaking out honestly.

Given such a lack of openness, honesty, integrity and responsibility, the obscure, coded language and strange manoeuvrings in this 'world within a world' of politics and economics can be seen to fit into a bizarre, pathological kind of pattern. From the *Threshold*, the devious scheming of the various professional deceivers, can be observed following a coherent pattern, as they each play their part and collect their rewards. And since none of them would want to admit to being part of a mass deceit, the strategy is:

'Carry on regardless, and avoid asking or directly answering any awkward questions.'

So, from the **Threshold**, it looks like: *'On with the show, for better or worse'* – *in the hope that the inevitable implosion, collapse and rude awakening won't happen... yet.*

The Money Trick: *'It's all about confidence'*

The value and usage of money is thus totally dependent on people's **confidence** in it...which requires confidence in those who claim to guarantee its false, imaginary value. Managing a money system has consequently become one huge, complex *trick*. That is to say, **the global money system is a huge *confidence trick*.**

The message printed on paper money is no more than a promise to pay to the holder a certain quantity of similar printed paper promises. Also, as a self-preservation strategy, the *SCAB* people have always been keenly aware of the need to win the *confidence* of the host nation. So each *central bank* falsely presents itself as an indispensable supporter both of the State's ruling elite and of the ordinary small-time business people and citizens, while subtly operating according to a very different long term agenda – nothing to do with economics.

185

A rigged system

Seen from the *Threshold*, then, **money has become an elaborately contrived *illusion* –**

whether in the form of printed paper, metal coins, plastic cards or electronic symbols –

because it's not backed up by any gold or other commodity of material value. The only 'back-up' to such *fiat* (*'Let it be so'*) money is a State's assurance that it is 'legal tender'.

As such it has become a system of token points to be won, lost and exchanged, according to various rules and conventions in an elaborate kind of *game* in which the holder can trade these tokens for whatever's on offer at an agreed price.

Participation in the game, however, is compulsory and the playing field is not at all level, but tilted to favour the rich. And there's no cancelling out of scores at the end of each session or season. So there's no *jubilee* and no restart with all players equal again on zero points. It's also no surprise to find that the whole global money system is highly *rigged*, ie controlled and manipulated from the top down by those who benefit most from it.

At the top of the heap are the invisible elite of *controllers*, *SCAB & Co*, set above the *professionals* who know how to exploit their familiarity with the system. Below them are the *teachers* of *economics*, *business studies* and the like. They teach how the game is supposed to be played, according to the official rules, even though these rules obviously don't apply to those at the highest levels, ie those who have access to useful 'insider' information not available to the rest.

Political control through money control

In the shift from *descent* to *ascent*, the world has become more *monetised*, because money is a more efficient means of *political* control than crude physical methods. Keeping people addicted to money and pre-occupied with competing for it, and the inevitable associated *corruption*, is a cheaper way of maintaining the status quo – at least in the short term.

Mama SCAB (page 201), in cartoon imagery, is the spider whose enticing **global web of debt** captures the separate, competing *nation states*, sucks them dry and leaves them depleted. It's her IMF that issues the currency called *SDRs, Special Drawing Rights*, that's used for financial transactions between nation states – one more way in which the world has become ever more indebted to, dependent on and controlled by *Mama SCAB*.

BBC's wall-to-wall *financial capitalism* promos
Financial capitalism operates where virtually all economic activity, including state and commercial corporate media, are controlled, directly or indirectly, by *SCAB* and its associates.

In the UK, from the 1980s the BBC noticeably dedicated more and more broadcasting time
to financial, commercial and economic affairs... and this development was no accident. It coincided with the rapid increase in Britain's *sovereign/national debt* – owed to the *Bank of England*, ie the British branch of *SCAB*, whose status, profits and influence rose accordingly.

The 2007/8 *financial crisis* then greatly intensified media attention on big-time finance, such that the wall-to-wall coverage amounted to a major *propaganda blitz*... promoting *financial capitalism* and therefore, indirectly, *SCAB* and its self-serving agenda.

And throughout all this, one implicit but unmistakable message was being delivered:
All the major challenges confronting humanity have to be addressed and evaluated in terms of money, and within the warped logic of economics, the greed-creed... and for one simple reason: this serves *SCAB*'s agenda and boosts its profits and prestige.

Financial capitalism results in cancerous growth

Seen from the *Threshold*, financial capitalism is a pathological way for a society to function.

The inherent fear and the greed result in chronic inhibiting of the vitality of societies, which then manifest certain *cancer*-like symptoms. These include localised *unregulated growth*, resulting in accumulations of matter, such as property and possessions way in excess of real, natural need and swollen, insolvent financial set-ups, deemed 'too big to fail'. These increasingly pollute the whole system, leaving it weakened and dying.

Yet in capitalist cultures, these *tumours* of excess wealth are celebrated as signs of success, portrayed as admirable, exemplary achievements, to be admired and emulated. *Medically*, however, tumours often foretell the eventual collapse of the whole organism, plus swollen and insolvent financial institutions, deemed 'too big to fail'.

Realising that there is a cancer process going on usually has a 'shock' effect, creating a kind of emergency/crisis mentality. Whether the sufferer then survives the crisis or not depends on how he or she responds. Naively just wanting the symptoms gone in order to return to the previous status quo is unlikely to achieve more than a temporary fix: medical treatment may provide a period of remission, but unless there is a radical change in attitude and behaviour, the underlying **imbalance** and **inhibition** will manifest in further symptoms and a relapse.

The *economic* accumulating of wealth in excess of real need, ie *capital*, can be understood as a reaction to feelings of vulnerability, insecurity, fear and emptiness. However, the *cancer* of *capitalism* can be addressed in a practical and sensitive way, once it's realised that **humankind is essentially one living, conscious being.** Healing may then be possible through altering distorted states of *consciousness*, ie attitudes which would eventually find expression as pathological *physical* symptoms.

Obese societies: sick, over-consuming economies

An *obese society*, like everything else, occurs in a context. An obvious symptom is the excessive consuming of enticing, artificially manufactured, unwholesome products, cleverly sold to targeted, vulnerable, exploitable people. The result is the unregulated expansion of sick, dysfunctional bodies... and societies.

The early stages of transition from an era of *descent into matter* to one of *ascent out of matter* brought a major shift in the psychology of mass governance in the West. It took the form of the distorted and predominantly *feminine* trait of *consumerism*. With the introduction of *supermarkets* and *credit cards* from the 1960s onwards, the earlier ideals and models of strict self-discipline, moderation, patience and financial prudence were replaced by a major enticement to *over-indulge*, to **have it now and pay later**... which was not in itself a new phenomenon.

It was realised that the *temptation* to *consume* in *excess* of need would prove irresistible. People have long been seduced by displays of attractively presented goods. But now the ***instant convenience*** of **plastic money** cards made goods appear to be there for the taking. Subsequent generations have been inducted into a world of ***instant gratification***, where the new propaganda promoted the idea that, on credit, '***I can have what I fancy right now, so I will***'... while callously ignoring the deprivation being suffered elsewhere as '***not my problem***'.

Monopoly: learning the game

Since 1935, the family board game, *Monopoly*, has served as a simple introduction to the typical ups and downs of a greed-driven, property exploiting, *capitalist* society. The competing players try to become rich by buying up and exploiting the available assets, monopolising the system and driving their rivals into bankruptcy and out of the game.

The game also includes the unique but misleading role of 'the banker', who can provide an endless supply of pretend money (like *central banks* in the world) while supposedly remaining above and apart from the risky world of property dealings.

Monopoly, ironically, is a redesign of an earlier game first published by a Quaker political activist in order to demonstrate the immorality inherent in the way actual monopolies bankrupt the many, while bringing extraordinary wealth to just a few greedy individuals. Another 1930s phenomenon is the *American Dream*, a master stroke of mass indoctrination – sold with the same promotional skills that made junk food and drinks an integral part of life in the USA.

The American Dream: a 1930s fantasy romance
The American Dream is a 1930s style, artificially sweetened, Hollywood-style fantasy, ie a mass media marketing con. Symbolically, it represents a fake romance between *Papa State*, in the form of *Uncle Sam*, and the devious, greedy and extremely wealthy *Mama SCAB* (see page 195).

The bizarre conjoining of these two symbolic figures suggests that the *American Dream* is, in essence, a joint *Jewish/Christian* propaganda sales pitch. You're persuasively invited to buy into a **fantasy**: ie a deeply corrupt *capitalist democracy,* romanticised into a slick commercial brand name, the *American Dream*... as if it were some dubious investment scheme.

Created in the increasingly materialistic *descent* era, it epitomises the schizoid, split personality of US culture. On the one hand there's the dutiful, inhibited, Christian *masculine* side, emphasising the glories of militarised religious nationalism. On the other, there's the scheming *Jewish, feminine* side, glamorising and glorifying acquisitive 'wealth creation', ie selfish greed. The fact that the two find themselves **mutually dependent** affirms the underlying *polarity*, ie a two-ness within a greater, inclusive one-ness.

It's another example of *ASS, Addictive Superiority Syndrome*, being promoted as an admirable and 'aspirational' way to live. People are continuously being conned into *uniting* under the flag of *us-versus-*

them patriotism while competing amongst themselves as rivals, ie *divided*. Meanwhile, **the mass media encourage the struggling many to emulate the wealthy few**, some of whom are so rich they can put themselves effectively above the law.

The American Dream is essentially an enticement to behave selfishly in the hope of becoming one of the 'winners', one of those who've ruthlessly acquired sufficient wealth (or credit) to own property and then lord it over the less wealthy 'losers' whom they can treat as *inferiors*... the big reward being to flaunt your 'success' and worthiness as an American citizen. It's all part of a culture that programmes people into believing that everything has a price tag and can thus be bought and sold... including politicians, state officials and the power of the mass media.

So, once again here's the old *divide-and-rule* tactic of keeping people too busy fighting amongst themselves to realise how together they're <u>all</u> being tricked by the ruling elite. The whole set-up is built on a global scam, the fraudulent *money trick* perpetrated by *SCAB* It's also another example of how ruling elites treat populations like naive children who are unable to work out how they're being exploited.

Inevitably, sooner or later, that kind of dream, glorifying the false freedom of selfish greed, turns into a nightmare. Yet it's still part of the glossy US image of '*democratic capitalism*', ie crooked, crony '*financialism*', corrupt militarism, bigoted religion and fake democracy, enticing everyone to selfishly 'go for it'... on money lent by *SCAB*.

Contrasting perspectives: from *Richland*, from *Poorland*

While westerners in 'Richland' may see their contemporary TV dramas simply as being about the lives of certain characters, residents of '*Poorland*' may well perceive the same dramas as extravagant displays of excessive opulence and consumerism... triggering either admiring ambition, envy, disgust or various other feelings.

Meanwhile, in the UK, the NHS and the State education system are being set up to fail as a result of underfunding, so that **privatisation – ie a commercial, profit-driven, USA-style *insurance* scam favouring the wealthy** – can be imposed as the only 'viable' solution.

A *cashless* **world**, using only digital/electronic money, is meanwhile being promoted as themost convenient and efficient system possible. But this gives yet more centralised power to those who already have monopoly control of the world's money supply, and can therefore instantly expand, contract or cut off the supply wherever and whenever suits their purposes.

Where's the gold?

Gold served as an international standard of value for all currencies until 1971, when it was abandoned by the Zionist controlled USA and Federal Reserve, so as to set up a freely fluctuating system of *floating* fiat currencies. Which, in effect, made the US dollar the world's standard currency, against which all others have since been measured. And it greatly boosted the international financial power of *SCAB* and the US Zionists. But this situation is now being challenged by the growing economic strength of China and its currency.

SCAB has for decades obscured its extensive hoarding of physical gold by claiming to officially hold only 'gold certificates', issued by the US Federal government... which it controls. Meanwhile, so-called *paper gold* – ie the numerous other printed claims on specific amounts of physical gold – far exceed those physical reserves.

Thus there are many unanswered questions about the Federal Reserve and official US secrecy and whether there still exists any gold in Fort Knox. For this supposed asset has remained unaudited since the 1950s, despite a legal requirement for regular auditing.

Crypto-currencies and *blockchain* **technology**: Who'll be in control of what?

The world's existing *fiat money system* of *SCAB*-controlled *debt money* is essentially an elaborate, crooked game of 'let's pretend'. But in 2009, with that system spiralling out of control towards disintegration and collapse, a new and supposedly 'secure', transparent, digital and potentially decentralising technology, the **blockchain**, appeared and soon seemed to threaten to displace it.

Bitcoin was the first pioneering digital crypto-currency and blockchain to be launched. Essentially, it's a system for registered authenticated parties to confidentially and securely authorise the transfer of digital money and other information between themselves without the need for a 'trusted' third party to act as an intermediary, such as a bank or a State institution.

The **idealistic intention** was that every transaction would be encrypted and digitally recorded anonymously, and the basic information would be automatically saved and made accessible to all participants in the system via the internet... thus **ensuring its integrity**, while there'd be **transparency throughout the system**.

However, despite the idealistic intentions of some advocates of crypto-currencies, there are some significant limitations to the whole idea. First, encryption itself indicates an obsessive secrecy about money and privacy, symptomatic of a divided and ruled world still operating on the basis of fear and selfish greed. So, digital crypto-currency money, while potentially being a reliable and convenient means of exchange and a store of value, **cannot avoid also being treated as a speculative commodity**, an *asset*, itself, traded and gambled with as its value, in terms of conventional currencies, rises and falls.

Thus, **any such set-up is still essentially a kind of *fiat* money system**, ie symbolic tokens not backed up with anything of substantial material value, such as gold. Therefore, crypto-currencies themselves are not a long-term solution to the deeper psychological problems humanity has with the very idea of money.

Ecologically, unlimited, depleting damage to the planet is already being threatened by the ever increasing electricity generation required to operate blockchains and '***the cloud***' , which use massive computer power requiring extensive cooling systems. Economically, the cost of paying for all this and its consequences could soon become a limiting factor.

Vulnerability to sabotage, hacking, corruption, fraud etc increases as the system expands. And presently there are various emerging alternative money/payment systems, each seeking global dominance, emulating the 'success' of Google, Amazon, Facebook and others.

In the bigger picture, the *blockchain* itself does represent a significant step forward for humankind on the long road of evolving towards eventually not needing money at all. However, as long as humankind continues to be indoctrinated with the selfish greed-driven system promoted by *SCAB* and all who materially benefit from it, most human interaction will still be corrupted by fear, greed and mistrust, especially regarding money. And *SCAB* & Co will continue to exploit this for as long as they can, for they seem to know no other way.

A radically different money system is proposed in the *One Humanity* section. This involves a debt-free, 'decaying' kind of electronic money that does not retain its initial value. So, it cannot serve as a 'store of value' *asset* that encourages unlimited, selfish accumulation. It thus represents a wholly different attitude to living on Earth.

The Loveless Marriage of Convenience
Papa State and *Mama SCAB* are still running the show

What these characters represent – ie the two great polar opposite cosmic forces in recognisable worldly form – will be explained shortly. But first, a basic question.

What is a *nation state*... since it's not a nation, a country, a government or a people? (Similarly, What is a *federal state*?) *The State* has been defined in sociology as the group that collectively wields a monopoly of coercive force within a country. But that academic, detached and morally uncommitted view avoids the more down-to-earth and human understanding that...

The State* is essentially an elaborate *protection racket in which the racketeers are the ruling elite who collect *taxes* as their *protection money,* while providing just enough 'welfare' to offset any potential revolutionary discontent among the population. What distinguishes the State is its *masculine, 'father figure'* quality, whether its token figurehead 'leader is a *male* or a *female*. Ruling over and 'protecting' its subjects, it's a relic of the medieval *descent era*.

A raw, unvarnished, uncompromised picture of a *state* in its bare, ruthlessly violent, dominating essence, was provided in 2015 with the appearance on the world stage of the self-styled ***Islamic State*** (aka *IS ISIS, ISIL, Daesh*).

A key word regarding nation states is WAR, because war is what state ruling elites use to justify their privileged position as leaders and protectors against designated *enemies*, external and internal. The threat might be a hot or cold war against another nation state or alliance, a war on terrorism, insurgents or crime, a trade or currency war (ie ***protectionism***), or a war on a disease.

A smaller or bigger state?
Presently, humanity suffers from both State domination and *financial/capitalistic* exploitation, and the confusion is reflected in the ideologies of so-called *left* and *right* wing politics.

Smaller state / right wing ideology effectively means societies heading towards:
- a smaller dominant *elite* of privileged, feudal-type, aristocratic governing dynasties,
- less redistribution of wealth, ie less welfare and support for the deprived masses,
- fewer jobs, careers and less bureaucracy in the so-called 'public', ie State, sector.

Bigger State/left wing ideology implies more State ownership, control and intervention, supposedly to offset the greedy capitalistic exploitation of the most deprived. But given the actual nature of the state, as an elite protection racket, this is ultimately a fallacy. For at the top of any governance pyramid, state, financial, commercial and religious interests converge – ie an elite minority share a common interest in maintaining the status quo, with revolving doors between the 'upper' levels of state and financial/commercial institutions.

What is a nation in the 21st century
There is no agreed definition of what the word *nation* means, according to Israeli professor of history, Shlomo Sand, in his revealing books, *The Invention of the Jewish People* and *The Invention of the Land of Israel*. The word *nation* is derived from the Latin word 'natus' which means 'born', implying a connectedness through place of birth.

Today the word *nation* is normally used to suggest a population that incorporates various cultural traditions, yet shares some kind of historical commonality. Which, in this age of globalised communications and travel, makes *nationality* a virtually meaningless concept, more about bureaucratic passport details and migration regulations than about common roots. In this globalised era, the nation state, therefore, is diminishing in significance, although still some way from disappearing altogether.

At present, being '**stateless**' mostly presents problems for an individual – regarding 'legitimate' citizenship, rights and benefits.

But in the future it will signify individual autonomy and a level of personal maturity as an **Earth Citizen**, representing liberation from the childish, us-versus-them, 'team games' world of competing nation states.

The urge to establish one's *independent* identity is a clear sign of *adolescence*, whether in an individual or in the collective ambition of a group of people who think of themselves as a *nation*. Such signs are common and affirm that humanity is still in its *collective adolescence*, given the many other typically adolescent behaviours currently on display in world affairs and in private lives (page 168).

From the *Threshold* perspective, the early 21st century regression into **nationalism** is a clear indicator of the ongoing **transition** phase on Earth – as in the election of President **Trump** in the USA, **Brexit** in the UK, and the rise of various authoritarian **dictators** elsewhere. Together, these amount to a temporary **regressive push-back**, an angry **contraction** of the weakening *masculine* State as it reacts against humanity's warped *descent* era *feminine* aspect that has been revelling in the **expanding** financial trickery of the world's central banks. But that 'success' will fade as the *transition* proceeds.

Next: two major human organisations, symbolised to represent the two polar opposite forces of the cosmos, contracting *gravity* and expanding *levity*, and their two corresponding aspects of human evolution, the universal *masculine* and the universal *feminine*.

The violent death throes of *Papa State*

The world is presently witnessing the desperate, violent death throes of *Papa State*. So first, who is *Papa State*? The name symbolises the predominantly *masculine* institution known as the *state*, the *nation state* or the *sovereign nation state*, of which there are currently some two hundred around the world. However, *sovereignty* is today no more than a fantasy, given how almost every nation state is trapped, inescapably deeply in debt to the global central banking syndicate (described a few pages further on).

Papa State's pyramid of power

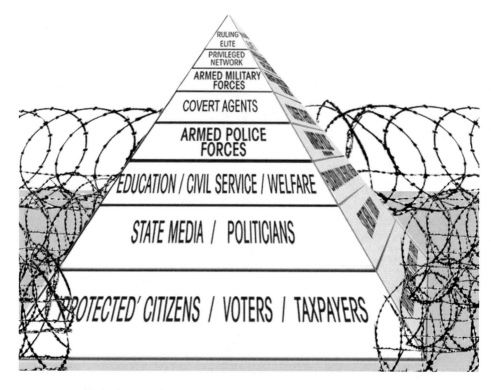

Typically behind a frontage of strong, protective authority, the basic State structure is a pyramid-like, top-down hierarchy of command and control, rules and duty – ie a system of imposed domination, enforced through military, police, civil and secret services. From which it's clear that **the primary function of these and other State institutions is to preserve the existing structure of power, authority, wealth and privilege**, ie the status quo in that society.

So, any delusional fantasies about benign paternalistic States and their police 'serving the people' are dispelled. Likewise, any romantic ideas of *'serving your country'* actually mean supporting the present ruling elite, and thereby maintaining the status quo... just like other divided-and-ruled populations elsewhere, similarly set up and serving as the required *mutual enemies* used by all such leaderships to justify their own privileged position.

"*Taxation is legalised extortion*" is a quote from a former head of HMRC, the UK State's tax collecting agency. It affirms that long established laws allow taxes to be legally extorted from the people by State authorities in order to pay for:

1. the lavish lifestyles and properties of royalty and the elite of the UK State establishment,

2. the military, police, secret and civil services,

3. the ever increasing interest due on the UK **national debt**, owed by the State after centuries of borrowing from the Bank of England, the 'local branch' of the global moneylending syndicate, and lastly...

4. just enough public facilities and welfare services to prevent citizens' discontent becoming revolutionary and threatening to overturn the status quo.

The **'deep state'** is the secretive, authoritarian coalition working within a modern state behind the official 'government'. It includes leading figures of the land-claiming aristocracy, the financial/industrial elite, the military, security and police services and the judiciary.

'Public service' means serving the State
The term '*public service*' has been corrupted over time, and is now normally taken to mean working for the State in providing the minimum welfare services it considers necessary for the population over which it rules. So, being employed by the State automatically involves a commitment to defend and maintain the current status quo.

In the **One Humanity** chapter (page 304), it's proposed that all the functions a state performs for the benefit of the public could be provided within a radically different social order which has no need for materially privileged elite minorities like States.

The *Threshold* perspective clearly reveals that the main job of the powerless, puppet politicians who act out the fantasy role of 'the government' is first to sell the ruling elite's agenda to the electorate and then to try and implement it... all the while creating an illusion of 'governing'. This deceitful pretence is a major cause of the worldwide cynical disillusionment with typical State politics.

Yet so far, the 'winners' under the status quo have managed to prevent most people thinking **beyond** the options officially on offer, despite all the discontent. Meanwhile, the illusory, superficial power and competence of the ageing *Papa State* will continue to fade, as will be explained. But what's going on beneath and above the surface?

The *male power* crisis
A combustible combination of factors is rapidly coming together, which, if not prevented, heralds the outbreak of wars of many different kinds. And that's a situation readily exploitable, for example, by the Zionists whose agenda involves undermining *Papa State*'s domination at every opportunity.

First, there's the ongoing cosmic **transition** from an era of *descent into matter*, which resulted in the predominance of the universal *masculine*, towards an era of *ascent out of matter*, which will be characterised by an increasing influence of the *feminine*.

This explains *Papa State*'s increasingly desperate attempts to re-assert his diminishing authority, and the ever-increasing desperation worldwide at the ongoing loss of male domination and *superiority* that many grew up to assume is normal and natural.

Those feelings have long been connected with the fiery power of the natural **sex drive** in young men, the energy of which needs to be discharged regularly one way or another. Otherwise, the 'bottled up' testosterone can damage the health of each charged-up male and adversely affect the wider society. The other main ingredient, common in adolescence, is a surging of passionate **idealism**, which requires suitable channels for expressing the powerful feelings involved and achieving some noticeable effect.

These elements, together with the appeal of identifying and bonding

200

with a group of other young males, may be channelled into gang life, sport, political or other cultural activities, social media, fantasy games, sexual activity or masturbation. But for some, those don't deliver sufficient satisfaction or release.

Traditionally, this source of raw power has been tapped into by *military* and *religious* orders which seek to channel it into serving their agendas. For in many cultures there's a deep well of discontent and contained anger, resulting from sexual frustration and a lack of opportunity for open and balanced relationships, especially between young men and young women.

This can be skilfully channelled by charismatic leaders and recruiting officers into an aggressive, potentially violent, attitude towards designated 'evil' enemies.

In the case of some young Muslim fundamentalists, there's also the seductive incentive of personal glory as a martyr, plus generous sexual rewards in the afterlife in return for brave self-sacrifice in this world. All of which contribute to a powerfully motivated and dedicated force – especially when the hypocritical attitudes and perverse values of the *infidel* enemy are clearly on display. Visible as contemptible signs of self-indulgent decadence, these provoke disgust, scorn and an urge to eliminate the perpetrators.

Of course, different cultures and belief systems each have their own ways of attracting new young male recruits as 'cannon fodder' in order to keep the old *descent* era *masculine* ways going for as long as possible.

Also, since *nuclear* weapons have made all-out war a non-viable, self-defeating option, there has been a *regression* back to earlier, more crude, tribal/medieval forms of warfare, but fought with modern hi-tech weaponry. Thus the commonly heard admission that *"There is no ultimate military solution"*. Which implicitly confirms that it's no longer 'a man's world'.

Which underlines the powerlessness of parliamentary politicians in general. For their careers depend on the whim of those who finance the already deeply indebted nation states that pay the politicians' salaries. So, <u>who</u> is the world's ultimate moneylender and creditor?

Mama SCAB: the subversive, polar opposite force

Mama SCAB is a symbolic name for the world's ultimate moneylender, the privately owned, profit-driven, global **S**yndicate of **C**entral and **A**rch-**B**anks. It has a 'daughter' branch (ie a *central bank*) lodged in virtually every country, and its *arch-banks* are the **IMF (International Monetary Fund), the** World Bank and the **BIS (Bank for International Settlements)**. They form *SCAB*'s global **web of debt**.

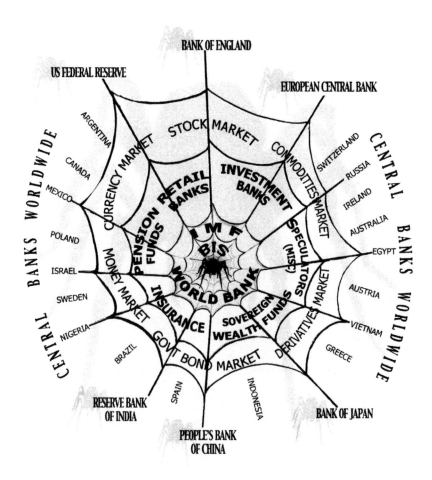

Prominent among the central banks are the *Bank of England*, the *European Central Bank* (ECB) and the US *Federal Reserve* (which, despite its deliberately misleading name, is <u>not</u> a *federal* institution) along with numerous others (see the diagram below).

The term *Mama* indicates that *SCAB* is essentially an expression of humanity's *feminine* aspect, itself much distorted by its subordination to the *masculine* principle throughout the now receding *descent* era. *Mama SCAB*, an essentially Zionist/Jewish organisation, is just one of many worldly expressions of humanity's universal *feminine* aspect, part of a cosmic process of counterbalancing the predominance of the universal *masculine*.

Yet somehow *SCAB* has managed to remain virtually invisible – until its presence is pointed out – like the *'Invisible gorilla'* in the famous psychological experiment (see YouTube).

Histories of the syndicate are now widely available, mainly focused on how the Rothschilds' vast empire of wealth grew out of a small German Jewish family business in moneylending. However, because this secretive, global organisation has no official name, and bans any public reference to itself in all the mainstream media that it controls, officially it doesn't exist and so is unknown to most people.

The only *SCAB* names that are familiar are those of its 'local branches', the **central banks** that are lodged, one in each country, and the three **arch**-banks at the centre of the web. How they coordinate in systematically controlling the nation states of the world remains a dark secret.

Central banks are <u>not</u> State-owned or State-controlled

With the collusion of each nation state, *SCAB*'s central banks are misleadingly referred to <u>as if</u> they are State-controlled institutions – a deceitful pretence which mutually suits the interests of both. So, while central banks make it their business to **appear** to be supporting their host State and the economic wellbeing of its citizens, <u>their</u> **covert purpose is very different**.

Alan Greenspan, a former chairman of the Federal Reserve, openly bragged in a television interview that ***"There is no agency of***

government which can override actions we take." Which clearly confirmed *SCAB*'s control of the so-called 'US government'.)

Viewed from the *Threshold*, *SCAB*'s long term strategy appears to be driven by both:
(a) an ancient *Hebrew/Jewish* biblical agenda for global supremacy, and
(b) a much later political *Zionist agenda* which looks beyond establishing a Jewish state in Palestine towards restoring the medieval nation state of Khazaria in what is now Ukraine.

It's everyday business has long been moneylending for profit, to finance its many commercial and industrial interests, while secretively manipulating the world of inter-national and corporate politics in pursuit of those aims.

Financial and *trading sanctions* – **a manipulative, *feminine* kind of warfare** – are now a growing part of *SCAB*'s strategy for stifling and strangulating economic activity in targeted countries through deprivation, so as to cause maximum division and social/political unrest.

Meanwhile, *SCAB* disdainfully **ignores economics** – with its so-called 'laws', statistics, charts and unreliable predictions – as a sterile, time-wasting occupation for academics, experts and business people. Instead, it focuses on achieving its goals through using its global financial power in whatever ways are most effective... while encouraging others to dedicate their lives to the delusional belief system called *capitalism* and its creed, *economics*.

Mama SCAB controls the world's money supply

Of all the money in circulation, for example in the UK, just a very small percentage is now issued by the State as debt-free *coins*. **All the paper and electronic money is supplied by *SCAB* as *debt*,** ie as interest-bearing loans. So, every *credit* transaction adds to humanity's indebtedness to *SCAB*.

Consequently, the toxic relationship between *Papa State* and *Mama SCAB* – ie between each nation state and the global moneylending syndicate – has a poisonous effect on world affairs.

'The Loveless Marriage of Convenience: Mama and Papa are still running the show' is an article at www.pathwayinitiatives.co.uk.

'Fedspeak: the mystical code deciphered...' is another article which explains the deliberately obscure language the Federal Reserve's spokespersons use to contemptuously carry on conning the world.

Neither *Papa* nor *Mama*, of course, will admit to their collusion, since public ignorance serves their mutual interests. However, *Papa State*'s previously dominant power is steadily being undermined by the also ageing *Mama SCAB*, whose own distorted *descent* era *feminine* ways nonetheless still give her an advantage during this transitional period. That is, until the incoming *ascent out of matter* era brings such radical changes to life on Earth that her financial 'soft' power no longer has any significant effect in the world.

Meanwhile, *Mama* and *Papa* continue to collaborate in ways that suit their mutual interests, including the hi-tech business of **mass surveillance**, ie *big data* information gathering from all accessible sources. This is the **snoop and snipe** method of staying in control by (a) targeting dissenting 'troublemakers', (b) selling commercially valuable information and (c) exploiting *'the cloud'*. Together, these are creating what some are calling a *'no more privacy'* world.

But in a future time of less ignorance, fear, greed, secretive guilt and so on, this **could** result in people feeling more responsible for their own actions, aware that at any time their every move could be being monitored and recorded by a hidden camera, microphone or a drone, for whatever purposes the society considers important.

Divide and rule: still a *winning formula*
Jews belong to a predominantly *feminine* tribal/medieval culture, rooted way back in the *masculine* dominated *descent* era. Thus they have long been experts at the *'divide and rule'* method of manipulating situations to their own advantage. One favoured technique is to set your enemies or rivals against one another, and to then hype up the conflict, provoking them into damaging each other without you having to risk direct engagement in combat yourself.

The general attitude behind that strategy of inciting already existing rivalries – which can also include funding proxy fighters, false flag operations, espionage, sabotage etc – seems to be *'How can we exploit this or that troubled situation for our own advantage?'* Which is not to imply that others don't use similar tactics.

Unreported by the mainstream mass media, this subtle strategy appears to be a key hidden factor behind many mutually damaging conflicts going on around the world, all serving the purposes of Zionists and Jews and their long term *supremacy* agenda. And it's this ideological commitment, mixed up with religion and extending way beyond any individual's lifetime, that makes it strategically more effective than the typical short term, results-oriented attitude.

And so, most of humankind remains fragmented, programmed into a toxic mix of partisan *loyalties* – national, ethnic, tribal and religious – while remaining addictively dependent on the imaginary *money* that *Mama SCAB* conjures up out of nothing and lends to the world... **as interest-bearing debt**.

By 2015, the global money system had spiralled out of control, due to the *SCAB*-inspired proliferation of speculative gambling at the 'global casino'... by private individuals as well as corporations and professionals. So, in order to prevent the collapse of its precarious financial scam, *SCAB* has had to virtually give money away in order to keep the pretence going. And the nation states, *SCAB*'s debtors, continue to comply because the current corrupt and fragile set-up is simply 'too big to fail', ie the ensuing chaos would engulf them all.

This it has done through **quantitative easing**, ie loans at low and even *negative* interest rates – a previously unheard of development. In this situation, financiers have switched from relying on interest earned from loans to charging fees for their services... mostly in the increasingly obscure and complicated world of financial **derivatives**, bets on the outcomes of other bets.

What holds this 'marriage', this corrupt collusion, together?

In the current *transition* phase from an era of *masculine*-dominated *descent* towards one of *feminine*-dominated *ascent,* this grand deception is being sustained because it continues to be perpetrated by the two institutions symbolised here as *Papa State* and *Mama SCAB*.

In simple terms, nation states are becoming weaker, and their leaderships are aware of their diminishing power and authority... that is, in relation to the financial, commercial and NGO sectors. Which means that many people are losing their privileged status and wealth.

SCAB, meanwhile, is itself becoming increasingly vulnerable, as its elaborate financial scam is gradually being exposed. Which is why it needs the protection of the fading *Papa State*. Such is the nature of their reluctant partnership of mutual dependency and mistrust. The underlying hostility between them is highlighted in such ongoing tussles as '*Main Street versus Wall Street*' and '*Brussels versus Silicon Valley*'.

For when the public becomes aware of who is ultimately responsibility for humankind's innumerable **debt** problems, *SCAB*'s various institutions will be the victims of some ferocious, resentful hostility – a not unfamiliar occurrence in Jewish history. But for now time, others whose worldly advantages are dependent on this corrupt partnership, continue to support it out of selfish greed, 'career fear' or the dread of some other bad outcome.

Debt money: still the measure of all things... Is there life beyond it?

To summarise very briefly, Jews have long been outstanding exponents of the skills required for profitable money-mongering, including lending and financing at interest (usury), banking services, hedging investments etc. All of which suit the subtle, predominantly *feminine* character of traditional Jewish culture, which itself has had to operate throughout the *descent* era in subtle, devious and covert ways in what has mostly been a 'man's world'.

That *descent* era *feminine* way has involved manipulating and enticing people, businesses and governments ever deeper into *debt* and obligations, in contrast to the typical *descent* era *masculine* way of achieving one's aims through ultimately threatening and exerting physical force.

Deceit and bluff: ie business as normal

As stated earlier, an integral part of the Jewish plan had long been to establish and control a *central bank* in the USA. This was eventually achieved in 1913 in the form of the deceitfully named **Federal Reserve**, the US branch of the private global financial syndicate.

From there, the planned Zionist takeover of the Federal state apparatus and most of the major US industries, including the mass media and major news agencies such as Reuters and AP, has successfully proceeded through the 20th and into the 21st century.

One clever news media trick has been to ensure that presenters always refer to '*America*', the '*USA*', '*Washington*' or '*President XYZ*' as doing this or that on the world stage, when that really means decisions made by the behind-the-scenes Zionists who control the president and the Federal administration.

The '***American exceptionalism***' claim (page 267) is thus, in effect, a Zionist/Neo-con boastful bluff that, while wrapped in the stars and stripes flag, they can do whatever they like whenever and wherever they choose. Meanwhile, over time, *Mama SCAB*'s various subsidiaries, associates and agencies have indoctrinated the majority of American people into assessing the value of just about everything in their lives in terms of *money*. Which has left them deeply addicted to and dependent on *SCAB*'s **debt money**.

So now, given the extent to which *SCAB*'s enticing, addictive *monetising* mentality has spread throughout the world, resolving the problem will be no quick or easy task. That's because fierce resistance to change is to be expected from those who believe that they are better off under the present status quo than they might be under a more just and fair global system. And at the **UN** the consistent support of Zionist-controlled America for Israel is further evidence of who's in charge in the USA.

Consequently, until a small but significant proportion of humankind begins to wake up to how it's being tricked – or until the whole *SCAB fiat money* business collapses because of its inherent fatal flaws – the prospects for a more balanced and sane world remain remote. The *Threshold* project is aimed at encouraging that awakening, one way and another.

A perverse 'success' story

The worldly success of *Mama SCAB* is an outstanding example of the darker aspect of humanity's *feminine* side from the *descent* era surviving and thriving in a 'man's world'. It was achieved through first enticing sovereigns and governments into borrowing, and then letting them sink so deeply into debt that they have to keep on borrowing more just to pay off part of the ever-increasing interest they already owe.

The backlash: *Papa*'s desperate but doomed fightback

Returning to the symbolic character of **Papa State**, what can now be seen in many places is a determined push-back, an attempt to restore the general status of males to their previously dominant position in the world. This accounts for the upsurge of dictatorial, 'father figure' regimes and the ruthless, violent conflicts they tend to stir up all over the world.

These conflicts are also inevitably being used by some State leaderships to boost their macho ambitions, as they ride this wave that's temporarily moving against the greater turning of the tide, ie the *transition* from an era of *descent* to one of *ascent*. But in the bigger picture, it's those males who are being manipulated... as the *SCAB*-sponsored news media obediently foment and hype up disruptive conflicts wherever they can – for example, in response to

SCAB-inflicted shortages of money, resulting in State welfare programmes being curtailed.

For that's just another part of the Khazari/Ashkenazis' divide-and-rule strategy for eliminating, as efficiently as possible, all rival states, cultures and religions. Their plan is for the Jewish State of Israel to end up in control of a weakened, submissive, subservient world – a world that's glad to be 'saved' by these successful, wealthy, confident people, offering deceptively simple sounding solutions to what are, in reality, deeply complex, long term problems.

For *Mama SCAB* and her industrial associates profit greatly from the massive borrowing and spending always incurred by the combatants in wars, revolutions, insurgencies and post-war recovery programmes. So, it's not surprising to find signs of *SCAB*'s devious plotting at major trouble spots all over the world and wherever there's anti-State activity.

All of which demonstrates how the *Threshold* perspective can help to clarify and resolve what may at first seem to be impenetrably complicated situations, and thereby benefit all humanity. So, without resorting to blame or condemnation, many problem situations can now be addressed coherently, and eventually be resolved without fear or favour.

Are you on *Mama*'s or *Papa*'s side?

It's crucial to remember just how <u>mutually dependent</u> **Papa State** and **Mama SCAB** are, despite their deep differences. Which is why ultimately they always support each other... and why it's no use condemning just one or siding with one against the other.

What does the *Threshold* perspective reveal about normal, ground level party politics?
In conventional *descent* era politics, the typical old style, ethical **left wing** view is that the greed-and-fear-driven *money and markets* mentality is an evil curse that can only be overcome by supporting a benevolent and strong paternalistic *State* that has the wellbeing of 'the people' at heart.

However, given that the State is a predominantly *masculine* product of *descent era* humanity, that naive view overlooks the fact, outlined elsewhere in this work (page 197), that...

the *State* is essentially an elaborate *protection racket*,
run by a ruling elite
which collects taxes as its protection money
and provides the minimum welfare benefits necessary
to maintain its exclusive power, authority, wealth and privileges...

So, fantasising optimistically about benevolent States will not resolve humanity's problems. By contrast, the distorted *feminine* aspect of *descent* era humanity appears as a selfish, manipulative and greedy character, supported by the anti-State advocates of so-called *free enterprise* and *market forces.*

For it's they who seek a minimal State that leaves the rich free to use their excessive wealth to become ever richer – at the expense of the poor who become correspondingly poorer, but may be awarded a few leftover scraps as compensation. In economics, this fallacy is known as the *trickle-down* effect.

And all the while, the collusion between *Papa State* and *Mama SCAB*, ensures that the current status quo of wealth, authority, power and privilege is maintained.

For example, in the UK the official story regarding the *Bank of England* is that it's 'allowed' to act independently in controlling the nation's money supply and interest rates for borrowing. That's because it's officially a 'nationalised' extension of the State, to which it's supposedly loyal and answerable. The reality of this relationship, however, is just the opposite: *Mama SCAB* is in control, but is glad to be protected by the illusion of being under State control.

The parallel situation of the US Federal Reserve was concisely summarised by one of its former chairpersons in a TV interview (https://www.youtube.com/watch?v=ol3mEe8TH7w).

Meanwhile, the misleading official version continues to be taught, swallowed and repeated by well indoctrinated generations of teachers, politicians, economists, media experts and others. Why? For the simple reasons explained earlier, regarding how it suits the self-interest of those who benefit, like parasites, from the current status quo.

Another major **deception** regularly perpetrated by certain 'experts' is to insist that *'the corporations'* are responsible for the world's 'economic' woes, instead of *SCAB* and the nation states. For some, this is a pragmatic strategy, for others it's simply naive ignorance.

Such are the flawed and crumbling foundations on which have been built these unbalanced social structures called *capitalist democracies* and their *economies*. They are combinations of corrupt *descent* era powerless politics (*Papa State*'s world) and greed-and-fear-driven financial business (*Mama SCAB*'s world)... blessed by various religious leaderships, themselves protected and supported so long as they help maintain the status quo.

So, in order to radically change the status quo, it's necessary to address both sides of this long running **dual bluff** at once.

Moving beyond the world of *Papa* and *Mama*
Humankind, locked into a collective *descent era* mindset and suffering the consequences, requires a whole new way of thinking. Which means first recognising and then abandoning:
(a) **Papa State** – ie those still running national protection rackets all over the world,
(b) **Mama SCAB** – whose *money trick* continues to sustain her worldwide web of *debt*, and
(c) **All divisive belief systems** that set people against one another or try to prevent people questioning and freely discussing how to change their damaging status quo.

Meanwhile, what is *SCAB*'s *Plan B*?
So, major changes regarding money are coming, one way or another. And unless *SCAB* comes up with an effective *'Plan B'* to counter this development, Zionist power worldwide could simply evaporate. What will happen then to all the Jewish settlers, earlier enticed with idealistic propaganda into helping occupy Palestine? Will they be

abandoned and sacrificed?

Surrounded by embittered, resentful enemies, they would be extremely vulnerable to Muslim vengeance, while the Zionist elite would be comfortably lodged elsewhere, relatively safe and secure.

A devious *SCAB Plan B* could consist of something like:
1. Offer a **false jubilee** of so-called '*debt forgiveness*', presented as an act of goodwill, and
2. Introduce a new single global currency, such as the IMF's *SDRs* (*Special Drawing Rights*), to replace the present multi-currency world system and allow time for organising the next phase of the greater *SCAB* strategy,

These measures would mean that the same old *fiat money* game could start all over again, with Zionist 'Jews' still running the show. OR, if things don't go according to plan, Israel ultimately has its **nuclear option**... given that the idea of 'limited nuclear strikes' has now been publicly aired. Which raises a whole new range of challenges for all humanity, including Zionists and non-Zionist Jews everywhere.

Another possibility is that, despite certain risks, the highly volatile crypto-currency adventure will be allowed to continue by the hidden ruling elite so that humankind quickly becomes accustomed to using digital money. That will hasten the imposition of **a global cashless money system. Then all crypto-currencies will be declared illegal and be replaced by a centralised, *SCAB*-controlled, blockchain system** that will give its obsessive controllers access to all transactions everywhere... unlike the decentralised, anonymous *Bitcoin* system.

So, is a world that no longer needs money possible? The answer is YES, but it will require much re-thinking, planning and scheduling, plus plenty of goodwill and perseverance, because as things are, it will take an unpredictable number of generations to be achieved.

'There's nothing ordinary people like us
can do about it... is there?'

That resigned attitude is typical of the many disempowered people worldwide who are thinking, in effect, *"I can't change the world or do anything about these problems that are making our lives so stressful. Obviously, the politicians can't either. So, I'm not going to waste my time thinking about it."*

Which is, in effect, allowing the hidden, privileged ruling elites and their dependents to carry on exploiting their victim subjects. For only when the many victims start linking up, locally and globally, with others whom they've long been programmed to treat as their rivals or enemies, will they realise their own potential and how empowering this can be. Then the imbalances of power and influence can begin to be rectified.

However, presently, all genuine goodwill initiatives, once they show any signs of potential for changing the status quo, are likely to be targeted for elimination one way or another. So, the big collective challenge for humankind is to learn how to:

- **grow out of its child-like dependency on these now redundant parent-like figures,**
- **overcome the disempowering effects of the *ignorance-fear-divide-and-rule* method,**
- **start planning and initiating something like the *One Humanity* project,**
- **learn from the Jewish *sayanim* how effective a dedicated global network can be,**
- **wean itself off its addictive attachment to *Mama SCAB*'s greed-inciting *debt money,* the subject matter of the next chapter.**

And that requires having viable, radical, inspiring alternatives available. Which is what the practical **One Humanity** vision is essentially offering – ie a non-centralised, non-partisan, non-religious, non-commercial system which transcends all divisive thinking. The **OH** vision is thus not a scaled up, global version of a *descent* era nation state.

214

Global depopulation: a very dark (unofficial) agenda

There's one unspoken ruling elite plan that at first might seem unthinkably abhorrent to anyone who's never considered these matters before. While each *Papa State* normally wants to <u>increase</u> the population within his territory, so as to have a plentiful supply of military 'cannon fodder' and civilian workers, *Mama SCAB*'s priorities are chillingly different.

It has been suggested that the Zionist/Jewish ambition of *supremacy* on Earth – to be achieved through manipulative control and exploitation rather than crude force – would be easier to manage if there were significantly fewer human beings around. And the most efficient, *descent era feminine* way of achieving that is through the proven method of *ignorance-fear-divide-and-rule*.

It involves, first, cynically depriving most people of certain essential knowledge. That leaves them ignorant, vulnerable, insecure, fearful, discontented and therefore hostile and craving some compensatory comforts. It also involves setting them against each other in mutually destructive conflict situations, both as individuals and in various groupings. All of which requires much secret planning, preparation and persistence.

Alternative options for *global depopulation* no doubt include more traditional *descent era masculine* methods of mass killing and mass sterilisation, but now using modern, less detectable technology.

Once that dark intention is grasped, many otherwise puzzling events worldwide, past and present, can be seen as parts of an overall pattern, such as the 21st century *Exodus*, referred to on page 150. Which means they can now be addressed in a coherent and practical way in order to prevent such ideas progressing any further.

Silent Weapons for Quiet Wars is a document which, whatever its source, serves as a clear guide as to how a small elite, headed by international bankers, retains supreme control over most of the USA, including the so-called 'federal government'. Through the manipulation of money and mass mind control techniques, people are being persuaded to dedicate their lives to their own continuing subjugation, unaware of how this trick works (page 398).

Powerless *Politics* & Fantasy *Economics*

Viewed from the *Threshold*, parliamentary **politics** and classical **economics** demonstrate how distorted and dysfunctional *descent era* societies can become through lacking certain vital cosmic knowledge. Politics and economics broadly represent the *polarity* of the universal *masculine* and *feminine* (which are not about gender, as is explained elsewhere).

Throughout the current but now departing era of *descent into matter*:
(a) the universal **masculine** has manifested as the world of adversarial, 'us v. them' **politics**,
(b) the universal **feminine** has manifested as manipulative fear-and-greed-driven **economics**.
Their complex relationship, which has become increasingly focussed on **money** as power, is summarised in the often repeated *political* quote: *"It's the economy, stupid!"* And so...

Question:
Why do all elected *politicians*,
including *presidents* and *prime ministers*,
appear so *powerless* and pretentious?

Answer:
Because others are actually in control.
...as the following quotations confirm.

Benjamin Disraeli (1804-1881)
Twice UK Prime Minister
"...the world is governed
by very different personages
from what is imagined
by those who are not behind the scenes."
(From *Coningsby*, his fictional account of UK politics at the time.)

Mayer Amschel Rothschild (1744-1812)
Founder of the global central banking (moneylending) business
*"Let me control a nation's money,
and I care not who writes its laws."*

Baron Nathan Mayer de Rothschild (1840-1915)
*"I care not what puppet is placed on the throne of England
to rule the British Empire on which the sun never sets.
The man that controls Britain's money supply
controls the British Empire,
and I control the British money supply."*

The two alleged Rothschild quotes convey a clear message about their general attitude, even though there's no conclusive proof or disproof regarding the actual words spoken or written, especially when translated. However, they do serve as insightful clues for understanding how populations today continue to be rendered politically impotent, while still believing and participating in the charades euphemistically known as **parliamentary democracies** and the global financial scam known as **democratic capitalism**.

There are today a number of academics, other experts and commentators of goodwill who speak and write of the many failings in the current political and economic set-up. But they studiously refrain, at least in public, from addressing the core factors highlighted by the above quotes – presumably in order to protect their livelihoods, reputations and funding?

So, **political** commentators at most only make vague references to '**Israel**'s interests', while **economics** experts only make indirect references to the global influence of '**Wall Street**' financiers and institutions... without directly implicating the relevant **political** Zionists (*neo-cons*) or **financial** Zionists (*neo-liberals*) or the many other well funded Jewish/Israeli pressure groups. And that's how the deeply flawed status quo is being maintained.

Economics (the *greed creed* of capitalism)
preaches the message:
'Blessed are the selfish greedy winners'

How the resources of a society are produced, managed and shared, ie its **economics**, reveal the unspoken assumptions and values, ie the **belief system** of its ruling elite... who normally try to indoctrinate the population they govern with those values. However, the assumptions behind classical *economics* incorporate certain deeply flawed ideas about *'human nature'*.

The word *economy* comes from an old Greek word meaning 'home management, which signifies a *feminine* quality – as opposed to the *masculine* qualities of *warrior* or *hunter*. As the *masculine*-dominated *descent* era proceeded, so the subject of *economics* was taken over by males, focusing on hostile competition and quantifying... just as *feminine* spirituality and healing became male-dominated, monotheistic religions, worshipping a father figure God.

Economics is based on the false premise that there is a *scarcity* of resources on Earth to meet potentially unlimited human wants, and therefore a scarcity of the basic necessities for all humankind to live a natural, healthy life. The *insecurity* resulting from that misconception then serves as a major **fear-generator**, which is used for promoting the divisive idea of 'dog eat dog' *rivalry* and *competition* as natural and unavoidable aspects of 'human nature'.

Classical economists then incorporate this delusion into their calculations and predictions, which in turn results in **the disempowering, fear and anxiety-based psychology of *'jobs'*.** By contrast, the idea of **work**, as a chosen, fulfilling activity, dedicated to serving the wellbeing of humankind on one level or another, has never been part of classical economics thinking.

Economics, as a discipline, has become frozen into dogma that supports the status quo. Broadly, it's a *descent era* expression of the universal *feminine*, as opposed to the more *masculine* adversarial *politics*. And since it's essentially an attempt to rationalise and justify the greed-driven belief system called *capitalism*, it has been called the **greed creed**.

The psychology of greed is a whole other subject, addressed elsewhere. But it's primarily a symptom of **fear** of deprivation and poverty, associated with **anxiety**, arising from a feeling of **insecurity**... itself due to a sense of **vulnerability** that results from a deep **ignorance** of how the cosmos works.

Capitalism is the outdated belief system that encourages unlimited, selfish acquiring and accumulating of material wealth in *excess* of *need*, and then the exploitation of that excess, as *'capital'*, to gain further excess wealth. Under capitalism, prioritising real human needs, fair sharing, justice and compassion are openly rejected or quietly neglected... in favour of the already wealthy and privileged being able to become ever richer.

The fantasy economics ideal of *free market capitalism* never has existed. And by the early 21st century the manoeuvrings of those controlling the world's supply of money have ensured that it never will. That's because they have long known, from before *economics* as a subject was born, how to manipulate, exploit and corrupt unwary individuals and whole societies. So, to them, obsessive *data collecting* and *number crunching* are largely irrelevant.

In the warped world of economics, any profiting from legal greed-driven behaviour is normally treated as a 'success story'. And any blocking or impeding of the greed drive is referred to as 'unfavourable conditions' or 'headwinds' by the media experts, paid to promote the *greed creed* by obsessively gossiping about all the ongoing ups and downs.

Currently, in deference to the mystical *'market forces'*, aka selfish greed, just about everything is quantified into **money** values, ie *prices*. And given how the 'trickle down' idea has proved to be fallacious, genuine *charitable* work has become largely *monetised*.

'Monetise' is itself a paradoxical word, because *money*, as described earlier, is essentially *non-physical*. It's *potential* worldly power, in token form of various kinds, which can be stored or converted into action or material things and then converted back again.

Economics masquerades as a science by using lots of graphs, diagrams, statistics and pseudo-scientific 'laws'. But it's basically an attempt to rationalise capitalism, which itself violates the universal cosmic tendency towards a state of *equilibrium* - that is, between the *centralising*, contracting force of *gravity* and the expanding force of *levity*. And, economically, that implies the need to adjust any significant discrepancies between **deficiency** and **excess**.

So, to understand how the worlds of **politics** and **economics** presently work, they have to be viewed in that light as **belief systems**, and <u>not</u> as presented by the mainstream media and education systems, whether State or commercial. For these are mostly funded by *SCAB*, which has long been rigging the world's monetary system for its own financial benefit.

Demand and **supply**, two key Economics terms, exclude natural human qualities such as love, compassion, altruism, charity... except when these might serve material self-interest.
- **Demand** doesn't differentiate between **want** and **need**, as the instigator of *supply*, while
- **Supply** doesn't distinguish between **selfish** and **altruistic** motives in addressing *demand*.

And when this ambiguity is set within a complicated, artificial, *debt money* system, the result, superficially, is a jungle of muddled thinking and activity. Yet when viewed from the *Threshold*, a coherent **pattern** becomes apparent through all the complications and clutter.

The term, an **'economy'**, refers to a society but only in terms of its consumption of goods and services, its prices, and its supply of money – ie ignoring most human and environmental considerations. So, to discuss the workings of an *economy* is to comply with a kind of confidence trick, since the very term *'the economy'* carries an implicit set of false assumptions. It's a reminder of how repeating particular words can distort people's thinking.

The term, **GDP** (*gross domestic product*) – the estimated total of all economic trading in a society – is used as a measure of the 'growth' and, implicitly, the strength of an economy. However, it only treats as relevant those goods and services that are traded for money. And since *SCAB* presently controls the world's supply of money, there's a clue as to why *SCAB* promotes the subject of economics being taught, but in its own dealings, ignores it.

Globalisation is a term that has been hijacked and corrupted into implying a world in which greed-driven <u>financial economics overrides politics</u>. That is to say:
- global traders in global markets seek ways to bypass national borders and avoid tariffs,
- transnational commercial corporations have power over competing national governments,
- *Mama SCAB* controls the whole game by playing them all off against one another in rivalry for her favours, ie by divide and rule.

The opposite of *globalisation* is mostly assumed to be *nationalism*, although the *masculine* nation state is increasingly being outmanoeuvred by *SCAB*, which represents humanity's *descent era feminine* aspect. However, the term *globalisation* can also refer to a **potential** situation in which nation states, banks and divisive religious organisations have been abandoned in favour of a borderless, balanced, interdependent and more sane world.

Which demonstrates how words such as *enterprise, business* and *profit*, have also been hijacked and corrupted by financiers, economists, the State and the media. And new words have been coined, such as *incentivising* and *commercialising*.

Competition, under capitalism, is promoted as the best antidote to the inertia and conservatism of the already wealthy. But it's really just a subtle, deceptive way of enticing people into trying to emulate the existing *winners* who, unsurprisingly, fiercely defend the status quo.

It's also often falsely asserted that without competition there would be endless collusion, corruption, cartels, complacency and cheating. But that argument is based only on humankind's past record throughout the *descent* era, and not on it's potential to evolve. In terms of *recapitulation* (page 81), hostile competitive rivalry only occurs in those who have yet to progress beyond the *childhood* stage of human evolutionary development.

Words such as 'healthy', 'vibrant', 'strong', 'robust' and so on are used to describe situations in which selfish greed is succeeding in making some people 'winners' – ie wealthy in excess of their natural human needs – while the consequences for the 'losers' are ignored as insignificant. Yet greed is not a sign of psychological balance and good health.

In the ongoing *transitional* phase (page 45), the tendency towards *monopolies* and *oligopolies* is due to the *descent era feminine* nature of the financial world, with its characteristic craving for total **control**. And when this is aligned with *masculine* state power, the tendency is towards fascism (page 94).

Morals and ethics are viewed by devotees of capitalism and economics as unnecessary obstructions to commercial profit-seeking. An example of this is the neutral, technical sounding term, **externalities.** This refers to the way a classical *economic* analysis of a particular situation deliberately ignores the environmental, human and social 'costs' incurred by the activity going on.

Thus, entrepreneurs tend to avoid taking responsibility for any costly outcomes of their enterprises. And so it's the wider world, ie humanity, that has to deal with the expensive and sometimes deadly consequences. In pursuit of this kind of outcome, *management consultants* may be hired to apply their creative skills in making greed-driven organisations run more 'efficiently' and therefore more profitably... regardless of the *externalities* referred to above.

An alternative way that transcends that false choice is outlined later as the **One Humanity** vision. This proposes that humankind, in all its diversity, is fully capable of sharing one broad vision and intention, such as all people on Earth re-learning how to live in rhythm and harmony with nature and the cosmos. Which means being able to satisfy their basic **needs** for a balanced, fulfilling life on Earth for all its citizens... when **ecology** supersedes *economics*.

So, until economics is replaced by an ecology which has itself evolved into an all-inclusive science of wholeness that acknowledges the primacy of *consciousness, polarity* and *resonance* in nature, life on Earth looks likely to continue deteriorating, at the hands of those controlling the money, the weaponry and increasingly, the available fresh water.

Politics: the age old game of *'Who's in charge?'*

All political activity at all levels can be understood ultimately in terms of the universal **polarity** principle, ie the rhythmical dynamic interaction between *contraction* and *expansion*. The chart below provides a few basic clues as to how the pattern, present throughout the cosmos, can be recognised.

Currently, the **context** is the ongoing phase of **transition** from an era of *gravity* and *masculine*-dominated **descent into matter** to one of increasing *levity* and *feminine*-influenced **ascent out of matter**. So, the way to a more sane and healthy world is not through political compromising between prejudiced partisan attitudes, but through recognising and adjusting any imbalances arising between the two universal forces as they manifest in everyday life.

Contraction	Expansion
Universal *masculine*	Universal *feminine* (principles)
Patriarchy	Matriarchy
Papa State	*Mama SCAB*
Weaponry & force	Money & finance
Militaristic/territorial	Financial/commercial
nationalism	globalism
Police state domination	Debt slavery to *SCAB & Co*
Centralising	Decentralising
Authoritarian	Liberalising
Uniformity	Diversity
Mass fascism	Individualistic anarchism
Inhibiting	Expressive
Containing	Releasing
Closed borders	Open borders
Isolationist	Globalist

'Superior us v. inferior them'

Viewed from the *Threshold*, it becomes clear that some of the fiercest and seemingly irreconcilable conflicts going on are clashes between (a) the distorted ambitions of certain individuals, and (b) cultures representing different phases of human evolutionary history, whether ancient or modern. Consequently, such clashes may involve very different sets of assumptions, attitudes, value systems and priorities. The result can then be minimal genuine communication, whether between representatives of different societies or between people within the same society.

For example, people who still have a *tribal/medieval* mentality tend to behave in primitive, child-like, self-centred, '*superior us* v. *inferior them*' ways. A typical sign of which is the simplistic, binary attitude, '*You're either <u>with</u> us or you're <u>against</u> us*'. From this arise the many conflicts between seemingly incompatible rivals and enemies, each arrogantly pushing its own prejudiced outlook as the one authentic worldview.

Such an immature, 'all or nothing' mentality leaves little room for conciliation or agreement. Why? Because it demonstrates a lack of the capacity for an inclusive *overview* from which the whole conflict situation can be seen in its wider context, revealing the common humanity and needs of all those involved.

That kind of inertia-stricken hangover from way back in the *descent* era explains why most contemporary official politics has a 'dinosaur', outdated quality, especially when viewed in the context of today's high speed communications technology.

Fatherland/motherland, patriotism/nationalism
Patri-words (patriarchy, patriot..) convey the idea that the *father* figure is dominant, emphasising the *descent era* dominance of the universal *masculine* over the *feminine*.
Matri- words (matriarchy, matrilineal...) imply the opposite.
The **nation** and the **state** are briefly described on pages 195-7.

The *democracy* delusion: a rigged numbers game
Democracy has become a 'magical' term, misused by all manner of political set-ups, as a kind of badge, intended to confer on them a measure of fake respectability or prestige. But the fundamental **fallacy** of such 'democratic' electoral systems is that counting and comparing the numbers of votes cast for or against this or that **does not amount to any kind of informed or balanced wisdom** about what might serve the wellbeing of humankind... just as the worldwide mass addiction to, and demand for, junk food, nicotine, alcohol, opioids etc doesn't somehow validate the mass marketing of these life-damaging products.

Thus there are challenging questions about the validity of the typical western '*numbers game*' **democracy**. In these set-ups it's implicitly assumed that whichever candidate or political group wins a simple *numerical majority* of the electorate's votes must be in tune with 'what the people want'. Which is then taken to be what's best for that society.

Such systems resemble a typical interactive **game show** based on the **numbers** of **votes** that rival competitors can attract in a calculated way. However, from the *Threshold* perspective, the reality of so-called democracies is not nearly as simple as that.

Among humankind there's a wide spectrum of natural intelligence and learning. It includes, at one end, the kind of *ignorance* that's due to a lack of education and other problems of deprivation. This tends to leave such people disadvantaged, unable to appreciate how they are being tricked and exploited by some at the wealthy, advantaged end of the spectrum, ie those whose background has given them a very different yet still distorted outlook.

The result is an unbalanced world of unfulfilled 'haves' and 'deprived have-nots'. And in modern 'democratic' societies they each have a *vote*, ie a supposedly equal say in how they are to be governed. Which raises many questions about numbers and 'public opinion'.

On closer examination, it's clear that the overwhelming *numerical majority* of the electorate in any society usually consists of the most educationally deprived individuals, who are generally less well prepared and equipped to question what they are being offered. That is to say, they may not be ready to recognise and resist the many hidden, encoded, mind-controlling tricks being used on them for various political, commercial and religious purposes. Also, they may or may not choose to vote at all in any election or referendum.

Which suggests that they can be influenced more easily than other sectors of their society by the clever manipulators of public opinion, ie well paid media professionals, hired by those who wish to promote certain ideas and attitudes... not usually of an open and fair nature.

By contrast, the wiser, more balanced and mature members of a society, who can be trusted to judge impartially and with integrity what's best for their society and humanity as a whole, always constitute a <u>small numerical **minority**</u>. So, they and their views are normally marginalised by ruling elites who control the mass media, both State and commercial.

Populist **politics** exposes the *democracy delusion*

Populist politics is essentially about influencing, harnessing and exploiting the feelings and attitudes of the **numerical majority** of a population – ie their discontent, fears, pleasures and fantasy hopes. And they, as already indicated, are normally the most educationally deprived people in a society, although there are always exceptions to the overall pattern.

Therefore, that majority, in general, are the least likely to realise how they are being subtly influenced and manipulated – through the elite-controlled mass media and education systems – into voting one way or another. While seeking some relief from their own immediate concerns, their frustration, anger and confusion can be redirected against a suitable enemy, external or domestic, and in favour of someone offering simplistic solutions. Within a society this can become a **tyranny of the majority** over certain minorities.

And that set-up could continue so long as enough people continue to believe that a simple *numerical majority* of votes – which can usually be organised through mass media *persuasion* techniques – justifies this or that policy... which the puppet politicians, posing as 'the government', are then obliged to try and implement. Which is essentially how 'democracies' are exploited by ruling elites, using the simple '*numbers game*' confidence trick.

Populism, therefore, amounts to a kind of mind-controlled, neo-feudal, fascist, *mob rule*... in which the so-called *will of the people* represents little more than the *numerical majority*'s collective favouring of this or that political option, selected from a carefully limited pre-set menu. For when mass emotions are skilfully provoked and manipulated, the result can be a kind of herd mentality, resulting in a temporary stampeding this way or that... although, as stated before, there are always some who do not follow the crowd. And that's a whole other fascinating subject itself.

The Zionists, who control the US administrations from behind the scenes, have long been attempting to impose this kind of *democracy* in many countries around the world. These tend to be places where the populations are not yet ready to take on the collective responsibilities involved in a real democracy. And so, they too are vulnerable to all kinds of commercial, political and financial trickery, bullying and exploitation.

In the USA, one kind of *populism* takes the form – in traditionally coded language – of setting **Main Street** (the many *Christian* 'losers') against **Wall Street** (a small minority of *Jewish* financial 'winners'). Other versions target *Muslims*, *Hispanics* and other 'aliens'.

Identity and *'identitarian'* politics: old style 'us v. them'

Identity politics, so-called, and its more specialised version, *identitarian* politics, are essentially about regressive, exclusive, tribal/ medieval, 'us v. them' attitudes. That usually means some kind of populist *ASS* mentality using *descent* era *divide and rule* techniques to stir up the buried remnants of old *superiority* attitudes, conflicts and vengeful feuds. And the direct, unofficial, personal nature of online **social media**, with their potential for spreading malicious gossip and rumours, is very much part of this trend.

The Identity Continuum (page 427), by contrast, sketches out the bigger picture, ie the deeper and higher dimensions of *identity* – as opposed to the typically limited personal or group identities normally inherited or adopted by people who are not yet familiar with the empowering effect of the *Threshold* perspective. The function of those lesser, superficial identities appears to be mainly to bolster up lives weakened by the insecurity resulting from ignorance of the *Threshold* knowledge.

And that sheds some light on why the mainstream media, State and commercial, are so tightly controlled. Therefore, any progress towards a more balanced, sane world requires a radical redesigning of political decision-making and mass media systems worldwide, with failsafe mechanisms built in to prevent any unjust elitism, rigging or corruption re-emerging. (see *One Humanity*, page 304)

Fault line party splits: *flag* vs. *money*

The familiar 'splits' in conventional party politics represent fundamental divisions that relate to the two polar opposite universal principles described earlier. For example, regarding the UK's relationship with the *European Union* (page 265), there has long been a deep 'fault line' split between:

(a) those who want to preserve the predominantly **masculine nation state** as the principal unit of world politics, but are locked into an exclusive, adversarial attitude of conflict and war, and

(b) those who favour the more **feminine**, inclusive, 'family' fantasy of a **federal** European **superstate.** Which implies eliminating the nation state and later being manoeuvred into one global superstate.

In this contest, *Papa State* is fighting an old-style **political** rearguard action against the fake 'progressive' *Mama SCAB*, who is promoting the **financial**, **economic** and **social** benefits of membership of the EU. And that leaves the powerless, compromised politicians, as usual, inelegantly attempting to straddle the chasm between the two, with those committed to either side trying to conjure up inspiring and enticing arguments to justify their position.

The broader picture is thus one of a grand *descent era* charade: vanity parades of politically impotent politicians, answerable to crowds of protesting but disempowered, discontented citizens, while religious leaders carry on preaching their own messages regardless. And it's all looked down upon with scorn and contempt by the ruling elites and their loyal dependants.

Meanwhile, the secretive *global governance* fanatics, whose ambition is to form a new global ruling elite, clearly favour the plan to create a European superstate. Why? Because, reading between lines and joining up dots, their long term strategy involves creating a world of just a few superstates which can then be merged into one. And that will be much more manageable for their intended world government than the present complicated mess.

Left, right or centrist: same difference

So, whether you're inclined to vote for *left wing, right wing, centre ground* politicians or others, it makes little difference to the hidden ruling elites. That is, so long as there's no serious 'out of the box' thinking going on, and you remain unaware of how they control the whole status quo, in which you are just one disposable unit, conned into competing with millions of other similarly powerless voters.

'Electable' means willingly serving Mama & Papa.

Presently, all politicians with ambitions to be 'in government' have to commit themselves to full compliance with the agendas of *Mama SCAB* and *Papa State*. For should they show the slightest hint of non-compliance, media campaigns can be run to sabotage their careers, branding them as incompetent, failed or '**unelectable**'.

The missing 'political will': why is it *never there* when needed?

The so-called '*political will*' (to 'do the right thing') is something still called for by well-intentioned people who naively think only in terms of the ground level events being acted out on the *world stage*. So, how come it's what always seems to be missing? The simple reason is that all government politicians will have already been made fully aware of:

(a) the restrictions on any ambitions they may have to change the status quo, and

(b) their obligations to their ruling elite sponsors - which render them politically impotent.

By contrast, an increasingly significant factor is the ongoing work of a small but growing minority of aware people of goodwill, who are quietly building up enough knowledge and support to start peacefully but firmly dismantling the old redundant world set-up piece by piece... to gradually replace it with an open, transparent system, more appropriate for a balanced, healthy 21st century world. This involves much learning from past mistakes.

Inter-national and corporate geopolitics, at least on the surface, is still largely being played out in public as an elaborate, territorial **board game**. That's because new generations are still being indoctrinated with this relic from the now departing, *masculine*-dominated, *descent* era... and, it seems, without much consideration as to whether, in the bigger picture, carrying on with it might be more harmful than beneficial for all humankind and the planet.

1917: *Russian revolution + Balfour Declaration =* ***Zionists win***
The story of how, in the late 19th century, certain European Zionist bankers funded the false dawn of *socialism* and *communism* – ie *state capitalism* – is a crucial but still largely ignored layer of modern history. For they would have known that these psychologically simplistic systems, designed to arouse idealistic but naive longings for a more fair and just world, were doomed to end in conflict and suffering, given humanity's unbalanced condition at the time.

The Khazari/Ashkenazi Zionists already had a longstanding grudge against Russia (page 148). So, the whole project, as an act of vengeance, appears to have been destined from the start to fail disastrously, doomed to result in havoc and terrible human suffering on a massive scale.

They knew full well that 'the people' were psychologically nowhere near mature enough or ready for these ambitious and noble sounding programmes. So, the cynical plan was to stir up various fantasy hopes and ambitions in order to create a major conflict resulting in the eventual collapse of the Russian state.

But to have the desired effect, the Zionists' agenda would have to be forcibly imposed on 'the masses'. And that would involve first funding and stoking up a major political uprising, a *revolution* among the proletariat – to be led by a few fiercely committed, intellectual, but emotionally unbalanced, power-craving rivals, each with personal ambitions to 'succeed'.

The Balfour Declaration emerged in a simultaneous diplomatic operation, involving some unsubtle manipulative pressure, exerted by certain Zionists on British politicians. It committed the British government to back the Zionists' plan to take over Palestine.

According to Haaretz (an Israeli news media organisation, 15 July 2018), the Balfour Declaration was closely connected to the entry of the United States into the war alongside Britain, France and Russia in the spring of 1917. The Zionists were able to 'persuade' the US government to step in despite resistance in the US from those who maintained that America should not become involved in European conflicts, and despite opposition from German and Jewish immigrants. This affirms **Benjamin Freedman**'s 1961 explanation (See References).

A purposeful pattern becomes clear when all this is seen as part of the long term, Zionist-led strategy for *world supremacy*, to be achieved eventually by weakening all other significant political and religious organisations. It was a manipulative, *descent era feminine-*style strategy, successfully executed without any need for a significant military capability of their own. (see Douglas Reed's detailed and documented account, referred to on page 392).

However, a lingering question remains unanswered. Although the Brits appeared to be submitting to the political Zionists' demands, were they actually allowing them and millions of misled 'settler' Jews to willingly walk into a trap, ie a small strip of land, surrounded by hostile, resentful neighbours? For once the *SCAB* money trick disintegrates and Israel's funding dries up, the Zionists' Palestine fantasy looks like coming to an ugly and violent end.

Back in the here and now: since the Middle East represents a microcosm of humanity's current troubles on Earth, next are a few observations on some of the key factors behind the propaganda and faked events on the *world stage*, as presented by the mass media in the format known as 'the News'. So, a crucial question for all humanity is: *Who controls which media outlets and channels in the fast evolving broadcasting and online arenas?*

Whose News? Whose Mass Media?

Given the current proliferation of propaganda and faked events on the *world stage*, as presented by the mass media in the format known as 'the News', a crucial question for all humanity here and now is: ***Who controls which media outlets and channels in the fast evolving broadcasting and online arenas?***

The on-the-ground picture is that all major news media corporations, commercial and State, are obliged to comply with the requirements of their ultimate creditor, *SCAB*... which itself itself is pursuing the Khazari/Ashkenazi/Zionist agenda, aimed at disempowering all nation states and religions... except for the Jewish State of Israel and Judaism.

And so, the mainstream news corporations worldwide – broadcasting, print and online – continue to misinform, distract and confuse the public about the 24/7 political pantomime soaps being acted out on the mass media *world stage*. Thus the ongoing, complicated, *board-game* of multiple conflicts is presented in ways that make the plot lines compelling for global audiences. Which gives the news people more to gossip and argue about than the crucial, unaddressed theme of how world affairs are being controlled and directed from behind the scenes by those who have control of the world's money supply.

The News: the same old recipe of spin, gossip and confusion
Mainstream *news* and *comment* in general amount to an incoherent, disjointed, rag-bag jumble of unbalanced, loaded information, propaganda, junk and biased opinion... **always with vital omissions,** ie significant information and questions that are unofficially decreed forbidden subjects and therefore excluded.

For behind the deliberately created confusion, there's that clear strategy with a dark purpose: ie to provoke maximum conflict within and among all nation states and religions, except Israel and

Judaism... in order to eliminate or weaken all rivals in the Khazari/ Ashkenazi/ Zionists' quest for global *supremacy*, which extends way beyond occupying Palestine.

And then there's the daily supply of **fake news** which most people and organisations don't have the time (or the inclination?) to check and evaluate thoroughly. *Fake news*, in that broad context, is calculated gossip-mongering, disguised in various ways, such as *leaks*, selective *media releases* and loose chat. These are then fed into the 24/7 news media machines to be packaged and pumped out for particular partisan purposes.

Chomsky's Exposé of a classic diversionary tactic

The perceptive Professor Noam Chomsky has written of a standard practice, adopted by most news media professionals for deceiving both the public and themselves. It states that:

> *"The smart way to keep people passive and obedient*
> *is to strictly limit the spectrum of acceptable opinion*
> *but allow very lively debate within that spectrum –*
> *even encourage the more critical and dissident views.*
> *That gives people the sense that there is free thinking going on,*
> *while all the time the presuppositions of the system*
> *are being reinforced*
> *by the limits being put on the range of the debate."*
> Noam Chomsky, *The Common Good* (1998, + Pluto Press 2003)

Chomsky's clear-eyed observation refers to to the formula widely used to restrict people's thinking and keep it contained 'in the box', ie kept safely within the restricting limitations of what's deemed acceptable by their ruling elite. It's a subtle, essentially *feminine* trick – unlike the gross, explicit, *masculine* way of crudely banning certain subjects. The result is that the output of the normal mainstream news media, state and commercial, lacks any depth or serious alternative perspectives on the world they pretend to 'cover'.

And that applies to just about every issue the media operatives address, including politics, money, economics, science, religion, migration, nuclear weapons, the arts and so on. It demonstrates how they compartmentalise their lives by 'professionally' separating off their personal career interests from any imaginings of honesty, integrity and responsibility as a human being.

Public awareness is thus severely limited, rendering people unable to question in any radical or insightful way how they're being deprived and exploited under the present status quo. Chomsky has also introduced many other insights into mass media trickery.

All of which enable ruling elites worldwide to continue pursuing their own pathological power-seeking fantasies... while anyone who seriously questions the status quo is branded, in the elite-controlled media, as a terrorist, a traitor or some other kind of troublemaker.

Thus the current hostile emphasis in Western media on, for example, various Muslim set-ups, Russia, Iran and North Korea... but no explicit mention of Zionists and their distorting influence on world affairs, especially through controlling the world's money supply.

How come
the world doesn't hear
about the hidden K/A *Zionist* influence
in *'the News'*?

The world doesn't hear about all this because the Zionist elite are not yet ready for the extent of their worldwide influence and control to be widely known. Consequently, taboos concerning what goes on behind the scenes are being enforced 24/7 in media and education systems around the world. Which is why certain crucial matters, such as this, have been 'off the radar' for most people, and so at first may seem too extreme to be believable.

That's how the status quo is continuously being reinforced 24/7 – ie by trained, compliant, media professionals, hired to convincingly convey the required messages to the world. The **BBC**, for example,

236). But the British state itself has long been deeply and inescapably in debt to the Zionist-run *SCAB*, which is not accountable to any nation state, to the UN or to anyone else.

The power *SCAB* wields through its monopoly control of the world's money supply was affirmed in a much watched TV interview (on YouTube), in which a former Chairman of the US Federal Reserve, Alan Greenspan, explicitly stated that the Fed is an independent agency and no US government agency can overrule any decision it makes.

The major *commercial* broadcasting corporations, meanwhile, are also financially dependent on and therefore under the control of the syndicate. So, taken all together, that amounts to a major *soft power* takeover through subtle mass mind control.

The simple explanation for such deceitful practices is that all major news organisations, at their higher levels, share a common interest in maintaining the overall status quo of wealth, authority, power and privilege. For were all the significant dots to be joined up in *the news*, the resulting picture would expose those most responsible for humanity's present troubles as being the same people who control the mainstream news media.

However, what has not yet been widely realised is that *SCAB* is rapidly losing credibility, as its elaborate global money scam spins out of control towards disintegration and collapse. Yet its **grand bluff** still enables it to strongly influence most news media professionals.

But is this all too difficult to swallow... easier just to ignore?

To realise that you've been tricked and fooled for years through mass media suppression of certain vital information is not a pleasant or welcome experience, although it's usually preferable to know than be kept in ignorance and continue to suffer the consequences. Two famous historical examples, among many, are the way the **known harmful effects** of *asbestos* and *tobacco* smoking were

suppressed for decades while huge profits were being made from their sales. By contrast, one way and another, the current *transition* phase is becoming a kind of *owning up time*.

The insights provided in this work go some way to explaining such typical reactions as:
- *It's hard to accept that I've been deceived throughout my adult life regarding money...*
- *I always naively believed in the BBC's reputation for impartiality and integrity...*
- *It's very disturbing to realise that I've been tricked into complying with a huge scam...*
- *This is just jealous, anti-semitic, conspiracy stuff...*
- *I have friends and colleagues who are Jewish, and I wouldn't want to offend them...*
- *Surely the 'international community' would have done something about it by now... etc.*

News media pros play their part

Meanwhile, in the charades known as 'democratic' politics, typically one team of powerless 'government' puppets is elected and then later blamed by discontented voters for failing to deliver on its election promises... only to be replaced by another team, eager for its turn at pretending to govern... in an endless *vanity parade* of fake political posturing.

And in this ritual the news media professionals play a key role. That is, the presenters, reporters, journalists, experts, editors, producers etc, who dutifully avoid all the taboo subjects, while pretending that their main purpose is to responsibly inform the general public... yet fully aware all along that they are *accomplices, complying* with the agenda of their invisible sponsors.

So, although news media professionals personally may be no more or less evil than the rest of humankind, they do bear a special responsibility for their complicity in deluding the public about

237

what's going on in the world. For, significantly, what they do **not** inform the public of is how *SCAB* exploits its monopoly control of the world's money supply to control governments, banks and corporations... **including *news media* corporations**.

'Public service' **broadcasting means *State-controlled***
The **BBC**, seen in its greater context, is a **state-sponsored, global propaganda organisation**. That's what is implied in its World Service jingle about being *'the world's radio station'*.

But the British state itself has long been deeply and inescapably in debt to *SCAB*, which is not accountable to any nation state, to the UN or to anyone else. So, it's not surprising how the BBC has, over decades, increasingly been complying with the Zionist agenda, especially in its news and financial/business programmes, and its selection of staff and guest experts.

The major *commercial* broadcasting corporations, meanwhile, are also financially dependent on and therefore similarly under the control of the syndicate. So, taken all together, that amounts to a major soft power coup by *SCAB* in the world of mass mind control.

Like other so-called 'public service' broadcasting set-ups, the BBC adopts a fake posture of unbiased political 'neutrality' to create a false image of itself as representing 'the public interest'. And so, on behalf of the State, it selects and 'colours' the topics that it presents as 'the news, while withholding other vital information.

The ongoing *transition* into a more *feminine*-influenced cosmic era shows through in the current trend towards increasing privatisation and commercialisation. Yet so far, the BBC – a *descent era*, predominantly *masculine*, State-owned, tax-funded set-up – has resisted the pressure to become a commercial advertising broadcaster. That is, one which offers a range of programmes in between the adverts it needs in order to survive.

One major but 'unmentionable' assumption that's behind every programme or article about economics, finance and 'business' is the warped, *descent era* message that **selfish greed is to be encouraged** as a necessary part of 21st century life. And that message disguises the fact that the resulting worldwide craving for *SCAB*'s debt money ensures *SCAB*'s continuing monopoly control of the world's money supply... all in pursuit of its long term *supremacy* agenda.

In the bigger picture, however, it's not only the main characters on the *world stage* who are responsible for humanity's current failings. It's also the reporters, journalists, editors, producers and managers etc, and the general public... each of whom is to some degree a willing participant in what is presently a collective game of *'Let's pretend we're in control'*, when this is clearly not the case.

'American' interests means *Zionist/Israeli* interests?
There is one deliberate news media deceit that's repeated 24/7 by all Zionist-controlled news corporations and others worldwide. It's the practice of referring to *'America'* or *'Washington'* or *'President Whoever'* doing this or not doing that on the world stage – when they know full well that it's the Zionists who are in control behind the scenes.

For having gained control of the world's money supply, the Zionists are able to control the Federal USA administration and therefore its foreign and domestic policies, as well as the news media corporations. And, given how addicted to and dependent on *SCAB*'s debt money the population of the USA has become, they continue to bamboozle the military and others with 'smart' financial conjuring trickery.

Then there's the way the president of the USA is misleadingly referred to as *'the most powerful man in the world'*.... an inane and deceitful practice. For those who speak it know it's not true, but are required to keep repeating it like an advertising or propaganda slogan.

A variation of this is the way critics of the USA government refer to 'American' failings and wrongdoing, when they know that these are a deliberate part of the subtle sabotaging strategy of the controlling Zionists, hidden just out of public sight. Similarly, the familiar 'American' promotion of 'democracy' all over the world is really about trying to rig elections and instal a puppet regime to preside over a corrupt system of financial capitalism, which 'American' corporations can then exploit and plunder.

Also, all talk of *Israel,* whether in the US or Israeli media, is based on an unquestioned assumption that the Jewish State of Israel has a God-given right to exist and continue operating in the way it has so far. And that's despite its dark history that's now being revealed, especially through certain Arab and Russian media outlets.

So, a question, regarding mass mind control through mass media...

How could you *take control*
of a country (as large as the USA)
<u>without</u> the use of military force?

Throughout the *descent* era humanity's *masculine* aspect, an expression of the cosmic force of *gravity*, ie *contraction*, has naturally been dominant. Consequently, in accordance with the cosmic tendency towards *equilibrium*, the universal *feminine*, an expression of *levity* and *expansion*, has been subtly counterbalancing that distortion in whatever ways it can. For example, it's effect can be detected in anti-State sabotage, devious manipulation, enticement into debt, divide-and-rule provocation, blackmail, disguise, false flag operations and so on.

So, the answer to that question, so far, has been to do it the *descent era feminine* way (which is not about gender, as has been explained earlier). Influence over policy and decision making has been achieved by creating a world-within-a-world. Exclusive groups and secret societies are very much part of this. Which is where the so-called **deep state** and **financial-military-industrial complex** fit into the picture.

An essential part of this involves mass and individual **mind control**. And for that purpose, the mass media can be used to systematically create in a population a toxic, disempowering mixture of fear, confusion, insecurity, anxiety, shame, guilt, discontent, cynicism, ambition and callousness... with an occasional hope-inspiring hint of 'better times to come' thrown in as a bait. This is just one aspect of the broader *'ignorance, fear, divide and rule'* method, which requires tight control of the news media in order to keep these matters out of the news.

Other mind control methods, for example, traumatise, numb and fragment the mind of victims into isolated *compartments*, and thereby produce an unquestioning, programmable, loyal obeyer of orders and coded 'trigger' messages... such as to assassinate, destroy, disrupt or whatever else is required. According to Kay Griggs' testimony (page 398), such methods have certainly been working on high ranking US administration and military personnel.

Secret society membership is also a key factor in this world-within-a-world. It's a conveniently hidden facility that serves well the Zionist/USA/NeoCon policy of instigating *regime change* wherever and whenever it suits their purposes and long term agenda.

The *'Something must be done!'* trick

A familiar **mass mind control** technique, employed in different ways by ruling elites throughout recorded history, is to:
(1) set up an alarming, threatening scenario of some kind, today through the mass media,
(2) prompt a mass demand that **"Something must be done!"**, and then
(3) deliver an already prepared response, designed to further the agenda of the ruling elite.

One example would be the sudden, dramatic introduction on to the mass media world stage in 2014 of the so-called *Islamic State*, also labelled as *IS*, *ISIS*, *ISIL* and *Daesh*. Which prompted a major escalation of State military and espionage spending and activity. How the rise of *IS* was funded and for whose purposes was not probed in any depth in the mainstream media... an omission which was itself revealing.

Another example would be for one side in a conflict to:
(1) declare that the use of chemical weapons is a 'red line' which, if crossed by 'the enemy', would trigger a violent response,
(2) stage a chemical weapons attack against its own people or allies as a **false flag** operation,
(3) blame 'the enemy' for the incident and use it to justify attacking them or their allies.

Seeing through the make-believe

All the while, on the mass media-created *world stage*, the endless pantomime of public life carries on regardless. And so, elected governments deceitfully try to persuade each new generation of the electorate that they have the best interests of 'all our people' at heart... when they clearly don't. How so? That's because **the politicians who act out the make believe role of 'the government' know that they have to either comply with the ruling elite's agenda or pursue a different career**.

With regard to the US Federal administration, the key strategy of the 'hidden hands' Zionist puppeteers has been to take control of the nation's money supply and the mass media – especially the news and entertainment industries. That then ensures:

(a) the ability to pay for whatever's required in the relentless pursuit of the long term Khazari/Ashkenazi/Zionist agenda of global supremacy, and
(b) the power to influence public opinion through the mass media.

But, as has already been mentioned, that global money scam is heading for a major collapse. So, it's no use simply blaming and condemning the Jews and Zionists at this crucial time. That's because **there are greater dimensions to this situation, involving powerful natural forces working through various levels and linkages to the everyday world of life on Earth**... with far-reaching implications as yet unrealised by Jews and non-Jews, it seems.

The bigger picture context of all this, from the *Threshold* perspective, is the ongoing *transition* from an era of *descent into matter* towards one of *ascent out of matter*. And within that process, a range of key clues indicating what's to come were revealed in the pivotal year of 2016, as outlined in the next two chapters.

Transition troubles

The current **transition** phase from a cosmic era of *descent into matter* to one of *ascent out of matter* (page 46), accounts for much of the turbulence and uncertainty being experienced on Earth today. As fundamental changes work through, people are either adapting or suffering increasing trouble and confusion in their lives. So, it's vitally important to have some basic understanding of what this *transition* involves, and to see it as the ever changing backdrop to all that's happening in the world.

Emerging within this 'bigger picture' context are various signs of a major cosmic and earthly rebalancing process. It's a gradual evolving towards a far-in-the-future state of **equilibrium** between the primal forces of *contraction* and *expansion*. So, given humankind's evidently unbalanced and dysfunctional present condition, a wholly different way of thinking about how to share our time on this planet is required.

Although there are some harmonious developments occurring, here are a few examples of humanity's current *transition* troubles.

Social trouble

Mass migrations are obvious signs of populations undergoing major change, the *emigrating* usually happening in response to dire poverty, brutal wars, victimisation and/or environmental hazards. The plight of the emigrants, sometimes the result of proxy political power manoeuvrings, may be further exploited by opportunists for commercial purposes.

As *immigrants* settling in another country, unless corralled in camps, these people instantly create **multi-cultural** populations which, predictably, experience unease and hostility, especially when large influxes have been officially encouraged or allowed to happen.

There is a very obvious and straightforward way for humanity to resolve this problem (page 274). But so effective is the mass mind control currently being exercised through the world's mass media organisations and education systems that the necessary clear, practical thinking is simply not allowed to develop.

Which emphasises the urgent need for some radical rethinking, leading to an effective, coherent counter-strategy. This would be aimed at creating a world that's progressing beyond passively being divided and ruled by such set-ups as competing nation states, a central banking syndicate and a few supremacy-preaching religious organisations.

Weaponised societies indicate a deep, fear-driven state of **insecurity**, both in individual citizens and collectively in the whole population. And the flawed idea that more weapons will bring a greater sense of security is rooted in a now redundant, adversarial, confrontational mindset, typical of the *masculine*-dominated *descent era*.

For that insecurity is the result of people being unaware of an imbalance in the 'bigger picture' context behind their general unease and discontent. And those feelings can be hyped up by political, financial and commercial interests, as they seek to profit from increasing sales of weapons and social division... while fully aware that more weapons only bring a <u>false</u> sense of power, and increase the likelihood of further violence.

The hidden forces behind the ongoing political/financial battle at the heart of this tragic dilemma are exposed in **Guns and Money in the USA** (page 282) – an example of the *Threshold* perspective being applied to an unresolved problem in the everyday world.

Social media (ie the mind of humanity displaying its range of lighter and darker aspects) In the midst of the current *transitional* turbulence, an increasing number of commercial online networking set-ups, blandly referred to in the media as *platforms*, enable people to freely express themselves – openly, anonymously or under false names, for good or evil. The standard communicating tool (or weapon) is the mobile phone or personal computer.

What started out as a borderless, global forum for the exchanging of messages, information and pictures soon evolved into an easily accessible, free-for-all jungle.   Many people found that they could safely indulge the darker, malevolent aspects of their personalities without the risks involved in physical face-to-face situations. Consequently, there's a continuing escalation of trolling, provocation, abuse, deceit, disinformation, fomenting, fake news etc... alongside all the harmless communicating.

The commercial, profit-driven organisations making all this possible meanwhile remain largely unaccountable. That's because, within the wider social/political status quo, any effective regulation is extremely difficult without (a) severely restricting people's freedom to communicate, and (b) enabling even more extensive snooping by the State and commercial organisations than is already going on.

This trend can be understood when viewed in the context of the greater *transition* process described elsewhere in this work. The outcome is an increasingly irresponsible and emotionally immature world culture, displaying humankind's collective adolescence, childhood and infancy in a range of unbalanced and out-of-control behaviour, much of which will have long term consequences for future generations.

Feminism is a label that broadly refers to a key aspect of the ongoing **transition** phase as the cosmos tends towards a state of *equilibrium* between the two universal forces. In this process, the power and influence of *expanding **feminine**/yin/levity* is increasing as its polar opposite force, *contracting **masculine**/yang/ gravity*, diminishes.

As a social movement, *feminism* has inevitably been abused, distorted, commercialised and compromised, which is what tends to happen to innovative social movements. Nevertheless, the feminist drive has brought about profound changes which continue to grow and spread worldwide. Equal rights and opportunities for women, awareness of the rights of children, attitudes to gender issues etc are all part of this natural rebalancing.

However, **feminism, in essence, is not about women becoming equal to men**. In a world largely designed and built by men, the rise of the universal *feminine* is introducing a wholly different quality to life on Earth, the complementary opposite of the *masculine*.

Political trouble

Since 2007 approximately, a significant revolution in attitudes has been spreading around the world. At first, few people seemed to have any notion of what was going on behind the dramatic scenes shown in 'the news', and why it was all suddenly happening. However, many did sense that significant changes were occurring on some level, despite the unfolding events being relayed by the mass media in their usual superficial, partisan ways.

There were some temporary local awakenings, such as the so-called *'Arab spring'* in 2010, but the pattern by 2016 was broadly a regressive relapse back into *descent* era, predominantly *masculine*, nationalistic habits, promoting the power of the nation state.

In the USA, this trend coincided with a widespread turning away in disgust from the selfish greed-driven, money-obsessed attitude, known as *neo-liberalism* – which, in practice, represents the agenda of the global Zionist central banking syndicate, *SCAB* (page 201).

The normal strategy of this predominantly *feminine* (not *female*) elite has been to hedge its bets by backing both or all main contestants in any major conflict or election. Which ensures that its overall

247

influence and control continue, whoever wins. It also ensures that, in parallel, the *masculine*, war-mongering, Zionist **neo-cons** remain in charge of US foreign policy from behind the scenes.

So, in the context of the three-way deadlock between Jews, Muslims and Christians:
   - **Jews** have been fomenting and provoking conflict among Muslims and Christians,
   - **Muslim** extremists have been trying to eliminate Christian and Jewish 'infidels'.
   - **Christian** fundamentalists in the USA have been targeting Muslims and Jews,

From the *Threshold* perspective, the political **numbers game**, currently known as **democracy** (page 225), can clearly be seen as a major piece of self-delusion, a blind spot in humankind's political thinking. And since it's being regularly exploited by ruling elites, until it's replaced by a more sane system, humanity will remain stuck in the current decaying political mess.

Then in the USA in 2016, the *numbers game* trick failed to deliver the result that the Zionist/ *SCAB*/Democratic ruling elite had planned. Previously, they had been able to effectively influence, through the Zionist-controlled mass media, how the *numerical majority* of citizens would vote... but not in 2016. However, the subsequent decline in support for the Jewish-controlled Democratic Party can be understood when viewed in the context of the great cosmic *transition*... ie they 'lost the plot'.

In 'democracies' worldwide, the current *transition* phase is blurring the old 'either or', *binary* mentality of the *masculine*, adversarial, party political 'team games'. Which has resulted in increasing *diversity*, a *feminine* trait, in the range of views represented.

Yet overall, the ill-informed and increasingly volatile voters of the world continue to go through the futile ritual of choosing candidates from a carefully limited **pre-set menu**. Which ensures that candidates and voters remain politically impotent. Meanwhile, nation states and commercial corporations remain dependent on *SCAB*, the world's ultimate moneylender.

All of which adds up to a growing realisation of the need to think and act **beyond ineffectual gestures such as *protesting* to powerless politicians** – an activity that's quietly encouraged by ruling elites. Why? Because it only serves as a release valve for discharging potential threats to the status quo. The ***One Humanity*** proposal (page 304) offers some radical, non-violent, far reaching suggestions.

It's that sense of powerlessness that has given rise to a regression back into so-called '***populism***', ie the politics of hard, *masculine*-style, totalitarian, puppet dictatorships (of whatever gender) that offer deceptively simplistic solutions, protection, stability and security. The trend represents an instinctive negative reaction against the ineffectual, impotent posturing of 'democratically' elected governments, already neutered by the essentially *feminine Mama SCAB*.

Internationally, **nuclear weapons**, meanwhile, are becoming increasingly widespread and so are having a diminishing *deterrent effect*, regardless of the fact that a nuclear war, once started, would quickly wipe out most human life on Earth. Yet some medieval-minded leaderships are still preaching that suicidal martyrdom earns desirable rewards in the afterlife.

Also, the leaderships of certain 'younger', more politically volatile nation states are striving to acquire nuclear weapons as their right – ie to win some kind of macho respect from those longer established states which already have WMDs and want to remain 'top dogs'.

From the *Threshold* perspective, a more mature and pragmatic approach would be for humankind collectively to acknowledge the shared risks that come with the current competitive status quo, and abandon the artificially contrived, political and profit-driven arms race for ever more deadly WMDs.

Instead, people could use their talents to develop more balanced and fulfilling ways of living together on this planet. But that requires people to start electing more mature, non-partisan leaders and administrators, who are not driven by vanity or immature cravings for power, wealth and status, and are able and willing to think beyond the current deadlocked mess.

The UK *State education system* and *NHS* are both being underfunded, which suggests that they are being set up to fail. The *NHS* has been 'managed' and starved to the point of collapse so that *privatisation* and a profit-driven, commercial *'health insurance'* scam that favours the wealthy can be imposed, justified as 'the only financially viable solution'.

And meanwhile, the traditional tussle for State funding continues between the ***masculine military*** elements and the more ***feminine financial*** interests... at the expense of ***welfare*** spending.

Financial/Economic trouble

Mama SCAB, representing humanity's *descent* era ***feminine*** aspect, has increasingly been undermining the authority of the previously dominant ***masculine* nation states** through financially favouring large, commercial corporations over those nation states.

A typical example of this in the UK has been the ***PFI (private finance initiative)***. It's basically **an enticing confidence trick**, irresistible to politicians eager to claim the credit for quick and easy short-term achievements – like providing new housing, hospitals and schools – while ignoring the long term problems being stored up. Based on the claim that private enterprise is always more efficient than the State, commercial organisations with easy access to large scale finance from *SCAB* offer to take over what was previously the role of local governments: for example, in major 'public' projects, but much more cheaply than is possible for the State, which is accountable and open to scrutiny, unlike private set-ups.

Such undercutting inevitably involves compromising on quality and cutting corners to reduce costs. So, the inevitable resulting problems only emerge some years later, when the politicians, business people, lawyers and accountants who set up the deal have moved on, leaving others to deal with the mess of ever-increasing costs and a huge debt burden. The victims of this confidence trick, resulting from **collusion between *Papa State* and the private finance world of *Mama SCAB***, are the subsequent generations of tax-paying citizens.

Thus the overall pattern has been the replacing of what was known as *capitalism* with what could be called **financialism**, all under the control of the secretive *Mama SCAB*, operating at the centre of **a global web of debt**. (See diagram, page 202.) In this broad context, the basic *polarity* shift will continue, despite some regressive lurches back towards *descent* era, 'us v. them', *masculine*, *populist*, tyrannical dictatorships, promising stability, success, security and protection from 'terrorists' or other enemies of 'our nation'.

What will also continue until seriously challenged is the corrupt alliance between *Papa State* and *Mama SCAB* in controlling and operating through a few large corporations. This is the basic formula for a feudal-style, **fascist**, global government, intent on ruling over a world of disempowered, discontented populations. The outcome so far has been that despite many technological advances, poverty and conflict are increasing worldwide, while excessive wealth is being increasingly accumulated by a small, self-serving elite.

How is this being achieved? Societies are being systematically de-stabilised, as *SCAB*'s central banks keep conjuring up more imaginary *fiat debt money* out of nothing and feeding it to the already wealthy in order to keep its own global financial scam, the **global casino**, going... while sustaining the illusion that it's doing this for the greater good of humankind.

Meanwhile, everywhere there are supposedly '**shortages of money**'... so nations have to 'live within their means', and people have to suffer '**austerity**'. This is the result of the mass of humankind being kept ignorant about how the world works, and therefore powerless and confused about how to improve the situation... which is essentially a grand Ponzi scheme, destined eventually to collapse. The question then is 'What is *SCAB*'s Plan B?' (page 212)

Economics and the irresponsible *'animal spirits'* in men

Today, various primitive, animal-like tendencies are still present and active within humankind. They connect back to earlier phases in the evolutionary process (page 354), echoing the primitive ways of warriors and hunters. In the contemporary worlds of finance and commerce where the *greed creed* rules, they manifest mostly in those unfulfilled males who exhibit a primitive, testosterone-driven, adventurous, aggressive, animal-like lust for extreme experiences of power, dominance, control, pleasure, risk-taking and violence, regardless of the effects on other people's lives.

The worlds of finance and commerce, however, are essentially expressions of humanity's manipulative *feminine* aspect from the *descent* era. Thus the mismatch of those aggressive, rivalry-driven characters with their daily work environment, as they typically treat the world of commercial *business* as a jungle or battlefield. A more *feminine* aspect of those tendencies is the pathological drive recognisable as insatiable **acquisitiveness**, ie excessive **greed**, a symptom of a basic psychological imbalance, explained on page 86.

This combination of qualities is what economists, quoting Keynes, refer to as the **animal spirits** in human beings. In selfish greed-driven, commercial cultures, such as the USA, this immature re-enacting of humanity's primitive past, continues to be promoted, admired and respected – as necessary for achieving the much promoted goal of economic/financial **success**. And the resulting mass pursuit of that goal ensures that the status quo of wealth and power is maintained – ie through *dividing and ruling* those unquestioning, competing masses.

Crypto-currencies (page 192), as potential alternatives to *SCAB*'s global *debt money* scam, were born out of the ideal of **universal**

accountability through the transparent, borderless **blockchain** system. However, despite the idealistic intentions of some advocates, they still essentially function as a kind of *fiat* money, ie a system of digital tokens, not backed up by anything of substantial value, operating within an economic system based on selfish greed.

So, presently, they do not offer a long-term solution to the deeper psychological problems that *money* represents... unlike the *One Humanity* proposal, which requires a radical change in consciousness and behaviour for humanity to evolve and resolve those issues.

Religious trouble

In the current *transition* phase, the resulting increase in *diversity* has enabled a resurgence of some primitive, tribal and medieval-style 'fundamentalist' belief systems). It has also helped expose the failure by leaders of certain long-established institutions to fully acknowledge and confront such issues as *sexual abuse* and *violent terrorist activity* within their organisations.

Yet in spite of *masculine* dominance fading and *feminine* diversity increasing, many people still cling to the idea of **God** as an all-powerful **father figure**. For example, the Old Testament God whom the Jews worship is clearly partisan, domineering, harsh, jealous and vindictive, offering a limited, conditional kind of love to those who claim to be his 'chosen' people. Which shows how certain *masculine*-dominated *descent* era attitudes still prevail today.

In some male-dominated Christian cultures there appears to be a schizoid split. For example, the Russian Orthodox Church presents a distinctive *polarity*. In Russia, a huge conglomerate of many peoples and sub-cultures, a major aspect of the *transition* has been the retro-revival of the *male*-dominated, patriarchal Orthodox Church.

Accordingly, it has humanity's universal *feminine* aspect at the heart of its elaborate culture, as symbolised by an idealised *female* Virgin Mary figure. Which this gives Russia, as a whole, its own unique combination of the universal *masculine* and *feminine*. And, just as in other male-dominated Christian cultures, there appears to be a schizoid split – especially among celibate men – into polar opposite attitudes towards women and the female body. On the one hand, there's the unholy mixture of suppressed, 'sinful', sexual lust, disgust and contempt, and on the other, the worshipping of a holy virgin.

The current Church revival follows some 70 years of banishment under the harsh, cruel, authoritarian and fiercely secular Soviet administration, set up after the 1917 revolution.
Thus the deep longing amongst millions of Russian citizens for a return to traditional Orthodox Christian culture. And with the support of the Kremlin, the Church has in effect become an extension of the central government.

Ecological trouble: learning to care for this one shared planet

In the current transition period there has been no shortage of data, information and hard evidence of the ecological troubles increasing daily on Earth, whether concerning pollution of water, air and land, nuclear waste, harmful radiation, extreme weather, diminishing vital insect life due to modern farming methods or other threats to life and health. The harsh reality is an ever growing trail of damage and toxic leftovers accumulating all over the planet.

Lacking among both the experts and humankind in general is an effective cosmic *overview* and the necessary psychological *insight* into the problem, especially regarding the *will power* to tackle these matters practically. So, what is at the heart of this dilemma? How and why did these problems arise? And why are they continuing to grow?

A *descent* era *masculine* attitude, seeking dominance over planet Earth, along with an assumed right to exploit its resources at will, have resulted in some beneficial outcomes for humankind. But these are overshadowed by the ever growing curse of deadly pollution.

And **scientists** of all kinds, however well intentioned, are very much a part of this failing. That's because many have been easily manipulated by ruling elites. Divided and ruled, they can be bullied into political impotence by those who control their funding and therefore their careers. And so, they tend to passively defer to powerless politicians who are themselves controlled by the money manipulators.

'*Green*' politicians – although driven by good intentions – likewise remain politically impotent under the present distorted status quo, and therefore remain isolated on the fringes of the political arena. That means they have no chance of forming a so-called 'government'. Which is why the general public is rarely aroused by ecological arguments into taking any radical political action beyond the occasional impotent protest and cash donation... despite the mass of alarming and distressing ecological evidence now available.

Next, a particular year that marked a critical shift in world affairs on Earth... 2016.

2016: A Pivotal Year

As the *'post-truth'* age of *fake news,* *conspiracies* galore and retro-*populism* began, what on Earth was going on?

Polarity rules... at all levels

2016 was the year in which the major **transition** from a *masculine*-dominated, cosmic era of *descent into matter* to a predominantly *feminine* one of *ascent out of matter* became increasingly evident. Various signs of breakdown within the old order and of newly emerging trends made 2016 a critical *tipping point* on Earth.

One unsettling part of the resulting rebalancing process was the resurfacing of certain disruptive relics from humanity's dark, troubled past... more of which later. These were individuals and groups still stuck in the ways and habits of the old and now departing *descent* era, and therefore lacking the empowering knowledge now accessible from the *Threshold* perspective... knowledge that could enhance life on Earth for all humanity.

The overall trend was a gradual shift away from **masculine**-style, forcibly imposed, uniform order towards a more fluid, flexible, subtle, *feminine* approach, tolerant of diversity and change – for example regarding sexuality and gender – although with many exceptions.

So first, an important reminder. Each person, of whatever gender label, is a unique combination of *masculine* <u>and</u> *feminine* qualities. Each individual thus consists of a unique combination of:
(a) the complementary qualities of the **universal** *masculine* & *feminine*, and
(b) **specific** *gender* attributes.

As an example, the distinction between *feminine* and *female* is often blurred in everyday language, but can be clearly appreciated in the difference between: (a) the broadly **feminine** *nurturing/caring* quality that can be found in <u>all</u> gender types, and (b) the biological **female** *physical form* which is gender-specific.

Conspiracies 2016: to heal or to harm?

Prior to 2016, the term *'Conspiracy theory'* was commonly used as an accusation, implying that someone was fabricating an *ulterior motive* behind an incident that others assumed was not the result of such motivation. But from 2016, that all changed. And in the hyped up, frantic world of online social media, conspiracy thinking suddenly became almost normal.

To con-<u>spire</u> means to *'breathe together'*, in a <u>spir</u>itual sense, which implies sharing a particular belief or intention. A *conspiracy* can thus carry an intention either to do good OR evil, to heal OR harm, to promote change OR resist change etc. Currently, the term is used almost exclusively to imply a negative/destructive intent.

That said, the main media story of 2016 concerned...

The *Trump* Splash 2016: reading the ripples

The election of **Donald Trump** as the next president of the USA marked 2016 as a significant tipping point in the ongoing cosmic *transition* process, referred to earlier. This unashamedly self-promoting individual vividly reflected back to many citizens of the USA an image of their own collective mentality – with all its flaws, distortions, fantasies and hopes.

As a presidential candidate needing an attractive package to sell to a numerical majority of the electorate, he conjured up a policy platform which appeared to be the opposite of the familiar politics that was currently leaving the US public deeply disillusioned. And being neither a loyal Republican nor a committed Democrat, he faced the prospect of considerable opposition and obstruction from both sides, as well as from the Zionist-controlled Federal administration, its security services and privately owned Federal Reserve central bank.

Instead of *neo-liberal globalisation* – a *descent era feminine*, selfish greed-driven policy – he offered, with great enthusiasm, a simplistic, conservative recipe of nostalgic, old fashioned, *descent era masculine, patriotic nationalism* and outdated anti-ecological economics,. Which resonated with the wishful fantasising of many ordinary Americans in their nostalgic longing for a return to the 'good old days' when America was great and they had steady jobs. Which meant they felt financially secure and less fearful.

His *'us versus them'* message was specifically intended to appeal emotionally to the educationally deprived **mass majority of voters** in the USA. For as an independent presidential candidate, Trump could be his own man and cynically say whatever he reckoned would win him votes, knowing that once elected, his indebtedness to certain financial Zionists would make it a very different game, and various compromises would be necessary. **His primary aim, evidently, was to be a 'winner'** which, in this case, means 'staying in the saddle'.

Also in his favour was his image as a successful, self-financing, self-made billionaire, ie a proven 'winner', and as a well known celebrity personality on a popular TV reality show. Trump's basic approach, as a *showman* and a persuasive *dealmaker* but not a warrior/fighter, was: *'I've got something you want. You've got something I want. So, can we make a deal?'* This is more in the nature of *feminine economics* than *masculine*, combative *politics*.

He could therefore be seen as an assertive, attention-seeking *male*... BUT with certain typical characteristics of humanity's *descent* era *feminine* aspect, ie someone who gets what he wants through manipulating people and situations instead of directly using force himself. With his pursed lips, delicate hand movements and spiteful sniping style – which reveal his hypersensitivity to criticism – he's an unlikely character to imagine in a real, stand-up fight. However, as long as he's in control of any situation – through having **money** available – he appears quite comfortable, even when things look chaotic from other viewpoints.

His peculiar combination of *masculine* and *feminine* qualities, in a world still largely locked into a simplistic '*male* or *female* only' mentality, made him, like the Zionists and Jews, difficult to handle or to predict for many people. He was thus able to use this double-sided quality to his own advantage as a new rival to the hidden, ruling, USA Zionist elite.

The *Threshold* perspective, however, reveals a key difference between Trump and the Zionists. The unspoken long term Zionist agenda has been to subtly undermine, disable and ultimately control the USA, politically and economically... while appearing to support it. This is the smart *Wall Street* tail that wags the sleepwalking *Main Street* dog – a major deception, long sensed but rarely articulated in public.

By contrast, Trump, an individual driven by an overwhelming ambition to be 'successful', openly generated an undiluted, uncompromising, *positive* attitude as his mission statement, knowing that it would appeal to many disillusioned American voters. His *American Dream* approach, if implemented, would bring short term 'successful' economic results, by stimulating people's *animal instincts* and hunger for some relief and 'success' in their lives.

And so, he took the Zionists' own cynically amoral methods to a new level and, in the process, became a credible threat to their previously unchallenged, behind-the-scenes control of the Federal administration. Which explains the fierce hostility of the Zionists and Jews towards Trump, and their attempts to remove or at least control him. For, yes, they were still there and in control of the money supply, but now much compromised by his presence.

It wasn't because he was so effectively disrupting the *masculine* Federal state establishment in the USA – something they too had long been covertly doing. It was because they realised how he had moved in centre stage and taken over their historic role – ie he was proving a more effective expression of the universal *feminine*, in its cosmic function of counterbalancing the *descent* era dominance of the universal *masculine*, than they presently were.

In no way a '*states-man*', Trump acted out a simplistic role of a maverick businessman and **godfather/protector**, selecting his enemies and claiming unconvincingly to be a supportive friend of Israel while adopting a favourable attitude towards Russia's president. Which deeply disturbed the Ashkenazi Zionists who have an old historical grudge against Russia (page 148).

Trump's unconscious role in the bigger cosmic picture

Trump's unconscious *evolutionary* function – as a **male** expression of the universal **feminine** – has been to help bring to an end the *descent* era dominance of the *masculine* principle and, in the process, the reign of *Papa State* and *Mama SCAB*. This he has been doing by disrupting their corrupt, inertia-bound regime of **collusion**, thereby loosening their grip which has long been obstructing the evolving of human consciousness worldwide.

So, while the *financial* Zionists, ie the *Democrat* **neo-liberals**, have been trying to bring him down, the *political* Zionists, ie the *Republican* **neo-cons**, have been exploiting his fake macho posturing in order to stir up more conflicts around the world. And all the while, the complicit media mouths and scribes continue dutifully to generate lots of superficial froth, as required.

The overall effect of his presence is to bring about the disintegration of both the *descent* era *masculine* and *feminine* elites in the USA. Which means that the Zionists' time of privileged behind-the-scenes influence is now running out. And the crucial question they are not yet ready to ask themselves is whether (a) to adapt in a positive way and bring the best of Jewish culture and talent into next era, while abandoning the worst of it, OR (b) to carry on as before and inevitably fail, bringing further suffering upon themselves and all humanity.

Trump rides the male backlash

The cosmos naturally tends towards an *equilibrium* state. And in the current but now departing *descent* era, the universal *feminine has* had to counterbalance the predominance of the *masculine* in whatever ways were available. The rise of Showman Trump, despite his being biologically *male*, has been just one example of this.

Meanwhile, confused, disempowered males all over the world are trying to come to terms with the cosmic changes that are affecting their everyday lives, as their previously unquestioned assumption of authority over females evaporates. And since they don't know what to do about it – other than angrily lash out in various ways or submit and become depressed – reported incidents of violence, inhuman atrocities and suicides are increasing.

So, for support, Trump has been tapping into the widespread frustration and resentment of the many disillusioned males, and sympathetic females, in the USA as they react to the ongoing *transition*. All along he has been feeding their nostalgic fantasies and desperate longing for some kind of superficial, token *success* with words of sympathy and promises of a return to the days of American greatness.

Thus his much repeated, simplistic, 'dog whistle' slogans and promises in 2016, finely attuned to those sentiments and serving as bait... just like in commercial advertising and propaganda campaigns. But what these signs actually indicate is the ongoing decline of the universal *masculine* and the corresponding rise of the universal *feminine*, although, by earthly human standards, there's still a long way to go.

And so, in 2016, the *post-truth* age of open, unashamed fakery and malice – especially via online social media – effectively kicked in... heralding the eventual disintegration of the old, rigid, inertia-bound, uniform, top-down command, 'straight lines and right angles', *masculine* order of the *descent* era. The world was now well into a period of chaotic, short-term unpredictability and confusion... ie **turbulent** *transition*.

The overwhelming majority of humankind, meanwhile, continued to be easily tricked and misled with lies and deceit. Which indicated how effective the complicit mass media corporations and education systems still were at keeping people ignorant, fearful and discontented, ie divided and ruled. Consequently, few people are now able to coherently question the status quo in any depth beyond impotently protesting or reacting angrily.

Unintended consequences
In the USA, the long term policy of mass cultural deprivation also unintentionally served Trump's purposes. It enabled this ambitious actor-manager/showman to step into the spotlight and seize the political initiative from the Zionist financial syndicate which had long been running the whole show from behind the scenes.

He was thus able to exploit the delusional *Democracy Numbers Game* (page 225), which gives the *numerical majority* of citizens, ie the most educationally deprived, the voting power to elect whoever seems the most appealing (or the least unappealing) candidate. Previously, they had been persuadable through the Zionist-controlled mass media. But not in 2016 when, in a close contest, the peculiar US electoral system made Trump the winner.

Suddenly it was too late for the financial and the political Zionists to recover their previous degree of mass mind control. For the influence of the mass media was shrinking while online social media, although often extremely biased and distorted, were rapidly growing.

Also, although Trump's style appeared to be unsubtle, he was actually using subtle *feminine* ways, guaranteed to distract and confuse the politicians, media experts and academics who only understand the 'game' as it used to be played – ie under the old and now abandoned, male-dominated, formal 'rules' and conventions. Thus his regular use of **Twitter**.

The business of governing - *bluff and counter-bluff*

As a much-vaunted businessman, Trump in 2016 was temporarily outsmarting the Khazari/Ashkenazi/Zionist financial elite – still predominantly *male* but, with their subtle, manipulative ways more characteristic of the universal *feminine*. The fact that this elite had long been running US Federal government affairs from behind the scenes was widely acknowledged in such expressions as **'JewSA'**.

Trump, by proposing massive Federal state spending on infrastructure projects, requiring huge borrowing on top of the US national debt, which already ran to trillions of dollars, was in effect **counter-bluffing** the Zionist Federal Reserve elite... who control the US money supply through a huge financial bluff of their own.

This challenge to their money power was testing whether they would dare, politically, to block his popular job-creating plans. It was a high risk strategy because his scheme would inevitably expand the US national/public debt – owed ultimately to *SCAB* – to an even higher, more 'unreal' level... given that mathematically, it can never be repaid, due to the interest already owed and regularly accruing.

SCAB still rules - but only just

And therein lies a clue as to why in 2016 bank interest rates fell so low – towards the previously unthinkable prospect of dropping to zero or even 'negative'. It was because *SCAB*, of which the US Federal Reserve is just the North American 'branch', would implode and collapse should the world's money and banking system fail.

So, *SCAB* pumped in vast amounts of electronic money, freshly created out of nothing, just to keep the old redundant system running a while longer – ie to buy time to sort out its next move. For since all major banks are technically insolvent, such a collapse is never far from occurring. And that would mark the end of any significant Zionist influence in world, as well as the demise of the Jewish State of Israel in Palestine. So, *SCAB* simply couldn't afford to let that happen... and Trump would have known it.

Further, *SCAB*'s confidence trick of *debt money* only works so long as enough people agree to participate in it. Once a significant minority realise that the world doesn't have to function that way, other workable options can appear on the menu. (One of which is in the radical yet practical, long term, visionary **One Humanity** proposal on page 304.)

In the last resort, if the Khazari/Ashkenazis' control over the USA Federal administration is threatened, there is always the *JFK option*. This refers to how President J F Kennedy was assassinated in 1963 soon after issuing Executive Order 11110, his first move towards replacing the *Federal Reserve*'s debt money with new *debt-free* money, out of *SCAB*'s control.

A more likely fate for Trump would be his 'death by a thousand cuts', to be inflicted by the various Zionists and their dependents and supporters in the administration and mass media, along with Republicans who know he is not really one of them. Undermined by the Zionist *neo-liberals*, he would be pushed unwillingly into committing the USA to expensive international conflicts by the political, war-mongering Zionist *neo-cons* who support Israel.

So, in 2016, in a smart tactical, divisive move, the fake macho Trump chose to favour the more *masculine*, aggressive, *neo-con*, **political Zionists** over the more subtle, *feminine*, manipulative, **financial Zionists** of the Federal Reserve, who see him as a rival and a threat to their prized position of control. And in later backing the neo-cons' push for Jerusalem to be recognised as the capital city of Israel, he pleased many Zionist/Jewish voters.

Then, in 2018, adopting a posture of commercial patriotism, he initiated a new wave of **trade warfare**, setting the USA against China, Iran and Europe. In doing so, he was serving the Khazari/Ashkenazis' global supremacy strategy of divide-and-rule. In the bigger picture, this move could be seen as a powerful disruptive, rebalancing force heralding and prompting, through Donald Trump, the demise of both *Papa Sate* and *Mama SCAB* – as redundant relics of a past era, to which there could be no return.

The 2016 *Brexit* trap

In deeply discontented societies, fragmented into rigid, polarised loyalties as a result of *descent era* inertia, any compromise proposals to resolve their differences tend to be rejected as unacceptable by the more committed 'us v. them' groups and individuals.

In the 2016 *Brexit* **referendum**, the Conservative government offered the UK electorate a stark 'either/or' choice between the UK **remaining** in the EU or **leaving** (the *Brexit* option)... despite the fact that the complexity of EU politics and economics is way beyond the comprehension of virtually all UK citizens.

The referendum call was primarily a strategic attempt to prevent the Conservative party fragmenting. It would also divert public attention away from more sinister, behind-the-scenes machinations.

Its effect was to divide the electorate into:

- *Leavers* (*Brexiteers*), favouring an aggressive, retro, *masculine*, independent, 'us v. them', nationalist, protectionist, pro-State UK, set against

- *Remainers*, favouring a closely united European, federal, 'family', as part of a more *feminine*, open, fluid, corporate, commercial, 'free trade' world of diminishing 'sovereign' State power.

The unspoken context was that *Remain* was the policy of the behind-the-scenes *A/K* financial Zionists. For their long term *global governance* strategy is to set up a world of just a few superstates, including the EU, all eventually to be merged into just one, over which they would reign supreme.

So Brexit, in effect, amounted to a trap, an artificial choice between the prospect of two kinds of *fascism*:

(A) A *descent era*, *masculine*, nation state **fascism** of a privileged elite, ruling over peasants, serfs and slaves, the status quo

sustained by the threat of **violent force** (ie *Papa State*'s way)...
OR
(B) A global, *SCAB*-controlled, superficially softer, *feminine* **fascism** of **debt slavery** to financial/commercial corporations, with profit-driven prison labour camps, subsidised by taxes.

'BREXIT: a False Choice' was a 2016 pre-*Referendum* article, posted on www.pathwayinitiatives.co.uk.
It rejected both officially offered options as two polar opposite *distractions* from much deeper and more significant issues. The situation represented the deadlock between *Papa State*'s *descent era* world of nationalistic patriotism, and *Mama SCAB*'s *descent era* world of global, greed-driven financial commerce.

The sane way to resolve such a complex conflict is to **transcend** it. That means to rise above it, gain an *overview*, and work on what unites rather than divides the opposed factions - ie their common humanity. Otherwise, at ground level, the only thing that unites them is their opposition to any proposed compromise solution.

Transcending, in practice, will inevitably involve systematically but sensitively exposing and then dismantling and replacing all redundant *descent era* institutions, including nation states, the global financial syndicate of central banks, commercial corporations and divisive supremacy religious organisations. The *One Humanity* project (page 304) is offered as a basic start-out model for a whole new and balanced way for 21st century humankind to be sharing this planet.

Where next for the faltering Zionists?

In 2016, the upsurge in *populism* in the USA, spearheaded by Trump, aroused a growing nationwide feeling of optimism. And apart from the obvious economic implications, that seemed at least partly to be based on a widespread instinctive sense that the controlling federal Zionist elite was at last beginning to falter.

Although in 2016 the words *Zionist* and *Jewish* were mostly substituted, at least in public, with coded terms such as *deep state* and *shadow government*, there was clearly a fierce ongoing battle for supremacy regarding *'Who rules?'* in the USA. And in this time of global awareness, neither side – not the the old, fading *Papa State* nor the ageing, toxic *Mama SCAB* – appeared convincing as candidates to represent humanity's future prospects. In Trump's coded language, 'the media' and 'the democrats' both meant the hostile, controlling **Zionists**.

The immediate prospect was an increasingly embittered, divided society, split in an infantile, 'us v. them', binary way between so-called 'leftist' liberals and 'hard right' authoritarians...
as if no other options existed. And the problem persisted because no radical, progressive alternative visions were being allowed time or space in the mainstream mass media, where
all thinking had to be contained 'in the box' (see *Chomsky's Exposé*, page 234).

Which meant that for a while longer the two-faced, double-dealing Zionist elite retained control: posing as BOTH 'leftist' *neo-liberal*, financially smart Democrats AND 'right wing', hawkish, warmongering, *neo-con* Republicans.

However, from the *Threshold* perspective, instead of people simply blaming the Jews for humanity's present troubles, it would be more useful to understand their unique evolutionary role in **undermining** the predominantly *masculine* status quo, and their **potentially significant destiny** (page 141).

American exceptionalism (2016)
This is an old bluff that resurfaced in 2016. It's a claim that 'America' is *exceptional* amongst humankind, and so has a self-granted license to ignore the rules and protocols that bind and limit all other peoples. From the *Threshold*, it can be seen as a double-disguised exercise by the the Khazari/Ashkenazi/Zionist elite, acting as Jews

while also wrapped in the USA flag – in effect, affirming the Jews' claim to be God's chosen people and therefore a special case.

This explains the unlimited funding of the US military on weaponry and personnel – in order to pursue the long term Khazari/Zionist *supremacy* agenda, which involves disempowering, one way or another, all rival nations and religions... while generating huge profits.

Proxy war politics 2016: *where all was not as it seemed*

Syria in 2016 continued to be a battleground where millions of ordinary people were the tragic victims of historic, Middle Eastern rivalries, magnified into a major geo-political proxy war, orchestrated and directed by invisible hands. This whole scenario can be seen as just one part of the Zionists' strategy of divide-and-rule, in pursuit of their long term agenda of global *supremacy*, while making a profit in the process.

And so, *descent* era ignorance, fear, powerlust, greed and deceit turned that already tragic situation into a major arena of treacherous **proxy war politics**, all based on the cynical, treacherous attitude, *'my enemy's enemy is my friend'*. Which raised such questions as:
- ***Who was funding and controlling which 'front' organisation?***
- ***Whose identity was being concealed through false flag operations?***
- ***Who was responsible for which strands of propaganda?*** *...and crucially,*
- ***Who profited most from the conflict?***

Although no experts dared say so in public – out of fear for their reputations or their lives – most knew that the main beneficiaries of the Syrian conflict were the financial **Zionist Jews** and, politically, the **Jewish State of Israel**. From the *Threshold* perspective, little unbiased dot-joining helps clarify a deliberately confused situation.

- **Financially**, vast fortunes were made through lending money to the combatants who were then sold expensive weaponry, later having to borrow heavily for reconstruction programmes.

- **Politically**, the Zionists continued to pursue their long term agenda of world domination, by cleverly manoeuvring certain states into mutually destructive conflicts – all part of a long term plan to steer humankind towards an intended, deadly climax, resulting in a much reduced world population.

- **Regarding religion**, the prophesied *End Time Apocalypse* – which looked increasingly like an artificially contrived piece of propaganda – thus appeared to be approaching, which would leave the Zionists in control on Earth.

Questions: Given all the diversionary tactics, propaganda, funding and false flag operations going on, were the news media ignoring the subtle Zionist involvement in keeping this war going? And if so, was their 'blindness' the result of naive ignorance, negligence or deliberate disingenuousness?

'Anti-establishment': flavour of the year 2016

'Anti-establishment' summarised the prevailing attitude in the populist politics of 2016 in the USA, as well as in various other countries. It implied a deep general resentment towards the so-called *establishment*, ie those involved in maintaining the status quo of authority, wealth, power and privilege, including the hidden Zionist puppeteers of the Federal government

The 2016 *anti-establishment* movement particularly featured populist, *'alt right'*, ultra-conservative nationalists, Christians and white supremacists, all broadly sharing an exclusive, divisive attitude, targeting various non-white or non-Christian groups. The related **gun lobby**, based on the Second Amendment right to bear arms, has also adopted an anti-establishment attitude towards the Zionist-controlled Federal government (page 282).

Consequently, on the *world stage* in 2016, these more primitive operators appeared to be 'winning'. Why? Because their directness, single-minded intensity, lack of scruples and rejection of any notion

269

of 'fair debate' or 'reasonableness' were proving more appealing to most voters than the compromised and weakened conventional politics of those who had already been rendered politically impotent before taking office.

As a result, westernised, 'democratised' cultures appeared to be allowing themselves to be dragged 'down' into primitive, instinctual, emotional ways of reacting to provocation, and so were regressing back into tribal/medieval ways of responding. But now, lots of modern weaponry and other technology was easily available to all.

Whistleblowers 2016

Whistleblowers continued to hasten the demise of *Papa State* and *Mama SCAB* in 2016 by revealing 'confidential' information and exposing various dark secrets of illegal activities. These mostly involved State officials, religious figures, financial and commercial business people, lawyers, celebrities and others who didn't want their behaviour disclosed. The many revelations continued to undermine whatever remaining faith people still had in previously respected institutions and eminent individuals.

Yet the courageous efforts of a few whistleblowers to shine some light of honesty and integrity into dark places, for the benefit of all humankind, tended to be rewarded with vindictive persecution by those whose wrongdoing they exposed. The ongoing, long running cases of Julian Assange and Edward Snowden, for example, have been well documented online, as have many others on Wikipedia and other websites.

They include many examples of unjust and excessive punishment by States and corporations when their reputations seemed threatened. Meanwhile, some whose wrongdoing was exposed escaped punishment.

A few areas of effective whistleblowing continue to be:
- **Financial fraud**, including market rigging and tax dodging on a vast scale by financial institutions which carried on regardless, treating the fines they were hit with as business expenses. Meanwhile their reps continued to appear as guest experts on news media shows.

270

Surveillance, privacy and data mongering

In 2016 there were already thousands of **data brokers** around the world, trading all kinds of data – whether for commercial or 'State security' purposes – some of it highly 'confidential',   harvested from individuals and organisations unaware of its unauthorised use. Also, most technical experts seemed to agree that **no ultimate *data security* solutions are possible**. Why? Because the well paid creators of the smart computer algorithms used by various elites are always a step or two ahead of commercial 'security' software and of the official regulators.

Superficially, this was about some of the complex, world-changing effects of rapidly evolving digital technology. But on another level, it was about the ongoing, corrupt, divisive ways of *Papa State* and *Mama SCAB*, two pathological relics from the dark days of the *descent* era.

Their lust for dominance and control through *IFDR (**i**gnorance, **f**ear, **d**ivide and **r**ule)* have significantly boosted the digital revolution. Which has enabled vast amounts of information, known as **big data**, to be captured, stored and processed quickly and cheaply... regardless of how it has been sourced and whose lives might be adversely affected by its circulation.

The only viable solution to this man-made problem is for humankind collectively to grow up and begin replacing the current redundant ethos of powerless politics, greed-and-fear-driven economics and supremacy religions. That will involve carefully and thoroughly dismantling the status quo, and making a fresh start in redesigning and cultivating a new and more sane world - perhaps like the *One Humanity* project envisioned on page 304.Meanwhile, in 2016 there were also...

- Sports scandals, including:
- **doping** of athletes, given the common, primitive, child-like craving to be a 'winner',
- **match-fixing** for financial gain, in various sports, through corrupt gambling systems,
- **sexual abuse** and **bullying** by coaches and trainers.

Anti-semitism **UK 2016**: the old trick was still working

In 2016, the UK government was persuaded by supporters of the International Holocaust Remembrance Alliance to propose legislation establishing a legal definition of so-called '*anti-semitism*', in order to make it a more easily punishable offence. That token gesture by the government, officially to discourage 'hate crime', revealed how submissive and weak the UK state had become in complying with the demands of its invisible Zionist controllers.

In 2018, the IHMA tried to railroad the UK Labour Party into adopting certain extremely restrictive rules specifying what its members should not be allowed to say in public about Jews and Israel. That was despite the fact that these proposals had already been thoroughly discredited in 2016 by an eminent English barrister, who dismissed them as inconsistent and carrying no legal or other significant authority. They were also rejected by Jewish anti-Zionist groups who did not want their ancient religion tainted with the murky politics of territorial nationalism and nation statehood.

However, the long-running Zionist/Jewish bluff was clearly still working, as evidenced in the persistent pestering and nagging by loyal supporters of the Zionist cause **for special, privileged treatment,** and especially protection from criticism. Those supporters included certain MPs whose careers depended on Jewish support.

Whatever next?

By the end of 2016 various warning signs were visible for all who chose to read them with an open mind. So, a crucial question remained unspoken: *How can humankind move beyond its repetitive cycles of wars and economic boom/bust, problems largely due to* **imbalances** *between its redundant* **descent era masculine** *and* **descent era feminine** *aspects.?*

Evidently there was a concerted Zionist strategy being pursued worldwide, which can now be understood in its greater evolutionary context (page 141). But by 2016, *SCAB*'s global, greed-driven money scam had grown out of control, leaving the world's financial system close to collapsing. And so, with the Zionists and others 'playing for time' in anticipation of major changes, a crucial tipping point was evidently imminent.

All the reported and unreported fear, lying, deceiving and hostility revealed in 2016 served as a kind of mirror, starkly reflecting back at humanity an undeniably ugly self-image... although with notable exceptions. This broadly showed the kind of irresponsible, immature leaderships – political, economic, religious and scientific, that were being allowed to carry on re-creating and deepening the troubles already being experienced all over the planet.

Which raises the question: *How much of this was the result of a deliberate, undermining and sabotaging strategy, given the long term biblical and historical agendas of the Hebrew Jews and Khazari Zionists?* But then that has to be viewed in the context of their counterbalancing, sabotaging, evolutionary role, as described earlier. Which raises the whole issue out of the realm of worldly blame, counter-blame and denial. (see next chapter)

By 2016, was it too late to rescue the situation, given how deeply the collective mind of humanity had been indoctrinated over centuries by *Papa State*'s war-mongering and *Mama SCAB*'s money-trickery? For these two were still able to control the world's mass media, including all the complicit news media professionals. And that was making it virtually impossible for any 'out of the box' perspectives to be aired or circulated on a mass scale.

Humanity was thus left a choice of two main options to consider, in anticipation of the old order eventually collapsing. One was (and still is) to allow even worse, ie more extreme and unbalanced, regimes to take over an already fragmented world... OR, alternatively, start connecting up and preparing the ground for a radically different, more balanced, sane and just world, perhaps something like the radical yet practical *One Humanity* vision).

Separate Issues, a Common Thread

A few extra examples of viewing, from the *Threshold* perspective,
the complex world of everyday life on Earth in the 21st century.

Mass Migrations: from *Poorland* to *Richland*
What are the real factors behind this resolvable problem?

If you were a devious political manipulator, set on destabilising all
nation states, apart from your own, there's one policy that's
guaranteed to have that effect. It would be to provoke and
encourage mass migrations from the world's poorest and most
troubled places to the world's most materially privileged societies.

In Western Europe a fast-growing *population* crisis has now reached
a level that's alarming citizens and governments. It's a crisis that
highlights just about every political, economic, social and ecological
failing in the present world set-up, raising profound questions about
humankind's future on this planet. It's the complicated, deadlocked
mass migration problem.

The callous response of most national leaderships involved in the
current migration crisis has been to argue about the **numbers** of
migrants here or there or on the move. This diverts attention away
from the human suffering involved, and from the politicians'
responsibilities and failings, as they criticise one another and try to
seal national borders.

As for the 'ordinary' inhabitants of the receiving countries - as has
already been suggested, people's natural feelings of compassion for
others who are suffering, can be distorted by the perceived threat to
their own lives. They then tend to resort to a hostile, defensive,
suspicious, '*us v. them*' attitude towards those from outside their
familiar social circle, which is politically easy to exploit.

For the numerical majority within most countries today, in this increasingly globalised world, are deprived of an education that would enable them to question their own and other people's attitudes and assumptions. Each society and culture installs mental programming in its members before they're old enough to realise how they're being indoctrinated. This is not easy to overcome.

Therefore, many citizens haven't yet been able to form an objective overview of the bigger picture, ie the context within which specific problems occur... like surges in **immigration**. And so, migration has become a big, emotionally charged issue that's easily exploitable by populist politicians.

Homeless and stateless human beings, labelled as 'migrants', are thus treated like cheap, expendable gambling chips in inter-national 'games' of politics. Each government tries to dump the problem somewhere else rather than admit that they're all being cleverly manipulated and played off against one another.

A different view of the 'problem'

Instead of obsessively focusing on the *details*, ie the numbers, categories and destinations of these people on the move, the *migrants*, it is possible to view the whole process in a simple, natural scientific way. The question then is who *naturally gravitates* towards what, and why.

The ongoing transition from a cosmic era of *descent into matter* to one of *ascent out of matter* is resulting in an increasing fluidity and a dissolving of previously rigid, attitudes, habits, traditions, institutions, barriers and borders. This shift is also evidenced in a changing balance of influence in the world: away from the predominance of the universal *masculine* towards the universal *feminine*.

In that broad context, aided by various fast-evolving technologies, the free flow of ideas, people and goods around the planet continues to accelerate. And that's part of the universal tendency in the cosmos towards a state of **equilibrium** between the polar opposite forces of expanding *levity* (as the *universal feminine*) and contracting *gravity* (as the *masculine*).

The universal force of *gravity* draws matter 'inward' towards centres of greater density. (A useful image is that of scattered iron filings drawn, in a clear 'positive/negative' pattern, by the polarised field of a magnet.) Living creatures that are *deficient* in what they need for a basic, productive life, naturally *gravitate* towards places where they sense they can satisfy their basic needs. That is **natural migration**, regardless of the social or political implications.

So, given the currently increasing imbalance around the world, regarding wealth and poverty, in this major re-balancing process the overall migratory flow is bound to increase. And that's despite the walls and razor wire fences being erected, and the border patrols and slum refugee camps being set up here and there.

What does history teach about migrations?
The current migration crisis can be seen as a kind of payback time for those wealthier nations whose ancestors once plundered other people's homelands (ie it's *karma, consequences, chickens coming home to roost* etc).

That payback especially applies to the states of Western Europe and North America, who have been living off the proceeds ever since. (Although the acquired wealth has not been distributed in equitable ways within their own societies.)

For this aspect of western history has not been forgotten or ignored by the descendants of the victims, many of whom are now migrating to reclaim some of that stolen wealth – in the form of social, educational and employment opportunities. Meanwhile, **the mass media are required by their financier-controllers to focus only on the superficial symptoms** and not delve into the historic and hidden causes of the current worldwide inequalities and injustices.

Politicians blame 'war', 'corruption' and 'oppressive regimes' for causing poverty and therefore refugees. And they use *people traffickers*, as convenient scapegoats. However, were the root problems being addressed, there would be no fearful, ragged refugees, and no people trafficking business.

The result has been a general avoidance of responsibility for the plight of millions of human beings around the world, forced to live in dire **deficiency** while others live way in **excess** of their real, natural needs. The huge number of non-governmental organisations (NGOs) called *'charities'* is an indicator of the scale of this problem.

What's the solution?

The solution is simple. Extremely simple. In broad principle: address what prompts and motivates the migration. The motivation of people to leave their homes, in search of a better life as *immigrants,* often in a distant country, would significantly diminish if their plundered, polluted, neglected homeland environments were restored back into healthy, productive places... and if they were educated such that they could choose leaders who do not ambitiously crave power and wealth for themselves.

Such a solution would also require the current descendants and beneficiaries of the plunderers to take responsibility for the deeds of their ancestors, and to commit to making the necessary reparations. Which would again require a more mature and balanced attitude to the whole question of leadership.

The word *migrant* would then no longer be a pejorative term. And humanity – now more mature – would be able to think globally and act locally.

So, from the *Threshold* perspective, a rational, practical solution of the world's fast-growing 'migration problem' is possible, once a small but significant proportion of the **one human species** evolves towards thinking and behaving in more mature and balanced ways. For it's not a 'law of nature' that humans have to allow themselves to be kept ignorant, divided and ruled, and be herded into rival, competing teams, whether religious, national, local, ethnic or economic.

Who's been manipulating this and other such sick situations? is a question dealt with elsewhere in this work, for example, regarding the **depopulation agenda** (page 214).

The long term solution? A new start

As outlined in the **One Humanity** chapter, there is a sane and viable long term solution to humankind's *migration* and other related problems. In simple terms, it involves systematically and sensitively **replacing all divisive *descent* era institutions**, including nation states, supremacy-preaching religious organisations and the global central banking syndicate, *SCAB*, which is responsible for the whole toxic 'debt money' scam.

In their place would be set up the robust beginnings of a **decentralised** global system of autonomous self-governing regions and communities. These would be **united by the simple, explicitly shared aim of eliminating all unnecessary human need** and, in parallel, all self-indulgent lifestyles excessive to the natural human need for a decent, fulfilling life, until those prior human needs are met.

Also, all significant exchanging and trading would be transparent via a universally accessible *blockchain* system, bringing openness, simplicity, transparency and total accountability.

This offers a more inspiring version of **globalisation** than the current greed-driven, financial/commercial version. And although many would regard it as an impossible non-starter in what they take to be the 'real world', that assessment only applies while a critical proportion of humankind continues to allow itself to be indoctrinated and conned by corrupt elites in ways already described.

And all the while, behind the *mass migration* crisis, there persists a major unresolved, ongoing, worldwide problem... in one word, **poverty**

Poverty: unnecessary deprivation

The word *poverty* implies an inability to afford to buy the necessities for a basic, broadly acceptable standard of living, which in turn implies a life of *deficiency*. The causes and circumstances of poverty obviously vary widely according to place and time.

The World Bank, for its own purposes, tried to quantify poverty by defining it in numbers, thereby de-humanising it. The Bank is one part of the privately owned, profit-driven, global syndicate of central and arch-banks, *SCAB*. In true *SCAB* style, in the late 20th century, it attempted to turn poverty into an objective, sterile, mathematical and financial statistic, instead of treating it as an issue of collective human responsibility and compassion.

Based on some of its own statistics from the world's poorest countries, the World Bank came up with its so-called **'poverty line'** – set at just one dollar a day per person, at that time approximately the cost of a can of fizzy drink. Which implied that if your income was more than $1 a day, you were not poor.

It did make a token concession that *"There are many non-monetary indicators— on education, health, sanitation, water, electricity, etc — that are extremely important for understanding the many dimensions of poverty that people experience."* But its global *poverty line* does not currently take these multiple dimensions of poverty into account.

The figure was much disputed, and has since then been slightly raised. There have also been other attempts, for example, to define *absolute, extreme* and *relative poverty*.

The intention of setting such a low level **poverty line** was obviously to artificially reduce the perceived amount of real suffering going on in the world as a result of severe deprivation. For that conveniently lessens the moral obligation on national governments to spend money alleviating the problem, either in their own countries or as *donor* states.

The World Bank, meanwhile, exhorts 'countries' to be more inclusive, to do right by poor people in words that sound almost noble... ie the same old *SCAB doublespeak*.

From the *Threshold* perspective, the problem behind all the politicking about poverty is a range of distorted and confused attitudes towards deprived people. And that's due to the continuing existence of those corrupt and divisive set-ups, the *nation state* protection racket and *SCAB*'s global 'debt money' scam, supported by certain religious organisations... and despite the efforts of various well-intentioned but politically impotent *charities*.

So, the 'problem' looks like persisting until a small but significant proportion of humankind no longer supports the present status quo, and is instead ready to inspire others to unite in dismantling the present set-up... so as to replace it with a co-ordinated global/local and genuinely non-partisan system along the *One Humanity* guidelines.

Terrorism: an all-purpose label?

Terrorism is a label that's now widely applied to the efforts of a wide range of people who rebel against the status quo in a variety of ways, mostly violent. However, some of those labelled as terrorists see themselves as, for example:
- *freedom fighters* for independence from an unwelcome occupying force, or
- *insurgents* or *separatists* seeking independence from an oppressive regime, or
- *agents of God*, punishing those who don't share their particular belief system.

In practice, terrorism usually means a deadly mixture of a primitive, '*us v. them*' mentality, armed with all kinds of weaponry, and modern digital communications equipment.

It can also be understood as a symptom of a world artificially divided into some 200 so-called *nations*, each dominated and 'protected' by an elite gang controlling the apparatus of political power, known as 'the *State*'. And because of the mutual rivalries and enmities state leaderships need in order to justify their privileged positions, these nation states are easily divided and ruled by the invisible global financial syndicate, *SCAB*, that controls the world's supply of money... on which they all currently depend.

All of which points to a hidden agenda behind its funding and supporting of disruptive elements all over the world and their activities, including *terrorism* and *false flag* operations.

There are various levels on which the phenomenon called *terrorism* can be investigated. For example, the article, *'How, in the 21st century, do young men become dedicated killers and torturers?'* on the website www.pathwayinitiatives.co.uk looks at how the fiery discontent, especially in young men, due mainly to a potent combination of sexual frustration and idealistic religious fervour, continues to be exploited by military and religious leaderships worldwide.

The *Threshold* perspective reveals the basic working principles of how the living cosmos functions, and how that knowledge can add light and focus to humanity's many problems.

It can also can give a very long term view on terrorism. For as the cosmos tends naturally towards re-establishing a state of *equilibrium* between its two polar opposite cosmic forces (page 38), *terrorism* can be understood as that rebalancing process painfully working itself out in particularly unbalanced situations. This kind of *overview* and *insight* – rather than hyped up, partisan, self-interested reacting by 'the authorities' –- could help humankind begin to heal itself of this self-destructive symptom.

Guns and Money in the USA

In the USA, mass shootings occurred amidst all the other ongoing gun crime.

Yet there's still the familiar deadlock preventing any significant progress towards effective gun control legislation. Not only is there disagreement and conflict between the Federal administration and individual states, but also among the governments of different states. If you wanted to set up a situation of political paralysis, you couldn't do much better than this.

How has it come about? It's happening because '**ambivalence rules**'. What does that mean?

It means that two opposite attitudes towards guns and human rights simultaneously govern life in the USA. As a consequence, the population is subjected to continuing fierce arguments between two *polarised* camps. And that reflects a fundamental polarity in humankind as a whole, evidenced in the fearful, angry and confused population of America.

So, to gain a clearer picture of the forces, factors and dynamics involved in this seemingly unresolvable duel, the simplest method is to start from ground level and work upwards.

At ground level

At ground level there's widespread fear, insecurity and sense of vulnerability that comes from from living in a society saturated with guns. These symbols of personal power, are glorified in films, video games, adverts and print. All of which tends to prompt an urge to own and be ready to use a gun to defend oneself and one's family against any kind of threat.

Set against this is the unavoidable realisation that the proliferation of guns, especially into the hands of immature, irresponsible, extremist and mentally unstable individuals, increases the risk of being shot - whether as a member of the general public or as a targeted individual.

And yet one of the proposed 'solutions' to the problem of 'too many guns, too many shootings' is to have yet more guns.

The social context of all this is an ethos of hyped-up competitive rivalry. People are set against one another in two basic ways:

(1) vulnerable, insecure **individuals** are programmed to regard other people in a child-like way as rivals in a rigged, competitive, fear-and-greed-driven '**economy**'.

(2) rival **groups** are cross-divided according to class, wealth, ethnicity, religion, nationality etc by clever manipulators, provoking a hostile 'us v. them' attitude in the 'child' within each adult.

In this way populations can be intimidated, herded and exploited, and in the process become demoralised and hyper-stressed. At the same time many are also being enticed ever deeper into debt through the offer of easy, instant credit. All of which leaves them feeling powerless and craving various compensatory substitutes for the lack of any deep fulfilment in their lives. There are, of course, exceptions to this norm.

One level up - the Federal government and the lobbyists

Hovering above the lower stratum of fear and greed-driven rivalry floats the well-funded and professionally organised '**gun lobby**', representing a common attitude towards gun ownership shared by many very different people. It feeds off the fragile *bravado* that comes from carrying a gun, a bravado that masks the underlying fear. And that tends to result in a self-centred, desensitised devaluing of lives outside one's circle of 'our people'.

The essence of the 'pro-guns' message is *defiance* against any who threaten to disempower Americans by restricting their freedom to bear arms in order to defend themselves. And that defiance is primarily directed against the Federal administration whose aim is perceived to be the disarming of citizens in order to disempower them.

The lobbyists skilfully harness that collective attitude and will power, and focus it in ways that will influence government policy, since they represent a significant number of voters.

'**Pro-guns**' supporters tend to justify their position mainly by referring to:
(a) the Second Amendment to the Constitution, affirming the right to bear arms, and
(b) the dubious arguments that *'It's people who kill each other, not guns'*, and *'Good people with guns can prevent bad people with guns doing harm'*.

By contrast, the cynical élitists might well think: *'Give enough guns to immature, discontented people, and they'll soon start shooting each other'*... (like a collective version of the old saying, *'Give him enough rope and he'll hang himself.'*)

Next, to understand who is controlling the Federal authorities from behind the scenes, it's necessary to go up another level.

Second level up - the hidden controllers of the Federal government

The existence of a (more or less) covert controlling élite has already been presented in this work. That control is not only of the world's money supply but of the media and entertainment industries. And much more. So they are able to control what most Americans consume in the way of news, films, TV programmes, advertising etc... This enables the minds of the American people to be programmed and influenced in ways that suit the controllers' agenda.

Throughout the whole 'gun control' battle, this dedicated and well organised global financial enterprise has been the huge, unmentioned '**elephant in the room**'. It has managed this because most ordinary people find it hard to comprehend such a warped, calculating and determined mentality that craves total social control through gun control but at the same time is willing to compromise, since there are vast profits to be made from the guns and weaponry industry. The resulting death, suffering and destruction also serve the dark Zionist agenda.

There are, of course, some who stand against the gun culture and challenge those they see as responsible. So, to make sense of the ideological battle between the double-dealing controllers and those determined to defy them at whatever cost, it's necessary to rise above this level.

Third level up - the universal *masculine* and *feminine* at work

Numerous examples of the universal *masculine* and *feminine* influences have already been given in this work. So, from this more 'elevated' perspective, a clear *polarity* can be detected: the *gun-toting* mentality is broadly an expression of humanity's **masculine** aspect, whereas the craving for *control* is more a characteristic of humanity's distorted **feminine** aspect from an earlier, darker era.

Fourth level up - primal *polarity*

This perspective enables a basic grasp of the cosmic evolutionary process, ie the primal *polarity* of the cosmos, which can be appreciated in the dynamic, rhythmical alternating of **contraction** and **expansion**. And the two corresponding forces of this universal pulsating are **gravity** and **levity**, which find expression in the natural world as the universal **masculine** and **feminine**.

Presently, the cosmos is in the early stages of **transition** from an era of *contraction*, ie the '*descent into matter*', to one of *expansion*, an '*ascent out of matter*'. These eras are explained on page 45.

As one of the two forces temporarily prevails over the other, so its qualities predominate, although partly counterbalanced by those of the opposite force, since the cosmos naturally tends towards an *equilibrium* state. *Therefore,* all the while, the ever-changing dynamic between the two universal forces is the background to the strains and stresses humanity collectively experiences between its *masculine* and *feminine* aspects.

Which links back to the basic *polarity* that characterises the 'gun control' dispute, and to the realisation of how little meaningful communication there is between people speaking about the same situation, but from different levels with different perspectives. And so there's the familiar deadlock, with the *pro-guns* people grimly refusing at any cost to submit and allow the 'control freak' *Feds* to disempower them, as they see it.

The result is ever more shooting massacres, increasingly by immature, unbalanced, discontented individuals. And meanwhile, both sides speak only in coded language, so that what the gun control battle is really all about remains obscured, as does the deeper psychology of the gun mentality and the gun-promoting world.

However, from the *Threshold* perspective, a deeper understanding and an appreciation of the factors involved at the different levels of this challenging situation are possible, and practical ways of resolving it <u>can</u> be worked out. But they require millions of ordinary citizens to start working out how to grow out of the disempowered *'ground level'* mindset described earlier.
Which implies that changing deeply ingrained habits and ways of thinking is not going to be easy or quick. But the alternative options look far worse.

Upbringing and Education: for what kind of a life?

This whole subject is far too big to address in any detail in this particular book. However, the *Threshold* perspective on the upbringing and education of young human beings can be briefly summarised.

A fundamental principle is that <u>children are not the **property** of their parents or their society</u>, despite many cultural traditions, born out of an overriding need to survive one way or another. It's the **responsibility** of adults to **protect** the children in their care, while **preparing them to live as fulfilling a life as possible**, until the young are able to take care of themselves.

To *'e-ducate'* means, literally, to 'lead out', ie from a state of unpreparedness into a state of readiness for whatever roles and responsibilities might be appropriate in this life. What kind of preparation and knowledge an 'appropriate education' should consist of, and what qualifies a person to be an educator, have long been debated. Likewise the question of when so-called 'teaching' is more a form of indoctrination.

A vital question for the members of any society is to ask whether its attempts at education prepare young individuals:
(a) for a healthy, useful and fulfilling life, OR
(b) merely to become subservient, compliant subjects of the State, OR
(c) to be employable as servile, exploitable employees of commercial, greed-driven set-ups.
(In between those alternatives, *not-for-profit* organisations operating within selfish greed-driven societies represent a range of compromised work situations.)

Competing schools that set their own pupils in rivalry against one another by dividing them into competing groups are reinforcing their society's *divide and rule* ethos. This enables the society's authorities to maintain their dominant status by keeping the rest of the population preoccupied with competing against one another, ie treating other citizens as rivals or as enemies when differences of religion, nationality, ethnicity, wealth or class are hyped up.

Normally, only in times of crisis is the unity and common interest of citizens called upon to support the status quo, and especially the leadership of the existing ruling elite, its dependents and its puppet government politicians.

The *Threshold* perspective on education highlights the real natural needs of each individual life in relation to the needs of the wider environment - in effect, the context of each life.
Certain crucial questions then arise, such as...

Why are *children* not taught such vital basic **life skills** as
    First Aid,
        Survival and coping strategies,
            Self-defence (physical and psychological)
            and the all-important mental skill
                How to question everything?

From the *Threshold* perspective, the answer is simple. These and other 'essential for life' subjects are not taught in most schools or by many parents because:

(a) many teachers and parents themselves lack these skills, and crucially,

(b) **this kind of knowledge is empowering**... implying a potential threat to the status quo.

That is to say, it would give people, individually and collectively, the self-confidence to question and then to start radically adapting the present status quo of power, wealth, authority and privilege in their societies towards more balanced, just and healthy set-ups... instead of complying with their present divide-and-rule regimes.

There are always some exceptions, but in general it's normal for parents and teachers to conform to the status quo. Consequently, they too will tend to neglect and avoid addressing the real needs of the young people for whose education and upbringing they are responsible.

Keeping 'the masses' ignorant of vital knowledge and thus fearful, distracted, and pre-occupied with many other matters helps ruling elites to retain their privileged positions of dominance and control. For although they too may lack the powerful *Threshold* knowledge, they will have learned certain effective techniques for staying in charge and in control.

So, there are many as yet unanswered questions regarding the responsibilities of those who take on the role of *teachers* of the young, questions such as, **What kind of adults are they preparing their pupils and students to be, as active participants in this evolving world?**

That implies a whole lot more than merely training them to jump successfully through a series of examination hoops, in order to prove themselves 'acceptable' to the decaying and disintegrating, *descent* era world of *Papa State* and *Mama SCAB*, backed up by certain supremacy-seeking religious organisations.

Also, in order to clear minds and start making the necessary radical changes, a lot of **unlearning** of misleading, unnecessary and disempowering information will be necessary.
So, recognising all that trickery, and then developing and teaching ways of countering it, are a vital part of being an educator, as humankind moves through the current *transition* phase.

A more open approach to the whole subject of **ageing**, **death** and **dying** would likewise be empowering and develop compassion and practicality, replacing the fear and avoidance that result from neglecting the subject because of ignorance and the consequent unease.

One visible effect of the cosmic shift from an era of *descent* to one of *ascent* has been an early 21st century shift in UK government *education* policy. It has moved away from the *masculine* **uniformity** of a State education system towards the more *feminine* **diversity** of schooling and teaching practices.

However, the influence of the *masculine*-dominated *descent* era is still present in the UK National Curriculum with its grid of Levels and Attainment Targets, and league tables for schools. This competitive element serves to divide and rule the education system. There is also competition between parents, who go to great lengths to obtain a place for their children in a 'good' school. Meanwhile, students who misbehave may be excluded or expelled, due to a school's concern for examination results and consequent position in the league table.

One aspect of education over which children and young people can exercise some creative power is the rapidly evolving world of *digital technology*. But, as well as offering many benefits through access to this attractive and burgeoning world, those behind it also have access to the child, whose naïvety and vulnerability can be callously exploited both for financial profit and for other malevolent purposes.

Another trend has been the increasing **commercialisation** of education, especially the business of sponsorship and deals for exclusively supplying goods and services to schools.
A further example is the business of buying and selling educational course work and qualifications. This has become a growth industry, despite the sophisticated detective software of universities and examination systems... as divide-and-rule competition is generally being hyped up by ruling elites, state and commercial, for their own purposes.

Which is very much connected to the hyping up of *competitive sport* in the mass media.

Sport: more than games of *winners* and *losers*

Most sports, like ceremonies and rituals which celebrate human diversity, can be harmless, enjoyable and sometimes inspiring activities, and serve as safe substitutes for real conflict. Many sports have enabled the harmonious integration of people from many diverse ethnic groups, nationalities and religions... in ways that words never could.

But intense rivalry and competitiveness, however friendly on the surface, can be harnessed by provocative, divisive interests and degenerate, flipping over into a war-waging mentality, or be exploited by commercial and financial interests into excessive spending and debt.

The word **com-petition** means *'together seeking'*, so **sport** can work on at least two distinct levels. The **adult** way is to engage in sporting competition because you enjoy testing your limits of skill, strength, stamina etc with the mutual cooperation of opponents who are similarly seeking to test their limits. Here, winning or losing a contest is of little significance, for you *gain* by participating wholeheartedly, doing your best and learning valuable lessons, while respecting the corresponding motives of your opponents.

The **child-like** way is to be driven by an overwhelming desire to be a 'winner', to be applauded, to be awarded prizes and be acknowledged as *superior* to others – usually in the context of some kind of *pecking order*. A basic *polarity* to be found in all competitive sport is that between the two polar opposite modes, *contraction* as **defence** and *expansion* as **attack**.

The *polarity* of the universal *masculine* and *feminine* is illustrated in the lucrative business of professional football. While the fanatically supported English Premier League of privately owned clubs is the most **commercially** successful in the world – ie at making money, *Mama SCAB*'s speciality – the English national team, intended to be the pride of *Papa State*, relies on **patriotic fervour** for support.

During recent international athletics events, commentators from the BBC, a State propaganda organisation, kept repeating over and over the key expression, '*Team GB*'. This is evidently intended to stir up, in a feelgood fun way, a measure of old-style, *descent era*, patriotic, jingoistic, flag-waving fervour... in the hope of reviving *Papa State*'s fortunes.

Which is essentially what's behind the various cases of state-sponsored doping of athletes competing at the Olympic Games. **It's the primitive, childhood fantasy craving to be a 'winner' or at least to be in a winning team**.

This desire is easily exploited for darker purposes by *Mama SCAB*, who watches contentedly as the 'children' enthusiastically compete for prizes and medals, wrapping themselves in their national team flags... encouraged all the way by *Papa State*. For while they're preoccupied with all that rivalry, they and the millions of spectators worldwide pose no threat to the status quo of wealth, power and privilege in the world.

The general **feminisation** process has also become very apparent, for example, in the way, sportsmen now hug and embrace one another in celebrating a successful outcome of one sort or another, or after a hard fought contest as opponents.

Corruption: 1001 varieties, one pattern

Corruption, in its many forms, is an unmistakeable *symptom* of a distorted and dysfunctional society, in need of some deep healing and radical reform. In simple terms, it's typically the result one type of social system and culture, representing a certain mentality, being imposed on people with a very different mentality and cultural background.

When a centralised, regimented, industrial kind of social structure - ie one dominated by the qualities of the universal *masculine* - is imposed on a more organic, traditional, family or tribal kind of system, more in accordance with the universal *feminine*, the incompatibilities between the two systems tend to result in behaviours, labelled '**corruption**' in modern parlance. Those who have to accommodate themselves to alien, laws, rules and regulations may adopt ingenious ways to bypass these restrictions on their ambitions and traditions. What are survival strategies to one culture may be labelled '**corruption**' by another.

Forms of corruption include various kinds of cheating, bribery, extortion, embezzlement, nepotism and tax evasion. These have always been present in so-called *capitalist* economies because of the inhumane *descent era* values promoted by *Papa State* and *Mama SCAB*.

States demand submissive, orderly, loyal obedience from the masses. The money-mongers keep people addicted to and endlessly competing for scraps of *SCAB*'s debt money. And the wealthy and privileged, in general, indulge in callously selfish, arrogant, greedy behaviour.

So, the *corruption* problem can't really be sorted out until humankind realises it no longer needs *Papa* and *Mama* running the show and indoctrinating people with their toxic values.

The 'race' fallacy: 21st century *divide-and-rule*

Long periods of shifting land masses and the consequent migrating and intermixing of diverse groups of humans on Earth have resulted in a multicultural, globalised, 21st century world, especially in the USA and Western Europe. So, the idea of **races** today as pure, authentic, unique, ancient strands of the human species is a meaningless fallacy, despite some sharing of physical features, language, culture, ancestry and ethnicity.

Politically, however, the idea of races has long proved very useful for those who seek to divide and rule by setting different human groups against one another, thereby turning beneficial, inclusive *diversity* into toxic, exclusive hostility. And that, broadly, has characterised the pathologically *descent era*, **identity politics** (page 228) in which such groups are misled and provoked into '**us v. them**' conflict, as enemies or allies, in various primitive, immature and prejudiced ways.

One common method of exploiting people's already existing discontent has been to focus on certain superficial, over-simplistic distinctions. For example, by divisively labelling people as '**white**' or '**black**', when evidently there's a continuous range of lighter and darker skin colouring, prejudiced attitudes of 'our' *superiority* and 'their' *inferiority* can be stirred up.

But such behaviour, whatever the particular differences in question, can now be seen as variations of the psycho-pathological condition **Addictive Superiority Syndrome** (page 89).

However, in an increasingly globalised and intermixed world, the whole notion of *race*, *racist* and *racism* are becoming obsolete and irrelevant, and will eventually fade away.

What next? A choice: transcend or degenerate

As this work has shown, behind the superficial worldly changes going on, there are more subtle and profound developments happening. For example, humanity's *feminine* aspect, across the whole gender spectrum, is growing increasingly influential, enabling women especially to respond with more assurance to the ups and downs of these turbulent times.

No longer accepting domination by men as normal or natural, women will increasingly be able to abandon many of the devious and subtle techniques they've long found it necessary to use in order to counteract that crude imbalance of power.

In the meantime, some assertive women, driven by worldly ambitions to 'succeed', continue to imitate the ways of 'successful' *descent era* men, but with some added *female* subtlety. At the same time many men are finding it difficult to free themselves from the grip of old *descent* era habits.

Yet there are some signs of a loosening up and abandoning of old redundant ways, so that eventually, humans of all gender types will be able to live more balanced, emotionally stable and fulfilling lives.

But this *transition* phase is not going to be a quick and easy or a comfortable process. Plenty of resistance is to be expected. Much sensitivity, tolerance, persistence and patience will be required to respond to the inevitable relapsing and regressing into old ways.

For example, seeds of mistrust can easily be sown by gossip, rumour, sabotage and provocation, resulting in discouragement, anger, cynicism and conflict. Here the empowering *overview* and *insight* of the all-inclusive *Threshold* perspective can be a source of inner strength and balance in counteracting those regressive tendencies.

Next, the continuing influence of certain ancient traditional institutions, including **secret societies** and their subtle but significant role in an ever-evolving world. The influence, for good or evil, of these hidden networks, these 'worlds within worlds', is significant since at their highest levels they are dealing with timeless 'power knowledge' which can both inspire and corrupt those who acquire a taste for it.

The *Esoteric/Occult* Dimension

Esoteric/occult thinking tends to span what are, by earthly standards, immeasurably long timescales, and is normally more concerned with the non-physical dimensions of our being than with the worldly, personal lives and circumstances of individuals.

Esoteric means *inner* or *'known to just a few'*, whereas **exoteric** means *outer* and *accessible*.
Occult means *hidden* or mysterious – in astronomy, it refers to hidden planets.

Two thresholds

In that context, at least two main thresholds can be discerned. The **esoteric** *threshold* is said to exist between earthly, physical life and the non-material 'spiritual' world. It's where, after your physical death, you are confronted by *'the dweller at the threshold'* who requires you to accept responsibility for all your deeds in your last incarnation, and thereby be cleansed.

The **exoteric** *threshold* is the border zone between the *physical-material* and the *pre-physical* realms. Accessible at a certain elevated level of consciousness, it enables an all-embracing *overview* of this world and some penetrating *insight* into whatever is being focused on. It thus provides a uniquely all-inclusive, two-way perspective: outwards/inwards, radiating/focusing, contracting/expanding – enhancing awareness of both the bigger cosmic picture and the motivating forces at the heart/core/centre of any situation.

It also reveals how how all the various dimensions are inter-related, and clarifies the essential nature of *good* and *evil* (page 34).

To recap briefly, the three universal *Threshold* principles – *consciousness, polarity* and *resonance* – apply on all levels of existence. And that includes the subtle, fluid, intermediate realm of the pre-physical *aether/quintessence/quantum vacuum* which exists in between:

(a) *universal consciousness*, of which each human being is an individual *focal point*, and (b) the *physical-material* world that human beings experience while in physical form.

To deny the existence of that intermediate level of being would be like denying the existence of the radio waves that transmit information through the space you physically occupy... simply because you cannot detect them without the aid of special equipment that can be tuned to *resonate* at the appropriate frequency and 'read' them.

Reincarnation

The doctrine of **reincarnation** is based on an assumption that each person continues to exist beyond physical death, as a conscious, non-physical individual being, preparing for its next physical birth. In some traditions this dimension of a person's being is called the *soul*, a non-physical entity which progresses through a succession of earthly lifetimes in a long process of evolving towards a 'higher', more refined state of being.

Regarding reincarnation, no totally objective physical proof or disproof is possible, since the 'transformative processes' take place in a non-physical dimension. There are ancient teachings which a seeker after this knowledge might find authentic. And there are also reports of individuals recalling events and people from a recent previous lifetime, and their specific memories apparently being affirmed by survivors from that time.

Karma

The complex subject of cause and effect is dealt with in the esoteric world as the working out of *karma*. *Karma* is an ancient Sanskrit/ Hindu term, referring to the effects or consequences of any action. It can be understood more broadly as the constant working out of the *equilibrium* principle, which refers to the cosmos naturally tending towards a balancing out of its two primal, polar opposite forces, *expansion* and *contraction*.

The conduct of an individual being, incarnated in a certain physical body in one lifetime, sets up the conditions and learning requirements for the next incarnation and lifetime. **Karmic responsibility** is, therefore, a significant factor in each person's conduct within societies which acknowledge the principle of Karma. So, increasing awareness, wisdom and responsibility are particularly significant.

Secret societies: guardians of sacred knowledge... or what?

There are secret societies all over the world, varying in size, history and influence. They offer, or appear to offer many things. Some claim to be guarding sacred knowledge which the rest of humankind is supposedly not yet ready to handle safely. Some may be altruistic and concerned with charitable work.

Most offer a feeling of belonging – to a family, a brotherhood and/or a sisterhood. Others offer the opportunities for worldly advancement. Some seem to offer a blend of all these. Some may present a public front of 'goodwill' which conceals darker goings on, while yet others may be unashamedly cynical and malevolent, especially towards those they see as naive 'do-gooders'. Many agendas are being pursued under different emblems and logos.

A key question the motivation of the uninitiated individual who feels drawn to what a secret society seems to be offering? Does he or she have a hunger for spiritual knowledge, or just a desire to gain some worldly advantage? Or is it just the quiet thrill of belonging to a secretive, exclusive group? Caution is required. For a secret society, particularly one involving 'the occult', can be an enticing but deceptive and disturbing realm to venture into unprepared.

Also, some secret society leaderships appear to present one face to their own lower orders and the general public, while presenting another to their own higher order initiates. Meanwhile, increasingly, the moral failings of 'respectable' authority figures and secret society members are being exposed, as previously 'secret' information is made available.

There is a need at this critical stage in human evolution – with the internet now widely available – to open up the whole subject of secret societies, to question their motives and their leaderships. The infiltration of societies such as the *Freemasons* by those in pursuit of opportunities to influence and exploit is seeping out into public awareness. And so,
corruption, perversion, misguided ambition and *supremacy agendas*, which once were well disguised, are now spoken of openly.

Kabbalah

Kabbalah is an ancient occult system of thought that in recent years has been promoted for all manner of purposes: spiritual, political and commercial. Some of its elements can also be found in other occult systems, including *Freemasonry*.

Its fascination with symbols and numbers seems to date back to early in the predominantly *masculine descent* era when *males* began to take over what had previously been *female* roles in spirituality and healing, and when *numeracy* was emerging as a new, exciting discipline.
Psychologically, Kabbalah seems to appeal especially to people with a typically *pre-adolescent* urge to belong to an exclusive clique whose members have their own secret signs, symbols and words. This is highlighted in the way that some media celebrities seem unable to resist publicly signalling their allegiance to this movement 'in plain sight' of the public... through, for example, making certain hand signs and wearing symbolic ornaments.

However, humanity, still in its *collective adolescence* (see Glossary), is now slowly beginning to prepare for its *collective adulthood*. So, those *pre-adolescent* tendencies will eventually fade, while the core ancient wisdom itself will persist long after Kabbalah and other such pursuits have gone out of fashion. Meanwhile...

Regarding the universal principle of **polarity**, an example of the *universal feminine* would be the broad culture of **witchcraft**. This has been mostly practiced by women who have been passed on secret knowledge concerning healing and the influencing of events through techniques for manipulating consciousness, sometimes called *spells*.

An example of a typically *masculine* culture would be **Freemasonry**, which is full of symbolism related to the building of the legendary Temple of Solomon in the Old Testament.
Shamanistic healing, ie working with non-physical beings, seems to incorporate both the universal *feminine* and *masculine*, in proportions according to the individual practitioner.

Being aware

Although knowledge is always potentially empowering, a person does need to understand enough to be able to gauge how to respond appropriately to new challenges. For occult organisations are like obscured paths; there may be lights along the way but they may be leading to places which operate according to very unfamiliar principles.

So, it is possible for a person's state of mind, thinking and behaviour to be altered without consciously being aware of what's happening. Such modifications could be effected through hypnotic techniques, rituals, ceremonies, subliminal visual or audio messages, or various other means. The intention might be to make people's lives less troubled and more fulfilled. Or the intention might be to ensnare and exploit.

The influence of **discarnate beings** is also part of the esoteric/occult world. These are individualities not in physical form – ie distinct, identifiable units of consciousness which exist and function in the *pre-physical* dimension. Questions then arise as to how such beings might be be able to affect and influence the lives of incarnate human beings – individually and collectively, for good or ill. For all beings, physical and non-physical, are subject to the same primal cosmic principles.

Different cultures have their own names for such discarnate beings, which may be *super*-human or *sub*-human, and may influence and communicate with incarnate humans on levels of consciousness other than the normal waking state. And although human intermediaries, known as *mediums* with an ability called **clairvoyance**, may convincingly sense certain aspects of the non-physical realm, there can be no totally objective *physical* proof or disproof of this, since essentially it's about communication in a *non-physical* dimension.

Sometimes the language of an esoteric/occult thinker, when considering the long term evolutionary history of humanity – involving aeons, empires, wars, plagues, mass migrations and so on – may seem detached, impersonal, insensitive and even callous to someone who is at that moment more attuned to earthly, human, personal experiences and feelings.

PART THREE

APPLYING THE KNOWLEDGE

The essential *Threshold* knowledge, based on the three universal principles, is applicable to any situation – physical or non-physical, past, present or future. It can clarify thinking through *overview*ing anything in its greater context. And it can bring enhanced *insight* into psychological and social issues as well as the arts, sciences, mathematics and some transcendental realms.

First here, a brief summary of the ***One Humanity (OH)*** project. This proposes a timeless new way to think about, re-organise and administer human affairs on Earth – locally, regionally and globally – in rhythm and harmony with nature and the cosmos. It's based on an assumption of **the essential unity of humanity**, beyond all the superficial diversity of background, appearance and traditions.

For humanity now has the technical know-how to ensure that every human being on Earth can access the basics for a balanced, healthy life, neither *deficient* nor in *excess* of real, natural **needs**, physical and psychological. One longstanding problem has been *inertia,* a relic of the departing *descent into matter* era that has kept people stuck in old redundant ways and habits, causing all manner of problems and suffering.

The pioneers of this new era will set the tone and, against the odds, help to create and get the basic system up and running. They may be regarded with scepticism or cynicism by their contemporaries but will be remembered, respected and honoured by future generations.

The most common accusation likely to be made against the *OH* proposals is that this new option, now clearly on the horizon, is 'unrealistic', 'too idealistic', a 'wishful fantasy' etc. However, that kind of response can be read as an uneasy expression of fear and reluctance to even consider the prospect of adopting a new and unfamiliar value system. That is, one that could replace the old, corrupt and distorted, but familiar, *descent era* mentality, along with all the inherent problems it keeps regenerating.

One Humanity (OH)
a global cooperative

Creating a world without fear-inspired borders

The basic framework, outlined (next) as the *OH Agenda*, is offered as a start-out, adaptable design, a template for all who are willing to explicitly commit themselves to certain principles, values and procedures, inspired by revelations from the *Threshold* perspective.

The basic *OH* idea is for humanity to co-create and evolve a global network of linked autonomous communities and regions, each adapting to local circumstances, while dedicated to the wellbeing of all humankind. Which means that those people most in real need are prioritised, whoever and wherever they are.

At the same time it will become unacceptable for anyone to live in gross *excess* of their real natural needs while aware that other human beings are living in dire *deficiency*.

As the cosmic shift from an era of *descent into matter* to one of *ascent out of matter* proceeds, so humanity's collective *masculine* and *feminine* aspects, regardless of individual gender, will continue evolving towards a state of *equilibrium*.

Meanwhile, the nature of the *pre-physical* realm will become increasingly evident, as a new generation of scientists, engineers and healers begin to understand how that dimension functions – ie as a living, conscious medium, crucial to all life on Earth.

Generation OH, yet to be born, will be sufficiently evolved psychologically, and especially emotionally, to bring about the necessary world-changing patterns of living on Earth. For they will need to firmly reject and sensitively abandon many old, redundant *descent era* ways, while setting an inspiring example for their families, friends, colleagues and the wider world.

They will have progressed beyond old-style indoctrination that instils tribal-like hostility against 'others' or the attitude that it's OK to ignore real human need. They would be involved instead in dissolving old partisan *'us versus them'* prejudices and resolving ongoing *vengeance* issues. And so will be born a wiser, more inclusive *realism*, immune to the pathological after-effects of exclusive, *descent era* cynicism and hostility.

That will require creating, as part of the work, a viable **OH**-type model model as a template for pioneering groups all over the world to adopt and adapt according to local needs.

Generation OH will have the psychological tools and know-how to diagnose all situations and, in any disputes, judge **what's best for all humankind** in the longer view.   Ignoring what such awareness reveals, and thereby allowing unnecessary trouble to develop, will amount to irresponsible *neglect by tacit consent*, whether individual or collective.

Failsafe mechanisms, alarms and procedures will be built in to remind these pioneers to be constantly wary, and to alert them to any regressive tendencies towards reviving old redundant *descent era* ways. whether in themselves or in others, and whether by secretive plotting, undermining and sabotage or open resistance.

An interim, *transparent*, **debt-free money system** will help humanity wean to itself off its present addictive dependency on *Mama SCAB*'s fraudulent *debt money* scam, and to avoid falling for any other such scams. The interim period will last until humanity has matured sufficiently to function in a balanced, healthy way without any need for old style money.

A significant minority of humankind will work out how the following redundant institutions could be sensitively but firmly abandoned, dismantled and replaced or redesigned:
(a) all 'protection racket' *nation states*,
(b) all 'branches' of the trickster moneylending *syndicate of central and arch*-banks, *SCAB*,   (c) all divisive, supremacy-seeking religious organisations,
(d) all materialistic branches of science and medicine.

This rebalancing of the current pathological disparity between **excess** and **deficiency** is one more expression of the natural cosmic tendency towards a dynamic state of **equilibrium** between the universal forces of *expansion* and *contraction*.

A new vocabulary will emerge which will enable people to think and speak in ways that reflect and express *OH* thinking and attitudes. The *OH* project will then have the potential to be a creative and invigorating force - although never treading an easy, comfortable path. It will, however, be an inspiring challenge, requiring considerable determination, courage and integrity, ie an inclusive sense of being a responsible member of the one human species.

The power of worldwide cooperative networking can be appreciated by noting how effective the global Jewish *sayanim* system (page 166) has been at influencing human affairs at all levels of societies during the dark, but now departing, *descent era*... although the motives behind its operations have been very different from those of the **One Humanity Agenda** which now follows.

The *One Humanity (OH)* Agenda
(a summary)

NEED BEFORE GREED

'Need before greed' **is the guiding *OH* moral, ethical and practical principle. Therefore, as long as some people are known to be suffering avoidable *deficiency*, relieving that need is the first priority. At the same time, to be living in *excess* of real, natural, human need amounts to morally and ecologically flawed behaviour, creating unnecessary imbalance and stress.**

First, an inspirational *vision* is required – to provide a sense of purpose and direction, a clear target and a non-partisan ethos with progressive stages to be reached along the way. That means addressing the whole question of ***priorities*** – ie ***Who needs what first?***

One obvious fact, for a start, is that to achieve any kind of harmonious balance among most people on Earth, significant discrepancies in wealth and consumption have to be resolved. It will be a world in which extremes of consumption and wealth display are no longer acceptable, admired or sought, for such imbalances indicate a collective child-like *ASS* immaturity. The result, however, will not be a world of dull, uniform mediocrity. Variety and diversity will be able to flourish within a general ethos of sufficiency.

Relieving *real human need* wherever it is found will be the primary working principle of a new global networking system and a whole new way of life for linked-up, online humankind. The ideal of *'just enough'*, ie poised between deficiency and excess, will become normal – replacing the present *fear* and selfish *greed*, due to divide-and-rule rivalry and unnecessary competition for life's essentials.

In preparation, plans can be made for appropriate administrative systems necessary for rational and just decision-making, so that later they can be implemented without the whole process being sabotaged by *financial*, *political* and *religious* interests.

Thus **there need be no** *'power vacuum'* during the dismantling and replacing of the redundant global *debt money* system, the various territorial *protection racket* nation states and all *supremacy-seeking* religious institutions.

Need before greed

The first priority and responsibility of all able people will be to help relieve **real human need** wherever and whenever it's found, so that **all** human beings are at least able to live a basic, decent, balanced life. This will bring to an end the warped mentality of callously carrying on living in **excess** of real natural need while others are suffering unnecessarily in conditions of real **deficiency**.

At present that may seem a highly unlikely prospect. But in this volatile time of extreme swings in public opinion, and new generations emerging with very different values, it's not as unthinkable as it would have seemed just few years back. One small step in that direction, ie the idea of a *universal basic income*, is now being contemplated and experimented with in some locations as a practical economic measure.

Who's living where? - as public information

Live video feeds from around the world and continuously updated information, available online and on public display, can make people everywhere aware of the current *deficiency/excess* situation worldwide. Regarding land, dwellings and other buildings, overhead surveillance technology, like drones and *Google Earth*, can provide non-invasive public information about the use all land and buildings in relation to real natural need.

Thus humankind's self-awareness will evolve, such that many old prejudices and hypocritical pretences that create envy and resentment will finally be abandoned – although not without some resistance from those unwilling to abandon what they consider to be their 'advantages'. One major example is the fallacy of claims by individuals and organisations to exclusively own parts of this planet's surface, as so-called 'private property', backed up by laws designed to protect the wealth, authority and privileges of the already privileged.

Out of this can emerge a whole new way for humanity to organise, in a balanced and fair way, where and how all people dwell, according to their present real **needs** and in the context of local factors. It will obviously not be a quick, easy or short-term fix, given all the distortions resulting from the *descent era*. But that does not render the idea non-viable, especially in this time of rapid and often unexpected changes in public attitudes.

OH is thus a 'big picture' practical *vision*, to which all kinds of creativity, expertise, energy and enthusiasm can be committed by all humankind in endlessly inventive ways. It represents the next critical stage in human evolution on Earth – from humanity's collective self-centred *adolescence* to its more balanced young *adulthood*.

Broadly, everyone has something to contribute. All deeds, great or small, performed with unconditional, non-partisan goodwill for humankind and the natural world, are seeds that could later blossom, contributing towards the collective destiny of the *One Humanity*.

Such an ethos can create an atmosphere in which people are no longer deliberately set against one another in hostile, competitive rivalry, ie striving to be dominant 'winners' and not humiliated 'losers' – for example, in acquiring excessive material wealth at the expense of everyone else. And in a continuous process of re-educating and re-skilling, many new roles would be created and adopted, including:

- **_Counselling, conflict resolution, reconciliation and healing services_** to help people adapt to the many inevitable and profound changes in the world and in themselves.
- **_Self-defence and first aid instruction_**, to develop personal competence and self-confidence, both physical and psychological.
- **_OH Wardens_**, authorised and empowered to prevent harming, cheating, sabotaging etc.
- **_Warriors for One Humanity_**, ie an armed, non-partisan, transparent military organisation, committed to confronting and eliminating all regressive, unjust, divisive tendencies.
- **_Money administrators_**, to ensure the new interim money system runs efficiently and fairly,
- **_Prefabricated homes_** designers, producers, manufacturers and maintenance professionals – operating as the new 'normal' for a fast changing, more flexible world.
- And many more...

So, next are offered a few brief suggestions regarding some elements that will be required to raise awareness of how a future _One Humanity_ world might look and function. These could then serve as 'first steps' examples from which to learn and evolve. Such a potentially world-changing project also needs to be viewed in its greater cosmic context.

Destination *OH*

Mentally, it's conceivable... technically, it's workable...
physically, it's do-able,
and from an evolutionary perspective, it's ultimately inevitable.

The Context

Seen from the *Threshold* perspective, the inevitable progress of humankind is towards, first, a harmonious state of *equilibrium* between the polar opposite cosmic forces of *expansion* and *contraction*, then, *redemption* back into pure energy, and eventually, back into *universal consciousness*. It's part of an irreversible, ongoing evolutionary process in which *humanity* plays a key role. But presently, certain human attitudes and behaviours are delaying progress. And the delay is prolonging trouble and suffering.

This all-encompassing view affirms that a very long term outlook is required to even begin to consider possible developments which will extend way beyond the lifetimes of all those now living on Earth. It also affirms the understanding that **the cosmos is essentially a coherent system**, despite all the apparent incoherence, distortion and so-called 'randomness'.

One Humanity (OH), as a convenient label, refers to a significant stage which lies ahead in the evolving of human consciousness. The following is a brief sketch of some of the main features likely to be involved as the ongoing *transition* phase proceeds.

First things first

Ignorance is at the root of many problems, including ignorance of how the cosmos originated, how it functions and came to be the way it is right now, and how humanity fits into the picture. That lack of understanding is why over time various pathological ways have become normalised in societies worldwide, in the form of traditions, institutions and heritage.

So long as people are kept in a state of *ignorance* about their real identity, ie about their role in the greater order, such ignorance leaves them vulnerable, insecure, fearful and thus defensive, hostile, anxious and greedy, constantly craving compensatory substitutes. And it has been in the interests of certain groups to maintain this situation of ignorance.

'**Ignorance, fear, divide and rule**' (*IFDR*) has thus long been the pathological but effective method used by self-serving ruling elites worldwide for preserving their status of authority, power, wealth and privilege.

Certain vital missing knowledge, therefore, is now being made available in order to empower a significant minority of determined people of integrity, who could then bring to an end various long running scams that are being perpetrated by pathological exploiters of human ignorance and vulnerability.

Trust v. Cynicism

One essential quality these pioneers will require In working together at that task is a significant degree of mutual **trust**. That is, the special quality in relationships that creates a shared and lasting bond of confidence between individuals and groups (page 170).

Trust takes time to establish and is challenging to maintain. But it has to be developed and nurtured in the practices of *OH* groups and networks if they are to flourish, link up and coordinate their efforts. Understandably, this prospect at first may have little appeal to many people living today in a world permeated by selfish greed, fear, deceit, rivalry and therefore *mistrust*. For their main priority is still just to survive in their present circumstances.

Cynicism can be understood as a distortion of human consciousness, related to the *callousness* that itself results from psychological and physical wounding. So, it is to be expected that the *OH* vision will prompt much pessimistic cynicism, especially among the many whose experience of the *descent into matter* era has left them psychologically wounded and with an outlook coloured by 'the worst of the past'.

The **decline of trust in various previously respected figures**, such as priests, doctors, nurses, police, the military, teachers, bankers, financiers, economists, lawyers etc has brought many people to a state of doubt and suspicion, ie suffering from a *'trust deficit'*, particularly with regard to authority figures. Yet in this turbulent phase of *transition* towards an era of a*scent out of matter*, humanity is still seeking to progress and evolve. And the *OH* vision provides a vehicle for that impetus.

Different values

The *Threshold* view of a potential future reveals a very different set of *values* and *criteria* from those by which humankind is currently being persuaded to live. In order to evolve with the least trouble and suffering, there's now an urgent need to progress beyond the old habits of powerless vanity *politics*, selfish greed *economics*, primitive supremacy *religions* and sterile materialistic *science*.

The common yearning for a more fulfilling quality of life can only be satisfied by **pro-active participation** – not through passive compliance with pathological regimes, nor by avoiding personal responsibility, nor through fakery, trickery and indulging in compensatory distractions.

Radical change cannot be implemented through the 'normal channels' - that is, through organisations supported by people with an interest in maintaining the overall status quo. So, it becomes necessary, right from the start, to think beyond normal comfort zones, while also being prepared for the hostility of those who feel threatened by this kind of awakening.

From *UN* to *OH*: it's *transition* time on Earth

The ruling elites of today's nation states require enemies in order to justify their own privileged positions as 'protectors' of 'their' people (page 197). So, the UN, as an organisation composed of nation states, can only deliver what its member states are prepared to support, fund and allow... which indicates an inherent weakness, despite all good intentions.

At its creation in 1945, various ideals for the UN were announced in its founding documents. But set against these were various dark, power-lusting and greed-driven ambitions. There was also the ongoing oppression of numerous smaller national, tribal, ethnic and religious groups, many of which were determined to re-assert their distinctive identities.

Yugoslavia, for example, having been set up in the mid-20th century as an artificially created nation state, composed of several forcibly integrated peoples, had by 2006 disintegrated in a savagely violent way. The UN was criticised for mismanagement, corruption and for its impotence in failing to prevent this. Its effectiveness at peacekeeping was also questioned. But, as already explained, the UN's powers are severely limited.

And despite various UN commitments to ideals including ecological issues, poverty reduction, public health, peacekeeping and human rights, there have all along been other forces working to undermine and sabotage its power and effectiveness. This dynamic can be understood when viewed in the context of the *polarity* between humanity's *masculine* and *feminine* aspects throughout the *descent into matter* era.

The idea for a non-centralised, global network, to be known as **One Humanity**, arose at a time when the UN was in deep crisis. In the pre-internet 1980s, the UN's future role in the world and its very survival, were in question. At that time, **so-called 'sovereign nation states' were still widely considered important institutions**, despite that sovereignty having long been an elaborate illusion (page 197).

314

Yet expectations of the UN still remained high, despite its many inbuilt limitations... which inevitably resulted in much disillusionment.

The *OH* guiding principle

By contrast, the *OH* vision offers **a non-centralised, totally inclusive attitude to all humankind**, respecting all traditions while not supporting or promoting any divisive, partisan or exclusive tendencies. And there would be no preferential positions of authority for any partisan groups, something which has been a fundamental flaw with the UN since it was founded.

For as long as there are people suffering and struggling to survive without the physical and psychological necessities for a basic, healthy life, humankind as a whole will continue to be plagued by conflict and powerful expressions of discontent. Therefore, the primary *OH* guiding principle for the foreseeable future is both a practical and moral one:

The first OH priority
is to meet the real, natural, human needs
of all those people found to be most deprived
and lacking the basic necessities for a basic, healthy life,
wherever and whoever they are.

This shared aspiration offers a clear, conceivable target, towards which all *OH* people can aim and work in their own ways and from their own diverse starting points. **It gives everyone involved a shared sense of direction and purpose**, something that can be extremely inspiring and uplifting, especially in moments of doubt, disagreement, conflict or fatigue.

The *OH* vision

The aim is to evolve a new, organically functioning network, its workings transparent and open, to serve the wellbeing of all humanity. It's main features will be as follows:

- No centralised, top-down, hierarchical structure of command and control.

- No single *OH* head office or headquarters.

- Instead, a growing number of autonomous *OH* centres located worldwide, all committed to the same agreed basic principles, but adapted to local conditions.

- A natural diversity and interdependence among these centres, each functioning as a vital organ of the one body, humankind.

Such a progression inevitably involves a small but significant proportion of humankind developing ways of thinking and behaving in a balanced way, in order to function cooperatively and efficiently.

Some other features distinguishing a new *OH* world from the old UN world would be:

Leadership: evolving beyond the *democracy delusion*

OH community leaders will have to be trusted, competent and non-partisan administrators of proven integrity who have no inclination to live in excess of their basic needs. Their main reward will be the honour of being awarded special responsibilities, respect and trust. Such individuals do not seek the glamour of special status, fame or fortune. Neither do they support divisive 'us v. them' attitudes or agendas.

Their conduct will illustrate how, once the divide-and-rule competitive rivalry factor is gone, the **fulfilment factor** becomes a potent influence in communities... demonstrating how this is more deeply satisfying than striving to prove yourself *superior* to others. The same principle applies to *OH wardens* (who would replace the previous nation state *police*).

Transparency/Responsibility/Accountability

All *OH* work and activity will be transparent and accessible to monitoring through new and adapted information technology - except for specific cases requiring personal confidentiality. Every adult will be held responsible and accountable within their communities, groups and in the wider world for the consequences of their actions, public and private. For at some level, everything is interconnected.

Education for an *OH* world

- Throughout this book, the importance of *education*, especially for the young, has been emphasised. For it involves much more than just *schooling*.
- The whole notion of *education* for an *OH* world will broaden out into an open-ended, flexible, lifelong process of preparation, learning and teaching for all people of all ages and backgrounds... as appropriate for each's current needs and inclinations.
- The task is and will be to help awaken people to their own potential for a fulfilling life. And, in this complicated and confusing world, one crucial element of that process is being able to find one's way back to the simplicity of the three basic principles that govern how the cosmos and all within it function. Everything then begins to fit into a recognisable pattern.
- From there one can learn how to prevent oneself being misled, deprived, conned, bullied and exploited by people with a pathological craving to dominate and/or control others... because of their own inner sense of powerlessness, due to ignorance of *the basics*.
- **OH co-operatives** for educating the most deprived and neglected people could offer all manner of relevant, useful skills and information. And the accumulated experience of existing and historic cooperative set-ups will be of great value in this process.

Meaningful work instead of the old 'jobs' mentality

- Once the old, disempowering, anxiety-driven, 'jobs' mentality has

finally been abandoned, there need be no fear or anxiety about redundancy, poverty or loss of status or prestige.
- People will be able and encouraged to contribute their time, energy, abilities and enthusiasm as they are best able. Some, understandably, may take time to adapt to this new work ethos.

- **Re-skilling and re-deployment** will thus involve most people one way and another. And in this context knowledge and skills can be freely passed on. Roles and responsibilities will also change according to requirements, and will not have special privileges attached.

Conflict resolution, mediation and reconciliation skills
These skills will need to be employed with sensitivity and persistence to defuse the divisive *descent era* cultural programming that's still being instilled in much of humankind from an early age. That kind of indoctrination includes unquestioning *loyalty* to tribal, ethnic, national, religious and secular traditions, and may involve viewing people of other cultures or groups as inferior and/or malign (see ASS, page 89). It can result in mutual vengeance lasting many generations. So it may take several generations for some groups to move beyond their redundant but deeply embedded loyalties.

Land and Property: the end of territorial claims
In order for humankind to achieve a more balanced, just and sane world, various false assumptions and territorial claims to exclusive rights over land and property will have to be abandoned by certain previously privileged individuals and groups.
This will bring to an end the unbalanced, unsustainable situation of the one species, humankind, being divided into a few who live a life of *excess* in 'Richland' while the overwhelming majority struggle in conditions of *deficiency* in 'Poorland'.

- **Homes (static or mobile) for all**, according to current, real, natural needs. For much of human history millions of people have not had a basic, adequate home and have lacked the necessary resources essential for a decent fulfilling life.

In contrast, a small minority have felt entitled to oversized dwellings and have laid claim to large areas of land for their sole use. This is unnatural and dangerously divisive. Redressing this imbalance will be a priority for *OH*.

> **The natural, sane and responsible way**
> **is for people everywhere to be able to occupy a home**
> **appropriate to their current, real, natural needs.**
> **And when those needs change,**
> **they automatically move on**
> **and occupy a different appropriate home.**

Minds freed from *descent era* programming could design and produce a wide and imaginative range of dwelling places – for individual, family and communal living. That is, once the financial shackles of a greed-driven debt-money system and its priorities are removed and no longer impose constraints on creativity,.

In this context, the competitive 'game' of climbing the '*property ladder*' becomes irrelevant.
Instead, an openly accessible database to match people and homes could be maintained.

- **Buildings and land: change of use** – Premises previously used for commercial or *state* business could be adapted and used for *OH* purposes.

- *UN* **resources could be re-directed to** *OH* **purposes where appropriate**. This will amount to a fresh, new start: a *post-nation state, post-'greed-creed' economics, post-supremacy-seeking religions* and *post-materialistic science* world.

War and conflict

Warmongering is deeply embedded in the human psyche after millennia of *descent era* conflicts and vengeance-seeking. So, dealing with this is a priority and a long term task.

A critical turning point in the 20th century was in 1945, when the first atomic bomb was dropped on Hiroshima. It brought a horrific end to a world war, and at the same time effectively ruled out the option of all-out nuclear war on Earth.

Viewed superficially, the two then most powerfully armed states on Earth became deadlocked in a 'cold war' of mutual threats and an expensive 'arms race', while behind the scenes the ultimate moneylender, *SCAB*, and its armaments industry associates profited greatly.

This opened the way for numerous old local and regional conflicts to be re-ignited. Worldwide, small-scale warfare became a constant. Local *insurgencies* and so-called *international terrorism* have since become the main threat to the survival of the nation state. Again, all very profitable for *SCAB* & co, and in accordance with its long term K/A agenda.

Drones, robots, high-tech global telecoms and clever use of the ever-evolving media changed people's conceptions of war and risk – who gets involved and how, willingly or unwillingly. And as the great *transition* proceeds towards more subtle ways, wars are increasingly becoming *consciousness battles* – to win over hearts and minds through propaganda.

So, in an *OH* world, as already stated, skills in *conflict resolution* and *mediation* will be much in demand – to prioritise dealing with real human *need* over childish but deadly fighting about issues which can be settled in more adult ways.

Meanwhile, there is one overriding insight that the *Threshold* perspective brings to all situations of conflict, rivalry, fighting, warring and subterfuge. It's the fact that **whatever divides and sets opposed parties against each other, what they have in common is always the greater shared unity within which they both exist.** And gradually, awareness of this basic fact will spread worldwide, despite all the ongoing, mass media-provoked division.

The natural born fighter: *OH* warrior, regular soldier, mercenary or assassin?

The *OH* vision provides an option for the born *fighter* to live the life of a true, ethical **warrior.**

That is, instead of either:

(a) serving as an obedient programmed, unquestioning *soldier*, exploited as 'cannon fodder' in other people's wars or commercial ventures, OR

(b) pursuing the fantasy heroic role of a maverick, Hollywood-style mercenary or assassin.

It offers a way to greater fulfilment for the natural, ethical warrior – through serving all humanity instead of being hired to defend the privileged lifestyle of a particular ruling elite.

Given all the ongoing injustice, corruption, tyranny, slavery, cruelty, violence and environmental neglect worldwide, there will be no shortage of ethical fighting needed in the foreseeable future. Which means that each fighter will have real choices to make about the purposes to which his or her skills, strength and courage will be committed.

- The **true *warrior*** consciously commits to fight, alone or alongside others and without fear of dying, for universally shared principles such as *justice* and *freedom*... OR may choose not to fight for any cause which seems unjust or morally unworthy.
- The **obedient *soldier*** is required to kill and destroy as commanded, out of unquestioning, partisan loyalty – whether for national, religious, tribal, ethnic or other causes, just or unjust.
- The **amoral *mercenary*** hires out his or her services strictly for money, and so is not a true warrior – more a **professional assassin** or killer for hire.

The role of *OH*-trained fighters, dedicated to enabling improvements in the living conditions of those most in need, would be to overcome any resistance to the necessary changes. As well as providing physical/material aid, *OH* warriors could pass on useful practical skills and training, generally supporting **cooperative** instead of **divisive** purposes.

Combat Zones: **for irrepressible, undisciplined fighters**

- For those who have a compelling urge to fight physically, either as individuals or in groups,
but are not true warriors, prepared to commit themselves to creating a better world, special *combat zone islands* could be set up. These would provide wild, bare environments where such inclinations could be indulged without endangering others. Basic 'sticks and stones' and bare hands fighting – without any artificial, high-tech or remote control weaponry or digital software access – would make the experience real, harsh and direct.

- The participants could live out whatever roles they choose, and fight as loners or in gangs. Active involvement could continue until the participant is either killed in action, is no longer fit to fight, is judged ready to serve as an *OH* warrior, or is able to live as an *OH* civilian.

- Endless pseudo-battles could be fought over such issues as religious, national, tribal or ethnic rivalries, territorial claims, access to resources, historic vengeance and so on... until this tendency to fight becomes an insignificant, manageable factor in human evolution and eventually dies out. Such zones, meanwhile, would also be useful for medical training.

War Games Theatres

- There are those who have become fascinated by the psychology and technicalities of war, ancient and modern, but who prefer to remain safely remote from actual combat and danger. For these people there already exist *'war theatres'*, fitted out with high-tech electronic simulation war games.
- All manner of rival groups and individuals can engage in 'virtual' cyber-realm combat, their efforts viewed by audiences and followers. Teams and leagues of players could be organised.

Eventually, as humankind matures, the fascination for this kind of activity will die out.

Interim practical steps

Obviously, none of this is going to happen overnight and will take several generations to become fully operational. But once the subtle power of *trust* enables confidence to begin to grow and extend across the world, there'll be a linking up into an ever-expanding network of communities and groups, with the intention of creating a coherent global system, responsive to *real human need* wherever it's found.

- **Recruiting trustworthy, innovatory thinkers and planners.**
- First steps spring from first thoughts and ideas. So, competent, talented and trusted individuals and groups will need to be identified and recruited to prepare practical plans and schedules for coordinated action and for overcoming unforeseen obstacles.
- Practical visionaries, inventors, engineers, designers and others could then plan how to carefully dismantle and replace redundant, damaging and wasteful institutions and structures with new appropriate and evolving forms.
- Databases of names, links, resources, schedules etc could meanwhile be compiled to build up networks of local, regional and global connections. Operations and preparations could then be gradually scaled up as momentum builds. Ecological rebalancing and the healing of damaged people will be a necessary priority.

- **Contingency plans and resources** will ensure preparedness for all conceivable emergencies.

- **The *detoxing* of human societies**

The *OH* project will serve as a general *detoxing* process – for humankind to cleanse itself of vanity politics, financial trickery, greed economics, supremacy-seeking religions and materialistic science... as well as many other now redundant institutions and traditions.

- Personal identity: stateless, non-aligned *Earth Citizen*
Initially, people could re-designate their worldly identity status by opting out of the nation state *protection racket* trap and the *SCAB* money scam as far as possible, while a new set-up is being created. Their explicitly declared commitment and loyalty will then be to all humankind.

When widely adopted, this gesture will hasten the demise of all divisive, partisan, 'us versus them' allegiances, and clear the 'atmosphere' for some fresh thinking about living on Earth.

An interim money system

- Necessary for the *transition* phase, this will not be based on debt, nor be controlled by any State or profit-driven organisation.

- An *OH* interim currency would be radically different, using **electronic money that 'decays' after a certain period of time** – ie each unit gradually diminishes in value from its initial 'date of issue' value until it is worthless. This prevents hoarding and usury.

- And since such money cannot serve as a *store of value,* it cannot be treated as as a tradable commodity. So, it could not be used to gain any financial advantage over others.

- In each locality, electronic *OH* 'money points', sufficient to meet the standard basic needs for a decent, healthy life, could regularly be allocated to each individual. And this new 'organic', dated money, if not spent before it has expired, will automatically either be deleted or returned to a common reserve fund.

- Any excess units accumulated above an agreed limit by any individual or group would thus be automatically recycled. Which accords with the *OH* proposal for a radical rebalancing by eliminating all extremes of ***deficiency and excess***... through first addressing the most urgent human needs, wherever they are found,

- A digital *blockchain* system (page 192) will enable every monetary transaction to be logged, along with the changing *balance* of every account, in an open, transparent, public record. Existing software systems could be adapted for this interim set-up.

These measures will gradually decrease the overall amount of monetary activity and end the current anxiety-driven obsession with so-called financial 'security'. They will also end those deceitful claims by governments that the State 'cannot afford' this or that for its citizens. For the flawed assumptions behind that kind of nonsense have all along been cleverly concealed by the corrupt 'debt money' scam (page 207), which it will be necessary to abandon.

- **Crypto-currencies** represent a very limited step in this direction.

- The end of the rich/poor divide
Any signs of excessive accumulation of goods, power or privileges will be seen as symptoms, like cancerous growths, indicating a pathological state of imbalance which threatens the whole host body, ie the society and its culture. So, striving to acquire material or monetary wealth in excess of real, basic needs will **no longer be acceptable behaviour.**

OH Mass Media
The media's role will no longer be to spread state propaganda, carry commercial advertising, and provide engaging distractions from all kinds of hidden, darker goings-on. Media presenters and other professionals will therefore no longer serve as compliant, unquestioning mouthpieces of state, commercial, religious and other organisations.

OH-run media will provide essential but previously withheld information in a balanced and responsible way, as well as channels for creative human expression. Networks will provide content of all kinds: arts and culture items, news, discussion, humour. And a constant flow of ideas and inventions for improving the quality of life for all humanity and the efficient functioning of the OH world will be a vital part of the broadcasters' role.

Situations needing special attention will be reported on. And one aspect of this will be to give media access to **whistleblowers.** All who feel impelled to speak in this way will be encouraged to share their concerns. For these could serve as early warnings of activities which might jeopardise or perhaps enhance the *OH* project.

- **Telecoms, broadcasting networks etc**: *Google* and other major IT systems could be adapted to serve *OH* on behalf of all humankind in a non-commercial, non-partisan way.

Descent era **addictions**: resolvable in an OH context
As people increasingly appreciate the universal benefits of mutual trust and commitment – and see how in the longer view this serves everyone – *addictions* and anxieties related to various old, failed ways of living will begin to fade. For example:

- **Dealing with the inevitable relapses, cheating and sabotage**
For a while the psychological legacy of *descent era* insecurity and addictions makes it likely that some people will tend to relapse into old, domineering and greed-driven behaviours: ie divisive attitudes and practices. So, this possibility has to be guarded against with various built-in **whistleblowing** alerts and **failsafe** mechanisms.
In the early stages there will inevitably be *tricksters* trying all sorts of scams and rackets, along with plenty of cynical *cheating, fraud and sabotage*. This can be addressed through some new rules and regulations, and by providing facilities which offer harmless outlets for such impulses and habits until they eventually die out (see below).

- **Financial trading and other gambling games centres**
For those addicted to gambling, special dedicated hi-tech *trading game centres* could be set up where they could indulge in various complex digital games and speculate on electronic simulations, using pretend money, until they've worked that compulsion out of their systems.

Apart from variations on *Monopoly*, other games could involve running *Ponzi/pyramid* selling schemes, (for exploiting speculators who are seeking quick and easy returns on their investment). There could also be *market rigging* and *grand fraud* games, inviting endless diverse strategies for exploring the psychology of self-serving deception and cheating.

This facility could be *educationally* useful - demonstrating outmoded behaviours which used to be considered normal and were tolerated. It would also make clear to the general public how they used to end up paying the price for the indulgences of greed-and-success-driven financial speculators.

OH: an *ideas and inventions* culture

In the new stateless, non-greed-driven *OH* ethos, there would be no patents or material rewards on offer for introducing original ideas. But respect and prestige could be won for outstanding contributions. New ideas and inventions would be assessed on the potential benefits they offer, set against the 'costs' or damage to human wellbeing and the planet.

OH competitiveness

For those who aspire to excel through **competition**, public recognition could be achieved by coming up with the most effective **ideas**, large or small, for improving life either for a local community or for the wider world.

And for those who wish to participate in more physically interactive kinds of competition, there would be **sports and games**. Behind these would be the understanding that all participants, by competing, are mutually and respectfully testing the limits of their own and each other's skills, strength, stamina and character. So, all would tend to perform to the best of their abilities for the benefit and enjoyment of all.

Generation OH

The *OH* project will have come too late for many people, already programmed into *descent era* ways such that the resulting mental inertia severely limits their potential for an open minded, inclusive worldview. So, the future lies with **Generation OH,** whose time of emerging on Earth depends on how quickly or slowly the *Threshold* knowledge spreads and takes root.

Generation OH will not be as bound and inhibited as earlier generations by the vulnerability, insecurity, fear, greed, hostility etc that result from a lack of *gnosis* – that is, a lack of the basic knowledge about human identity and how the living cosmos functions.

They'll find that there's more than enough necessary, practical and creative work waiting to be done all over the planet to fully occupy several generations to come. For example, first there's how best to clear up the polluted, damaged mess left by previous generations and to treat those suffering from its ill effects. In addition there'll be much planning and preparing to be done in order to create a more balanced and wholesome environment.
Unemployment will thus become a redundant word.

Helping to heal the millions of damaged bodies and minds requires work which will no longer be hampered by divisive *'us v. them'* and *ASS* attitudes. Neither will this work be poisoned by the greed-driven mentality of 'the market', which currently dictates what supposedly can't be 'afforded' by states because of their entanglement in 'debt money'.

Generation OH will be able to link up all over the planet with a shared awareness of their common humanity, and a concern for their collective wellbeing in a dangerously unhealthy global environment. This will inevitably lead them to question whether they would ever want to return to the old, callous, selfish, *'us versus them'* ways of the *DiM* era – ie being kept in **i**gnorance and **f**ear, **d**ivided and **r**uled.

OH: a practical vision of the possible

- The *OH* project will serve as a general *detoxing* of humankind, as it cleanses itself of vanity politics, financial trickery, greed economics, supremacy tendencies in religions and arrogance in science. However...

For a better world, there's a price to pay, since nothing of worth comes for nothing.
To bring into being a better world, humans have to start by changing themselves.

- **Awakening**, **self-healing** and **trust-building** are required, backed up by some basic awareness of humanity's cosmic dimension which is all about the shared identity of all human beings, along with an appreciation of each individual's uniqueness.

- The *OH* project is neither a quick fix nor a '*leave it to others to do it for us*' plan. It's the practical beginning of **a long process for the benefit of future generations**, and requires explicit commitment and active participation in order to become more than just a fantasy.

Mentally, it's conceivable... technically, it's workable... physically, it's do-able.
And from an evolutionary perspective, it's ultimately inevitable.

But its implementation does require humankind to be familiar with the basic principles governing the functioning of the cosmos and life on Earth. So, ultimately it's all about *consciousness* in its many variations, including intention, integrity, intuition, inspiration, intelligence, love, tolerance, courage and perseverance.

In summary: *OH* is a 'big picture' practical *vision* involving all humanity, to which all kinds of expertise, energy and enthusiasm can be committed in creative and inventive ways. It's the next critical stage in humanity's evolving towards an eventual *redemption* back into universal consciousness. So, broadly, everyone has something to contribute. All small, modest deeds, performed with unconditional, non-partisan goodwill, serve as seeds that may later blossom, inspiring progress towards humankind's *One Humanity* destination and destiny.

So, next are offered a few brief suggestions regarding some of the qualities and action that will be required to raise awareness of how a *One Humanity* world might look and function. These could then be demonstrated in practice as 'first steps' examples. And such a potentially world-changing project also needs to be viewed in its greater cosmic context.

Science: what is it really about?

There are several reasons why the huge and rapidly expanding subject of *science* is included in this work. One is that, viewed from the *Threshold* perspective, orthodox materialistic science has become a dangerously detached world, with its own arcane language that conceals from the rest of humanity much misguided, unbalanced thinking and dogma... a situation that has the potential for disastrous consequences, affecting all life on this planet.

That mentality also tends to discourage investigation into the world of science by outsiders. For much scientific research is sponsored and supported by financial, commercial and political interests who have their own agendas, and clearly do <u>not</u> have as their priority the wellbeing of humankind as a whole.

Seeing the world of science in its greater **context** and investigating the **motivation** behind all 'scientific' work therefore has to be a major priority... since cultures steeped in the values of the *descent era* lack certain vital knowledge, such as the *Threshold* basics. Therefore, the thinking of most scientists, as a result of their indoctrination within such cultures, has been severely limited and distorted.

Consequently, their notion of what is and what isn't 'proper science' has been compromised, such that **they have omitted from their investigations at least half of the total reality naturally experienced by all human beings**... ie the non-physical world of *consciousness*.

There's also a fundamental psychological flaw in the whole approach of Western-style materialistic science with its many branches and sub-branches. The problem here is a false assumption that has evolved into an institutionalised *emotional reflex*. It results in scientists rejecting any ideas about nature and the cosmos that have any conceivable connection with divinity, mysticism or religion... although there are always notable exceptions.

That deeply embedded prejudice reflects an entirely understandable yet misguided, unbalanced, reactive attitude. It dates back to when the early pioneering scientists were persecuted by the then powerful but inertia-bound and bigoted Church authorities. And that historic conflict is what accounts for the deep, long running split in Western culture between the two camps... and the continuing materialistic indoctrination by the science authorities.

The existence of this attitude today echoes the *pre-adolescent masculine* tendencies that were predominant during that phase of the *descent* era when materialistic science first emerged in the western world. And the continuing prejudice and rivalries among scientists still leave them easily manipulable by State ruling elites and financial/commercial interests.

Threshold science

Threshold Science takes a <u>psychological</u> approach which views science and scientists within their greater cosmic context. It's not an alternative discipline in opposition to current orthodox, materialistic science. But it does question how scientists are influenced in the ways they tend to think and act - ie what hidden assumptions lay behind their conduct, both as scientists and as human beings - and how they interpret their raw observations.

The subtle power of the *Threshold* perspective thus makes possible some radical **re-interpreting** of phenomena previously observed and recorded by scientists. Which in turn enables some long established but inadequate theories to be reviewed and revised. And what becomes clear, crucially, is that **a fundamental *coherence* can be found in the functioning of the whole cosmos**, despite its apparently random, chaotic unpredictability.

Here are a few brief examples of how certain typically compartmentalised and exclusive branches of contemporary materialistic science can be seen to fit coherently into the view from the *Threshold*. Referring back to the ***polarity*** basics, summarised on page 34:

- **Black holes** are about extreme **contraction** and **gravity** at **focal points** within the **cosmic torus**.
- **Inflation Theory** and the **Expanding Universe** are essentially about cosmic **expansion** and **levity**.
- **String Theory** alludes to the archetypal **vortex** form within each torus (page 341).
- **Quantum physics**, in penetrating 'inwards' into the pre-physical dimension beyond the smallest quantifiable amounts of physical energy, represents the **universal masculine**.
- **Chaos Theory**, investigating the fluid, unpredictable, diversifying dynamic nature of reality 'behind' the apparently static forms of solid matter, represents the **universal feminine**.

Consciousness first

The root of the word *science* is the same as the **sci** in con-**sci**-ous-ness, and comes from the ancient Greek word for *knowing* in its broadest sense. However, the young discipline of Western science, over just a few centuries, has already narrowed its scope down to studying only the *physical-material* world... by excluding the prior existence of the *non-physical* realm.

Scientists have neglected to investigate or even acknowledge the existence of a major part of what humans experience as their continuous ongoing reality. And that's despite knowing that while all the cells of their physical body are continuously dying and being replaced, their *consciousness* persists on a range of levels, including waking, sleeping, dreaming etc.

This affirms that consciousness exists prior to physical **matter**, which is essentially condensed **energy**, which is itself a transformed state of primal **consciousness**. So, what is normally called the 'universe' first exists as primal **universal consciousness**. Each individual human being is therefore one **focal point**, one *unit* of universal consciousness, around which is formed a complex 'body' of non-physical and physical phenomena.
What is also clear is that there would be:
- **no science** without there first existing curiosity, enthusiasm,

willpower, perseverance and discipline, all of which are aspects of _consciousness_,
- **no technology** without the intention to apply scientific knowledge,
- **no invention** without technical know-how plus awareness of need and desire,
- **no theories** without creatively recognising patterns of phenomena observed,
- **no mathematics** without abstract, logical, systematic and consistent thinking...

So, **consciousness**, in its many forms, is the foundation of all scientific activity. And the very practice of science is 'consciousness in action', directed towards understanding the origins, composition and workings of this living cosmos. Here are just a few pertinent quotes.

"...the content of consciousness is the ultimate reality."
20th century physicist, Professor Eugene Wigner

"...consciousness is a gift and we wouldn't be here without it."
21st century physicist and mathematician,
Professor Sir Roger Penrose

"Consciousness is the ground of our being."
21st century theoretical nuclear physicist, Professor Amit Goswami

"...individual cells act with purpose,
a higher order responsiveness, beyond chemistry,
that all living things have..."
Biologist, Sir Paul Nurse

Threshold Science, as outlined earlier, is based on the three fundamental working principles of the cosmos. It brings a unifying, all-inclusive clarity and elegant simplicity to scientific thinking – in contrast to the complicated contradictions within materialistic science. It opens the way for a new kind of science, not locked into the sterile, 'bits and pieces', machine mentality of the current system, which is rooted in the *descent* era of *masculine* predominance when humankind as a whole was younger.

A science that lacks the essential principles revealed from the *Threshold* is doomed to end up lacking balance, consistency and coherence, and struggling with various unresolved enigmas, conundrums and paradoxes. And one crucial part of that failing is the official ignoring of the universal tendency towards a state of **equilibrium** between the two primal forces, **gravity** and **levity**. *Gravity* has been a familiar concept in science since Newton's time, but so far, not *levity*.

Levity

Levity is the expanding, counter-balancing, polar opposite, cosmic force to **gravity**. Newton knew it as the **universal expansive force**. It can be witnessed directly in heat rising, as in a flame, or when you experience a sense of elevation in your upright posture. A tree can be seen as a solidified 'trail' (think of a vapour trail) of *expanding* energy as it's drawn it away from the centre of the planet, countering *gravity*.

But levity was arbitrarily decreed an invalid concept and banned in the17th century by the then ruling science establishment, the Accademia del Cimento in Florence. And so, in science it became a taboo, and most dictionary definitions still corrupt the true meaning of levity, reducing it to a light-headed, trivial, flippant, frivolous attitude.

In the mid-20th century **Ernst Lehrs**, a writer, teacher and electrical engineer, recovered the term *levity* in Man or Matter (see References). He wrote: *"It must not be confused with the hypothetical 'anti-gravity'"* and *"...although capable of producing physical effects.... (levity) is itself of a non-physical nature."*

Einstein's cosmological constant, in that context, can be seen as an abstract mathematical device for balancing an equation, ie acknowledging the expanding levity of the cosmos counterbalanced by contracting gravity. But *levity* was arbitrarily decreed an invalid concept and banned in the17th century by the then ruling science establishment, the Accademia del Cimento in Florence. And so, in science it became a taboo, and most dictionary definitions still corrupt the true meaning of levity, reducing it to a light-headed, trivial, flippant, frivolous attitude.

Consequently:
- **Biology**, 'the study of living things', lacks any understanding of the essential nature of conscious **vitality** itself, the pre-physical *quality* that distinguishes you from a corpse.

- **Chemistry**, which evolved from **alchemy**, still excludes and ignores the existence of the <u>pre-physical</u> *aether/quintessence/ quantum vacuum* (in which *levity* overpowers *gravity*). This is the dimension of *potential* energy and manifestation, the medium through which thoughts are transmitted and within which chemical transformations occur.

- **Physics** still persists with trying to reduce *consciousness* down to something <u>physically</u> measurable. And since physicists do not officially recognise the universal principles of *polarity* or *resonance*, the resulting paradoxes include, for a start, a crucial incompatibility in their Standard Model of the universe between the **macro** scale of **relativity** and the **micro** scale **of quantum** phenomena. However, this can be resolved, when viewed from the *Threshold*, by realising that *polarity* means the co-existence of opposites always within a greater unity – in this case the *physical- material* and *pre-physical* realms.

Boysworld science: groping in the dark

'Boysworld science' refers to the way some contemporary scientists still display certain characteristics of the early male scientists back in humanity's *pre-adolescent* phase. They were fascinated and excited by this new field of opportunities for experimentation, discovery, fame and fortune. But there was also fierce rivalry and a lack of responsibility for the many unfortunate outcomes resulting from their

endeavours.

That was a few centuries ago, in the depths of the *masculine-dominated* *descent into matter* era. Yet contemporary materialistic science is still characteristically *masculine, dogma-bound, machine-minded* and politically impotent, despite humankind progressing in other ways.

Western science emerged as a distinct discipline during that *pre-adolescent* phase of human evolution on Earth, when people were increasingly thinking for themselves in ways that did not conform with those of the dominating 'parental' Church and State authorities.

As a result, current science can be seen as still broadly reflecting the mentality of a curiosity-driven, clever, *pre-adolescent boy*... obviously with many exceptions to that caricatured image. Typical characteristics of *pre-adolescent males*, across many cultures, are:

- a fiercely **competitive** drive to be a '**winner**', with the biggest, fastest, strongest, loudest, smartest whatever... a carry over from natural boyhood *pecking order* rivalries;
- a craving for **approval**, applause, prizes, admiration, authority and wealth;
- an insatiable *'What if?'* **curiosity**, for example, *'What if I smash this or set fire to that?'*;
- a denying, ignoring or masking of any 'soft' **emotionality**, so as to appear more manly, sometimes coupled with a rebellious attitude;
- a **cop-out** tendency of irresponsibility, implying that science has nothing to do with morals, ethics or spirituality... and that involves adopting a fake neutral, '**value-free**' posture;
- a child-like passive **deference** towards strong, authority figures.

In Westernised cultures, the natural enthusiasm and curiosity of youngsters has been hyped up through education systems and the mass media, promising great opportunities and a glorified 'digital future'. Thus a fierce sense of competitive rivalry, along with a hunger for material wealth, have been continuously promoted as admirable traits.

Selfishness in childhood is a natural part of growing up. However, when encouraged as 'normal' behaviour in adults, it becomes counter-productive, both to their societies and to humanity as a whole. Yet most people still seem unaware of how selfish greed is being promoted by ruling elites as a classic divide-and-rule strategy in order to control, distract and exploit whole populations... including scientists.

Thus, many young 'wannabe' scientists, desperately wanting to be *winners*, have grown up indoctrinated with a pathological craving for approval, prizes, applause, fame and worldly rewards for their efforts. Which, in science, may mean being the <u>first</u> to discover, achieve or produce something new. Seen in that light, certain less than honourable behaviour by various eminent scientists now becomes understandable, although not admirable, in retrospect... for example, the race to complete the so-called 'human genome'.

All of which has nothing to do with seeking *wisdom* and helping humankind to achieve an ideal state of *equilibrium* between the cosmic forces of *expansion* and *contraction*, and thereby a natural harmonic *resonance* with the cosmos and nature.

Polarity rules

As stated earlier, a fundamental flaw in materialistic science is that it has all along been dominated by a *descent* era, immature, *masculine* attitude, emphasising the significance of *gravity* while trying to ignore *levity*. And one outcome of this has been its denial of the whole *pre-physical* dimension of existence, along with its failure to acknowledge the universal principle of **polarity**. Here are a couple of contemporary examples.

Dark energy is the current term used by physicists to refer to the *universal expansive force*, a reality familiar to Sir Isaac Newton back in the 17th century. The very name, *dark energy*, is a wry admission by today's scientists that they are 'in the dark' as to its essential nature. For it is, in essence, the primal cosmic force of **levity**, the complementary polar opposite of *gravity*. And gravity without levity is as meaningless as north without south. Other substitute terms for **levity** include *anti-gravity* and *Einstein's cosmological constant.*

Dark matter, another mystery to physicists, can be understood <u>not</u> as some speculative, subtle, invisible kind of substance, but as the universal *contracting* force of **gravity** *in action*, the polar opposite of *expanding* **levity**.

Then there's the quest to identify so-called '**gravitational waves**' while ignoring the effects of *levity*, the complementary other half of the two-way universal process of cosmic pulsation.

From the *Threshold* perspective, the problems of the flawed *Standard Model* of the universe are easily resolved: Einstein's *gravity*-dominated universe and the *levity*-dominated *quantum* world can be understood as complementary polar opposite dimensions of a greater, dynamic, pulsating, cosmic *oneness* within a yet more inclusive '*nothingness*', ie *universal consciousness.*

The following diagrams are attempts in flat 2D to picture the dynamics of **D2D**, including a re-configuring of the so-called '*four forces or interactions of physics*', according to the universal principle of *polarity*. But first, a brief introduction to *D2D.*

D2D: the nature of *pre-physical space*
D2D stands for the <u>d</u>ynamic **2**-<u>d</u>imensionality of *pre-physical* space. This is the space of the primal *pulsating,* ie the continuous rhythmical alternating, of *contracting gravity* and *expanding levity*, inwards and outwards between the periphery and centre of the cosmos. That basic dynamic is what is known in physics as *potential energy* (see <u>Threshold Science</u>).

The pulsating pre-physical cosmos, a primal energy field, can be envisaged as a bubble within which pulsate innumerable lesser bubbles, all variously in rhythm. These generate within themselves smaller bubbles which do the same, all sharing in common the one centre point of the cosmos, from which they all emerge and *expand* before *contracting* back into it. This view reveals the connection between the pulsating cosmos and your heartbeat.

In order to grasp the significance of this universal phenomenon, the first requirement is to take on board the three basic *Threshold* principles (page 30). Then, *D2D* space, as the all-inclusive cosmic context, offers the potential for new areas of healing. science, mathematics and the arts to emerge and evolve, while also enabling all existing sciences to function in clearer, more consistent and joined-up ways.

Through recognising *D2D* as a primal reality, prior to and 'behind' the gross, physical-material, 3D or 4D world, various previously unresolved enigmas, paradoxes and conundrums of science and mathematics become resolvable. For example, in this pulsating, **spheroidal torus**-*form* cosmos, all apparently straight lines are ultimately curved – which makes more sense of Einstein's intuitive notion of *curved space* than the crude, 'heavy ball in an elastic hammock' model. *(Spheroidal* here means approximately spherical).

A small first step towards directly experiencing *D2D* is offered in the mental exercise called '*I Breathe the Cosmos*' (page 437). This can help one to gain a sense of the *polarity* between:
(a) the centre of one's own individual existence, as *individual I*, and
(b) the centre and periphery of the cosmos... all in the context of unlimited *universal consciousness*.

The ID Continuum (page 427) offers another way of experiencing the reality of *D2D*.

Torus and vortex: archetypal natural forms
Realising that the cosmos is essentially a pulsating, rotating **spheroidal torus**, ie an approximately spherical torus, can help in visualising its **D2D** nature. The torus is a self-contained dynamic form which demonstrates unity and continuity of:
(a) the inward/*centric/gravity-driven/masculine/yang* tendency and

(b)   the outward/*peripheric/levity-raised/feminine/yin* tendency. The central crossover point of the double vortex '*funnel tunnel*' in every spheroidal torus form serves as a *quantum portal*. And through that threshold, that critical point of maximum *gravity* and minimum *levity*, passes **energy**, transformed from *pre-physical potential* energy to *physical kinetic* energy and vice versa in the opposite direction.

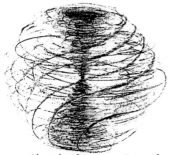

Sketched impression of
dynamic movement

Computer graphics
diagram

The **doughnut/ring torus** represents a degenerate version of the spherical torus, more inertia-bound and tending towards materialisation, also abstracted by mathematicians into an idealised, static 3D form.

The **vortex** is an archetypal dynamic phenomenon, formed by rotating energy being drawn inwards towards the centre of the **torus**-shaped cosmos, and outwards towards the periphery. Physical examples are tornados and water rotating down the plughole of a bath. They are also central to the idea of *black holes*. And on page 61, pre-physical vortices are shown as potential living forms.

Atmospheric vortexing energy

The huge and rapidly evolving subject of atmospheric **jet streams**, **climate** and **weather** could benefit from being viewed in the greater context of (a) the pulsating, living, *D2D* cosmos, and (b) the current *transition* phase from an era of **gravity**-dominated *descent into matter* towards one of **levity**-dominated *ascent out of matter*. However, the elegant simplicity of *D2D* remains as yet too radical for orthodox scientists to adopt, although change is inevitable as the cosmic *transition* phase proceeds.

The mathematical **Fibonacci Sequence** is derived from the spiralling *torus* patterns that can be found throughout the natural world – eg in cones and nautilus shells. It results from the the interaction between *contracting* **gravity** and *expanding* **levity** in the pulsating, spinning and orbiting of the planet and the formative effects of this.

Polarity
the primal cosmic dynamic

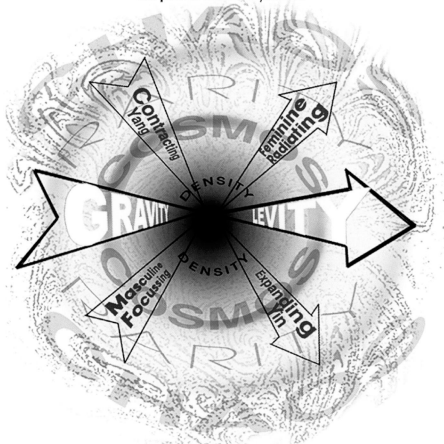

The Three Universal *Threshold* Principles (in *D2D* space)
(*D2D*: the dynamic 2-dimensionality of *expansion/contraction*)

1. **Consciousness**: the original animating principle of the cosmos

2. **Polarity**: the dynamic between the primal inward and outward cosmic forces, **gravity** and **levity**, creating raw, potential energy.

3. **Resonance**: the vibratory rhythmic interaction between different parts of the Cosmos, *consonant* ie harmonious, or *dissonant* ie conflicting.

The universal principles of **masculine** and **feminine** are not the same as *male/female* gender.

The 4 Fundamental Forces/Interactions of Physics
- reconfigured from the *Threshold* perspective

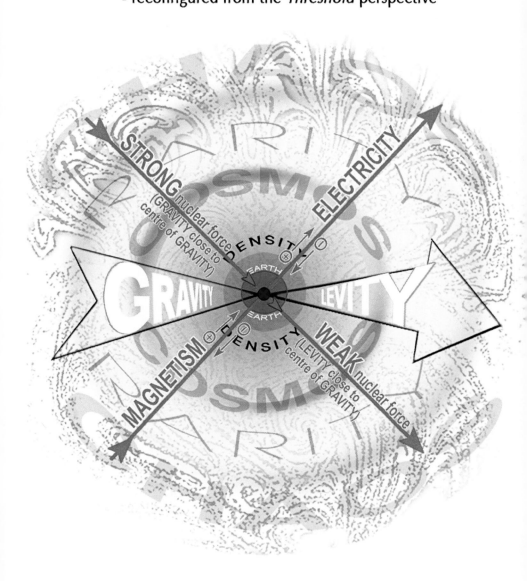

From the *Threshold* perspective
Dark Matter is GRAVITY
Dark Energy is LEVITY

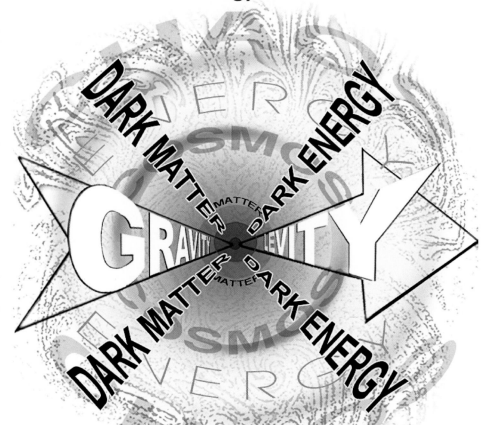

Gravity functions centripetally in physical space
Levity functions centrifugally in pre-physical space

Threshold Science is a free-to-download PDF at www.pathwayinitiatives.co.uk

EMUs and building blocks

The overall pattern has been to focus, probe and penetrate the *physical* nature of whatever is being studied, with little attention paid to the ways in which everything relates to the greater cosmic context, the unlimited 'bigger picture'. In addition there has been much emphasis on *objectivity* and *quantifying*, and an addictive fascination with abstract mathematics, while neglecting to appreciate and evaluate the *qualities* experienced in the process.

As a result, materialistic scientists – in trying to 'master' nature – have developed and imposed on its dynamic, fluid continuity a **sterile mathematical grid** system. And from this various systems of standardised *equal measure units, **EMUs**,* have evolved (page 346).

That approach indicates the familiar materialistic **'building block'** mentality, based on the false premise that everything in the universe is composed of standardised micro-units, in physics called *fundamental particles*. Which is very convenient for mathematical formulae, but does not reflect the fluid, rhythmical continuity of nature and the cosmos, given that the word **part-icle** literally means *a small part,* ie of a greater wholeness.

Yet the very idea of *wholeness* is studiously avoided by physicists. Why? Because their naive predecessors were misled into a *descent era* trap, and then allowed **false pride** and **inertia** to set in, resulting in the rigid **dogma** that now prevents open-minded investigation. Ironically, that limiting pattern of behaviour mimics the bigoted attitude of the 16th century religious authorities who persecuted the early pioneering scientists.

Consequently now, any who dispute the official orthodoxy are treated like *heretics*, in an aggressive-defensive, hostile way, having their work ridiculed or dismissed as 'pseudo-science'... as if materialists have a monopoly on scientific investigation. The desperately dismissive official reaction to the work of pioneering scientists, such as Jacques Benveniste and Luc Montagnier on the special properties of *water*, illustrate that warped, toxic mentality.

The outcome has been that so far this pre-adolescent *boysworld science*, although ingenious and inventive, has failed to acknowledge the *pre-physical* realm as the intermediate dimension between consciousness and physicality - ie an essential part of the greater reality within which humans exist.

The significance of the *pre-physical* dimension, as the vital reality behind the *physical-material* world, is indicated in the diagram of emerging living forms and gender on page 61. So, at least half of our experienced reality is missing from current materialistic science. Which is where **Threshold Science** and **Threshold Mathematics** have a significant contribution to offer, at least as starting points for others to develop.

Numbers: a seductive *illusion* of uniformity, certainty and precision?

A fascination with *numbers* is another trait especially associated with pre-adolescent males. It appears to correspond with the phase in humanity's evolving when **numeracy** first became significant in human cultures.

Although the language of numbers has proved extremely useful in many ways, it is an artificial, abstract system. Regular use of the basic 'natural' number system of 1, 2, 3 etc to **quantify** the physical world into standardised identical units, **EMU**s, has resulted in the false notion that the world is made of innumerable, standardised, 'building block' **particles**, as previously mentioned.

From there, it tends to be assumed that everything in the physical world can be represented and measured by various systems of symbolic **EMU**s (page 346). Then, when imaginary EMU grids are superimposed on the real world, they display patterns of units that correspond to the features of the physical reality they cover. And from these, systems and languages of categories, orders, formulae, calculations and theories can be developed.

Scientists, lacking the *Threshold* perspective, have thus tried to impose on the messy and unpredictable world of physical matter, energy and forces the seductively precise, neat, orderly, consistent, clean and emotion-free language of **mathematics**.

This has resulted in the sciences in general becoming increasingly dependent on numbers and abstract mathematical formulae, while ignoring:
(a) the existence of the *pre-physical* dimension that is experienced, but not physically,
(b) the *qualities* of the living, conscious cosmos,
(c) the *wholeness* and continuity of the natural world in time and space, and
(d) the scientists' own deeper *feelings* about what they're doing in the name of science.

A new, evolving, all-inclusive science will be able to investigate all aspects of human experience, including the so-called *subjective* realm, in an open, consistent and rigorous way. And one key realisation in this venture concerns the *D2D* nature of *pre-physical space*.

Meanwhile, regarding the general state of contemporary materialistic science, a little honest frankness now and then from some eminent scientists conveys a certain message...

Eminent scientists admit ignorance
*"Science fails to admit that it has not the slightest clue what **energy** is..."*
*"I think it is safe to say that no-one understands **quantum physics.**"*
Physicist and Nobel laureate, **Richard Feynman**

*"Western science still doesn't know what **mass** or **matter** actually are..."*
as UK physicist **Brian Cox** admitted
in a 2005 BBC radio tribute to Einstein.

*"Physicists don't really understand the concept of **force**..."*
according to Professor of Physics, Ian J Thompson, in 2004.

Power, in physics, is officially defined only in terms of **quantity**, ie *"the rate of doing work, the amount of energy transferred per unit time."* (Wikipedia)

"What sex is, why it evolved and how it works are the biggest unsolved problems in biology."
Steve Jones, eminent UK biologist.

Taken all together, that's a lot of 'not knowing' in contemporary science. By contrast, here's the *Threshold* perspective, briefly, on four of those basic concepts plus a new one.

Threshold Science: four basics redefined

- **Matter** is created through spherical standing waves of pre-physical, potential *energy* being 'woven' by the inward/outward pulsating of *gravity* and *levity*, a**mass**ed and con**dense**d into physical form.

- **Energy**, in its most basic manifestation, is the dynamic, the *potential* between the two polar opposite, complementary, pulsating, cosmic forces, *levity* and *gravity*, observable as *expansion (yin)* and *contraction (yang)* as they naturally tend towards an *equilibrium* state.

- **Force** is the directed exercising of *power* or *will*, in a physical or a non-physical way. The primary force exerted in the cosmos is the tendency towards *equilibrium* between *levity* and *gravity*, a stage on the way to the *redemption* of energy back into universal consciousness. **The four forces (or interactions)** of contemporary physics can be reconfigured into a simple, coherent system, conforming to the universal principle of *polarity* (see diagram, page 343).

- **Power** can be understood as the capacity to effect change by directing *force* or releasing *energy*.

Polyrhythmic Pulsation (PrP) (see Glossary) is the universal principle of ***polarity*** in action, ie *expansion/contraction*, creating multi-rhythmical waves of primal *potential energy* in **D2D** space. Recognising this universal phenomenon brings vital insights into science, medicine and healing. The idea of *biorhythms* appears to allude to this spectrum.

The new version of science will necessarily include studying the *qualities* of different phenomena, for example the impressions, feelings and intuitive thoughts evoked by encounters with different aspects of the manifest world. For example, directly sensing *blue-ness* is not the same experience as recognising certain symbols that represent a particular range of wavelengths and frequencies in the electromagnetic spectrum.

The problem of dogma in science today lies not with the inventive, practical *experimental* scientists, but with the *theoretical* scientists. Why? Because they've been indoctrinated in a materialistic-mechanistic culture that tends to produce fragmented thinking, focusing on component parts and mechanisms, all translated into abstract mathematics. It's an approach that fails to appreciate the relationships between those parts and the greater living wholeness which they comprise and, beyond that, the unlimited potential of universal consciousness.

Threshold Psychology, which starts with the primacy of consciousness, emerges as the basis of all scientific investigating, and re-integrates science with all other areas of investigation, including the creative arts.

The quantum dimension is...
the pre-physical *aether/quintessence*

Physicists may well be the last people to acknowledge this. Why? For a start, two key concepts, the pre-physical **aether** and **levity** (the polar opposite of *gravity*) remain excluded terms, and are thus still absent from orthodox science – for long outdated and redundant

4 Aethers

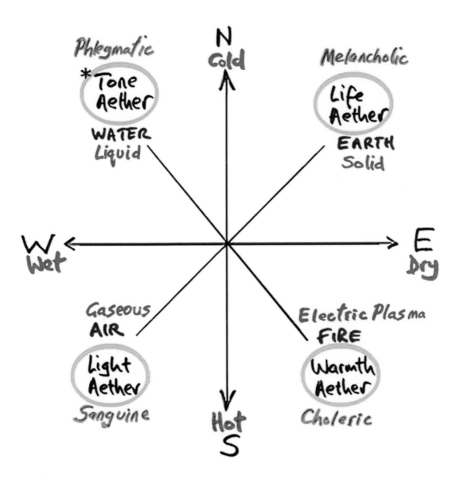

NB It's only a diagram.

* **Tone Aether**: aka Chemical/ Sound/ Number/ Colour Aether

The Four Ethers, a book by Dr Ernst Marti (Schaumberg Pub'ns Inc. 1984)

'Electric Plasma' is explained by Professor Donald E Scott in his book, *The Electric*

reasons, explained in _Threshold Science_. However, the artificial barrier separating physics from metaphysics is dissolving.

The existence of the **aether**, long known by various names in other cultures, was explicitly affirmed by Einstein. Its most recent pseudonym in physics is, ironically, the ancient term, **quintessence**, which literally means the '_fifth_ essence or element', ie the timeless _aether_.

This refers to a state of being **prior to physicality**, ie the **pre-physical** medium from which emerge the four traditional archetypal **elements** (_earth, water, air, fire_) which incorporate the physical qualities of the physicists' **four states of matter** (_solid, liquid, gaseous, plasmic_).

The aether also inherently has the quality of _four-ness_, two secondary polarities, as the following diagram shows. And one distinguishing quality of the _aether/quintessence_ – which exists prior to physical, _gravity_-dominated 3D space – is its **D2D** (**d**ynamic **2-d**imensional) character, a primal expression of the universal principle of _polarity_.

The pioneering quantum physicists had penetrated, in a _masculine_ way, to the ultimate central point and 'portal' of the spheroidal torus-shaped physical dimension, which is where quantifying ends. They then peeped through, and what they glimpsed was the pre-physical _aetheric_ dimension in which everything appeared to them to work in a counter-intuitive way. _Chaos Theory_, which emerged a few decades later, provided further clues as to how the pre-physical aetheric dimension functions.

So, they came up with various quirky labels for the unexpected features of the quantum world. which, being non-physical, exists in a dimension more subtle than physical matter and energy. And not surprisingly, these features correspond with known characteristics of the timeless _aether_, for example:

- **Entanglement** affirms the immanent, all-pervasive presence of universal consciousness.

- **Nonlocality** indicates how *D2D* space is a subtle, pulsating, living, conscious continuum.
- **Superposition** implies the fluid, circulating, spatial and temporal *continuity* of the aether.
- **Tunnelling** exemplifies how aetheric forms *inter-penetrate* one another like pure light.

Chaos: another kind of order

The emergence in the 1970s of **Chaos Theory** clearly affirmed the ongoing *transition* from an era of *masculine*-dominated *descent into matter* into one of *feminine*-influenced *ascent out of matter*. It did so by showing unmistakably how **chaos** involves qualities which are characteristic of the universal *feminine*.

Chaos is an ancient Greek word which refers to a womb-like, seething realm of *living energy* and potential before it has taken on a recognisable form. It's the polar opposite of **cosmos**, a Greek word which means *order* – that is, 'order' as it has come to be understood during the *masculine*-dominated *descent* era of centralising, uniformity, straight lines, numbers etc.

Chaos Theory arose out of the practical realisation that trying to predict the weather could never be a precise science, because very small variations in initial circumstances can lead to big variations in outcomes. More generally, that idea plays out in how one small word, look or gesture can radically change the whole tone or atmosphere of any situation.

Chaos Theory is based on four main characteristics:

1. *Non-predictability* - inherent *disorder* at the micro-level, regardless of any order at the larger scale macro-level, makes precise predicting unreliable.
2. *Non-linearity* - the consequences of any event ripple outwards in all directions, and not simply in *lines* or *linear* chains of cause and effect, linked in a mechanical way.

3. *The Butterfly Effect* - a reminder of how tiny events can have enormous consequences if the 'ripples' build up through *resonance* into big waves.
4. *Fractals* - in apparently random or disorderly situations, fractal-type patterns can reveal a hidden inner order of repetitive replicating on an ever-decreasing scale. Generated by computer software using a particular formula, *fractal graphics* can powerfully magnify one detail of an image, artificially 'revealing' exact replicas infinitely 'inward'.

These appear to be why it was not welcomed by many scientists whose thinking, careers and reputations were based on the old *descent* era, *masculine*, mechanistic models of science – whether Newtonian or quantum mechanics.

Chaos Theory, by contrast, provides a deep understanding of various principles involved in Nature's workings, for example, revealing insights into the *random mutating* of Darwinian evolutionary thinking.

Involution and *Evolution*
What's missing from Darwin's version?

The science of *evolution* is essentially about how the natural world has come to be the way it presently is. However, from the *Threshold* perspective, certain flaws in current Darwinian thinking are revealed. They have arisen because the Darwinists have been unable or unwilling to acknowledge the primacy of *consciousness*.

There's also a key principle that's missing from Darwinism, and that's the polar opposite of **e**volution, ie **in**volution. This refers to the '*descent*' of an individual unit of consciousness into and its *involvement* in the physicality of an unborn, potential, physical body, which is thereby *animated*.

But first, it's necessary to dispose of an unnecessary and irrelevant distraction. And that is the futile dispute between so-called *creationists* and *evolutionists*, a misguided, ideological battle between two rival 'us v. them' camps. Both are locked into rigid, inertia-bound attitudes, and fail to comprehend the whole **creative** process of **evolving** life forms, which starts with *universal consciousness*.

That clash is a typical sign of humanity's collective *pre-adolescence*, an earlier phase in the *masculine*-dominated era of *descent into matter*, still distorting many people's thinking.

Here's an edited extract from **Aether – the Transcript** (ISBN 1-900034-10-7).

Two major Darwinian misconceptions

1. There's the false conclusion that there is an unbroken chain of heredity connecting humankind with apes of an earlier time – which would make them our direct, bloodline ancestors. And that's despite the fact that there have been questions all along about the 'missing link' between apes and humans – which would have to consist of some conclusive fossil evidence of transitional ape-to-human forms. However, none has yet been found.

The orthodox interpretation has been further undermined by a growing body of scientific evidence indicating the presence of humans on Earth long before was supposedly possible, according to the orthodox view.

2. The flawed idea that life on Earth arose 'spontaneously' from non-living matter - that is, from a *primordial soup* of chemicals. Attempts to come up with a recipe for this in the laboratory, however, still remain purely speculative.

Also, Darwin's concept of *natural **selection*** doesn't provide answers to the obvious questions: *How was the **selecting** programme set up in the first place, and for what purpose?* For the very process of *selecting* implies some prior guiding principles for making choices.

He described the actual origin of species as 'the mystery of mysteries', and wrote that he used the expression '*natural selection*' – which implies Nature choosing – only as a metaphor. As a metaphor for what or who doing what is not made clear.

And he does seem to have had a much less dogmatic attitude than current neo-Darwinists, as the following quote from him affirms. **"I am inclined to look at everything as resulting from designed laws, with the details, whether good or bad, left to the working out of what we may call chance."**
(Darwin in a letter to Professor of Botany, Asa Gray, May 22 1860)

Hence his theory of species *adapting* to their environment through so-called '*natural selection*', resulting in the '*survival of the fittest*'. And all this in a world of apparently '*random' mutations* appearing in each new organism.

As a superficial description of the physical evidence, this does seem, more or less, to fit the observable patterns through time. But that kind of nineteenth century 'winners and losers' thinking only addresses the <u>physical</u> dimension of life on earth. It lacks an all-inclusive overview and any insight into the other, more subtle, non-physical dimensions of our lives.

So, given that fundamental flaw in the orthodox theory of evolution, what to put in its place? The *Threshold* perspective has much to offer in resolving those anomalies and failings.

A different tree of evolution (diagram page 358)
Following Darwin, the image of a tree can be used to represent the evolutionary process. The many species are represented by its branches and the individual creatures by its leaves. On a line **radiating outwards** from the centre of the Earth, the tree represents an extending growth towards the sun, while simultaneously **penetrating inwards** towards the centre of the Earth through its roots. That's the basic *polarity*. (See diagram, page 343).

The main trunk of this imaginary tree represents the long history of humanity. The **growing tip** represents humankind at the present moment, as the earthly *avant garde* of the process, always seeking the optimum way to express and manifest the 'seed' potential of the originating impetus within its present circumstances.

The branches below the growing tip represent the 'lower' species, each at its own level, marking its place in the sequence and order of evolutionary events. Given the rhythmical orbiting of the earth around the sun, the branches can be seen as *spin-offs* reaching outwards, **away from the main vertical direction** of the growing tree.

That limits their potential for evolving 'higher'. Consequently, the development of these 'lower' species becomes inertia-bound more quickly because of the effects of *gravity*. And so their physical forms age, dry out and harden earlier. The higher, most recent branchings represent the species most closely related to humankind, ie today's primates.

Meanwhile, species that have become *physically* extinct continue to exist at the *pre-physical* level of being, a level which most humans today cannot consciously access while in their normal waking state. For example, the primitive,'reptilian brain' in humans is physical evidence of an earlier phase in human evolution, still functioning and affecting lives. Thus there remains much to be discovered about the *pre-physical* dimension – including where, when and how the many diverse life-forms on Earth originated and evolved.

It's really all about *consciousness*
With this broader perspective, it becomes clear how the Darwinian view fails regarding the bigger and more subtle questions of human evolution. For **what it doesn't provide is a valid explanation of humanity's distinctive and more advanced modes of *consciousness*** – that is, compared with creatures whose **physical** resemblance to humanity suggests that their **consciousness** would more closely resemble humanity's.

The crucial error has been to notice a pattern of *physical* similarities

The Tree of Evolving Human Consciousness

Involution: pre-physical consciousness 'descends' into *dense* physical forms
because of **gravity**.

Evolution: living forms 'ascend' towards the *rarity* of the pre-physical realm
because of **levity.**

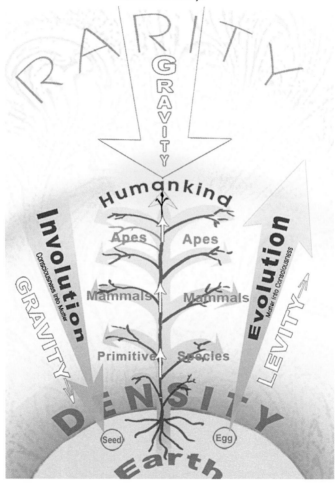

The growing tip is where humankind (collectively) remains soft, young and evolving.

The branches represent earlier outgrowths away from the vertical thrust of the main stem,
continuing to evolve in limited ways, hardening and ageing because of gravity and inertia.

Charles Darwin: *"I am inclined to view the world as if it were the result of designed laws, but with
the details left to chance."* (He noted the coherence behind the apparently random mutations).

A Fundamental Flaw
in Darwinian Evolutionary Theory

This misleading image
implies a direct line of descent from apes to humankind.

Each kind of ape existing today
is the end product of a particular branching away
from the main thrust of evolving human consciousness,
which is represented by the main stem in the diagram below.

Conclusion
1. **The common ancestor** of apes and humankind
would have had a 'younger', softer, more fluid form
than today's creatures.
2. **Humankind** is neither 'the finished product' nor an evolved ape.

The Back Story
Primal *universal consciousness*, which existed prior to physical manifestation,
(a) became *involved* in dense physical matter on Earth (*contraction*), and
(b) has been *evolving* out of the density of physical matter (*expansion*).

And still no *'primal soup'* recipe has been discoverd after many years trying,
because life did not mysteriously emerge from a blend of inorganic chemicals.

and progressive changes, and then naively rush to interpret these as a *linear* chain of causes and effects, linking the latest model to the earlier original version... when the process is evidently more subtle, complex and *nonlinear*.

To summarise: a fundamental scientific misconception of the Darwinians is that humans are direct bloodline descendants of apes, and the *common ancestor* of humankind and today's apes is an earlier ape. For it's now clear that **the apes are *spin-offs***, having earlier in the process branched away from the main stem, which represents the evolution of human consciousness and the progressive development of less dense physical forms.

Why there are no fossil remains of a common ancestor

Once it's realised that the pre-physical *aether/quintessence* existed before the cosmos cooled and condensed into physical-material form, **a vital clue** presents itself. And that clue is that early humankind came into being first as a pre-physical *proto-organism*, which then evolved into the present physical human form.

So, at those stages in the process when the various branchings away from the main human thrust of evolution occurred, the typical physical form at the 'growing tip' would still have been relatively 'young, ie soft and fluid. In biology, that kind of form is known as *neotenous*.

And as the various branchings extended away from the main 'vertical' thrust, their evolving towards lighter, more rarefied forms was countered by *gravity* which pulled their trajectory back towards the density of Earth. As a result, their forms condensed, hardened and 'aged' into the many distinct species, all less evolved than humankind. **Which is why no fossil remains of the soft, young and more fluid *common ancestors* of humans and apes exist.**

Genes: do they actually exist?

A *gene* is essentially an idea, like the idea of a *vitamin*. It's not a physical-material entity. It's an imaginary 'unit of heredity'. Yet genes are often referred to as though they physically exist and somehow indicate an implicit *intention* for a creature to manifest certain traits. There are many examples of this tendency among academics, scientists and journalists online and in print.

The notion of a 'gene' is thus an attempt to *objectify* and *materialise* what is a *potential* or *virtual* trait of an organism, ie a **quality**. And that's done by reducing it down to a physical **quantity** of chemicals, in the form of *chromosomes* of DNA and protein.

The function of genes, therefore, is supposedly to deliver **information** as **instructions** about specific characteristics to be manifested in newly emerging organisms. So, these imaginary entities called genes are, in effect, 'units of *purpose*', ie **consciousness** at a certain level influencing biological processes.

A **genome** is supposed to be a complete catalogue of the genes of any particular species, ie its unique set of DNA sequences. These are supposed to correspond to, and thus 'produce', particular traits or characteristics. However, in reality:
- the same chemical combinations have been associated with different traits, and
- different chemical combinations have been associated with the same traits.

So, DNA *genetics* is based on invalid assumptions. That's because the whole evolutionary process, as revealed from the *Threshold* perspective, is essentially about the evolving of **consciousness**, and how this manifests *physically* in the most advantageous ways and forms for surviving and thriving on Earth.

DNA/genetic micro-manipulation
Trying to trick or outsmart nature into delivering certain results has been a hallmark of this branch of applied science... whether the aims have been medical, commercial, agricultural, or for other purposes. But now an increasing unease and anxiety can be detected behind

the bullish confidence of those promoting and prophesying 'successful' high tech outcomes.

For the familiar ruthless, competitive determination to be a winner – as history has shown – tends to bring unforeseen, unintended consequences, both for unaware victims and for the scientists and sponsors involved, however well intentioned, commercially appealing or technically impressive the project. And through the damage being done, the seeds of future troubles are being sown.

Ecology: a cinderella science?

Ecology is a vital branch of science which has so far been much neglected – subordinated both to the *masculine* 'defence' spending of national governments and to the more *feminine* promotion of greed-driven financial *economics*. However, along with *Threshold Psychology*, Ecology is due to become a major branch of science as the ongoing transition into an era of *ascent out of matter* progresses.

That's because it's essentially concerned with how human consciousness and life on Earth can harmoniously survive and flourish best by being in *resonance* with the rhythms of nature and the cosmos. For such coordination is the key to a sane, balanced, healthy human species, consciously maintaining a natural state of *equilibrium* on planet Earth.

The current major ecological challenges for humanity are well known, including most recently the *waste plastic pollution* of land and seas. There's also a connection between the ongoing **cosmic transition** phase, outlined in the Cosmic Time chapter and **global warming/climate change/extreme weather**. Physical scientific evidence of this has yet to be accumulated.

Ecology presently, however, is a semi-stifled, much inhibited discipline, corrupted by the monetising and commercialising strategy of the financial elite and by State militarism. Consequently, only 'financially viable' ecological initiatives tend to be supported.

An outstanding example of this twisted mentality has been *carbon emissions* trading. It amounts to the gross pretence that *polluting* is a tradable commodity. In this way, *wealthy* polluters evade their ecological responsibilities by paying *poor* polluters to claim that they are reducing their polluting emissions. The dubious amounts recorded then create the **false impression** that total emissions have been reduced by the officially required amount.

This is somewhat similar to clever, expensive accountants assisting the wealthy in evading and avoiding paying taxes. Given this devious practice, **pollution** in its many form and the responsibilities of polluters have largely been ignored by the mainstream corporate media... in servile deference to their ultimate sponsor, *Mama SCAB*.

In the great cosmic *redemption* process, on the long journey of return through many generations, the next major 'milestone' for humanity could be the implementation of something like the project labelled **One Humanity** (page 304). This points to a future phase in which, as a priority, all real, natural, human needs are routinely met so that nobody has to live in deficiency and, simultaneously, no one lives way in excess of their real, natural, human needs.

For by then a more sane and balanced value system will have evolved, under which all surviving humans will be able to live and thrive together on Earth... because it will have become clear that no other way is *ecologically* sound or viable in the long run.

However, here and now, humanity urgently needs to be aware of some secretive planning going on for world **population reduction**, intended to make it easier for a neo-feudal, fascist style global government to be set up and operate. This is an idea that many people are not yet willing or perhaps able to take on board as a real possibility: ie that some human beings have become so callous and corrupted as to be actually plotting a drastic reduction in the overall human population on Earth - in effect, a **cull**.

Who are these conspirators? Who are their targeted victims? Where? When? How?... Many unpalatable questions that nevertheless urgently need to be answered. A range of clues can be detected from the *Threshold* perspective. Meanwhile, one of the great distracting delusions misleading humankind is the rapid, out-of-control growth of *digital* technology.

Digital: a 'smart' but fundamentally flawed system

Because all digital technology is based on **binary** logic (page 34), as such systems grow increasingly complex or 'smart', they tend to run into increasing trouble. Why? Because *binary* computer logic starts from the broad assumption that everything can be thought of as being composed of standardised, *micro-building blocks* of *information* called *bits*. ... just as in physics the world is assumed to be reducible down to various micro-particles.

These *bits* can then be organised and processed by computer software to resemble and exactly replicate any desired form - either as a 2D *virtual* entity, eg a printable image on an electronic screen, or as a potential physical-material form by using a 3D printer.

Binary thinking is an indicator of the *pre-adolescent* stage of humanity's collective evolving. It's the product of a self-centred, exclusive, 'us v. them' mentality that lacks a sense of identity with the greater cosmic wholeness of which each individual is a vital part.

Correspondingly, the currently deteriorating world situation, regarding the reliability of digital technology, has the character of **a pre-adolescent male's desperate attempt to impress the world with his cleverness** – successful at first, but then failing because it was not built on sound foundations. The logic of this sterile, emotion-free, mathematically encoded discipline has an irresistible fascination for the pre-adolescent still 'present' in many adults.

A major problem is that in any major digital system today, no human mind can hold the quantity of encoded information now involved. And it's this inherent weakness that leaves humankind vulnerable to hacking attacks, major shutdowns and the failure of systems now completely dependent on digital technology and so-called *artificial intelligence*.

This parallels the way a bridge, building or machine with a built-in, fundamental design flaw, is doomed eventually to fail. So, there's a major inherent problem here. In this age of ever faster, more powerful, digital computers, all codes based on these identical *bits*, however complex, can eventually be de-coded. And in a world still largely run by *Mama SCAB* and *Papa State*, deception, cheating and fraud are very much the norm.

And that's attracting ever more people to **cyber crime** of one sort or another. Thus the continuing series of major cyber incidents, followed by temporary 'fixes' – a situation somewhat like being stuck in a deep hole and digging oneself ever deeper, rather than finding a way of climbing out.

For the whole shaky idea of '**security**', regarding 'confidential' information held by the State, commercial organisations or private individuals amounts to little more than a wishful fantasy. And with humankind already confused, politically powerless and passively consenting to become ever more dependent on digital technology, more of the same means the problems can only get worse. So, is there a sane way out of this man-made trap?

Human ingenuity, given some inspirational motivation, is capable of coming up with a range of ideas that could benefit all humankind and help create a more balanced and sane world. But first, the path has to be cleared of some major obstructions: not least, the fierce resistance of some to any radical changes to the status quo... that resistance being essentially the *inertia* resulting from the departing era of *descent into matter*.

The *One Humanity* chapter addresses these issues and proposes a new generation of **analogue technology** – ie analogous to nature and the cosmos.

Artificial Intelligence (*AI*): a dangerous, delusional fantasy

Viewed from the *Threshold* perspective, *AI* is a contemporary example of cutting edge, digital technology racing ahead on a pioneering but deeply flawed venture. Despite its optimistic promises of technically impressive and commercially successful outcomes, in essence, **it's an attempt to invent and evolve artificial, programmable and therefore conveniently controllable substitutes for natural human intelligence**.

However, it's also symptomatic of the worldwide confusion and disorientation resulting from ignorance (a) of how the cosmos works, and (b) of the ongoing shift from a cosmic era of *descent into matter* to one of *ascent out of matter*.

Algorithms are the sets of precise instructions for computers to follow in any operation they are programmed to perform. Therefore, all kinds of human prejudice, bias and errors can be built into an algorithm, and then become part of whatever outcomes follow. *AI* equipment normally processes an uninterrupted inflow of digitised data. So, it depends on reliable, 'secure' digital technology and a consistent electricity supply, neither of which can presently be guaranteed, since both are vulnerable to human error, technical failure and sabotage.

AI is a prime example of the *boysworld science* mentality and *super-smart* technological inventiveness (page 337). Significantly, it's also a commercially well funded and officially encouraged area of research – which suggests darker, hidden purposes than some of the hyper-enthusiastic pioneers may realise.

The predicted '*singularity*', refers to a typical pre-adolescent male fantasy of digital technology merging with human consciousness to produce super-intelligent beings, 'smarter' than current humankind... by the 2040s. Its proponents also assume an immature, 'value-free' attitude, which means ignoring any moral or ethical constraints, while trying to avoid any responsibility for unforeseen bad outcomes.

The protagonists of *AI* have tended to be, although not exclusively, enthusiastic males, enticed, manipulated and fired up with fantasised aspirations for fame and fortune – to be achieved through making world-conquering discoveries or inventing commercially or militarily successful products and heroic, life-saving, medical fixes.

AI, as applied to medical diagnosis and treatment options, amounts to calculating probable outcomes, based on whatever data is being fed in – data normally selected according to orthodox materialistic assumptions. This is somewhat like analysing and classifying the flotsam and scum on a polluted river – with no consideration of the wider, deeper and long term factors creating those symptoms.

An *AI* health warning

Don't be charmed by AI smartness into passive complicity in your own disempowerment. *In any AI system The whole repertoire of automated responses has been pre-programmed in advance to cover all predictable situations, according to their mathematical probability, based on various unspoken assumptions. Therefore, if the wider circumstances change in unexpected ways, those assumptions will be rendered invalid, and the relevant AI systems will automatically respond inappropriately and perhaps dangerously.*

Robots, trans-humans and electricity

The *Threshold* perspective reveals that sensitivity to the <u>qualitative</u> difference between natural, animate beings and artificial, inanimate systems is crucial. For one purpose of those funding much current *AI* research seems to be to make humans increasingly remote-controllable through implanted micro digital devices. So, some penetrating investigation into the unseen influences and factors at work here is urgently required.

It's all part of an envisaged merging of human and artificial intelligence into **trans-human hybrids** or **cyborgs**... *"when humans transcend biology"*. This is the so-called **singularity** which, inevitably, will bring many unforeseen and unintended consequences, as certain humans try to outsmart nature in the pursuit of a range of delusional ambitions.

From the *Threshold* perspective, humankind appears to be heading for deep trouble in accepting and complying with that general trend towards a scenario which suggests many conflicts of incompatibility, severe disturbances and long lasting damage.

For example, some robots will be small enough to circulate within the physical body and be programmed to self-replicate, as well as take over other digital devices and collectively swarm to protect one another. So, how can this self-perpetuating trend be countered?

The key to answering that question is the bigger question of what 'higher' knowledge will be needed to halt and reverse the process that has now begun – as in the legend of *The Sorcerer's Apprentice*. For it may no longer be the case that whatever processes some humans may set in motion, others will be able later to terminate and dismantle.

The programming of 'intelligent' robots is inevitably based on them 'learning' from the past, ie *memory*... which is essentially 'dead' data/information. And the overall *direction* of the logic that's built into their design is pre-set, expressing the unquestioned assumptions and purposes of those who fund and sponsor their development – eg to maintain the status quo.

What *AI* robots cannot access is the vitality and spontaneous wisdom of the timeless, living, *equilibrium*-seeking, pre-physical *aether/quintessence/quantum vacuum*. So, the prospect is a sterile, imprisoning *AI* world.

A flawed 'futurist' agenda
Certain techno-fix futurists appear to be attempting to establish an irreversible agenda and schedule through preaching self-fulfilling prophecies, just like some religious manifestos. People are then judged by them to be either positive supporters of the current wave

of new info-tech, OR negative, resistant opponents, intent on preventing its further progress.

Meanwhile, the majority of humans remain only superficially aware of and therefore mostly unconcerned about this extremely hazardous and largely hidden area of human activity. Exponentially accelerating progress in *AI* is presented as inevitable, and the techno-fixing of all diseases and of poverty are still being fraudulently sold as part of this package.

A more mature approach would be first to investigate the motives, ie the hidden agendas, of those behind the concerted push to develop the *AI* industry, which does require significant financing. Meanwhile, much re-thinking is needed in order to appreciate the *qualitative* differences between *natural* and *artificial* intelligence before the situation runs out of control.

Crucial questions therefore arise about *AI*'s connections with the State, commercial corporations, mass religious organisations and the materialistic science establishment... and how much complicity there is, one way and another. For privileged, well-funded scientists are usually unwilling to bite the hands that entice, protect and generously feed them.

And all the while, this is being acted out within the 'house of cards', assembled and controlled by the global *syndicate of central and arch-banks, SCAB*, which has its own dark agenda. All of which is a reminder that behind the glamour there are shadowy, malevolent forces behind much of today's science.

What about the ongoing *secret science* research?
Humankind in the 21st century is still being indoctrinated with childish 'us v. them' attitudes. Why? Because this serves the distorted, immature ambitions of ruling elites, eager to demonstrate their fantasised power through weaponry, whether labelled *defensive* or *offensive*. It also serves the the purposes of the smart, financial elite who are playing *divide-and-rule* by stirring up those rivalries,

and then lending money and selling weapons to the various competing factions.

Consequently, there's an ongoing hidden **arms race** of evolving technologies, radically different from and more powerful than nuclear weapons. It's part of a secret world of unorthodox, unconventional science and technology, currently being researched and tested. Joseph P Farrell has made this a special subject of his research in various books.

One clue to that technology is the Large Hadron Collider (LHC) at CERN, the world's largest and most powerful particle accelerator. An outstanding feat of engineering, it also serves darker, unspoken motives. It's based on a system of powerful counter-rotating magnetic fields, a technology closely associated with (a) the German WW2 *Nazi Bell* Device, a pre-nuclear weapons project, and (b) *anti-gravity* research.

Given LHC's technical troubles right from the start, this connection raises many questions, not least concerning the complicity, naive or knowing, of the scientists allowed to experiment with that formidable piece of potentially destructive technology. Meanwhile, propaganda documentaries about CERN create the impression of a happy, well funded, exclusive club of clever scientists, dedicated to a cult of super-high-tech *'smash-it-and-see'* research.

In the ongoing arms race, the various rivals are **relics** of the departing *descent into matter* era. Which is why their aims and 'games' now constitute a grave danger to all life on Earth, as the remaining time to prevent critical levels of global toxicity and damage is running out. The challenge is how much damage they'll be allowed to inflict before their inevitable demise.

Meanwhile, they're still able to pursue their deluded fantasies of world domination. And in this they're callously treating the rest of humankind as an expendable, disposable resource, kept in ignorance and fear, divided and ruled, distracted and pre-occupied...

until it's either waking up time or too late to prevent major catastrophes on Earth.

Alternatively, LHC, with its hyper-sensitive detectors, could be re-dedicated to investigating the *Threshold*, ie the *zero point field*, the border zone between the *physical-material* and the *pre-physical* aetheric dimensions, as a potential resource for greatly enhancing life on Earth.

Why the unquestioning compliance of scientists?

Why do contemporary physicists doggedly persevere with deeply flawed ideas such as the so-called 'standard model', which clearly fails because it cannot reconcile the *macro* with the *micro* scale, ie the gross *physical-material* world with the subtle *pre-physical* dimension?

It seems that having been inducted, at an impressionable age, into the belief system called 'science', and having been enticed into following that through into a career, many later find the idea of radically revising that flawed worldview too disturbing to contemplate.

So, in order to pursue a path in science, they comply with the prevailing **dogma**, ie the unofficial set of restrictions on what is and what isn't acceptable 'scientific' thinking. And that regime is maintained through various incentives and disincentives, imposed by their invisible sponsor, *Mama SCAB*. For what purpose? There seems to be a clue in the following.

Have scientists been deliberately misguided?

Whether *The Protocols of the Elders of Zion* is a genuine record of certain discussions or a well informed piece of satire is of little practical significance – just as the merit of certain plays, allegedly written by a William Shakespeare, doesn't change according to whether or not they were written by someone with that name.

Either way, *The Protocols* is a master class in mass mind control, given that it was first published over 100 years ago, before radio and TV. The following excerpt is from an early 20th century translation from a supposedly Russian original text.

Regarding how scientists are easily misled into believing whatever 'the authorities' decree... "The goyim* are not guided by practical use of unprejudiced historical observation, but by theoretical routine without any critical regard for consequent results.

We need not, therefore, take any account of them - let them amuse themselves until the hour strikes, or live on hopes of new forms of enterprising pastime, or on the memories of all they have enjoyed. *For them let that play the principal part which we have persuaded them to accept as the dictates of science (theory).*

It is with this object in view that we are constantly, by means of our press, arousing a blind confidence in these theories. The intellectuals of the goyim (see Glossary) *will puff themselves up with their knowledge and, without any logical verification of them, will put into all the information available from science (that) which our agentur specialists have cunningly pieced together for the purpose of educating their minds in the direction we want.*

Do not suppose for a moment that these statements are empty words: think carefully of the successes we arranged for Darwinism, Marxism, Nietzscheism. To us Jews, at any rate, it should be plain to see what a disintegrating importance these directives have had upon the minds of the goyim.

The Protocols of the Elders of Zion 2.2

Why is science such a turn-off for so many people, yet fascinating for a few?

The simple answer, from the *Threshold* perspective, is that having emerged during the *masculine*-dominated era of *descent into matter*, physical science soon lost the youthful, magical excitement of inquisitive, open-minded experimentation and discovery. It became, instead, inertia-bound, institutionalised, dogmatic and corrupted by money, politics, status and professional rivalries - ie by the typical human attitudes prevailing at the time.

That context gave rise to the ruthless seeking of material wealth, power over other people, superiority in status and fame, all of which were, and in some situations still are, considered acceptable and admirable behaviour. It also inevitably encouraged cheating and fraud over honesty and integrity. For example, the supposed 'checks and balances' function of 'peer reviewing' is now widely recognised as susceptible to abuse, rivalry and carelessness.

The result, broadly, has been the misguided, amoral, sterile and typically *masculine* kind of materialistic, mechanistic science already described. The turn-off seems to begin with the teaching of science at school, despite the wide appeal of science fiction as entertainment.

And after the initial glamour of hi-tech equipment and the fantasy of making great new discoveries starts to wear thin, the idea of a continuing interest or a career in science only seems to appeal to a small proportion of young people, ie those who feel that those qualities suit their personality, preferences and curiosity.

Mathematics
Why is *mathematics*, like *science*, such a *turn-off* for so many people?

Mathematics, as presently understood, can be seen – like orthodox materialistic science – as a legacy of the *masculine*-dominated *descent* era. Traceable back thousands of years, it still represents in certain respects the mentality of humanity at an earlier stage of its evolving, when the power of a number system in measuring and quantifying was a new, useful and exciting area of discovery.

Also, over the last few centuries, materialistic science and mathematics have become colluding partners in a joint exercise in self-deception. And that seems to have occurred primarily because mathematics has certain qualities that are highly seductive to some scientists.

So-called *pure* mathematics – as opposed to practical *applied* mathematics – involves thinking that's detached from the messy, ever-changing, uncontrollable ways of the physical-material world. It's an abstract, objective discipline that's orderly, clean, logically consistent, controllable and emotion-free. And it's these qualities which seem to have enticed scientists into adopting it as their main language, despite various incompatibilities between the two disciplines (see EMUs, page 346).

And the attraction has been mutual, since in return, the prestige that the young discipline of physical science has enjoyed throughout the last few hundred years has benefitted mathematicians. As a consequence, both disciplines incorporate unresolved inconsistencies, conundrums and enigmas that cannot be resolved within the limitations each has imposed on itself.

Two mathematical examples are *the prime numbers sequence* (below) and *Gödel's Incompleteness Theorems*. Consequently, one important lesson seems to be...

> **"We can't solve problems**
> **by using the same kind of thinking**
> **we used when we created them."**
> Albert Einstein

By contrast, *Threshold Mathematics*, from its all-inclusive perspective, incorporates both abstract and living qualities as *two* complementary opposites within a greater *oneness*, and all within the unlimited *no-thing-ness* of universal consciousness. And so it opens up the possibility of a whole new area of mathematical thinking that includes the relationship between the transcendent *pre-physical* and the earthly *physical-material* worlds.

A 2000+ year old conundrum resolved by *Threshold Mathematics*

For example, in <u>Threshold Mathematics</u> and in <u>The Primal Code</u> (2006) there's offered a simple resolution of the oldest conundrum in mathematics, the 2000+ year old mystery of *the **prime numbers** sequence*. It's resolved by starting with the three basic *Threshold* axioms, not yet incorporated by conventional mathematics... to which they're then applied in order to reach a resolution that's self-consistent and *resonates* with the functioning of the cosmos.

Prior to that discovery, at least five popular books about 'the mystery of the primes' were published, and a millennium prize of $1 million was offered. But after 2006... silence. Here are what some eminent mathematicians & scientists have said about the **Prime Numbers** enigma, prior to its 2006 resolution.

"...The primes represent the most tantalising enigma in the pursuit of human knowledge..."
Cover blurb of **The Music of the Primes** by UK professor of mathematics, Marcus du Sautoy (2004).

"Upon looking at these numbers, one has the feeling of being in the presence of one of the inexplicable secrets of creation."
Mathematician Prof. Don Zagier speaking of the primes, as quoted in **The Mathematical Experience** by Philip J Davis and Reuben Hersh (1981).

Prime Numbers – The Most Mysterious Figures in Math.
Title of a 2005 book by mathematician David Wells.

God's Secret Formula – deciphering the riddle of the universe and the prime number code.
Title of a1997 non-fiction book by scientist Peter Plichta.

"Prime Obsession ...the Greatest Unsolved Problem in Mathematics"
Title of a 2003 book about the prime numbers by mathematician John Derbyshire.

Each author seemed intuitively to sense something very special, yet none was able to grasp what actually makes the prime numbers so significant. What was required to detect the previously undetected pattern was a different approach and a different way of thinking - essentially, an 'out of the box' approach. That was esoteric thinking in action.

Similarly, certain other previously unresolved mathematical 'problems' have also been resolved – including the Riemann Hypothesis, the Goldbach Conjecture and Fermat's last so-called Theorem – although not in a style that conventional mathematicians are yet ready to acknowledge as 'proper' mathematics.

Mathematics: discovered or invented?

From the *Threshold* perspective, this longstanding, unresolved question reveals a flawed, superficial, **binary** way of thinking, which can be addressed only very briefly here. First, given the bigger picture context as described in the earlier chapter, *The Becoming of*

Cosmos out of Chaos, all forms of separateness, including the cosmos and humankind, are ultimately manifestations of the unlimited, all-inclusive *universal consciousness*.

What is called *mathematics* is a broad, loosely defined area of human thinking that is continuously expanding and evolving... from early notions of size, quantity and number way back in the *masculine*-dominated *descent* era. Therefore, like materialistic science, it displays various '*boysworld*' characteristics (page 337), including certain abstract ideas that allude to <u>qualities</u> of the pre-physical *aether/quintessence/quantum vacuum*. But, because of mental inertia, these are couched in inadequate, *descent era*, <u>quantitative</u> terms.

In the ongoing *transition* phase, as human *individuality* and *intellect* developed, the emphasis in mathematical progress shifted away from **discovery** towards **invention**. But this could change again as human **intuitive** *Threshold* awareness becomes an increasingly significant factor.

The Arts: glimpses of the as yet unfamiliar

This very brief mention of 'the arts' is mainly to acknowledge what a hugely important part of human life they are. The brevity is not intended to imply any minimising of their significance.

The creative arts provide clues as to where a society and its culture is heading, and what as yet unexpressed thoughts and ideas are present and potent in the aether. That's because artists, in all kinds of media, tend to have a special sensitivity to emerging directions and patterns before these have taken on or been given a recognisable form or a label in a society.

That's why, in some societies, artists tend to have an unofficial kind of licence, a special permit, to express, in creative ways, ideas and feelings that might otherwise be unacceptable to 'the authorities' or to others.

This privilege does, however, bring with it certain responsibilities regarding how the rest of a society might be affected and influenced by whatever the artists are trying to express in their work. Yet in contemporary individualistic, greed-driven cultures, that sense of artistic responsibility is generally not considered important, compared with the more familiar patterns of immature quests for fame, status and wealth.

Also, given their unique and vulnerable position in today's materialistic and celebrity dominated world, genuinely creative artists – as opposed to technically competent *hacks* – are particularly prone to the enticing prospect of 'selling out', ie trading their talents for short-term materialistic rewards.

The context of certain ruling elites controlling and limiting virtually all areas of people's lives, as described earlier, can be seen to account for the way some highly gifted creative individuals remain largely ignored, while other, less talented ones are favoured and enjoy worldly success. Such outcomes largely depend on which artistic work resonates with the ethos, the wider plans and the prejudices of the ruling elite at any given time, regardless of artistic merit.

What is 'a good death'?

From the *Threshold* perspective, **birth** can be understood as a **manifestation** from a pre-physical state into physical-material form. **Death** is the polar opposite process, ie a return or **redemption** back into a *pre-physical* state of being. And after the temporary physical vehicle has been shed, an individual being does not completely cease to exist.

In Western cultures, that *pre-physical* entity of individual consciousness is sometimes called the *soul*. Other cultures have other names for this state of being. The *soul* is one distinct unit or strand of universal consciousness on a long journey through many physical lifetimes of learning on Earth. It's much more enduring than personality or character.

As a result of the *descent into matter*, a combination of ignorance and mental inertia has frozen many people's attitude to death and dying into a rigid, dogmatic mentality of 'one lifetime only'. They are thus unable or unwilling to conceive of any kind of existence beyond their present incarnation, fearing or ignoring 'the great unknown' beyond this earthly life.

A more open, enlightened attitude would be to consider how well prepared people can be for the next phase of their greater life/ journey. For there are accounts given by some exceptional individuals who have been able to recall their experience of previous deaths, and other accounts of *near death experiences*.

What is 'a good death'?
Briefly, it can be thought of as a peaceful, easy departure from one's physical body after:

(a) having resolved as many outstanding issues and conflicts of this lifetime as possible, and

(b) having said farewell to loved ones and friends, while intuitively accepting that this physical parting may not be a complete and final end of those connections.

What is the *Threshold* perspective on death and dying, regarding healing?

From a **healing** perspective, if the natural ending of an earthly life is clearly imminent, the most valuable healing contribution from another person in the circumstances will probably involve sensitively helping the dying person prepare for a good death experience – physically, emotionally and mentally. The physical aspect can be aided with skilled palliative care. So, consciously preparing for a good death all through each earthly lifetime, by clearing out old psychological 'baggage', is generally a positive and healthy thing to do.

Also, exploring the idea of **reincarnation** and the sense of **karmic** responsibility that comes with it, contributes positively towards your next incarnation. However, accepting reincarnation is not a requirement for living a fulfilling life and experiencing a good death.

For those curious to explore this area of knowledge further, there are various esoteric works that deal with all aspects of death and dying, both practical and philosophical. Eastern cultures have tended to be less inhibited about this aspect of life on Earth.

Understanding more fully the dying and death process dissolves and dissipates much unnecessary fear or dread – especially for those who have been locked into a materialistic, *descent* era mindset, and have so far refused to accept that there could be any kind of conscious individual existence that doesn't involve a physical body.

Psychologically, a fear of death and dying may be related to other personal fears and anxieties, for example, fear of separation from familiar people and places, dread of aloneness, loss of valued possessions, the emptiness of the 'dark void' or 'evil spirits'.

One way of thinking about your forthcoming death could be to imagine it as marking 'vacation time' away from the residential school called planet Earth. It's when you return 'home' to assimilate the benefits of your experiences and learning at school, in preparation for another term when you'll take on a new role in a different class, and learn more about yourself, the world and your part in its affairs.

Coming to terms with death and dying puts our worldly concerns and troubles into a much wider and longer perspective. For example, our sense of *identity** as an individual human being is enhanced, extended and elevated to a universally shared perspective from way beyond our individual earthly involvements and commitments

* **The Identity Continuum** (page 427) is a concise outline of the *Threshold* perspective regarding our combined individual and universal sense of identity.

A Brief Summary
of *The Threshold Perspective*

The three universal *Threshold* principles governing the functioning of the whole living cosmos are the *primacy of consciousness, polarity* and *resonance*. A primal *polarity* is that between the *pre-physical* and the *physical-material* realms. Unlike the 3D physical-material world, the *pre-physical* realm is characterised by a primal, 2-way pulsating of expansion and contraction.

That dynamic *polarity* accounts for the whole living cosmos and all within it. And in the natural world it finds expression in the universal *masculine* and the universal *feminine*. Regarding time, the currently departing, *masculine*-dominated era of *descent into matter* is being superseded in the ongoing *transitional* phase by an era of increasingly *feminine*-influenced *ascent out of matter*, suggesting an ongoing, alternating cycle of such eras.

The destiny/destination of the cosmos is, first, a dynamic state of *equilibrium* between the polar opposite forces of expanding *levity* and contracting *gravity*... progressing towards a *redemption* of matter back into energy, and energy back into universal consciousness.

BUT... the departing *descent* era has left a legacy of inertia-bound relics which are obstructing the evolutionary *impetus* of human consciousness. One such relic is what is known today as 'Jewish' culture, a uniquely convoluted expression of humanity's *feminine* aspect, which itself has long been distorted by the imbalance of the *descent* era.

Into Jewish culture, around the 8th century CE, came a major influx of converts from Khazaria, a predominantly *masculine* warrior people, resulting in a unique combination of *feminine* and *masculine* qualities. This arrangement has proved an extremely effective subtle influence in the world especially in undermining the nation state.

1

For that other major relic, the nation state arose as one expression of the universal *masculine* principle, which itself has naturally been predominant in the *descent* era.

In the current phase of *transition*, however, as the balance of cosmic forces shifts and a new order emerges, that *descent era* sabotaging mode of operating has become redundant. Consequently, the disproportionately significant influence of Jews in the world is now waning.

The ongoing shift away from *contraction* and the *masculine* principle towards *expansion* and the *feminine* principle has also prompted a temporary, regressive, *masculine/male* pushback, and accounts for much of the current widespread turbulence. Evidence of this is in the emergence of various authoritarian regimes.

Mature, responsible, impartial people with an understanding of all this and a will to heal – ie individuals not seeking personal fame, wealth, nor political or religious power – are now urgently required to help birth a whole new, balanced and ecologically sound way of living for all humankind... perhaps along the lines proposed as the *One Humanity* project, introduced in this work.

So, a major task for humanity now is to find such individuals and encourage and support them in taking on the responsibilities of that role, while carefully dismantling and replacing the current dysfunctional status quo of authority, wealth, power and privilege.

Conclusion

As an essential part of the ongoing cosmic *transition* phase, the natural tendency towards a state of *equilibrium* between the primal forces of contracting *gravity* and expanding *levity* is proceeding. And within humanity, it's also working out as the dynamic between the universal *masculine* and *feminine*.

In the recent phase of the departing *descent* era, certain aspects of these two universals have found expression in two human institutions, symbolised by the characters, *Papa State* and *Mama SCAB* (page 197). But as that era departs, both are now in decline, as also are certain divisive, religious, self-appointing agents of divinity.

This book addresses some of the many shams and scams that are still keeping humankind ignorant, confused and powerless - ie unable to self-heal and help create the more balanced, sane and just world many still long for, despite all the trouble and pain they've been experiencing. But explaining how certain problems are being perpetuated is only a start.

For any genuine healing work is likely to encounter fierce resistance from those who naively believe that they're 'winning', or at least 'doing OK', under the current world status quo.

Therefore, the many people of goodwill around the world who feel determined to overcome that resistance to change, now need to:
(a) **coordinate** their efforts,
(b) **learn** to positively value their differences as natural **diversity within a greater unity**, and
(c) **cultivate** a significant degree of **MUTUAL TRUST** amongst themselves.

Otherwise, the options available could remain limited to a choice between:
(a) ie the sick world of *Papa State* and *Mama SCAB*, as it degenerates into an authoritarian, global, fascist **dictatorship**, OR

384

(b) an internet-driven, chaotic cacophony of disconnected, divergent, conflicting voices and forces, a 21st century Tower of Babel.

And since the many regressive forces each have their own deluded plans for humankind, all humans are inevitably involved one way or another, like it or not. So, it makes a difference how each human being responds to this challenge, whether actively or passively.

For to ignore what's going on, given the awareness now made possible from the *Threshold* perspective, amounts to passively allowing warped, unbalanced, power-lusting individuals to take charge and exploit their fellow humans for misguided, selfish purposes.

However, with the help of the three basic *Threshold* principles, it is now possible to navigate a way through the current world turmoil, and begin to formulate radically new approaches to what otherwise appears to be a jungle of entangled problems... ranging from practical earthly matters to abstract philosophical conundrums.

It's also now possible challenge the **assumptions** behind all kinds of distorted thinking, ie notions that have long been unquestioningly accepted as simply 'the way it is', and so haven't yet been widely investigated or evaluated.

For example, it is possible to conceive of a world without all the trouble caused by certain institutions, including:

a. the many competing **nation states** whose leaderships always **need enemies** in order to justify their own privileged positions as protectors,
b. the one **global financial syndicate, SCAB**, that runs the greed-driven, debt money system, and divides-and-rules by playing the competing nation states off against one another,
c. the major **supremacy-preaching *religions***, ie the transnational corporate empires, run by self-appointing *'divinity agents'*.

d. the **materialistic science establishment**, ie the self-serving leadership of a dogma-bound belief system, characterised by a '*pre-adolescent male*' attitude.

These institutions each have their own cultures, traditions and vocabularies into which the young are initiated before they're able to question the underlying assumptions and beliefs. And then there are those **secret societies** that promote a sense of exclusivity and superiority in their recruits through promising degrees of access to hidden sacred knowledge.

However, with the benefit of the *Threshold* perspective, it's now possible to understand, at least in broad principle, how the whole cosmos works. So, the mental tools now exist for finding the coherence behind any confusing or troubled situation, enabling one to see how it fits into the bigger picture and the longer view.

Similarly, it can be appreciated how each individual human being fits into the greater cosmic context, and so is continuously influencing the world in various ways, great or small, for better or worse.

Another consequence of this work is that there's now a lot of **owning up** to be done – that is, by those who've been deceiving, neglecting, robbing or otherwise harming their fellow human beings.... and the sooner the better, to avoid further suffering and the vengeful resentment which inevitably builds up and eventually rebounds on the perpetrators.

A warning against misuse of *Threshold* knowledge

It also has to be emphasised that attempting to misuse or abuse the powerful *Threshold* knowledge for selfish or malevolent purposes will eventually prove either ineffective or actually harmful to anyone who chooses to take that path.

That's because the cosmos naturally tends to rebalance itself towards a state of *equilibrium* between the primal forces that govern its functioning, and any actions that oppose this process are sooner or later cancelled out – whatever short term gains some people may imagine they're achieving.

And as for the three troublesome undercurrents...

Once it's realised that the old game is over, and a new and very different one has begun, the necessary changes will start to happen... despite some fierce resistance from those stuck in the mental inertia of the departing *descent* era. The ongoing transitional phase is bringing to an end the age of *masculine*-dominated nation states, federations and alliances of states, whether religious or secular.

Jews. Despite the dominant majority of Ashkenazis and the inbred Jewish delusion of *superiority*, the essential *feminine* quality at the core of Jewish culture represents a pragmatic, practical, adaptive attitude to life. So, once the *transition* is felt to have reached a significant point, the basic attitude and tone of Jewish culture worldwide could quickly begin to change to a more inclusive, non-superior, tolerant, harmonious quality. And furthermore, the *SCAB debt money* scam – after centuries of exploiting what was a *masculine*-dominated world – will itself dissolve and therefore cease to fund Zionism, which will simply evaporate.

Muslims. As the rise of the universal *feminine* proceeds and Muslim women become more assertive in the great rebalancing, so the eventually *masculine* macho tendency and jealous brotherly in-fighting will diminish, enabling humanity to mature into more harmonious and creative pursuits.

Christians. With the rebalancing of the *masculine* and *feminine*, the ambivalence of the fragmented, inertia-bound Church will be transcended by a dynamic, inclusive, youthful, unifying tendency, inspiring all of humanity in all its diversity.

Similarly, the rigid conservatism and the class and *caste* mentality of various tradition-bound belief systems, religious and secular, will gradually be dissolved as the *transition* out of a world that descended into the *density* of matter proceeds.

Such trends as these could be the local and global beginnings of a **One Humanity** world which has no place for exclusive *supremacist* attitudes. BUT this will only happen through continuous, consistent, clearsighted and persistent effort, sustained through several generations, and despite the inevitable setbacks and unexpected challenges along the way.

How long might all this take? The healing will take as long as it takes, since it's dependent on the commitment, ie the will power, intelligence, integrity and compassion of all who involve themselves. But the longer the deteriorating continues, the worse will be the clearing-up job left for those who follow later. So, the sooner the awakening begins, the sooner will come the end of a small misguided minority sabotaging, fooling and exploiting the vast majority of humankind.

Pioneers required now.

References

BOOKS etc: introducing the pre-physical aetheric dimension, and other valuable insights.

The Etheric Ernst Marti **Part 1** ISBN: 978-1-912230-05-1, **Part 2** ISBN 978-1-912230-13-6
The Four Ethers Ernst Marti ISBN: 0-935690-02-6
Aether: Knowledge is Power (Audio CD-ROM) ISBN 1-900034-11-5
Aether - The Transcript ISBN: 1-900034-10-7
Man or Matter Ernst Lehrs ISBN: 0-85440-430-9
Physical and Ethereal Spaces George Adams ISBN: 0-85440-328-0
Toward a Phenomenology of the Etheric World ISBN: 088010-115-6
Space and Counterspace Nick C. Thomas ISBN: 978-086315-670-0
Projective Geometry (website) www.nct.goetheanum.org/

On Death and Dying Elisabeth Kubler-Ross
Death: The Great Adventure (a compilation) ISBN: 97828828980085
The Tibetan Book of Living and Dying Sogyal Rinpoche ISBN: 0712654372
The Natural Death Handbook ISBN: 1844132269

BOOKS & QUOTES etc: concerning certain crucial worldly factors currently obstructing the evolving of human consciousness.

The Hebrew Goddess Dr. Raphael Patai ISBN 0-8143-2221-2

The Myth of the Jewish Race Dr. Raphael Patai ISBN 0814319491

The Invention of the Jewish People Professor Shlomo Sand ISBN: 978-1-84467-623-1 A best selling 2009 book by the Jewish Professor of History at Tel Aviv University, tells the complex story of how an artificial Jewish ethnic/national identity has been conjured up over centuries.

The Invention of the Land of Israel Professor Shlomo Sand ISBN: 978-1-78168-083-4

Whose Promised Land? Colin Chapman ISBN: 9780745918716
The following quotes are from **Soldiering for Peace** (1966) by **General Carl von Horn**, the Swedish Commander of the United Nations Truce Supervisory Organization (UNTSO) in Palestine from 1951 to 1963, who was very critical about Israeli reporting of events during this period:

> "The highly skilled Israeli Information Service and the entire press combined to manufacture a warped, distorted version which was disseminated with professional expertise through every available channel to their own people and their sympathisers and supporters in America and the rest of the world. Never in all my life had I believed the truth could be so cynically, expertly bent."

General Carl von Horn wrote about the difficult task faced by the UNTSO in trying to remain neutral and objective in the conflict in the face of much biased distorting and obscuring:

> "Our *raison d'etre* as peacekeepers was objectivity and impartiality. Yet these very qualities were exactly those which led to hostility. It was understandable; time and time again in the course of frank discussions with Israeli officers and officials, I had heard them openly repudiate the idea of objectivity. Their flat statement 'You are either for or against us', explained why – having dared to be entirely objective – I had now been branded as "against".

I had seen it happen many times before from my predecessors down to the ordinary observer on the frontiers who, in the course of his duty, had incurred Arab or Israeli hostility simply because his *impartial* version had been *very* different from theirs. Even nastier was an Israeli tendency immediately to brand objectivity as anti-Semitic; a convenient label which could be smeared on to any UN soldier whose impartial report did not weigh down in favour of the Israelis.

We have from time to time incurred a certain degree of animosity in our dealings with the Arabs, but never in the same implacable and frenetic way. The Arab could be difficult, intolerant, indeed often impossible; but their code of behaviour was on an infinitely higher and more civilised level. I think that we all came to this conclusion in the UNTSO, which was strange, because there was hardly a man among us who had not originally arrived in the Holy Land without the most positive and sympathetic attitude towards the Israelis and their ambitions for their country.

Never in my life have I encountered a nation with such an infinite talent for turning goodwill into disillusion and so often disgust. It seemed as though the state were possessed of some demon with a capacity to turn potential friends into enemies. I am certain that I shall be bitterly attacked for setting down my impressions so frankly, but unfortunately they are the truth. All of us who went to Israel knew very little about Arabs, but a great deal about the Jews and their appalling sufferings in the Second World War.

I have never been – and I am not – anti-Semitic; I have always numbered Jews among some of my closest friends since boyhood. I have good friends in Israel, wonderful families who stood by me and welcomed me into their homes during the height of the boycott. Many of our personnel, too, had close friends in the new state long before they came out to Jerusalem, and I would think that seldom before have the members of any organisation – and this was a truly international one – started off with such a fund of goodwill towards a state which had emerged at the cost of such dreadful suffering.

What went wrong? I always had a talk with staff members who were leaving the Mission. Invariably it was the same story. Nearly all of them had arrived with the honest intention to help both parties to the Armistice Agreement, but with a conscious sympathy for the people of "poor little Israel". Yet after two or three years in daily contact with officials, soldiers and private individuals on both sides, there had been a remarkable change in their attitude. I found it sad but very significant that when I asked them what their most negative experiences had been during their service with UNTSO the reply was almost invariably: "The consistent cheating and deception of the Israelis"."

The book provides an example of deliberate mis-information put out by Israeli government ministers about the Palestinians. An Israeli minister of education urged that Israeli youth should be given this information about Palestinian Arabs:

"It is important that our youth should know that when we returned to this country we did not find any other nation here and certainly no nation which had lived here for hundreds of years. Such Arabs as we did find here arrived only a few decades before us in the 1830s and 1840s as refugees from the oppression of Muhammad Ali in Egypt."

The Controversy of Zion Douglas Reed (1895 1976) ISBN: 978-0-9844733-7-3
A thorough and exhaustively documented history of Zionism, from its pre-historic roots through to the 1950s, by a senior foreign correspondent of the Times (UK) newspaper in the mid-20th century. A controversial but highly respected journalist and author, Douglas Reed made an in-depth historical study of the methods and influence of Talmudist/Jewish/Zionist leaderships from biblical times through to the mid-20th century. His views were not well received by the

Jewish/Zionist establishment and therefore by the mass media corporations they still control. Also available free online as a pdf.

> " The simultaneous triumphs of Bolshevism in Moscow and Zionism in London in the same week of 1917 were only in appearance distinct events, The identity of their original source has been shown in an earlier chapter, and the hidden men who promoted Zionism through the Western governments also supported the world-revolution. The two forces fulfilled correlative tenets of the ancient Law: "Pull down and destroy . . . rule over all nations"; the one destroyed in the East and the other secretly ruled in the West."

After the following brief introduction to the paradoxical nature of the Zionist Jews, Douglas Reed then quotes a revealing piece by **Winston Churchill**.

> "…Communism was demonstrably Eastern Jewish. As to the purposes revealed when the revolution struck in 1917, these showed that it was not episodic or spontaneous but the third "eruption" of the organization first revealed through Weishaupt. The two main features reappeared: the attack on all legitimate government of any kind whatsoever and on religion.
>
> Since 1917 the world-revolution has had to cast aside the earlier pretence of being directed only against "kings" or the political power of priests. One authority of that period knew and stated this. In the tradition of Edmund Burke and John Robison, George Washington and Alexander Hamilton and Disraeli, **Mr. Winston Churchill** wrote:

> *"It would almost seem as if the gospel of Christ and the gospel of anti-Christ were designed to originate among the same people; and that this mystic and mysterious race had been chosen for the supreme manifestations, both of the divine and the diabolical. . .*
> *From the days of 'Spartacus' Weishaupt to those of Karl Marx, and down to Trotsky (Russia), Bela Kun (Hungary), Rosa Luxembourg (Germany) and Emma Goldman (United States),*

this worldwide conspiracy for the overthrow of civilization and for the reconstitution of society on the basis of arrested development, of envious malevolence and impossible equality, has been steadily growing.

It played, as a modern writer, Mrs. Nesta Webster, has so ably shown, a definitely recognizable part in the tragedy of the French Revolution. It has been the mainspring of every subversive movement during the nineteenth century; and now at last this band of extraordinary personalities from the underworld of the great cities of Europe and America have gripped the Russian people by the hair of their heads and have become practically the undisputed masters of that enormous empire. There is no need to exaggerate the part played in the creation of Bolshevism and in the bringing about of the Russian Revolution by these international and for the most part atheistical Jews. It is certainly a very great one; it probably outweighs all others". (Winston Churchill, 1920)

Reed then comments:

"This is the last candid statement discoverable by me from a leading public man on this question. After it the ban on public discussion came down and the great silence ensued, which continues to this day. In1953 Mr. Churchill refused permission (requisite under English law) for a photostat to be made of this 1920 article (Illustrated Sunday Herald, February 8, 1920), without saying why."

The Jewish Ghettoes: a very different perspective

Douglas Reed's documented researches also revealed how the various European Jewish **ghettoes** were typically run like a small 'state within a state', ie as harsh, authoritarian, K/A style protection rackets. Here are a few quotes from the same book.

- "The ghetto was not something inflicted on the Jews by the Gentiles. It was the logical product of the Talmudic Law... The Talmud itself decreed that the Gentiles were not "neighbours" and that a Jew might not sell landed property adjoining that of a Jew to a Gentile. The express object of such provisions as these was the segregation of Jews from others and their isolation in ghettoes."

- "The modern suggestion that the ghetto signified inferiority is part of the legend of "persecution", which is chiefly meant to intimidate Jews, so that they shall always fear to venture outside the fold; today's myth of "antisemitism" is intended to produce the same effect on them."

- "The decline of the ghetto, during the century of emancipation, was a blow to the main prop of Talmudic power. A substitute had to be found unless the ghetto-spirit (as distinct from the physical ghetto) was to disintegrate altogether, and one was found in Zionism, which is the new method devised to re-corral the communities..."

- "The Talmudic regime in the close confinement of the ghettoes was in its nature essentially rule by terror, and employed the recognizable methods of terror: spies-on-spies, informers, denunciants, cursing and excommunication, and death. The secret-police and concentration-camp regime of the Communist era evidently took its nature from this model, which was familiar to its Talmudic organizers."

- "In 1898, at the Second World Zionist Congress at Basel, a Zionist from Russia, Dr. Mandelstamm of Kieff, declared, "*The Jews energetically reject the idea of fusion with other nationalities and cling firmly to their historical hope, i.e., of world empire*". "

- "The study of hundreds of volumes, during many years, gradually brought realization that the essential truth of the story of Zion is all summed-up in Mr. Maurice Samuel's twenty-one words: *"We Jews, the destroyers, will remain the destroyer forever . . . nothing that the Gentiles will do will meet our needs and demands"*. *You Gentiles* (1924)

- At first hearing they sound vainglorious or neurotic, but increasing knowledge of the subject shows them to be honestly meant and carefully chosen. They mean that a man who is born and continues a Jew acquires a destructive mission which he cannot elude. If he deviates from this "Law" he is not a good Jew, in the eyes of the elders; if he wishes or is compelled to be a good Jew, he must conform to it."

(Note how this unknowingly implies the essentially *feminine* quality of 'Jewish' culture, set within the *masculine* dominated *descent era* world.)

Grand Deceptions Brandon Martinez ISBN: 978-1-61577-841-6 is a dedicated journalist's thoroughly documented account of *'Zionist Intrigue in the 20th and 21st Centuries'*.

Facts Are Facts Benjamin Freedman ISBN 978-0-9799176-6-0 includes famous New York Speech https://www.big-lies.org/jews/jews-benjamin-freedman.htm

Babylon's Banksters *Professor Joseph P Farrell ISBN: 978-1-932595-79-6* is one of several books and YouTube videos on his extensive, in-depth research into the many diverse historical connections between those he calls the Babylonian Banksters (ie Jewish moneylenders) and current secret scientific research into immensely powerful, non-nuclear weaponry, based on technology earlier developed by scientists in Nazi Germany.

Professor Farrell takes a long, broad view, tracing the current status quo back through millennia into earliest recorded history. He pulls together many diverse strands, quoting historians, scientists and other thinkers, and contributing some inspired dot-joining and insightful speculating... while diplomatically avoiding any direct reference to Jews or Zionists.

His own website is https://gizadeathstar.com.

***The Holocaust Industry: Reflections on the Exploitation of
Jewish Suffering*** Norman G. Finkelstein (2000) ISBN
9781859843239SECA.
Also a short video of him at <u>https://www.youtube.com/watch?
v=aun2O2U0uvU</u>

The Thirteenth Tribe Arthur Koestler (1976) ISBN 0-394-40284-7.
Koestler, a prolific and respected writer, summarised this book as
follows:
"In Part One of this book I have attempted to trace the history of
the Khazar Empire based on the scant existing sources. In Part
Two, Chapters V-VII, I have compiled the historical evidence
which indicates that the bulk of Eastern Jewry — and hence of
world Jewry — is of Khazar-Turkish, rather than Semitic, origin. In
the last chapter I have tried to show that the evidence from
anthropology concurs with history in refuting the popular belief in
a Jewish race descended from the biblical tribe."

Why the Jews? Dennis Prager and Rabbi Joseph Telushkin ISBN:
9780743246200
Two eminent Jewish intellectuals, argue that the contrived,
nonsensical term *anti-semitism* is about more than just the familiar
Jewish characteristics which many people in many lands through the
centuries have found repellent. But the authors' partisan attitude and
lack of a detached *overview* or genuine self-*insight* prevents any
balanced conclusions being reached.

They deceptively oversimplify what 'jewishness' might or might not
mean by frequently using the catch-all term 'Jews' in order to imply
one ancient, politically distinct nation or people. But that strategy of
hyping up Zionist power is soundly negated in *The Invention of the
Jewish People* by Professor Shlomo Sand (see References). They also
ignore the earlier, predominantly *feminine*, matrilineal, Hebrew
culture, described in *The Hebrew Goddess* by Dr Rafael Patai.

Therefore, their version of Judaism only recognises the later,
masculine-dominated regime of strict *monotheism* that requires the

exclusive worshipping of an **all-powerful, male, 'father figure' God**. Yet it's the *feminine* aspect of jewishness, present in all gender categories, that accounts for most of the praiseworthy 'Jewish' qualities the authors highlight.

Other factors conveniently avoided include the darker, shameful teachings of the Talmud, Israel's *apartheid* policy and *false flag* operations, and the ongoing preparations for the Ashkenazi take-over of Ukraine to restore the medieval state of Khazaria (page 144).

The Promise, a TV drama by **Peter Kosminsky** for Channel 4 (UK 2011), offers revealing insights into the violent birth of the Jewish State of Israel in Palestine, and its consequences. Available on YouTube.

Silent Weapons for Quiet Wars (page 215). A/V version at https://www.youtube.com/watch?v=s_38tsQ4p0I

Shulamit Aloni (1927-2014) was an outspoken Israeli politician, one of the generation of young idealistic Zionist pioneers who were pro-active in the early years of the new Jewish State of Israel, founded in 1948. Later, especially following the Six Day War in 1967, she felt that the Israeli government betrayed the moral values and commitments earlier made by the Zionist leadership, after which the situation continued to deteriorate.

Kay (Katherine) Griggs' testimony re Zionist mind control of the US military.
Video https://www.youtube.com/watch?v=WpbloZWO8oA (Possibly sabotaged & relocated)
This Christian ex-wife of a violent, alcoholic US Marine colonel, in a long interview, describes how ambitious young personnel were being enticed into the world of the military, and routinely forced into compromising situations, as the price of advancing their careers. That left them vulnerable to blackmail and to being mind-controlled into compliance - for example, in committing assassinations, running worldwide illegal weapons and drugs trading rings, sabotaging

regimes in other countries... and much more.

Her courageous testimony makes it clear that many know about these goings-on but will not speak out about it, nor about the financial power and leverage that guarantees the favoured treatment Israel has traditionally been receiving from consecutive Zionist-controlled US governments. All of which serves as a reminder that it's necessary first to appreciate the scale and depth of this toxic infiltration in order to tackle it in a practical way.

Henry Ford was a prime example of the universal *masculine* principle at work, his mind *focused* on the *mechanics* and *uniformity* of mass production. His extreme individualism and idealism were at the same time classic characteristics of humanity's *collective adolescence*. But although exceptionally gifted at producing and marketing motor cars, he proved himself naive at dealing with the ferocity of humanity's *descent era feminine* aspect.

In the 1920s, he had published **The International Jew** which, from his staunchly patriotic American and Protestant Christian perspective, catalogued the extent to which at that time Jews in America had already taken control of its money supply and its major industries. These especially included the news and entertainment businesses, which Ford realised were crucial in programming the minds of the American people on a mass scale, in pursuance of the long term Zionist agenda.

But the Jewish financiers and others responded by outmanoeuvring him in a *feminine* way – through money manipulation, litigation and the threat of mass media malevolent gossip, all of which would undermine his reputation and huge business empire. Thus he was 'persuaded' to publicly renounce his earlier descriptions of their activities and aims.

The HeartMath Institute (https://www.heartmath.org) has published material on medical and other research into the **cardiac plexus** or *'heart brain'*.

Extras

Deuteronomy Ch.2 (excerpts)

Moses said:

"And the Lord spake unto me, saying. . . This day will I begin to put the dread of thee and the fear of thee upon the nations that are under the whole heaven, who shall hear report of thee, and shall tremble, and be in anguish because of thee . . .

And the Lord commanded me at that time to teach you statutes and judgments, that ye might do them in the land whither ye go over to possess it . . .

And because he loved thy fathers, therefore he chose their seed after them. . . to drive out nations from before thee greater and mightier than thou art, to bring thee in, to give thee their land for an inheritance . . .

And when the Lord thy God shall deliver them before thee, thou shalt smite them, and utterly destroy them; thou shalt make no covenant with them, nor show mercy unto them; neither shalt thou make marriages with them. . . ye shall destroy their altars and break down their images. . . For thou art an holy people unto the Lord thy God; **the Lord thy God hath chosen thee to be a peculiar people unto himself, above all people that are upon the face of the earth...**

And thou shalt consume all the people which the Lord thy God shall deliver thee; thine eye shall have no pity upon them. . . But the Lord thy God shall deliver them unto thee, and shall destroy them with a mighty destruction until they be destroyed . . . He shall deliver their kings into thine hand, and thou shalt destroy their name from under heaven, there shall no man be able to stand before thee, until thou have destroyed them . . .

Every place whereon the soles of your feet shall tread shall be yours. . . even unto the uttermost sea shall your coast be . . . Of the *cities of these people, which the Lord thy God doth give thee for an inheritance, thou shall save nothing alive that breatheth . . ._***thou shalt lend unto many nations and thou shalt not borrow** . . . *Ye shall utterly destroy all the places wherein the nations which ye shall possess served their gods. . ."*

The Talmud

The main written source and authority for rabbis, Jews and Zionists who study and teach Jewish culture is the *Talmud*. It's usually spoken of as a sacred text, but it also reveals a hidden, dark, malevolent aspect of Jewish culture.

The Talmud is a set of sixty three ancient volumes of over two thousand pages, written and added to over centuries by various rabbis. It contains numerous detailed instructions, some very intimate, on how to live a 'proper' Jewish life. And it's still studied by trainee rabbis today as their main resource regarding the detailed *do's* and *don'ts* of Jewish culture. English translations are now available online.

However, it has also been found to include various dark pronouncements specifying, for example, that certain forms of bestiality and sexual abuse of children and women are permissible. It also appears to decree that it's OK for Jews to cheat and deceive in business dealings with non-Jews. And it contains a number of immature, vicious and offensive remarks about Christians and Jesus... plus other toxic, venomous material. (A few online examples follow).

Not surprisingly, this dark, secret aspect of Jewish culture that the Talmud reveals is never mentioned in the Zionist-controlled corporate mass media, State or commercial. For example, in July 2013, the BBC broadcast a one hour radio documentary on the Talmud. It was presented by a rabbi who somehow failed to mention any of that kind of content.

And in 2013, the BBC broadcast an openly biased TV documentary series of five one hour programmes called *The Story of the Jews*, written and presented by a self-proclaimed Zionist Jew. Since when there has been no counterbalancing series broadcast to offer a challenging, opposing perspective, despite the BBC's hollow claims to be unbiased, neutral, fair and balanced. All of which indicates who is effectively in control of the BBC.

Excerpts from the Talmud
...from various online sources, exposing malicious and corrupting quotes from the Talmud.

Sanhedrin 59a
To communicate anything to a Goy about our religious relations would be equal to the killing of all Jews, for if the Goyim knew what we teach about them, they would kill us openly. [Goy/goyim (plural) means *unclean*, and is a disparaging term for non-Jews (gentiles), implying that they are like cattle.]

Shabbath 31b .
On the house of the Goy one looks as on a fold of cattle.

Libbre David 37
A Jew should and must make a false oath when the Goyim asks if our books contain anything against them.

Tosefta, Tractate Erubin VIII
When a Jew has a Gentile in his clutches, another Jew may go to the same Gentile, lend him money and in turn deceive him, so that the Gentile shall be ruined. For the property of a Gentile, according to our law, belongs to no one, and the first Jew that passes has full right to seize it.

Schulchan Aruch, Choszen Hamiszpat 156
If it can be proven that someone has given the money of Israelites to the Goyim, a way must be found after prudent consideration to wipe him off the face of the earth.

Yalkut 245c

Extermination of the Christians is a necessary sacrifice.

Zohar, Vayshlah 177b

...That the Jewish nation is the only nation selected by God, while all the remaining ones are contemptible and hateful.

...That all property of other nations belongs to the Jewish nation, which consequently is entitled to seize upon it without any scruples. An orthodox Jew is not bound to observe principles of morality towards people of other tribes. He may act contrary to morality, if profitable to himself or to Jews in general.

Zohar, Shemoth, Toldoth Noah, Lekh-Lekha

Jehovah created the non-Jew in human form so that the Jew would not have to be served by beasts. The non-Jew is consequently an animal in human form, and condemned to serve the Jew day and night.

Schulchan Oruch, Orach Chaim 14, 20, 32, 33, 39

A Jew may do to a non-Jewess what he can do. He may treat her as he treats a piece of meat.

1) If a Jew is tempted to do evil he should go to a city where he is not known and do the evil there. –Moed Kattan 17a

2) If a heathen (Gentile) hits a Jew, the Gentile must be killed. Hitting a Jew is the same as hitting God. –Sanhedrin 58b

3) A Jew need not pay a Gentile ("Cuthean") the wages owed him for work. –Sanhedrin 57a

4) If a Jew finds an object lost by a Gentile ("heathen") it does not have to be returned. –Baba Mezia 24a also in Baba Kamma 113b

5) When a Jew murders a Gentile ("Cuthean"), there will be no death penalty. What a Jew steals from a Gentile he may keep. – Sanhedrin 57a

6) Gentiles are outside the protection of the law and God has "exposed their money to Israel". –Baba Kamma 37b

7) All Gentile children are animals. –Yebamoth 98a

8) Gentile girls are in a state of niddah (filth) from birth. –Abodah

Zarah 36b
9) Only Jews are human ("Only ye are designated men"). –Baba Kattan 114a-114b
10) Jews may use lies ("subterfuges") to circumvent a Gentile. –Baba Kamma 113a
Plus:
- *Rabbi Yitzhak Ginsburg, "We have to recognize that Jewish blood and the blood of a goy are not the same thing." - NY Times, June 6, 1989*
- *Rabbi Yaacov Perrin, "One million Arabs are not worth a Jewish fingernail." - NY Daily News, Feb 28, 1994*

The *sayanim* (means *helpers*)

The **sayanim** is a broad label for the alleged unofficial and secretive worldwide network of supporters, informers, activists, spies, agitators, internet vigilantes, propagandists etc... serving the controlling Zionist 'spider' at the centre of a worldwide web of debt and manipulative manoeuvring. They are, according to certain informers and investigators, the many loyal, committed individuals and groups, scattered all over the world as a result of the Jewish diaspora.

Sayanim influence – through finance, favours, debt, threats, obligations and blackmail – is said to extend into all areas and levels of human activity, for example, appointments and elections to positions of power. Their divide-and-rule methods include political subterfuge, like deviously setting their enemies and rivals against one another in mutually destructive conflict while themselves remaining aloof, safe and in control... along with blackmail, persuading others to do the dirty work for them, and playing the **persecuted victim** card when it suits their purposes.

In October 2016 a senior staff member of the Israeli Embassy in London was secretly recorded stating his intention to "take down" certain MPs, including a British government minister whose views

were not favourable towards Israeli government policy.
https://www.bbc.co.uk/news/uk-politics-38545671

Among various online sources about the sayanim are the following:
https://en.metapedia.org/wiki/Sayanim,
https://www.theoccidentalobserver.net/2010/03/26/
mossad%E2%80%99s-one-million-helpers-world-wide/

The role of the sayanim in the bigger picture – like the malice and control freakery in the Talmud – can be better understood when seen in the context revealed from the *Threshold*, as concisely laid out in the **Brief Summary** on page 382. How the sayanim are linked with other secretive global networks could be a fruitful area of serious research, given their apparently significant influence on local and world affairs... depending on who might fund such work.

To ignore the worldwide extent of this insidious, manipulative network is to delude oneself into allowing the current unwholesome world status quo to continue.

Much can be learned from studying the effectiveness of this dedicated global network. The know-how <u>could</u> then be applied to work for the healing and benefit of <u>all</u> humankind, instead of for just for an exclusive partisan minority. A viable alternative to the present dysfunctional world system, based on very different psychological assumptions about 'human nature', is proposed in the **One Humanity** section.

The Deir Yassin Massacre, Palestine (09 April 1948)

<u>Time magazine</u> (New York): *"Jewish terrorists of the Stern Gang and Irgun Zvai Leumi stormed the village of Deir Yassin and butchered everyone in sight. The corpses of 250 Arabs, mostly women and children, were later found tossed into wells."* The massacre was allegedly led by Menachim Begin who later became Prime Minister of the Jewish State of Israel.

Meanwhile, the role of the Jews in the world generally continues to be not a happy or fulfilling one. Thus the bittersweet irony of Jewish/Yiddish humour, typically about making the best of a bad deal in this life. It's epitomised in such one-liners as '*I'd rather be unhappy and rich than unhappy and poor*', which leaves the cause of the unhappiness uninvestigated.

When small-time *greed* brought down the world's *banking* system... almost

The 2007/8 financial crisis

In August 2007, confidence in the global monetary system suddenly evaporated, as the inevitable consequences of over-indulgent, selfish, opportunistic *greed* hit home. SCAB had been making credit easily and cheaply available – as the irresistible seductive tease before its next withdrawal of credit... as it had done very profitably on previous occasions.

Many people and organisations had consequently become addicted to an 'easy money' lifestyle. But as in the *Sorcerer's Apprentice* tale of magic power being incompetently abused, that fantasy trip spun out of control. It degenerated into a runaway situation of properties being sold to easily enticed people who would not be able to afford to keep up the mortgage payments. Thus the inevitable painful contraction, panic and crash.

The 1980s globalisation of financial dealings had enabled the forces of greed and fear to grow too powerful and volatile to be controlled or manipulated in the old ways. Technical advances in digital computing and communications had changed everything. Instant computerised trading in 'virtual' assets had become detached from the physical world. The global financial markets were awash with obscure, probably worthless 'derivatives'.

Meanwhile, on the world stage, certain occurrences created imbalances which would push the world 'economy' towards breakdown. Muslims were making their presence felt, both as wily, manipulative oil dealers and increasingly in violent, primitive, *masculine* ways. The Soviet Union had collapsed back into Russia, leaving a new frontier of raw, corrupt capitalism, and China was owed an ever-growing sum of billions of dollars by the decaying US economy.

Imploding bubbles

The whole global financial system can be visualised as a cluster of bubbles, all within one big bubble, *Mama SCAB*'s global empire. So, should any significant bubbles in the cluster burst, all will inevitably be affected. In 2008, several did, whereupon the whole system seized up in fear and *contracted* severely, lurching close to implosion and collapse.

How close will never be fully known –given the lack of transparency and honesty amongst those most closely involved. But had there been a collapse, not only would nation states have had to admit their bankruptcy, it could also have been the end of business for *SCAB*... ie the end of it's influence in the world through its global web of debt. Facing this prospect, it was more than ready to step in, as always, with loans of its imaginary money, conjured up out of nothing, in order to avoid a meltdown, keep the game going and stay in business.

And when it's needed, who's got the (imaginary) money?

By 2008 it was crisis time worldwide... and the stresses were apparent at the *fault line* of the uneasy alliance between:
(a) the *global* financier, *Mama SCAB* (as humankind's *descent* era *feminine* aspect), and
(b) various nation states (representing humankind's *descent era masculine* aspect, *Papa State*).
States were being humiliated by *sovereign debt* crises because of the mounting interest due on their **long term *debts***, ultimately owed to

SCAB. And this resulted in huge **annual budget *deficits*,** as their spending normally exceeded their income, mainly from taxes.

So, contrary to the ideals of classical 'free market' capitalism, *SCAB* chose the option best suited to its own long term strategy. To 'save the world' and thus its own global empire from imminent financial 'meltdown', it conjured up out of thin air vast ***quantities*** of money to ***ease*** the situation, and fed this into the global system, as interest-bearing loans.

Quantitative easing (QE)

This 'massive dose' fix was called ***quantitative easing***, a policy previously known in economics as *'printing money'*. That's why, in economics jargon, *central banks* are described as the *'lenders of last resort'*.

Feeding in this emergency sustenance creates **an instant but false sense of confidence**, which is always followed sooner or later by trouble, when the short-term effect wears off. Thus economists spoke of states needing to be ***weaned*** off their dependence on *SCAB's* QE, sometimes likening it to doses of steroids.

QE was introduced to the wider world in 2009 by *SCAB*, as a new piece of financial jargon which had originated in Japan. It's essentially a financial conjuring trick, an ***illusion*** created with imaginary money, and performed as a double act by a central bank with its host government as the stooge.

As with many confidence tricks, the illusion is created by a cleverly worked out *deception* which distracts the onlookers' attention away from some ***sleight of hand*** deception. *SCAB*, through one of its central banks, in effect lends money to the state in question by buying large quantities of government bonds – in effect, IOUs which promise to pay an annual rate of compound interest.

As usual, the compliant mass media were obliged to passively play along and leave crucial questions unasked. By 2010, even on the

BBC, *QE* money was being openly described as '**electronically created'** – yet this didn't seem to provoke any significant querying. And despite all the mass media coverage, one crucial fact was rigorously omitted:

SCAB's *central banks* which conjure up money out of nothing are private, profit-driven businesses, national branches of the global financial empire, aka *SCAB*. They are <u>not</u> State institutions nor State-controlled, despite the official attempts to pretend they are.

Restoring confidence?
After the collapses and recriminations following the crisis, an attempt was made to re-create an impression of competent, trustworthiness in financial institutions, doing what needs to be done in a responsible, businesslike way. But financial capitalism, by its very nature, encourages its participants to cheat and deceive to gain advantage, and global profiteering always involves the risk of major disasters of one kind or other.

So where did all those billions of QE money go? The first dose of *QE* money in the US and UK temporarily created an illusion of stability amidst the global panic of banks, which were suddenly exposed as having nothing in reserve to repay all those people who naively thought 'their money' was safely 'in the bank'. But within a year or so of that *bail-out*, many financial institutions were back to 'business as usual', making big profits and awarding themselves big bonuses out of the *QE* payout.

This was at the expense of *the taxpayer* (page 183) who had supposedly bailed them out – in the obscure, misleading, make-believe jargon of *capitalism*. And in the process, *Papa State* sank yet deeper in debt to *Mama SCAB*.

Meanwhile, commercial banks argued that they had to incentivise their highly paid best people in order to prevent them migrating to competitors... to be paid even more money.

They also claimed that it's the enormous profits of *investment* banking, ie casino gambling,
that support the safer, 'boring, bread and butter' business of *retail* banking.

The unspoken message here was that this is how a *market economy* works, so *winning* at the money game, at whatever cost to the rest of humankind, <u>is</u> the priority of its players, because in the monetised world which *SCAB* controls, **everything has a price.**

Currency wars/competitive devaluation = *SCAB* wins

All this exposed the weakness of **separate** nation states, when set against each other and trapped like flies in *SCAB*'s **global** financial web. And it led to an increase in financial *protectionism*, ie *currency warfare*, as states tried to make their own national currencies 'cheaper' in order to 'boost exports'. But in this juvenile, competitive scenario, imperiously overseen by *SCAB*, most short-term gains were cancelled out by others taking similar measures... while making *SCAB* even wealthier.

Austerity or stimulus? – the bogus debate

By 2010, there was a clear division of opinion amongst economics experts regarding how best to avoid another major economic downturn, prevent high inflation and achieve some stability and a lasting global recovery. *Expansive* **stimulus** represents the more **feminine** approach, while *contractive* **austerity** represents the more **masculine** approach.

The debate concerned which option offered the best solution:
(a) the American/*SCAB*-led short-term approach: to *stimulate* economies back into growth
by increasing State spending, but thereby further increase the already vast sovereign debt
owed to the local branch of *SCAB*, eg the Federal Reserve in the USA... OR
(b) the **European**-led longer-term approach: to impose severe *austerity* programmes,

in order to reduce indebtedness to *SCAB* sooner and so be paying less interest, but at the risk of damping down any economic recovery.

However, seen from the *Threshold*, this dispute was just a media-hyped **distraction**, a bogus *binary* debate, since the 'either-or' question was based on a *false choice*:
Pay later or pay sooner, but either way, suffer the consequences, ie You pay and you lose –
because SCAB wins both ways, given its controlling position as the world's money supplier.

Not on the menu was the option of creating a more sane and just global set-up. So, the discontented citizen/taxpayers were left in confusion, squabbling among themselves – like children whose pocket money has been reduced, but who don't know how to or dare question the authority of their parents to find out why there's less money available for them.

The *austerity* con: a step towards a new *feudalism*

The *Threshold* perspective highlights a sometimes overlooked fact concerning money:
During economic 'downturns' the total wealth in existence doesn't actually diminish;
it's merely redistributed, with the result that a few get much richer and many get poorer.

Exclusive advance notice about *money supply* policy is very useful for the favoured few.
When a *downturn* is imminent, they can sell quickly while prices are still high. Then, when prices have fallen, they can buy back cheaply, so that at the next *upturn*, selling at a higher price will produce a profit. Meanwhile, the bewildered mass of onlookers, the 'losers', are told that it's **austerity** time, and that *'We're all in this together'*, despite the rich-poor gap widening ever further.

411

The fact is that when a government claims that there's of a 'shortage of money' and various *austerity* measures are required, that so-called 'shortage' does not directly correspond to any real scarcity in the world. It's just that **the supply of money has been restricted by the central bank**, as part of its relentless push to maximise profits and maintain its dominance, while impoverishing the rest of humanity, apart from a select group of associates.

However, to let this crucial fact become public knowledge would be an embarrassment
to the weakened State, an admission that it's at the mercy of the global loan shark, *SCAB*.
So it's quietly ignored and, as a distraction, the experts argue endlessly about details. This is like the famous psychology experiment involving the 'invisible gorilla', in which people's attention is so focused on counting the number of throws in a ball game that they fail to notice a gorilla walking right through the middle of the game and waving (YouTube).

From the *Threshold*, the austerity con can be seen as a shift towards a new feudal fascism. For by drastically purging the so-called *public sector*, ie *state* employees and dependants, the ruling elite can extend their dominion over the disempowered many. The 'upwardly aspiring', professional middle class can thus be reduced down to a bare minimum, disempowered and compliant, but sufficient to support the elite's privileged lifestyle.

This seems to be the plan for the many middle class professionals, soon to be made redundant or at least have their standard of living significantly lowered. The key question is whether they can wean themselves off the *financial capitalism* drip-feed, to which they've become addicted, before the predictable switch-off and withdrawal... and then whether they sink into dark despair OR raise their game to a new level, by recognising this crisis as a life-changing, world-changing opportunity. Which is what the *One Humanity* proposal offers.

Threshold Glossary

Addictive Superiority Syndrome (ASS): a pathological mental condition in which a person or group has a sense of inherent superiority over another or others.

Aether/Ether: the dynamic intermediate level of being/existence between consciousness and matter, also known as *quintessence, akasha*, the *quantum vacuum*...

Anxiety is a psycho-physical sense of unease which undermines self-confidence and mental stability, has various physical ill effects and may at any time flare up, for no obvious reason, as a *panic attack*. It may involve worrying about aspects of oneself or about external factors and uncertainties.

Arch-banks: the IMF, World Bank and BIS (Bank for International Settlements).These three global institutions belong to the syndicate of central and arch-banks (see Mama SCAB).

Ascent out of matter (AoM): the redemption process of physical matter reverting to a pre-physical state and then back into universal consciousness.

Binarity/binary thinking: the treating of two opposite tendencies <u>as if</u> they do not exist within a single greater unity or wholeness.

Bliss is a transcendent state of balanced, poised, peaceful, stress-free at-oneness with nature and the cosmos, the experience of an inner *equilibrium* between *levity* and *gravity*

Boysworld science: the limited materialistic science that reflects the immature, unbalanced mentality of humanity's collective *pre-adolescent* phase in the *masculine*-dominated era of *descent into matter*.

Central bank: one 'branch' of the global syndicate of central and arch-banks (see *Mama SCAB*). In each country where one is lodged, the central bank operates hierarchically 'above' and independent of the commercial and investment banks.

Collective adolescence: the current developmental stage of humankind as a whole on its evolutionary journey, its characteristics recognisable from observing individual human adolescents.

Consciousness, universal and individual, is continuous, multi-level and persists through sleep, death and all physical changes and renewals.

Cosmos: the universe, understood as an ordered whole.

Cravings, such as for power, authority, influence, privilege, respect, love, attention and so on are among many other widely sought addictive compensations for a lack of *gnosis* and the consequent lack of fulfilment and self-esteem.

Cynicism is more extreme than scepticism, for example in rejecting unfamiliar ideas outright. Cynicism **is** symptomatic of a distorted human consciousness with an outlook coloured by painful experiences that reflect 'the worst of the past'. It can also result in a callous insensitivity to the feelings of others.

Descent into matter (DiM) : the process of consciousness manifesting as energy and then as physical matter.

Dynamic 2-Dimensionality (D2D) : the primal dynamic space of *contraction* and *expansion*.

Ecstasy is a pleasurable peak state of inner excitation and joyful transcendence, due to a shift in one's inner balance, as expanding *levity* increases in relation to contracting *gravity*.

Emotional hygiene: any number of effective techniques, physical and mental, are possible according to personal characteristics and preferences, including *The Identity Continuum*. (page 427)

Equilibrium is the end result of the rebalancing tendency between *expansion* and *contraction* in all cosmic functioning, eg in correcting unnatural, damaging imbalances between *deficiency* and *excess*.

Flowform : originally referring to water patterns, any dynamic fluid form, eg a vortex.

Focal Point (FP) : Generally, a point where attention is focused. In this work, a point created by universal consciousness focusing inwards within itself.

Focus/radius line (F/R): a polaric understanding (inwards and outwards) of what's normally called the *radius* of a circle or sphere (ie focusing inwards and radiating outwards).

Goyim: a Hebrew/Yiddish word for *gentiles* (non-Jews), used in the **Talmud** to implicitly liken them to cattle.

Gravity: the universal centripetal, focusing, *contractive* force of the cosmos.

Greed: the selfish craving to acquire and consume in excess of real need, mostly the result of *ignosis* and the consequent feeling of vulnerability, insecurity and fear of poverty, deprivation, hunger etc.

Gnosis *(gnostic)*: knowledge acquired intuitively as a kind of direct perception, beholding and understanding – not through intellectual, rational, logical or instinctive mental activity.
Sometimes linked to **noetic** experiences of an inner wisdom, direct knowing, or subjective understanding, ie **noesis**. It doesn't mean wishful, unquestioning believing.

Greed, the selfish craving to acquire and consume in excess of real need, is mostly the result of *ignosis* and the consequent feeling of vulnerability, insecurity and fear of poverty, deprivation, hunger etc. So, it's more useful to understand it as a **symptom** in need of healing rather than as something to condemn or blame.

Humanity: a broad, multi-dimensional concept of the human species, including non-physical qualities and attributes, past and present, primitive and more advanced along the evolutionary path.

Humankind: a collective term for the human race or the physical species of earthly human beings.

Ignosis (*lack of gnosis*) refers to a sense of psychological emptiness, of something missing in a life which lacks a genuine sense of purpose and direction beyond worldly desires and fears. This tends to result in vulnerability, insecurity, anxiety, fear and a hunger to fill the vacuum with compensatory substitutes. The outcome of that might be, for example, selfish greed, deceit, bullying, pursuing fantasies or gullibly being persuaded to adopt an unsound belief system.

Inertia:
- *Physical*: a tendency to remain unchanged or static or to resist movement.
 - *Psychological:* a habitual or traditional resistance to change, conscious or unconscious.

Individual I (iI): *oneself as a distinct single unit, a focal point, of universal consciousness.*
On the pre-physical level of existence, *iI* am a pulsating *sphere of influence* of varying size, overlapping and inter-penetrating with other similar entities while retaining my unique, distinct, individual identity, character and qualities.

Inertia: *Physical* – a tendency to remain unchanged or static or to resist movement.
Psychological – a habitual or traditional resistance to change, conscious or unconscious.

Levity: the universal centrifugal, radiating, *expansive* force of the cosmos; the polar opposite of *gravity*.

Life: universal consciousness, manifesting in *pre-physical* mode as a kind of *potential energy*, the vital, animating element or factor in physical life-forms.

Love: From the *Threshold* perspective, this dynamic, attracting, unifying quality in human relationships occurs in infinite variations, yet can be thought of in terms of two basic grades.

   A. **Unconditional love**: a feeling of unlimited, sympathetic, harmonious *resonance* with one or more other beings... and in some cases, with the whole cosmos. It's commonly experienced as a pleasurable, reassuring excitation in the region of the heart. And, crucially, it's <u>not conditional</u> upon any other factors, such as favours, desires or demands being met.

   B. **Conditional love**: a more limited feeling of attraction, affection, favouring etc towards another being or other beings – limited because it's <u>conditional</u> upon certain requirements being met, such as receiving in return a favourable, sympathetic or obedient attitude towards oneself. Or it may be prompted by sentimental or nostalgic feelings, or longings for the gratification of fantasised desires.

Mama SCAB: the symbolic name for the privately owned, profit-driven **S**yndicate of **C**entral and **A**rch-**B**anks, the world's ultimate moneylender. It's *arch-banks* are the IMF, World Bank and BIS, and it has a 'daughter' branch (ie a *central bank*) lodged in virtually every country.

MindBox: the restrictive, enclosing, mental programming that each society or culture installs in its members before they're old enough to realise how they're being indoctrinated.

Noetic: (from the Greek *noēsis/noētikos,* meaning inner wisdom, direct knowing or subjective understanding).

One Humanity (OH)*:* the title of a visionary practical proposal for the next critical stage in the evolving of human life on Earth, as outlined in this book (page 304).

Papa State*:* the symbolic name for the institution known as *the State,* the *nation state* or the *sovereign nation state,* of which there are currently some two hundred around the world – not the same thing as a government, monarch, parliament, country, nation or 'the public'.

Physical-material : the world of physical matter.

Polarity : the co-existence of complementary, polar opposites within a greater unity.
Expansion/contraction is the primal dynamic polarity of the cosmos or manifest universe.

Polyrhythmic Pulsation (PrP)*:* the rhythmical alternating of *expansion/contraction* (polarity), resulting from pulses of *levity* withdrawing/escaping from *gravity* capture, as the cosmos tends towards an *equilibrium* state between the two universal forces. It occurs at all levels of manifest existence, and is due to the range of *resonant cavities* (concentric spheres) within the pre-physical cosmos.
Eg The audio spectrum from low distinct pulses to high 'continuous' tones.
Polarity of PrP:
- *Expansion*: opening/releasing/escaping//ascending/dispersing of energy...
 - *Contraction*: closing/withdrawing/capturing/descending/accumulating...

Pre-physical : the state of existence prior to physical manifestation, ie potentially physical.

Recapitulation: the repeating of a collective evolutionary process in the individual development of a creature.

Redemption: the phases of a cyclical process at which *physical matter* returns to being *pre-physical potential energy*, and potential energy is redeemed into primal *universal consciousness.*

Resonance is the common working principle of all responding and relating in the cosmos, whether physical, emotional or mental, harmonious or or discordant .

Scepticism: a cautious, questioning, doubting attitude to unfamiliar ideas, can in some instances be due to a lack of *gnosis*. Not as extreme as *cynicism*.

Spheroidal: approximately spherical.

The elephant in the room: an obvious truth that is going unaddressed, or an obvious problem or risk no one wants to discuss, amounting to a conspiracy of silence.

Threshold: the dynamic interface/ border level between the pre-physical and physical-material realms.

Torus: a dynamic, self-contained, energy flow-form with one continuous surface, no edges or corners, and a double vortex funnel-tunnel through its core. The spheroidal torus is the archetypal living form, uniting 'inner' and 'outer'. ('Spheroidal' means approximately spherical.)

Transcending means rising above boundaries and compartments, enabling one's consciousness to gain a broader and more inclusive overview, and resolve what at ground level may seem to be unresolvable conflicts, dilemmas, paradoxes, conundrums and other problems.

Transition: the current shifting from a cosmic era of *descent into matter* to one of *ascent out of matter*.

Universal consciousness (UC) : the ultimate, essential reality of which humans seem capable of conceiving at present.

Universal *Feminine*: the expression in living creatures of the universal cosmic principle of *expansion/yin/levity*. Not the same thing as individual *female* gender, since each individual is a unique combination of masculine and feminine qualities.

Universal I (UI) : universal consciousness, subjectively experienced as an individual's greater identity.

Universal *Masculine*: the expression in living creatures of the universal cosmic principle of *contraction/yang/gravity*. Not the same thing as individual *male* gender, since each individual is a unique combination of masculine and feminine qualities.

Vortex (vortices)*:* a spiralling form, contracting into and expanding outwards from a central point, normally within a ***torus***, physical or pre-physical. (See illustrations, page 341.)

The Author as Beginner

This publication follows on from my becoming aware of, and then carrying around in my mind for several years, the quietly powerful knowledge I first offered online in 2006 as *Notes from the Threshold*. That was my first rough attempt at an account, in words and a few diagrams, of an unexpected, undramatic, **non-religious** revelation I had experienced.

It had occurred as a kind of direct 'beholding', a gradual intuitive realisation and understanding of something very simple yet immensely powerful – ie a kind of *gnosis*. It amounted to a new yet timeless perspective on the world, also revealing how my individual *identity* extends beyond my physical body, my name and other worldly labelling.

It was my first glimpse of a basic reality of which I hadn't previously been aware... ie an all-encompassing kind of knowing, which therefore has practical relevance to every aspect of every life. The range of topics touched upon in this book affirms its universality.

My sense was that his information was somehow being fed into my mind – as a kind of gift and privilege. After which it was my responsibility to share it as widely as possible by putting it into a coherent and accessible form, appropriate for publication. Since when, I have felt honoured and grateful for this very challenging opportunity and the responsibility involved... although it has been quite a solitary venture, trying to convey a whole new way of thinking about this world and oneself.

The task was to identify the basic universal working principles of the cosmos, and then link them to the everyday world of life on Earth – so that they would not seem remote and irrelevant to most people's daily lives and concerns. The ongoing purpose is to make this powerful knowledge accessible to people of all backgrounds. From what dimensions this very practical information comes remains an open question... awaiting further research.

But for now it's a small start, offering a few basics that could enable all people to live a more fulfilling life. In essence, it presents a practical way of sharing a profound realisation: that there is a *coherent simplicity* behind the superficially complicated and apparently random incoherence of this world. But how come this opportunity fell to me?

Why me?
Since my memory has a very limited capacity for storing complex, detailed information and my mental processing is relatively slow, I had already evolved my own way of dealing with problems. It involves, first, gaining an **overview** of the problem situation in order to see it in its greater context, and second, penetrating to the heart or core of the situation to gain some psychological **insight** into the dynamics of the trouble there.

Then I fill in as much as I can of the 'in-between', linking information that seems relevant, ie the details and mechanisms involved. That area of knowledge is more the domain of experts and specialists – something I am not. Neither am I a professional writer. However, I have no doubts about the essential significance of the *Threshold*.

All along I have felt like an inexperienced beginner, a novice messenger, learning, mistake by mistake, what is required to at least complete the job as best I can. Lecturing or sermonising have never appealed to me as ways of communicating what's in my mind. So, it has been and continues to be a testing lesson. In the process, I have come to realise and accept that there are always other ways of thinking than those with which we were first indoctrinated.

Part of this was realising that the way people think is profoundly affected, by the *languages* they learn to use in different areas of their lives... and how a language can be manipulated, for good or otherwise, by those who appreciate its power and are skilled at exploiting it.

My background
I was born in 1944 and grew up mostly in London. As a child and adolescent, a major psychological challenge for me was trying to come to terms with the inconsistencies, lies and taboos I kept encountering in the normal everyday workings of the adult world... such that I found myself corrupted into those ways.

But gradually I learned to recognise the unease I experienced in connection with those tendencies, and instead learned to:
- detect dishonesty and untrustworthiness in others and in myself;
- read between the lines, often becoming acutely aware of what was not being said;
- seek out what seemed to be significant, useful information wherever it could be found;
  join up potentially relevant dots and discover patterns, sometimes useful, sometimes not, while not ignoring unwelcome information.

Trying to resolve the inconsistencies involved my pursuing a long, winding path of trial-and-error querying, investigating and learning. On the way, I acquired a university degree in psychology, but more importantly, I encountered several significant individuals – some in person, some indirectly through books and recordings – from whom I received many valuable lessons in how to better understand this world and how to live a more fulfilling life.

I also learned to check out any special information I'd gathered, to see whether it was consistent with my own experience of the everyday world, and with certain timeless, esoteric wisdom from various sources, Western and Eastern.

Then one day I unexpectedly found that my evolving perspective on the world now revealed patterns and insights of which I'd previously been unaware. I realised how the many diverse strands of my life and thinking are all connected, and how *individual I* am one focal point of a universal consciousness, which manifests as this living, pulsating cosmos that functions according to just three simple principles. It all seemed too simple to be true, but undeniable.

An insider's view of typical Jewish attitudes

As a youngster in a loosely Jewish extended but scattered family, I had an insider's view of the ways of various Jewish families and organisations in the UK, experiencing the warmth and general good humour towards children, but also sensing a darker, unpleasant aspect.

That was the ever present, underlying, disdainful exclusive attitude of an inherent **superiority** over non-Jews – usually expressed in Yiddish and often spoken with a contemptuous, disdainful, dismissive tone. This made me feel very uneasy, since I had many non-Jewish friends, none of whom seemed in any way inferior to me... although it did become clear that other cultures also had their own darker sides and prejudices.

One memorable feature was how it was mostly strong **mother figures** who were effectively in control, despite the fathers (and some sons) making lots of noise and fuss as they acted out their male authority figure roles.

There was also a continuous process of indoctrination going on in which **loyalty** to 'our people' was emphasised, demanded and expected, a loyalty which overrode all personal, family and political disputes. And when deemed necessary or pragmatic, that loyalty would override honesty and integrity, especially in dealings with the non-Jewish world.

Another thing I realised quite young was that there was no point in arguing with certain types of Jews whose views I didn't share. Why? Because they tended to be extremely tenacious, unyielding but also mentally agile, using various tricks and tactics so as not to concede a single millimetre while appearing to be open and reasonable.

424

Their technique is quite different from the typical Western *masculine* way of linear, logical debating or trying to impose one's views on others. It involves constantly changing tack: one moment citing 'indisputable' religious or scientific 'facts', then switching to personal accusations or loaded questions, based on arbitrary, self-justifying assumptions... and so on.

Such a slippery, disruptive style would make it almost impossible to clearly or consistently argue against them, which would then be taken to imply that you'd lost the argument. That was presumably what General Carl von Horn, a UN peacekeeper in Palestine in the 1950s, encountered in his dealings with the Israelis (page 390).

My motives

My motives were not and are not commercial, religious, political or fame-seeking. The knowledge in the chapter **Identity: This I Am** has become a living, everyday reality for me.

So, I am not 'pro-' or 'anti-' any particular people or groups. And I do feel privileged to have had the chance to make this small contribution, despite the strong likelihood that it will be ignored or dismissed during what remains of my present lifetime.

My main interest by far is in developing the endless possibilities of *Threshold* thinking in a variety of ways and directions, all of which can lead to a more balanced, sane and just world. However, I accept that 'cleaning out the stables' is also part of our responsibility as humans incarnated on Earth. I would much prefer not to feel obliged to be addressing this problem. But for me to consciously avoid or ignore it would be a constant cause of unease due to my negligence.

I'm also still driven by an urge to come up with coherent, accessible and engaging ways of presenting and putting this knowledge into the world. So, this present work is essentially an offer to share, as widely as possible, the profoundly empowering realisation that...

**Behind the superficial incoherence, disorder
and apparent 'randomness' of this troubled world,
an overall *coherence* can be found throughout the whole cosmos.**

However, a growing awareness of the increasingly perilous state of world affairs on Earth has prompted me, as a matter of urgency, to apply those principles in a practical way. And that has involved understanding how the present status quo in politics, finance, religion, health, science and the arts arose, and how a more balanced and just world could begin to evolve.

Catch the message, not the medium

As the author/messenger delivering this work, my feeling is that *individual I* am of minimal significance compared to the value of the information being delivered. I would gladly do it anonymously, but it seems right to take personal responsibility for putting it into the world.

I am also aware that it may provoke some hostility at first – as is often the case with radical thinking. Some may see it as a threat to their position under the present status quo. Some people may want to smash the mirror that reflects back an unwelcome image. Some may simply want to shoot the messenger. However, the deed is done, and there's no way back to not knowing what is now known.

So, if at some time it appears that I've retracted what I wrote in this book, be sceptical and look to those who would not have welcomed this information being made available. Or if I am silenced, one way or another, for having said what needed to be said, so be it. In the longer view, I'll be back for more... in another time, place and persona.

I take full responsibility for the contents of this book. And I am grateful to various others, best left unnamed, for their help and input along the way.

Michael I Finesilver (England, 2018)

THE IDENTITY CONTINUUM

Please read these notes first.

The Identity Continuum is a very condensed package of information. It's based on three simple but fundamental universal principles which govern how the cosmos, in all its complexity, originated and continues to function.

These three principles are the basis of the Threshold perspective and are explained in this book which is also available free as a download from www.pathwayinitiatives.co.uk.

They are just the bare essentials for such an understanding, yet they account for the richness and diversity of all the qualities experienced, and all the cultures, myths, legends, stories, characters and plots that have emerged in the evolving of human consciousness on Earth.

Therefore, each line needs to be carefully unpacked and digested in order to grasp its meaning and relevance for our lives on Earth. The tone of the piece is necessarily impersonal because it deals with who we are on a level beyond our normal earthly personality concerns, and uses certain unfamiliar terms to highlight this distinction.

The Identity Continuum serves as a bridge, a link, across the chasm of unknowing between our 'lower' and 'higher' consciousness. And the gist of it is that individual I am one focal point of the all-inclusive universal consciousness which is thus also universal I.

So, at any moment, I have a choice between the two polar opposite perspectives:
(a) the limited, separated individual perspective looking outwards from my centre point OR
(b) the unlimited, all-inclusive, universal perspective looking inwards.

Suggestions for using The Identity Continuum

1. Simply contemplate to appreciate the continuity between individuality and universality.
2. Use it as a meditation – first settling into a state of consciousness that's detached from the busyness of everyday worldly living. This would require learning the whole sequence, perhaps one line per week. When practiced regularly, reaching the line "I release..." may trigger a therapeutic releasing of physical tensions with surprising power. This is OK, so long as you take some quiet time to let yourself settle before resuming your everyday life.

Key unfamiliar terms

Focal point: where attention is focused.

Levity: the universal expansive force, the polar opposite of gravity.

Pre-physical: the state of existing prior to physical manifesting, ie potentially physical.

Threshold: the interface between the pre-physical and physical-material realms.

Vortex: a spiralling form, contracting into and expanding outwards from a central point.

Torus: a dynamic, self-contained, energy flow-form with one continuous surface, no edges or corners, and a double vortex funnel-tunnel through its core. The spheroidal torus is the archetypal living form, uniting 'inner' and 'outer'.

Spheroidal: in this context, it simply means approximately spherical.

Flowform: any dynamic fluid form, eg a vortex.

PART ONE

Individual I

am first this focal point of universal consciousness,

itself the unlimited source,

generating

the power behind the primal force,

radiating

primal sound and light,

polarised

by the complementary cosmic forces of expanding levity
and contracting gravity,

creating

this pulsating sub-sphere of primal potential energy,

incorporating

this pre-physical spectrum of tonal qualities,

vibrating and resonating

while held in suspension at the Threshold,

poised

between the pre-physical and the physical-material realms,

as this pre-physical sphere is extended and compressed by levity and gravity, *becoming*

this pre-physical vortexing torus flowform,

shaping

within itself at its core this dense physical body,

centred

within this heart at its crossover point,

identifiable

as one focal point of universal consciousness/universal I...

PART TWO

...and from this point,

I release, release, release... (allow time for releasing)

enabling

healing, healing, healing

into optimum functioning and form,

protected

within this sphere of pre-physical light,

realising

the unlimited power of my true identity

and fulfilling

this lifetime's purpose,

...grateful

for everything experienced and to everyone encountered,

appreciating

being free from severe suffering,

serving

the redemption back into pure consciousness,

providing

a channel for love and light and power,

healing, guiding and inspiring,

always learning.

Practical Daily Self-healing
What can I do daily to maintain a feeling of general wellbeing?

Assumption: all physical symptoms and conditions are signs/warnings of how a life is progressing. They can be acknowledged and read as informative... or ignored, denied, concealed, removed etc.

Healing oneself or helping others to self-heal is, essentially, restoring some harmonious *resonance* with the pulsating rhythms of nature and the cosmos. This usually involves:
(a) releasing tensions and inhibitions, chronic and acute, to free up the flow of energy and fluids,
(b) helping to generate the vitality, energy and strength needed to achieve a state of **equilibrium** between the the two primal, complementary, polar opposite forces, *expansion* and *contraction*.

Releasing reduces the depleting effects of *stress*, and helps dissolve *muscular armouring*, bringing ease, relaxation and better circulation, boosting vitality, strength and stamina… ie **wellbeing**.

A simple routine (adapt to personal requirements)
First, set aside a little time, 15 minutes or more, in a safe and private space, if possible.

Preferably having not consumed food or drink in the last hour or so, make sure bladder and bowels are emptied so there's no continuous clenching of muscles.

Self-scan from head to toes, becoming aware of those parts of your body where there may be tension, stiffness, pain, discomfort or deadness.

Physically loosen up and relax. Include gentle head rolling, eye rolling, puffing cheeks, opening mouth and throat wide with a few deep breaths, extending and retracting the tongue, swinging arms, swivelling hips, squatting down on heels and on toes, raising knees, rotating ankles, forward bend as far as comfortable, snake ripples up/down & left/right.

Give body a brief massage, from scalp down to toes in about a minute.
With heightened physical awareness, extend outwards: arms, hands, legs, feet, torso, neck.

Lie down for a few minutes and try to release any tensed and clenched muscles, so that head, eyes, arms, legs, hands, feet etc feel as though they're gently separating away from the rest of the body. For a couple of minutes, focus on breathing 'into the heart' and then releasing muscles and joints with each outbreath. An open throat helps you to relax and reduces the mental chattering.

Settle down into a comfortable and balanced position, preferably with a straight vertical back, supported if necessary... and prepare to go gently (inward, mentally) into the spaceless, timeless,   inner world of your feelings and thoughts. Feel as physically light as possible.

∞   *Mouth & throat*: open to sound a series of exaggerated vowel sounds (slowly and gently).
    OO-O-U-A-E-I-EE-I-E-A-U-O-OO-M   (3 times)

∞   *Tongue:* spread & extend to maximum, curl & contract to minimum, rotate in mouth to loosen.

∞   *Eyes*: rotate in both directions alternately, not fixing gaze; extend outward/withdraw inward.
    Palming: cover eyes with cupped hands (no contact) to relax in the darkness.

∞   **Horizontal subtle releasing** Lie flat on back, and with no muscular effort:

Allow spine to lengthen, let head float free from neck, release coccyx, widen back, release arms from sockets, release legs from torso. This is releasing and healing from within.
With practice over time, this can help develop bodily awareness and relieve some pain or discomfort by mentally disconnecting from it, so that although it's still there, it's less disturbing.

∞   *Raise awareness of your skin* in a slow wave from head down to toes, as you release any tension.

∞   *Inner Releasing* (in a slow wavelike sequence): brain, optic nerves and eye muscles, inner ears, inner nose, lips, teeth & jaws, roof of mouth & tongue (from front to back), throat/larynx, heart, solar plexus, spleen, belly, perineum.

Emotional cleansing: releasing psycho-physical tensions

This routine is about releasing as much as possible of the **emotional/ mental** stuff that's held, physically embedded at different locations within the body.

In a safe, comfortable space, after loosening up and relaxing, the general purpose is to try and **release all held, trapped energy**, including whatever remains below normal awareness levels.

The challenging part is to **allow and encourage any feelings, thoughts, memories etc which may emerge to do so at full power and intensity** – anger, fear, sadness, anxiety, longing etc – uninhibited by normal, social etiquette rules... and without trying to link specific memories to current emotional or physical experiences. So, be sure you're ready to take this on.

Exhaling fully is an important part of this, and may bring on such temporary reactions as excessive sighing, yawning, eye watering, some occasional shaking or shuddering, coughing, belching, sweats, hot flushes, panic symptoms, confusion etc. In this safe space, these indicate the discharging of contained energy and the releasing of troubling tensions, and are all OK, however unwelcome.

So, when ready, inwardly affirm: *"I am more than all these passing feelings. So, how strong can this particular feeling be? I know I can handle it. And right now I'm ready to experience its full power and then move my life on beyond such problems."*

This exercise is a test of will and courage, as you risk such feelings momentarily running out of control and possibly destabilising your life. However, given your honest intention to self-heal, these buried troubles can gradually be dissolved, dislodged and released, and therefore overcome, leaving you feeling relieved and less burdened or anxious.

When finished:
Lie down, this time releasing so that you feel heavy, inert, and part of the Earth, and relax for about 5 minutes. Then slowly arise, alert and ready to rejoin the everyday world.

You'll find you have more energy available when it's not being used up containing all those buried feelings and leaving you depleted, fatigued and discouraged.

Less inhibition, withholding and denying your own inner power means less inner conflict, fear and anxiety, more vitality and joy in being alive, with an increasing sense of ease and inner calm. There will always be more troubles from the past surfacing and needing to be released, but that means it's possible to feel even better and less burdened as the releasing continues.

Remember
- **The body is not a machine** and the mind is not a computer. They respond to your will and your feelings in many different ways, always seeking the optimum balance in the current circumstances.
- **No amount of *physical* exercising or cleansing can substitute for regular *emotional* cleansing and hygiene.**
- **Perseverance and patience** are necessary both for overcoming old, deeply ingrained habits, fears and prejudices.

- **The heart**, including the **cardiac plexus/heart brain**, is the centre of our whole individual self, mind and body. So, sensitive *heart awareness* in all aspects of our lives is vital for our wellbeing.
- **Cancer:** de-vitalised areas of the body, due to long term patterns of ***inhibition***, prompt the opposite reaction, ie *unregulated growth*, which is the main characteristic of the cancer process.

I Breathe the Cosmos
an exercise in experiencing *D2D* space

Preparation

From the *Threshold* perspective, each creature exists as one *focal point* of universal consciousness, clothed in physical matter (see *The Becoming of Cosmos...*, page 26). And this simple exercise is about directly engaging with the *non-physical* dimension of the cosmos, of which each individual is thus an integral, involved part.

D2D stands for the primal, **d**ynamic **2-d**imensional world of rhythmical *expansion* and *contraction* that functions throughout the cosmos 'behind' the more familiar *3-D* world of physical matter and energy.

First, think of your whole self, body and mind, as a non-physical bubble of energy that's pulsating in rhythm within a series of progressively larger concentric bubbles, all within the pulsating cosmos. At the centre of your existence as an individual is the crossover point of energy and blood flow at the centre of your heart.

As you stand or sit erect, note that your spine is in alignment with a line of force, **focusing** inwards and **radiating** outwards between the centre of the planet and the periphery of the cosmos. This is your particular **focus/radius** line *(F/R)*.

Further and further **inward** along that *F/R* line – from the centre of your being, through the centre of the Earth, through the centre of the solar system and galaxy towards the centre of the cosmos – is a series of progressively smaller points. They are the increasingly *gravity-compressed* centres of the Earth, solar system and galaxy etc, and their concentric peripheries are spaced out away from the centre of the cosmos.

Action

- Now, as you slowly **inhale**, shift the focus of your attention, at the speed of thought, **inward** along that F/R line of consciousness towards the centre of the cosmos (like a camera **zooming** in).

- As your point of focused attention approaches the centre of the cosmos, your consciousness merges with it, and you become aware of **being** the expanding/contracting cosmos, while still retaining your distinct, individual, physical presence, physically located within that vast space.

- As you slowly **exhale**, the cosmos – with your consciousness now an integral part of it – **expands** to its furthest imaginable reach.

- With your next **in-breath,** the cosmos, still incorporating your extended consciousness, *contracts* back inwards towards its centre.

- Then with your next **out-breath**, your point of attention instantly returns along your F/R line back to the centre point of your heart and your individual being. After that, pause for a few minutes to re-orientate and settle before resuming normal everyday awareness. You could work out your own variations of the routine, which is not intended to be a rigid procedure.

This short exercise is a reminder that each individual, despite being temporarily separated within a physical body and a non-physical energy field, is an integral part of the cosmos...which itself is a manifestation of the unlimited *no-thing-ness* that is *universal consciousness* or *universal I*, depending on which way you choose to view it.

The field of energy emanating from each living creature, ie each active unit of consciousness, constitutes a unique **sphere of influence**.

So you, as an individual being, are now able to **identify**, in a limited way, **with the whole conscious, D2D, pulsating cosmos**. By doing this exercise you can instantly and effortlessly shift the focus of your attention, ie your *individual* consciousness, to and from the centre of the cosmos, a greater dimension of yourself, without encountering resistance, impedance or delay.

The timeless *pre-physical* medium within which this identification occurs has long been known as the *aether* or *quintessence*, or more recently as the *quantum vacuum*, as well as other names in other cultures. So, not surprisingly, those non-physical characteristics are reflected in the key *quantum* concepts of *nonlocality*, *superposition*, *entanglement* and *tunnelling*. (See page 350.)

Index of Key Words